Munitions of the

For Professor Nicholas Pronay

Munitions of the Mind

A history of propaganda from the ancient world to the present era

Third Edition

Philip M. Taylor

Manchester University Press

Manchester and New York

distributed exclusively in the USA by Palgrave

Copyright © Philip M. Taylor 1990, 1995, 2003

The right of Philip M. Taylor to be identified as the author of this work has been asserted by him in accordance with the Copyright, Designs and Patents Act 1988.

First edition published 1990 by P. Stephens
Second edition published 1995 by Manchester University Press,
reprinted 1998 and 2002

This edition published 2003 by Manchester University Press
Oxford Road, Manchester M13 9NR, UK
and Room 400, 175 Fifth Avenue, New York, NY 10010, USA
www.manchesteruniversitypress.co.uk

Distributed in the United States exclusively by
Palgrave Macmillan, 175 Fifth Avenue, New York,
NY 10010, USA

Distributed in Canada exclusively by
UBC Press, University of British Columbia, 2029 West Mall,
Vancouver, BC, Canada V6T 1Z2

British Library Cataloguing-in-Publication Data
A catalogue record for this book is available from the British Library

Library of Congress Cataloging-in-Publication Data applied for

ISBN 978 0 7190 6767 9

This edition first published 2003

15 14 13 12 11 10 09 08   10 9 8 7 6 5 4 3

Printed in Great Britain
by Bell & Bain Limited, Glasgow

Contents

Acknowledgements

I am indebted to the British Academy for financial support aiding the research for the original edition of this book, and to the following colleagues for comments and suggestions: Dr Tracy Rihill for her observations on the ancient sections; Dr Graham Loud for his views on the medieval period; Professor F. R. Bridge for his comments on the early modern period. My research students over the years have extended my knowledge still further: Ilse Howling, Fiona Assersohn, Damien Stafford, Kate Morris, Dr Nick Cull, Dr Sue Carruthers, Dr Gary Rawnsley, Paul Rixon, Hossein Afkhami, Steve Bell, and Graham Cook.

A book like this takes many years of gestation and I am delighted therefore to acknowledge the assistance of many supportive professional colleagues and friends, especially Dr Tony Aldgate, Dr Steven Badsey, Philip Bell, Professor Robert Cole, Professor David Culbert, Professor David Ellwood, Professor Ian Jarvie, Professor John Grenville, Dr Frank MacGee, David Murdoch, Dr John Ramsden, Professor Jeffrey Richards, Peter Stead, Dr Richard Taylor, Dr Geoff Waddington, Professor Donald Cameron Watt, Professor David Welch, Dr Ralph White, Professor John Young.

My colleagues at the ICS in Leeds also deserve mention for bringing different disciplinary perspectives to my thinking: Dr David Morrison, Howard Smith, Dr Brent MacGregor, Dr Simeon Yates, Dr Richard Howells, Dr Steven Lax, Judith Stamper, Dr Robin Brown. Former students offered considerable help in various aspects of the research, especially Debbie Whittaker, Cheryl Johnson and Ian Bremner. But as a whole, my history students from 1978-90, and my communications studies students since 1990 will probably never appreciate how significant they have been in helping to shape my thoughts on this topic. At least my wife, Sue, knows of her contribution.

Preface to the New Edition

This book first appeared in 1990, with a second edition in 1995. It was, until recently, the only single volume history of propaganda from the ancient world to the present day. No such volume can purport to be comprehensive, but it has proved necessary to update the final chapters and to add new ones that embrace the Balkan wars (including the 1999) Kosovo campaign and, of course, the so-called 'war' against international terrorism. As I write this new preface, the world is gearing up for another possible war against Saddam Hussein in Iraq. Leaflets have already been dropped there. This book attempts to place the conduct of propaganda during these events within a wider historical context. It retains its main thesis that propaganda is a much misunderstood word, that it is not necessarily the 'bad thing' that most people think it is. As a process of persuasion, it is value neutral. Rather, it is the intention behind the propaganda which demands scrutiny and it is that intention which begs value judgements not the propaganda itself.

Much has happened since 1995, not least the terrorist attacks on New York and Washington on 11 September 2001, or '9/11' as it is now currently being described in shorthand. We are in the middle of another major propaganda campaign, although it is often difficult for us to identify it for what it is because we are living through it. News and views are all around us, speculation is rife, sides are being polarized. Indeed, the issue of Iraq notwithstanding, we may be on the verge of the greatest propaganda campaign ever seen as the West struggles to convince the Muslim world that this is not a war against Islam when many in the Islamic world genuinely believe that it is. President George W. Bush warns that the United States is in it 'for the long haul'. If so, then we will see a new global struggle for hearts and minds that may be on a par with the Cold War. This book should, until its next edition, provide some clues as to how to identify propaganda for what it is, how it has evolved and – most importantly – to judge for oneself the intentions behind those undertaking it.

Crag Bottom Farm, Two Laws
31 December 2002

Introduction

Looking Through a Glass Onion: Propaganda, Psychological Warfare and Persuasion

From the perspective of our modern information and communications age, the word 'propaganda' continues to imply something evil. For some it is a cause of wars; for others, it is an even greater evil than war. Writing in 1926, Lord Ponsonby echoed the sentiments of many when he wrote that propaganda involved 'the defilement of the human soul [which] is worse than the destruction of the human body'. For the liberal-minded, its continued existence remains a cancer threatening to eat away at the body politic of our increasingly free and globalized society; a disease which somehow afflicts our individual and collective capacity to make up our own minds about what is happening in the world around us. Propaganda, it is felt, forces us to think and do things in ways we might not otherwise have done had we been left to our own devices. It obscures our windows on the world by providing layers of distorting condensation. When nations fight, it thickens the fog of war. Propaganda thus becomes the enemy of independent thought and an intrusive and unwanted manipulator of the free flow of information and ideas in humanity's quest for 'peace and truth'. It is therefore something which democracies, at least, ought not to do. It suggests the triumph of emotion over reason in a bureaucratic struggle by the machinery of power for control over the individual. It is a 'dirty trick' utilized by 'hidden persuaders', 'mind manipulators' and 'brainwashers' – Orwellian 'Big Brothers' who somehow subliminally control our thoughts in order to control our behaviour to serve *their* interests rather than our own.

But who are these propagandists? We all know about Dr Goebbels, the 'Evil Genius' of Nazi propaganda. But where do his counterparts lie, because lying is, after all, what they do? Since they bear false witness, propagandists automatically break the Ninth Commandment, but to tell the Big Lie, they invariably invoke the Eleventh: 'thou shall not get found out'. This predisposition to remain hidden only makes them even more dangerous. In times of war, when passions and emotions run high and are thus more susceptible to manipulation by the conflicting parties, democracies are reluctantly forced to accept that they might need to fight fire with fire. Yet even then, propaganda is surely what the 'enemy' says and does because whereas 'they' tell lies, 'we' engage in the truth. Propaganda is thus something done by other, less scrupulous people; it is an enemy conducted by an enemy.

This book will challenge these various assumptions. Propaganda, as one British Foreign Office official put it in the late 1920s, is a 'good word gone wrong'. We are all in fact propagandists to varying degrees, just as we are all victims of propaganda. That statement will perhaps shock people who misunderstand the real nature of propaganda. The word carries so many negative connotations that this would be an entirely understandable reaction. But we need first to get rid of such baggage and start thinking in more objective terms. The questions that need to be asked are in a sense more revealing than any answers that may emerge. We will need to draw from several disciplinary approaches, transcending traditional arts-science divisions. Scientists, for example, use the word *propagation* in quite different ways. Botanists use it with reference to plants. Biologists talk of propagating germs and germ cultures. Social scientists, however, have tended to regard propaganda as being related more to biology than to botany, perhaps forgetting about how penicillin was discovered. Hence in political and sociological analyses of this subject, it tends to resemble a form of germ warfare on the mind rather than being about the cultivation of ideas. But if we begin by taking a leaf from the botanists, a new perspective on the subject becomes possible. Propaganda thus becomes a *process* for the sowing, germination and cultivation of ideas and, as such, is – or at least should be – neutral as a concept. The problem is that human beings frequently inject morality into processes. Yet before we can peel away the multifaceted layers of this glass onion, we first need to understand how it historically acquired a pungency it does not inherently possess.

When the Vatican gave us the word 'propaganda' in the seventeenth century to describe its organization to defend 'the true faith' against the challenge of the Protestant Reformation, the heretics shouted foul at such outside interference in the development of their 'natural' religious thought processes. The legacy of distrust against the word in Protestant societies remains to this day. But its recent pejorative connotations date mainly from the excesses of atrocity propaganda during the Great War of 1914-18 when the modern 'scientific' use of propaganda came of age. It was that development – and particularly its association with falsehood – which Lord Ponsonby denounced so vehemently. The odour got worse when it was employed by the Nazis, the Soviets and other thoroughly nasty regimes ever since. However, it is all too easily forgotten that it was the British who, during the First World War, set the standard in modern propaganda for others to follow.

As we shall see, falsehood was not a watchword of that experiment, the first to attract considerable scholarly attention. It was no more the policy of the official British wartime propaganda machinery to lie deliberately than it was to tell the whole truth. Facts were deployed selectively yet rationally, while falsehoods were eschewed in the belief that they would ultimately be exposed and thereby jeopardize the credibility of those facts that had been released. The government preferred to lie by omission, not by commission. The majority of wartime falsehoods – and there were many – were in fact circulated by a free and highly jingoistic press, not by the official propagandists, but the damage had been done. Nor were matters helped by the great praise subsequently heaped on the British use of propaganda by the likes of Adolf Hitler in *Mein Kampf* who went on to adapt the lessons of the British experience for his own, quite different, purposes. Moreover, in the United States, isolationist elements were quick to seize upon post-First World War revelations about the extent of British propaganda directed against neutral Americans between 1914 and 1917. Washington, they argued, had been 'duped' into joining the allied side and this, in turn, was used to reinforce their own arguments about the need to avoid future foreign entanglements. Propaganda thus bred propaganda. It might seem ironic, therefore, that it is the Americans who today stand as the masters of its art, science and craft. But even though both Britain and the United States, as pluralistic democracies, normally fight shy of the word, that does not mean that they do not engage in it. Nor does it automatically mean that they are wrong to do so.

The reason for this is that, before 1914, propaganda simply meant the means by which the converted attempted to persuade the unconverted. The converted were, and are, not necessarily nasty people with nasty ideas; nor were, or are, the unconverted particularly unreceptive or resistant to what they are told. After all, it takes two sides to form allegiances. Much propaganda in fact also takes place between the converted and the already converted. This is why the Bolsheviks preferred the word 'agitation' to describe the discourse between party and people, between source and target; 'propaganda' was used to describe the indoctrination of its party members, the already converted, before they went out to agitate amongst the people. But before we return to this, we need to consider some further aspects of propaganda's tarnished image. It is frequently charged with guilt by association with two time-honoured human activities: power and war. With the former, propaganda has always been an additional instrument in the arsenal of power, a psychological instrument, and it is its relationship to power which has attracted suspicion – mainly from the powerless or those resentful of power. Much propaganda in fact emanates from power rather like spontaneous combustion, as the British who started the century as the world's greatest power and the Americans who ended it having inherited that mantle know only too well. 'Power speaks for itself.' But in both countries it was equally recognized that propaganda by itself cannot win any struggle for allegiances – hence the need in many instances to back it up with force or coercion, which can range from the passing of mild punitive legislation to the imprisonment or extermination of opponents. The more extreme measures are especially characteristic of authorities – authoritarians – which are insecure about whether their messages will command, at best, general approval or, at least, popular acquiescence.

To be completely convincing, however, shadow does require some substance and myth needs to be rooted in some reality if propaganda is to succeed. Those realities can, of course, change and propaganda needs to adapt accordingly. In pluralistic democracies which purport to exist on the basis of consensus rather than coercion, persuasion thus becomes an integral part of the political process. And once we start talking about persuasion, we enter the psychological dimension of interpersonal, not to mention national or international, relations which has always been a significant element in the political, military, social or economic instruments of power. In the struggle for power, propaganda is an instrument to be used by those who want to secure or retain power just as much as it is by those wanting to displace them. For the smoke to rise, there must first be a spark which lights the flame. Propaganda is that spark.

This perhaps explains why propaganda and war have always been inextricably connected. Once war has broken out, propaganda has proved to be a weapon of no less significance than swords or guns or bombs. But it cannot normally be divorced from military realities. 'Victory generates its own support.' But propaganda does not itself kill people. Indeed, it can be an alternative to killing, the triumph of communication over violence. It can, however, create myths – not just about why wars begin, are won or are lost, but even on rare occasions transform defeats into victories (Dunkirk, 1940, immediately springs to mind). But words alone rarely win wars. The munitions of the mind, like other conventional weapons, have admittedly become more sophisticated with advances in technology, but yesterday's epic poem or painting is really no more than the equivalent of today's propaganda film or television broadcast. It is when propaganda is employed in the service of violence, however, that we begin to mistrust it, because it encourages people to kill people, or to acquiesce in that slaughter. Today it assumes the appearance of a devious weapon that once seduced the souls and the minds of men, exploiting their natural aggression to drive them periodically on to the battlefield.

To understand what drives people to violence would require at least another book. Here we can only begin to tackle the methods of persuasion which have been used throughout history to persuade people that violence is an acceptable course for them to pursue. We must thus beware the dangers of extrapolating twentieth-century perceptions on to our understanding of earlier periods. The same might equally be said for the notion of propaganda as we currently (mis)understand it – but only if we fail to regard it as a neutral process of persuasion. If we do this, we fall into the trap of labelling something 'good propaganda' or 'bad propaganda', as a persuasive process which we judge from the standpoint of our own core values. Thus the process earns approval because we agree with it, and disapproval because we disagree with it. Propaganda becomes something which is done by others we differ from who are selling a cause which we repudiate; hence they are telling lies or, at best, not telling us 'the truth' – and we are back to where we started from. When one person's beliefs become another's propaganda, we have already begun to take sides in a subjective manner. Propaganda analysis demands objectivity if it is to be undertaken effectively.

Although the scale on which propaganda has been practised has increased out of all recognition in the twentieth century, it is in fact an activity that does date back to the time when human beings first began to communicate with one another. Essentially, propaganda is really no more than the communication of ideas designed to persuade people to think and behave in a desired way. It differs – or should do – from education in that the imparting of information and ideas for educational purposes is to enable the recipient to make up his or her own mind on any given issue. Propaganda is about persuading people to do things which benefit those doing the persuading, either directly or indirectly. In wartime that usually means getting them to fight or to support the fight. I do not mean to imply by this that getting people to fight wars is right, merely that propaganda serves an essential role in persuading people to risk their lives for whatever the reasons or the cause. It is those reasons and causes which should be the legitimate objects of moral and critical analysis and judgement, not the propaganda itself. As such, propaganda can be used for 'good purposes', just as it can be abused. If the history of propaganda in the twentieth century appears to be largely a history of abuse, it does not follow that this has always been, and always will be, the case.

By propaganda, then, I mean the *deliberate* attempt to persuade people to think and behave *in a desired way*. Although I recognize that much propaganda is accidental or unconscious, here I am discussing the conscious, methodical and planned decisions to employ techniques of persuasion designed to achieve specific goals that are *intended to benefit those organizing the process*. In this definition, advertising thus becomes economic propaganda since the marketing of a product is designed to advance the manufacturer's profits. It may well be that those at the receiving end of the process also benefit, but in that case the word 'publicity' would be a more appropriate label. Public relations is a related communicative process designed to enhance the relationship between an organization and the public and, as such, is a branch of propaganda, albeit a nicer way of labelling it.

Similar euphemisms abound: 'public information policy', 'press/

media relations' or, more recently, 'spin doctoring'. The euphemism business is, of course, a response to the bad smell but merely serves to add more layers obscuring the reality. Because propaganda is here defined as a deliberate attempt to persuade people, by any available media, to think and then behave in a manner desired by the source, it is really a means to an end. The methods employed vary according to the communications media available. Communication with a view to persuasion is an inherent human quality. It can take place in a private conversation or a mass rally, in a church or cinema, as well as on a battlefield. It can manifest itself in the form of a statue or a building, a coin or painting, a flag or a postage stamp. Propaganda is simply a process by which an idea or an opinion is communicated to someone else for a specific persuasive purpose. Speech, sermons, songs, art, radio waves, television pictures, one person or millions of people – again, none of these matter here for purposes of definition. Communication, though essential to the process, does not by itself provide us with an adequate conceptual starting point. Communication, after all, is just as important for education or advertising. No, what distinguishes propaganda from all other processes of persuasion is the question of *intent*. Propaganda uses communication to convey a message, an idea, or an ideology that is designed primarily to serve the self-interests of the person or people doing the communicating. It may well be that the audience does not want to hear the message; but equally it may well be that it does. Unwanted propaganda, however, does need to be detected in the first place before it can be evaluated. For purposes of definition, it matters not whether the desired behaviour results from the effort; that is the difference between successful and unsuccessful propaganda. Success, however, also needs to be measured against the intention behind the process. But we cannot here involve ourselves in debates about whether the end justifies the means. When, for example, we talk of a 'Just War', then surely the propaganda designed to support it is justified? And if a war is 'necessary' then surely so also is the propaganda it engenders? The problem, when all else is said and done about any issue which arouses human judgements – whether they be historical, economic or moral – is that people seize upon answers that really depend on which side they were on in the first place. The Vatican was in a sense right to call its organization the *Congregatio de Propaganda Fide*, the Congregation for the Propagation of the Faith, because when all these issues are stripped of their theoretical flesh, perhaps human beliefs are really a matter of faith. Hence propaganda appears most effective when it preaches to the already converted.

This book is therefore concerned simply with means – with persuasive methods – not with ends. It does not address whether a product (such as a war or a religion) is itself needed or unwanted, or whether it is right or wrong, just or unjust. It simply examines the means by which those products were marketed, successfully or otherwise. There is no real point, in other words, in making moral judgements concerning whether propaganda is a 'good' or a 'bad' thing; it merely *is*. Rather, one needs to redirect any moral judgement away from the propaganda process itself and more to the intentions and goals of those employing propaganda to secure those intentions and goals.

Similarly, with psychological warfare – propaganda directed usually against an enemy – the same sort of pejorative connotations need to be peeled away before we can begin to understand the process fully. After all, why should there be such a stigma surrounding a process of persuasion designed to get people to stop fighting, and thus preserve their lives, rather than having their heads blown off? Today, as we learn more and more about the workings of the human mind in an era where nuclear weapons could readily destroy all human life on the planet, propaganda and psychological operations (as they are now called) have become genuine alternatives to war. As this book will argue, that is what the Cold War was really all about, as are indeed many of the contemporary 'information wars' which now accompany international crises. Propaganda is part of the struggle for perceptions in which words attempt to speak as loud as actions, and sometimes even to replace the need for action. It works most effectively when words and deeds (the propaganda and the policy) are synchronous, but the 'propaganda of the deed' is in itself a powerful persuader. When Rome destroyed Carthage, for example, or when the Americans dropped atomic bombs on Hiroshima and Nagasaki or when battleships are despatched to the coastline of a weaker adversary, such actions send powerful messages that form part of the persuasive process that operates in the psychological dimension of human communication.

But we do need constantly to bear in mind why we as individuals believe what we do. A great deal of theory works on the assumption that information is power, and whoever controls the flow of information therefore wields power over the recipient. Propaganda is thus a powerful tool for perpetuating power relationships. The problem in much propaganda theory is that the recipient is also felt to be empowered as well, in other words, he or she can reject the messages – provided they can be detected. This book might almost be regarded as a handbook to aid that detection. Although much modern propaganda appeals to reason, it is more usually felt to play on emotion, with the young being particularly vulnerable to such emotional manipulation. But are adults so immune? Scholars from a variety of disciplines have long pondered this question. Yet, regardless of whether the prevailing theory of the time was that we behaved the way we did because of 'God's will' or because we were 'possessed by spirits' or even because we have evolved into masters of our own destiny through a contest of the 'survival of the fittest', it has only been in the past hundred years or so, with the rise especially of psychology, that the focus of attention has been on the workings of the human brain rather than on the mysteries of the human 'soul'.

If war is essentially an organized communication of violence, propaganda and psychological warfare are essentially organized processes of persuasion. In wartime they attack a part of the body that other weapons cannot reach in an attempt to affect the way in which participants perform on the field of battle. However, in the centuries before nuclear technology and psychology, before the likes of Einstein and Oppenheimer, of Freud and Jung, neither propaganda nor warfare had been demystified or discredited. The battlefield was where individuals and States earned their place in history. It is important, in other words, to remember that because the cult of war is much older than the cult of peace, propaganda designed to get people to fight is a much older process than the relatively underdeveloped form of propaganda designed to get people to fight for peace.

Perhaps, in this current century, this century of the mass media as well as of Total Warfare, Cold Warfare and Nuclear Weapons, we have seen more of the horrors of war than any of our predecessors and we are therefore more aware of its consequences, with the result that we tend to place more emphasis on the merits of peace. Yet prior to this age, war was regarded as a normal, even acceptable and indeed glorious, method of resolving disputes, an extension of politics and diplomacy by other means. But did people then see warfare through the rose-tinted spectacles provided by propagandist opticians who wanted to masquerade its brutal realities? As consumers of the mass media, is it any different for us today? Just how realistic or authentic is the view of war held by non-combatants? Or are we just as blinkered as our predecessors were?

An essential characteristic of propaganda is that it rarely tells the whole truth. We do not need here to get into post-modernist theories about concepts of 'truth' or 'reality' to realize from this that censorship is the essential counterpart to propaganda. They are different sides of the same coin: the manipulation of opinion. The selective processes by which some information is disseminated and some held back is a problem facing all communicators, but where censorship operates – whether it be institutionalized or self-censorship – one needs to recognize how close one is sailing into the wind of propaganda. This is particularly true if the deliberate withholding of certain information is designed to benefit those who control the flow of information in the first place. However, censors of all persuasions take refuge in the notion that they are somehow protecting someone else from something that may do them damage. But invariably they are protecting their own interests for fear that information may indeed empower people to think and do things that might not serve or benefit those interests. This was why Hitler felt that it was pointless to attempt propaganda against intellectuals; they would always be able to identify propaganda when confronted with it. Hence the need for us to be clear on the difference between propaganda and education, although again the British experiment in the First World War, when foreign opinion-formers were the principal targets of propaganda emanating from Wellington House rather than public opinion itself, provides a salutary reminder of the susceptibility of even the most educated.

In wartime, censorship is today imposed with the justification that certain information which might serve the interests of the *enemy*, and thus jeopardize the lives of those doing the fighting on 'our' behalf, must be withheld on the grounds of 'operational security'. But it is no coincidence that modern military censorship coincides with the arrival of the profession of the war correspondent. Nor is it a coincidence that the advent of mass communications in the mid nineteenth century and the extension of political and military activity to a much broader population base have sparked off an explosion in the use of propaganda world-wide.

Ever since William Howard Russell's despatches for *The Times* during the Crimean War, the needs of military secrecy have clashed with the demands of media publicity and, with it, the battle to control the flow of information which might have an adverse effect on military *and* civilian morale. Modern censorship and propaganda are thus institutional responses to the 'communications revolution' which we are still undergoing today.

What that much used phrase actually means is essentially a shift from face-to-face communication towards mediated forms of communication in which a third party intervenes in the communication process between sender and recipient. Usually that third party is a medium such as a newspaper or television. If the consequence of this is that previous problems of distance and time between sender and recipient have been narrowed by the existence of the media, fourth parties such as propagandists and censors (and advertisers and other persuaders) also try to infiltrate the remaining space between them. With the arrival of instantaneous communication between sender and recipient – live television news reports, computer-mediated communications – there is no such space remaining. The challenge for today's propagandist/censor, therefore, is to gain control of information at source. If that does not work or is not possible, there is either a need to control the 'spin' on the information flowing out – crisis management – or to ensure that the information being received is done so by people who have already been sufficiently infused with propaganda over a long period of time so that they perceive it in accordance with a predetermined world-view. Hence unpalatable information falls on barren ground because people cannot see where it fits into their way of seeing and believing. Psychologists call this cognitive dissonance. French sociologist Jacques Ellul, who has produced one of the most stimulating conceptual examinations of propaganda, argued that the advent of the technological society was a major factor in the emergence of modern propaganda because that type of society conditioned people to a 'need for propaganda'. In his view, propaganda is most effective when it conforms to needs that already exist, but these are in fact 'pseudo-needs' created from childhood to cater for 'pseudo-satisfactions' created by an all-embracing propaganda society.

Previously, especially if wars were fought 'somewhere else', this required the creation of a perception gap between the image of warfare projected towards civilian audiences and its brutal realities as experienced by the soldiers. Today, that gap appears to have been substantially narrowed by the presence of the mass media, and especially television. But is this in fact the case? Or does it merely raise new problems for the projection and presentation of warfare?

The Roman writer Livy wrote that 'nowhere do events correspond more to men's expectations than in war'. Yet even volunteer, professional troops suffer from low morale and even panic if there is too wide a gap between the expectations of what war will be like and its realities on the battlefield. Factors such as bad weather, poor food and low pay can sap the morale of even the best-trained armies. Discipline and training designed to foster mutual reliance are essential factors in maintaining good fighting spirit, but this is difficult with conscripted troops reluctant to fight or fearful of their fate. Hence the use of incentives such as money, social status, personal or family or national glory, and even religious promises of everlasting life. A brave soldier who becomes a war hero might have all of these things; a coward would be denied them. Hence propagandists exploit both positive and negative incentives in order to persuade men to overcome their fear and risk their lives in the most brutal and terrifying of circumstances.

But what about the reasons for the soldier being there in the first place? Throughout history, great emphasis has been placed upon the justness of the cause for which men must go to war. Yet, as Lord Wavell wrote in 1939, 'a man does not flee because he is fighting in an unrighteous cause; he does not attack because his cause is just'. Wavell's view was that good morale was determined by the degree to which a soldier felt part of a cohesive unit, a small core of mutually reliant individuals, and the degree to which that unit identified with the society on whose behalf it was fighting.

Propaganda for and about war, therefore, cannot be studied merely by confining its analysis to the battlefield. It requires a much wider context extending into every aspect of society. At the end of the eighteenth century, Thomas Malthus wrote that 'a recruiting serjeant always prays for a bad harvest, and a want or unemployment, or, in other words a redundant population'. Motivating men to fight – for the history of warfare is largely the history of male aggression – has always been a major problem for history's recruiting serjeants. Hence the need to glorify and publicize military achievements to a wider public in order to increase the sense of mutual identification. Soldiers fight better if they know that their families, friends and the civilians who are waiting for news of their deeds from afar support their actions. With volunteers, there may appear to be little need for propaganda, although the pressures of society at war often make it easier to join up than it is to stay at home. (Hence the First World War campaign poster of 'What did you do in the Great War, daddy?'.) But there have always been men who enlist voluntarily for a variety of personal reasons that require little propagandist attention: the life-style, the physical training, travel, adventure, uniforms, money, family tradition, patriotism. In militaristic societies, such as ancient Sparta or eighteenth-century Prussia or in their twentieth-century counterparts, the central role of the army in society provided opportunities of wealth and status that attracted the ambitious. We cannot therefore discount the militaristic propaganda that permeated all aspects of life in such societies as a motivating force in recruitment. But nor, in other types of societies, can we discount propaganda surrounding 'the just war' or other justificatory themes. Soldiers may not attack because they believe their cause is just – although it must surely help. They attack because they are trained and disciplined to obey orders on command. But a just cause none the less has to be marketed to a wider audience in order to justify not so much 'why they fight' but rather 'why we must support them'.

We will never know for certain whether any given war might have had a different outcome if more or less propaganda had been conducted effectively by either side. We *do* know, however, that history tends to be written mainly by the victors, and to the victors go the spoils of historical judgement. Does this mean, therefore, that history is propaganda? Indeed to what extent are the educational systems of societies serving propagandist needs? Studies of school textbooks in Nazi Germany and Imperial Japan have demonstrated that history books in those countries said more about the time in which they were written than about the past. No one would doubt this any more in so far as the old Soviet Union was concerned now that archives are being opened to reveal the extent to which education was used as a form of social and political engineering. Democratic regimes, however, cherish the illusion that their history books do not overtly manipulate historical facts – even though a glance at American history books of the early 1950s or books written in Britain at the height of the Empire would indeed confirm this to be an illusion.

The difference, of course, is that no official propagandist body decreed that Anglo-American history or other books should be written to project a predetermined view of the past to conform with the political needs of the present. Even so, the scholars who wrote them were products of the times in which they lived and worked. And rarely has there been a time in history when the governors have not attempted to influence the way in which the governed viewed the world, including that of their own past. Information, whether current or redundant, retains its capacity to shape perception. For this reason, history has indeed proved to be an invaluable source of propaganda, and not just in dictatorships or authoritarian regimes. In societies which purport to cherish such notions as freedom of information, freedom of thought, word and deed, what then is the difference between propaganda and education? Perhaps the answer lies in the idea that propaganda *tells* people *what* to think whereas education *teaches* people *how* to think. The line is, however, much thinner in practice than in theory. Interestingly, modern dictatorships have never fought shy of the word 'propaganda' in quite the same way as democracies do. The Nazis had their Ministry of Popular Enlightenment and Propaganda and the Soviets their Propaganda Committee of the Communist Party, but the British had a Ministry of Information and the Americans an Office of War Information. We must not forget that all, however, practised censorship.

Historically, modern propaganda can be seen as a product of post-industrialization where people become consumers. But people do not like to think they would pay for propaganda, so propaganda has to be paid for by others – the State, say, or even the church – who spend money on this activity to suit their own needs, rather than the people's. The package is of course marketed in such a way that it is the consumers who believe they are the beneficiaries. Since the Enlightenment, consumers of ideas likewise prefer to believe that they can access information freely as and when they need it with minimum outside interference. In this way can propaganda be identified and then rejected. But is this notion also an illusion? Now, in an age that is witnessing a massive explosion of inform-ation – with its talk of 'information superhighways', digital data networks and global satellite television services – this issue remains one of the most central concerns of our time. How freely does that information flow? Is anyone controlling it in any way? If so, why?

Are we being told everything? Is what we see, hear and read an unfettered representation of what is really happening? What are we not being told, and why? Is the information on which we base our opinions and perceptions of the world around us free from the influence of propaganda? If not, is that to *our* benefit or advantage? Answers to such questions can emerge only slowly, whereas the technology is now moving so quickly that scholars who begin to tackle them barely have time to catch their breath before another new technological breakthrough commands their attention.

Yet such questions can only begin to be answered by a careful study of the way in which our information age functions and the ways it is developing. It is a study that needs to transcend traditional academic disciplines but one which none the less requires an historical framework. However, to reiterate, it must be borne in mind that the study of propaganda itself is not necessarily the study of something evil. The Ancient Greeks, after all, regarded persuasion as a form of 'rhetoric' and it was Aristotle who believed that the purpose of persuasion was to communicate a point of view and that knowledge and wisdom could only be secured through logic and reason. As we shall see, the most effective propaganda as it has evolved through the ages now bases itself upon 'facts' and credible arguments, upon as near (not as far) as possible 'the whole truth', upon reason rather than emotion. But whatever 'the whole truth' is or wherever it resides, the study of propaganda requires us first to look at ourselves: what we think, why we think it, whether we choose to think something because of some facet of our upbringing, our environment, our education or our individual experience or because someone else has suggested that that is the way to think for their benefit rather our own. Only then can we begin to understand whether our windows are in fact mirrors, or indeed whether the mirrors are prisms.

In so far as war is concerned, only the most optimistic of people can believe that it will ever be permanently eradicated from human behaviour. The continuing threat of nuclear weapons to human survival remains, however, a sobering reminder of the need to continue the effort. Rethinking the possible applications for propaganda is therefore an important element of meeting the challenge laid down by history to our contemporary age. As Albert Camus wrote earlier this century:

Over the expanse of five continents throughout the coming years an endless struggle is going to be pursued between violence and friendly persuasion ... Henceforth the only honourable course will be to stake everything on a formidable gamble – that words are more powerful than munitions.

Part One

Propaganda in the Ancient World

Chapter 1

In the Beginning ...

We still know so little about the dawn of mankind that it is impossible to identify precisely when Palaeolithic man began to use his tools for warlike purposes. Man's earliest days were undoubtedly violent, with the environment his greatest enemy. His struggle to master that environment was made easier after 8000 BC when the glaciers of the Ice Age began their retreat. Debate still rages among anthropologists as to whether early man was peaceful or warlike, but his struggle for mastery over his surroundings and his developing hunting and farming skills may have provided him with something wanted by others, and thus with something to fight over. We shall probably never know why he first began to organize himself for war. Yet even before he was learning to speak in a recognizable language, early man was appreciating the need to communicate, whether for peaceful or for warlike purposes. Anthropological and archaeological research suggests that before speech (organized language) all communication was visual. Primitive man communicated non-verbally via gestures and signals although sounds – cries and drum beats, for instance – were also important. Tribal man developed masks, war cries, and threatening gestures both to frighten his enemies and impress his friends.

Margaret Mead, the famous anthropologist of the inter-war years whose studies *Coming of Age in Samoa* and *Growing Up in New Guinea* throw much light on the behaviour of primitive peoples, suggests that visual symbols were used for very specific purposes. For example, one village might send a message to another in the form of leaves and weapons arranged in such a way as to suggest a danger from a third village, thereby hoping to forge an alliance. Equally, 'the omission of some small formal act of courtesy was, in earlier times in Samoa, the possible signal for an outbreak of hostilities between two villages'.

Mead also observed that a notched stick indicating a number of days, animals, or men would sometimes be 'preserved and displayed later to validate some political claim or counterclaim'. But essentially, historians have little evidence of early man's warring habits. We know he crafted weapons in the form of spears and clubs, but there is still uncertainty as to whether they were used primarily for killing his own kind. Cave drawings by Cro-Magnon Man suggest the celebration of primitive rituals and customs, but they usually depict features of the physical environment, such as animals or hunting scenes, and their purpose may have been purely decorative. If, on the other hand, they were celebratory and designed to impress others, either from the same village or from elsewhere, then they can be seen as a form of propaganda. It is only in Neolithic cave drawings from about 7000 BC that we see men using weapons against each other, making these drawings perhaps the earliest form of war propaganda. As the old saying has it, a picture speaks a thousand words.

It is only with the arrival of 'civilization' that historians begin to tread on firmer ground. The development of organized social systems, institutions, class structures, architecture, trade, and religion seems to have occurred first in the Middle East – in the Euphrates delta – around 5000 BC. By then, revolutionary weapons such as the sling, the bow and arrow, and the dagger had arrived. Pottery and seals attesting to individual ownership together with the sites of early temples in small Babylonian city-states such as Ur and Uruk, provide us with evidence of this development. Walls suggest danger from other, perhaps less well organized, tribes; the wall at Uruk was eventually nearly 6 miles long with over 900 towers, supposedly the work of its legendary king, Gilgamesh (later the subject of a resilient epic poem that served to throw light on the Mesopotamian 'world-view' or outlook). Certainly, the existence of such walls suggests that organized warfare – primitive though it may appear to us now – was well developed by the start of the Neolithic age. And it is only really with the organization of violence that we can begin to talk properly of warfare and of war propaganda.

The earliest surviving written evidence for social communication indeed comes from ancient Mesopotamia in the third and second millennia BC. Clay tablets yielding a primitive form of picture

writing known as cuneiform were found on the site of ancient
Sumer, the land between the Tigris and Euphrates rivers, dating
from around 3000 BC. The archaeological evidence of public
buildings, palaces, and temples indicates a well-organized society
based upon a hierarchical structure with a ruler at its head. Some
form of communication was necessary for that ruler to maintain
his position, to issue decrees and laws, to combat opposition, and
so on. But the Sumerian cuneiform tablets are essentially lists – of
animals, for example, pictorially represented. Yet the tablets do
yield signs denoting the professions of 'courier' and 'herald, crier'
and would appear to suggest that public opinion of a rudimentary
sort was an important factor in early political life.

The rise of interstate warfare between the cities of ancient
Mesopotamia was celebrated on stone and other monuments.
Elongated, rectangular stone monuments, known as stelae,
depicting the king with his god or with a subjugated enemy, often
with lengthy inscriptions, were erected at city gates or on borders.
An early example is the great stela of Eannatum of Lagash (*c*.2550
BC), a round-topped slab depicting Nin-girsu, the god of Lagash,
first capturing his enemies in a net and then in a war chariot. On
the other side, King Eannatum advances at the head of a well-
armed infantry phalanx crushing his enemies underfoot while lions
and vultures tear the bodies of the dead. His remaining enemies flee
before him and the death sentence is handed out to the defeated
king of Umma. Such relics, by their celebratory nature, indicate an
awareness of propaganda after-the-event; standards, decorated
shields and the like demonstrate its use during battle. Both Sargon
I (*c*.2276-2221 BC), who united his Semites from Akkad with the
Sumerian city-states into a single empire, and his grandson
Naramsin (*c*.2196-2160 BC), known as King of the Four Quarters
of the World, placed the name of a star before their names to
symbolize their divine character. During Sargon's many campaigns
his huge army of over 50,000 men could only survive by living off
the land, and the morale of his troops was mainly determined by
their ability to do this. An increase in the use of visual symbolism is
evident in Naramsin's stela, carved on a triangular stone and
depicting an upward surge of the conquerors and the falling of
collapsing enemies. Such stelae were often erected at invasion
points to deter future attacks; in the short term, such attacks would
have been futile since the land had been devastated by the foraging

armies; but once the land had recovered, the stelae served as a reminder of the defender's power – and of his ruthlessness.

By the middle of the fourteenth century BC, however, when the Assyrians were challenging the Babylonians for supremacy, they brought with them heroic military poems and hymns. The Assyrian Empire provides a much richer source of war propaganda than the Babylonian. One of the earliest, though fragmentary, epic poems was composed by King Adad-nirari I (1307-1275 BC) to celebrate his wars with the Kassites. Dating from half a century later, the 700-line Assyrian epic of King Tukulti-Ninurta I (1250-1210 BC) glorifies the king's military accomplishments and magnanimity towards the Kassites. It would appear that the events depicted in the poem were largely fictitious, that it was designed for public consumption and intended for oral recitation before large and illiterate crowds. This type of story-telling was also (and remains) a principal means of communication in Africa. Such stories were translated visually onto palace walls, as in the case of King Tukulti-Ninurta's friezes, which depicted the king amidst his soldiers in actual campaigns. Composed after the event, often long afterwards, epic royal poems and stories can be regarded as an example of celebratory war propaganda, being designed to praise and glorify the achievements or memory of a particular ruler.

But what about prior to battle? Cautionary tales warning of the dangers of a possible course of action were largely inspired by the priesthoods of ancient Sumeria who began to compete with kings for public loyalty. Omens, prophecies, and oracles were also forms of social persuasion and initially it was from religion that propaganda concerning the future outcome of wars most commonly derived. Invoking the gods was of course an ideal way to sustain the power and position of the priesthood in a superstitious society; but it was also a means of boosting morale prior to a fight if priests and king were of the same mind. But it was the king who instigated war and it was his partnership with the gods that legitimized his actions. War was undertaken in the name of religion rather than for booty or land – at least ostensibly. The Assyrians, for instance, maintained that they waged war against the enemies of the god Assur to demonstrate the glory of their deity, and they did so with such ferocity that many potential enemies conceded without a fight. Indeed, war was considered to be the very reason for a king's existence, and the Assyrians waged it ceaselessly.

By the first millennium BC, then, the rulers of the Assyrian Empire were perfecting the use of documents and monuments to create desired behaviour among their own subjects, to demonstrate divine support, and to consolidate their royal position. Fortifications and palaces, together with their decorations of statues and murals, all reflected the power and prestige of the king and revealed his preoccupation with war. Although religion provided war propaganda with its first real theme, a relationship which has remained a potent means of justifying aggression throughout history, the Assyrians were more warlike than religious. For example, on Eannatum's stela, the god is seen holding the net which captures the king's enemies, whereas on Sargon's stela the king himself is seen holding this recurring symbol. Palaces, rather than temples, became the major source of such celebratory propaganda. The ceremonies conducted within them ritualized the relationship between ruler and ruled and between one king and another. Assyrian royal inscriptions referred to warlike activities in reports on specific campaigns and in annalistic accounts. These accounts invariably describe the marching out to war of the king and his army, the battle and inevitable victory, the triumph and the punishment meted out to the vanquished, and the king's concluding report back to his god. Regardless of the reality, war was presented as a defensive or punitive measure, a glorious exercise in kingship whose triumph was made in the name of an increasingly formalized or symbolic deity.

Pictorial records of the Assyrian kings' campaigns were also depicted on glazed bricks mounted on stone slabs within the palaces. The purpose was to demonstrate the irresistible strength of Assyrian power by showing in detail that power in action. Charging chariots, marching armies, besieged cities, and retreating enemies are recurring themes in Assyrian art and architecture, whilst the god Assur is ever-present in supporting the king. A good example of these pictorial chronicles is the Black Obelisk erected by Shalmaneser III (859-824 BC) which commemorates the king's discovery of the source of the River Tigris after a military campaign and which bears the inscription: 'A mighty image of my majesty I fashioned; the glory of Assur, my lord, my deeds of valour, all I had accomplished in the lands, I inscribed thereon and I set it up there.' Royal power, demonstrated in war and depicted in great detail, was there for all to see. So was royal vengeance. From the mid sixth

century BC an inscription on the royal palace of Assurnasirpal II at
Ninevah describes how the Assyrian king punished the rebellious
city Suru and devised a method of warning against further revolts:

> I built a pillar over against the city gate, and I flayed all the chief men
> who had revolted, and I covered the pillar with their skins; some I
> walled up within the pillar, some I impaled upon the pillar on stakes,
> and others I bound to stakes round about the pillar; many within the
> border of my own land I flayed, and I spread their skins upon the walls;
> and I cut off the limbs of the officers, of the royal officers who had
> rebelled. Ahiababa [the rebel leader] I took to Ninevah, I flayed him, I
> spread his skin upon the wall of Ninevah.

Assyrian art reflects this brutality, and pottery took the images far
and wide. It was a policy of terror coupled with one of propaganda,
designed to keep conquered peoples down and to frighten potential
enemies with graphic propagandist imagery and brutal psychology.

The gradual shift from war fought in the name of a god to war
fought in the name of a king (with the god being reduced to a
symbolic presiding influence) may have been due in part to the
influence of the Egyptian kings, who developed their own forms of
propaganda, in particular spectacular public monuments such as
the pyramids and the sphinx. The Pharaohs were among the first to
recognize the power of public architecture on a grand scale to
demonstrate prestige and dynastic legitimacy. Yet, like the
Assyrians, their war propaganda was erratic and sporadic: there
was no coherent pattern or organization. Religion was used cynically by rulers to promote loyalty and fear among the ruled.
Undoubtedly superstitious themselves, ancient kings backed up
their propaganda with terror, both in peace and in war. In other
words, if religion provided the origins of war propaganda, terror
can be seen to have provided the origins of psychological warfare.
But these are modern terms and do not describe adequately the
persuasive activities of these ancient rulers. They imply an
organization and a philosophy which did not really exist. It is only
with the flowering of Greek civilization that we can begin to see the
introduction of both these factors.

Chapter 2

Ancient Greece

In Greece, all non-Greeks were *barbarians*, by which was meant people who did not speak Greek ('bar-bar' was the sound their language made in Greek ears). For the pre-Bronze Age period (before 2000 BC) our sources for ancient Greek society remain scanty, to say the least. We know that between about 1200 BC and 800 BC Greece entered a dark age, following the collapse of Bronze Age society. In the *Iliad* (probably written in the eighth century BC), Homer wrote of a war between King Priam's Troy and a confederation of Greek states (the Achaeans) under the leadership of the Mycenaen king, Agamemnon. Subsequent writers told of the way in which the war gave rise to one of the earliest examples of deception in war: the Trojan Horse. By this device, the Greeks were able to trick the Trojans into believing that they had abandoned the siege, and so defeat them when troops allegedly poured out of the wooden monument after it had been taken inside the city walls. The classical Greeks from a later period believed that the *Iliad* provided a factual account of their early history. In the nineteenth century the German amateur archaeologist Heinrich Schliemann used the *Iliad* to identify the actual site of Troy, and with the help of Aeschylus' fifth-century BC play *The Agamemnon*, which told of the murder of Agamemnon by his wife and her lover on his return from Troy, went on to excavate Mycenae. He made important discoveries at both sites, but his deductions were not always accurate. Moreover, Homer's account has been seriously undermined by the discovery of the Linear B tablets at Pylos, which provided a form of documentary evidence of much greater significance than Schliemann's deductions. Although it is therefore perhaps safer for us to regard such epic accounts as the *Iliad* as works of fiction, tales like that of the Trojan Horse do provide us with an insight into early Greek conceptions of war propaganda techniques.

After about 750 BC city-states emerged as the dominant political unit in Greece, replacing the tribal kingdoms of earlier periods. Reflecting this increasingly structured society, warfare also became more organized with the development of heavily-armoured citizen phalanxes and a wave of colonization. What can we deduce about early Greek war propaganda from this? The city-states were really united only by common language and the sea. Each one (*polis*) had its own gods and glorified its own achievements (Athens had Athena, Argos had Hera, and so on). Alliances were formed, but Greeks frequently fought Greeks. Warfare, however, was a seasonal occupation, with the volunteer soldiers coming mainly from farms which needed no looking after during the winter months. There was no standing army; all citizen-farmers were by definition soldiers whose military service was an annual event between sowing and harvest-time. Different city-states adopted different techniques to influence their troops. There was no unity between the fully-fledged independent city-states, simply common characteristics.

With a large expansion in trade, Greeks exported their goods in decorative vases. We admire these vases today as works of art, and it might be assumed that they served to project to a wider world the artistic achievements of Greek potters and, in turn, their images of Greek glory. This was not the case. Few decorated pots went to non-Greek communities and pot-painters were not highly regarded in ancient Greece. The majority were slaves and the pot was the tin-can of antiquity. It was the contents that interested the Greeks (olive oil, wine, grain, and the like) not the container.

Sculpture and architecture provide stronger evidence of a growing sophistication in the art of persuasion. Statues of gods and men became larger and more realistic as individual politicians strove to project themselves and their achievements before the population. But it is architecture that offers the clearest manifestation of propaganda in Classical Greece. Athens provides a notable example of the use of this medium to promote the glory of an individual or a city. In his *Life of Pericles*, Plutarch describes how in the fifth century BC the Athenian king 'wooed the masses' and how he promoted his own prestige by diverting Greek Confederation funds designated for defence against the Persians to work on the Acropolis, despite the objections of his allies who felt that Pericles was indulging in blatant self-glorification. Demosthenes spoke of the Propylaea and the Parthenon as symbols of Athenian honour at the expense of war against the Persians, and some of his own orations were designed as warnings on the dangers posed by Philip of Macedon. Monumental sculptures were also erected to commemorate victories, such as those put up by Attalus I of Pergamum and Eumenes II to celebrate their triumphs over the Gauls.

Athens' great rival was Sparta which, as is well known, revelled in the art of war. Trained to fight by the state from an early age, Spartan warriors had been fully indoctrinated with the merits of war and bravery in battle by the time they were despatched to the battlefield. During the so-called Messenian revolt against the Spartans, the second Messenian war which lasted for about twenty years after 640 BC, the Spartan armies were encouraged by the martial poetry of Tyrtaeus. (It was this revolt that prompted the creation of a standing army and the famous Spartan militaristic regime needed to keep down the helots.) Having conquered the southern Peloponnese in the sixth century BC and having established themselves as the dominant military power in mainland Greece by 500 BC, the Spartans were prepared to settle their differences and work with the naval power of the Athenians in repelling the successors of the Assyrians, the Persians under Darius, when they pushed into the mainland in the generation which followed. At the battle of Marathon in 490 BC, the Athenians triumphed against overwhelming odds without Spartan help, the Spartans having been delayed – significantly – by a religious festival.

Our main source for the Persian wars (490-449 BC) is Herodotus, who describes a series of omens which aided Athenian morale at Marathon. Despite this defeat, the Persians returned ten years later, now led by Darius' successor Xerxes. Local populations were by now less vulnerable to pillaging than in Sargon's time; Xerxes recognized the value of taking provisions with his armies and of not living solely off local supplies, while Greek farmer-soldiers were told to bring three days' supply of food with them. Warfare was getting longer both in terms of time and space. The omens this time were far less favourable for the Greeks (who were advised to take to the sea by the Delphic oracle of Apollo), despite the formation of a confederation of states. The Persians destroyed Athens in 480 BC, in spite of the heroics of the Spartans at the Battle of Thermopylae. The outnumbered Greeks were only saved by a series of brilliant deceptions on the part of the Athenian naval commander, Themistocles. There were so many Greeks fighting on the Persian side that disinformation was called for. Themistocles first left messages for Xerxes suggesting that Greeks in the Persian army were unreliable and on the verge of revolt. As a result, Xerxes chose not to deploy these troops. Then Themistocles sent a message to Xerxes suggesting that most of his Greeks at Salamis were planning to flee, whereupon the Persian deployed half of his fleet to trap them. Having thus reduced the size of both the Persian fleet and army, the Greeks were able to lure Xerxes into attacking them at Salamis on more favourable terms. Themistocles' actions had suggested that he was about to abandon the Greek cause – and Xerxes believed him. Why? The simple fact of the matter was that this type of defection was so common in ancient Greece that Xerxes had little reason not to believe Themistocles!

The formation thereafter of the Delian league under Athenian leadership finally defeated the Persians by 449 BC, whereupon they agreed not to stray from Asia Minor again. Against overwhelming odds, the Greeks had triumphed over the Persians, and the role played by superior morale and by heightened motivation stemming from defending their homeland against barbarian invaders cannot be overlooked as contributory factors. But at the decisive battle of Salamis in 480 BC, Themistocles had proved himself a master in the arts of propaganda and psychological warfare.

The Greeks fought their wars rather like mass duels; campaigns were short, battles were usually decisive, and their range of tactics was comparatively limited. The phalanx functioned through communal dependence, echoing the development of the city-state. Rows of heavily armoured hoplites, meeting head on, provided little room for individual heroics of the kind celebrated in the epic poems. With the exception of the militaristic Spartans, whose indoctrination from an early age perhaps shut their minds off from fear (or at least made fear of desertion greater than fear of battle), Greek armies required considerable morale-boosting. Fighting was a duty to the state, but it was also a terrifying business. Greek generals always addressed their troops before the battle in an attempt to raise spirits, and the Greeks shouted as they rushed into battle (with, again, the exception of the Spartans, who marched slowly into battle to music). Panic was not uncommon, which was one reason for employing professional mercenaries (often non-

Greeks) who were motivated by profit rather than duty. But in the main, especially when phalanx fought phalanx, fear and exhaustion in organized hand-to-hand fighting had to be compensated for by a combination of rigid discipline and pre-battle morale-boosting.

The role of religion in Greek warfare therefore assumed a psychological significance. Omens and portents – perhaps natural phenomena such as an electrical storm or a lunar eclipse – were used in psychological preparations for battle as signs from the gods. Oracles, like the most famous one at Delphi, offered mediation between humanity and the gods. As troops gathered from all over the Greek world at the start of a campaign, bringing with them a variety of superstitions and opinions, the Oracle provided a single viewpoint around which the soldiers could unite: a word from the gods to the people of Greece. The two Spartan kings were said to be accompanied by twin gods when they marched into battle, and the Greeks – according to Herodotus – sent a ship to fetch their war god before the battle of Salamis. (This may well have been a statue or an icon.) Contemporary accounts also refer to the gods actually appearing in battle. The heat of the moment, the rush of adrenalin during combat, combined with the religious background which dominated Greek life, may have caused the warriors to believe they were fighting alongside their heroes and gods – in short, to hallu-cinate. Alexander the Great even exploited this common Greek experience when, prior to a battle, he used a tame snake with a linen human head to demonstrate to his soldiers that the god Asklepios – often portrayed in serpent form – was with them. Other tricks were also used, such as dyeing the word 'Victory' on the liver of a sacrificed animal and showing it to the troops before battle as a sign from the gods. Alexander became obsessed with superstitious omens and could only have been psychologically disturbed by the series of omens which preceded his early death, such as witnessing the fighting of ravens with some falling dead at his feet.

Deception and disinformation, as we have seen, were also integral features of Greek warfare. Indeed if victory could be achieved with the aid of what we would now call propaganda, it often merited a more substantial sacrifice to the gods than would an actual military victory. But the principal medium for such activity remained religion. As Cicero later wrote: 'And what king or people has there ever been who did not employ divination? I do not mean in time of peace only, but much more even in time of war, when the strife and struggle for safety is hardest.'

Unfavourable portents were often kept from the soldiers. Those which could not be concealed – say a meteorite or even a sneeze – had to be explained favourably by quick-witted generals and their interpreters to convince their men that the omens were still with them. In the dawn before the battle of Salamis, according to Plutarch, an owl settled in the rigging of the Greek commander's ship. This boosted the morale of the Athenians because the owl was the symbol of their city. A century and a half later, before a battle between the Greeks and the Carthaginians, the Greek commander Agathokles quietly released numerous owls in his military camp to raise morale among his troops.

There are other examples where unfavourable omens – dreams or animal entrails – actually delayed battle or affected tactics. As one historian wrote as long ago as 1901: 'It is probable that the attention which the Greek commander paid to sacrificial omens was due rather to their effect on the minds and courage of the common soldier than to any undue trust which he placed in them as indications of the tactical policy to be pursued.' So common was the use of such psychological devices to raise morale in Greek warfare that W. Kendrick Pritchett, probably the subject's foremost scholar, has written: 'The problem is ... to explain why ruses and deceptions were *not* used when military advantages could have been gained.'

Following the defeat of the Persians, Athenian civilization began to flourish, particularly under Pericles (495-429 BC) and during the twenty-year Peloponnesian War with the Spartans (431-404 BC). The historian of that conflict, Thucydides (455-400 BC), was an Athenian who fought in the conflict and whose narrative provides a masterly example of seemingly objective history functioning as propaganda. He remains loyal to the Athenian cause while also criticizing where appropriate and presenting opposing arguments. Although more concerned with the details of the war and its battles and politics, Thucydides does provide valuable insights into Greek morale-boosting methods. For example, he describes the address of the Spartan king Archidamus to his troops before the expedition against Athens:

> Peloponnesians and allies, our fathers have engaged in many campaigns both in and outside the Peloponnese, and the elder men in this army of ours are not inexperienced in war. Yet we have never marched out in

greater numbers than now. And just as we are in greater numbers and in better spirit than ever before, so the city against which we are moving is at the height of her power. We must not, then, fall short of our fathers' standards, nor fail to live up to our own reputation. For the whole of Hellas is eagerly watching this action of ours ... Remember, then, that you are marching against a very great city. Think, too, of the glory, or, if events turn out differently, the shame which you will bring to your ancestors and to yourselves, and, with all this in mind, follow your leaders, paying the strictest attention to discipline and security, giving prompt obedience to the orders which you receive. The best and safest thing of all is when a large force is so well disciplined that it seems to be acting like one man.

As this speech reveals, many of the techniques of morale-boosting used in later periods were already known to the Greeks: the appeal to family and national pride; the reminder that the performance of troops was being watched by the entire population; the need for discipline and cohesion; respect for the enemy. Added to this was the role of the military commander and the incentive of booty.

The first people to describe the use of propaganda in the service of the state were the Greek historians and philosophers of the fourth century BC who were beginning to explain the universe in terms of the individual citizen and his relationship to the state. The growth of democracy had been accompanied by a process of humanizing the gods, thus undermining their propagandist role. In his discussions with his master Socrates at the time of the Peloponnesian War, Plato (428-327 BC) wanted to restore the sanctified position to the gods and advocated censorship of the epic poems, particularly those which painted a grim picture of the afterlife:

> Nor can we permit stories of wars and plots and battles among the gods; they are quite untrue, and if we want our prospective guardians to believe that quarrelsomeness is one of the worst of evils, we must certainly not let them embroider robes with the story of the Battle of the Giants, or tell them the tales about the many and various quarrels between gods and heroes and their friends and relations.

Similarly, in *The Republic* Plato stated that 'here again, then, our supervision will be needed. The poets must be told to speak well of that other world. The gloomy descriptions they now give must be forbidden, not only as untrue, but as injurous to our future warriors.' Plato then went on to advocate a policy of truthfulness, or at least the appearance of truthfulness. Yet he recognized the need for censorship and deception to be carried out by the rulers as an essential part of the *democratic* process.

Plato's pupil Aristotle followed this up in his *Rhetoric*, in which he laid down guidelines for orators who must base their persuasion upon the truth: 'the truth tends to win over the false'. He thus established one of the basic axioms of successful propaganda as employed by modern democratic regimes. But it was Xenophon, pupil of Socrates, who can lay claim to having made the first detailed study of morale in warfare. Writing at the beginning of the fourth century BC, Xenophon stated in his work *Anabasis*: 'I am sure that neither numbers nor strength bring victory in war, but whichever army goes into battle stronger in soul, their enemies generally cannot withstand them.'

The Peloponnesian war not only resulted in the defeat of Athens but also in its decline as the self-proclaimed font of civilization. Sparta, momentarily triumphant, was to follow suit within a generation. The renewal of the war with the Persians, continued 'civil' wars, and the defeat of the Spartans by the Thebans at the Battle of Leuctra in 371 BC thoroughly exhausted the Greeks. It took an outsider, Philip of Macedon (382-336 BC), to unite them, but not before he clashed with the Athenians. First in 348 BC and then in 339 BC, Athens under Demosthenes (384-322 BC) tried to resist Philip, but oratory – however brilliant – was no substitute for Macedonian military supremacy. Following the defeat of Athens, Philip formed the League of Corinth, which united most Greek states (except Sparta) and declared war on Persia in 337 BC to avenge the destruction of the Greek temples by Xerxes. Here was a religious pretext if ever there was one, since Greek temples were also Greek treasuries. In order to achieve his aims and enforce Greek unity, especially in view of the fact that Macedonians were not considered to be Greeks but barbarians, Philip introduced new levels of training and drill in his army and developed the Macedonian phalanx, which proved superior to the Greek. He constantly addressed his troops, urging them to be courageous, and he created the first real professional intelligence service. Indeed, the Macedonians were famous for their deceptions, their spies, and their ability to prevent valuable information from reaching the enemy. Philip's achievement on the battlefield, indeed, was matched only by his ability as a propagandist in his efforts to forge Greek unity.

Philip was assassinated in 336 BC and was succeeded by his 20 year old son, Alexander the Great, who took up both his father's military and propagandist mantles. Alexander's mettle as a commander is undisputed; his skill as a propagandist is less well appreciated. Alexander did of course become a cult figure and assumed a towering reputation as a military genius to stand along-side, and even above, the likes of Hannibal, Caesar, and Napoleon – who all admired him. Much of our knowledge of Alexander derives from that cult and there are actually very few contemporary sources of information about him. Even so, what does survive reveals an undoubtedly inspired leader of men and perhaps the first truly great military and political propagandist.

Following his initial successes against the Persians, Alexander publicized his victories in Greece as a triumph for the League of Corinth, even though the Greeks formed only part of his alliance and some, indeed, fought with the Persians. In his attempts to unite his Macedonians with the Persians, Alexander staged a symbolic act at Susa where he himself married Darius's daughter, eighty of his officers married Persian noblewomen, and 10,000 of his troops married their Asiatic concubines. Even his demands for deification as the son of Zeus can be seen as an act of political propaganda. Alexander's coins reflected this. The mint at Alexandria produced coins on which Alexander's face replaced that of Heracles, the 'real' son of Zeus. And, of course, cities from Egypt to India were named after him in the wake of his massive expedition to conquer not just Persia but most of Asia – all of which had been anticipated by his well known and widely publicized action at Gordium when he had cut through the Gordian knot, thereby convincing people that his destiny to rule Asia had been granted by the gods.

Like his father, Alexander employed Greek artists and craftsmen to depict him in bronze statues and in paintings, but most of the surviving portraits of him date from the period immediately follow-ing his death at the age of 32 in 323 BC. These portraits depict the deification of Alexander either in Greek or oriental styles and this stereotypical image was adapted by Roman generals and emperors who wished to emulate him. An essential ingredient of his success had been his attention to detail in matters of morale, not only among his troops but among his peoples. He realized that propa-ganda was an excellent substitute for his actual presence, which is why his image – on coins, buildings, statues, pottery, and in art –

was ever-present throughout his empire. The sheer extent of his conquests at a time when communication was slow and dangerous required the use of images and symbols of his power if he was to sustain his position as master of the world. Religion was used to explain his success: it also played upon the superstition of his peoples. The very fact that Alexander remains one of the greatest figures in history bears witness not just to the success of his propaganda during his lifetime but to the cult of personality developed around his war record by later historical figures. He provided the model for others to follow. Regardless of the reality, it was the image which captured the imagination.

War propaganda came of age under the ancient Greeks. Henceforth, it was to be conducted with growing sophistication. The Greeks had recognized the need for propaganda to galvanize and inspire their citizen-soldiers and had articulated its role within a civilized society. They appreciated the importance of public works as a psychological means of encouraging civic pride and popular loyalty and understood the need for censorship and propaganda campaigns to promote public support for specific military campaigns. The ancient Greeks, therefore, best remembered for their enduring contributions to civilization, recognized that propaganda was an essential ingredient of an organized and effective society. Subsequent civilizations ignored this legacy at their peril.

Chapter 3

The Glory that was Rome

Rome lacked the rich mythological sources available to Greek propagandists, so it created a mythology of its own to provide examples for its citizens to emulate. Indeed, the Romans were exceptional creators of mythological propaganda and their writings often tell us more about contemporary Roman attitudes than they do about the actual historical record. One story stated that Rome was founded by the survivors of Troy and the very best aristocratic families claimed to be able to trace their lines back to the arrival of those founding fathers. The other, better known, legend was that Rome was founded by Romulus and Remus, born of a virgin, orphaned by murder, and reared by a wolf – a story that reinforced Roman pride in their humble origins and that was especially useful at the height of Roman power to emphasize just how far they had come. But it was a violent story and fittingly so, for 'the glory that was Rome' was built on and sustained by violence.

War was an integral part of early Roman life and was the key to Roman expansion, first beyond the city boundaries into Peninsular Italy and then beyond into wider Europe, stretching eventually from Spain, Britain, and France in the west to Egypt, the Persian Gulf, and the Caspian Sea in the east. Military service (possibly as much as ten annual military campaigns) was an essential qualification for political office throughout the Roman Republic (510-27 BC) and, for a young aristocrat with political ambitions, selection as military tribune (of which there were six in each legion) was essential to his career in the Senate and to his appointment as consul (two per year) – a post which demanded military *and* political skills. The formative educational experience of such men was in the army. War, in other words, was the lifeblood of a Roman aristocrat's political and social well-being. In such an intensely ambitious atmosphere, there was no lack of motivation to go to war. As Sallust wrote:

> To men of this kind no toil was unusual, no ground seemed rough or steep, no enemy under arms seemed frightening: courage had gained complete control. But there was an intense competition among them for glory: each one of them hastened to strike down an enemy, to climb the rampart – and to be seen doing such a deed.

But how were ordinary soldiers and civilians motivated to support such warfare? At no time, it would appear, did the people oppose a Senate decision to go to war. So were they instilled with the same kind of war mentality as the aristocracy? Religion played its part, as the Greek writer Polybius recognized when he wrote that the Romans had wisely 'adopted this course of propagating religious awe for the sake of the common people', or as Cicero stated in about 45 BC: 'So in the beginning we must persuade our citizens that the gods are the lords and rulers of all things ... for surely minds which are imbued with such ideas will not fail to form true and useful opinions.' Thucydides and Plato would have warmed to these words. Rome's principal god was Mars, the god of war (naturally), and religion was used much more cynically as an instrument of social control than it had ever been in Greece. Polybius again: 'The Romans are very effective in moments of crisis at propitiating both gods and men.'

Before the battle of Zama in 202 BC, Polybius tells us, the Roman commander Scipio Africanus told his troops that if Hannibal was defeated 'they will obtain for themselves and their country incontestable dominion and power over the rest of the world'. Glory and honour were here being evoked as motivating ideals, not just for the city of Rome, but for the Republic as a whole in whose name the Senate governed (*Senatus Populusque Romanus* [S.P.Q.R] – The Senate and Roman people). Scipio, the eventual conqueror of Hannibal and a military genius in his own right, was well aware of the value of superstition and propaganda in motivating men to fight. As Livy wrote, 'he had worked on men's minds from the beginning' and he deliberately encouraged his image as a religiously-inspired superman. A story, for example that, like Alexander the Great, he was conceived as a result of intercourse with a snake, 'he himself never tried to scotch ... but rather enhanced it by skilfully refraining both from denial and from overt affirmation'. Such devices helped to enhance his mystique amongst his troops and supporters, thereby raising their confidence in a man whose youth might otherwise have raised doubts about his capabilities as a commander.

Many historians have pointed to Rome's repeated attempts to avoid annexation of overseas territories and to the fact that war was waged – at least in Roman minds – for defensive purposes. If so, then an important propaganda point was integral to Roman imperial expansion – namely, that right was always on Rome's side. On the rare occasions when Senate and people were not wholly in agreement over the declaration of war, it was usually the people who aggressively urged their leaders on to battle. Throughout history, war tends to be more popular when your side is winning and when the civilian population genuinely believes that right is on their side. The Romans usually did win, and victory justified the righteousness of the Roman cause and produced tremendous national pride. Yet, other than patriotism, a sense of innate justice, and pride in historical achievement, what else made the ordinary Roman citizen fight?

In the early Republic, Roman citizens had no choice but to serve in the army. The recruit needed to be a peasant landowner, a Roman citizen, and to be prepared to serve for between fifteen and twenty years. Clearly, his rewards at the end of his military career had to be substantial enough to compensate for the annual risk of death and the cost of his absence from his farm during the campaign season from March to October. Perhaps, rather like the Ghurka regiments in the British army of this century, army service was an important means of supplementing a farm income, as well as of acquiring family pride. At times of crisis conscription was used by Rome, but volunteer professional soldiers were the backbone of the Roman legions – men who saw the army as a career and whose motivation and morale were already high. Such men were in abundance in Rome until about the mid second century BC. Given the regularity of warfare, they knew that they were going to fight many campaigns, that battles would be fought fiercely, and that, if victorious, they would be expected to react savagely. Captured cities were harshly treated; Polybius described the indiscriminate murder and rape of civilians in New Carthage in Spain by Scipio Africanus' troops during the Second Punic War (219-202 BC): 'The purpose of this custom, I suppose, is to strike terror.' And so it was. The reputation Roman troops gained for their ferocity and savagery was encouraged and fostered by their leaders as a propaganda device to frighten further opponents. This was why Scipio Aemilianus, during the Third Punic War (149-146 BC), ordered that 400 rebels in Spain should have their hands cut off (although the same man is said to have wept at the sight of the total destruction of Carthage at the end of the war).

Roman historians certainly never depicted Rome as the aggressor. Rome always *defended* her interests and conquered foreign peoples to save them from themselves. Prior to any attack, envoys were always despatched in an ostentatious attempt to resolve the dispute in Rome's favour by means other than war, and only when this was refused did Rome declare war, 'justly' and after alternative means had been tried to 'save the peace'. Such pretexts (for pretexts they mostly were) enabled Rome to argue the rightness of its cause, not just to its own people but to its allies. However, given that war was the most effective means of ensuring wealth, power, and status, it would be unusual for Roman politicians and their followers to pursue policies designed to avoid war – although opening too many battle fronts simultaneously would have been a risky business inviting disaster. But caution is required when relying upon Roman sources that were often written to score party political points. Roman writers, especially Livy and Polybius, always maintained that Rome was the victim of aggression, especially in the Punic Wars against Carthage, when in fact the Roman seizure of Sardinia and Roman interference in Spain forced Carthage into declaring war. Rome knew that the demands of its legates to Carthage in 218 BC would be refused and, even thereafter, Roman sources praised the achievements of Hannibal (which were real enough) in order to portray the ultimate Roman victory over him as all the greater.

Such victories were the principal source of decorative and celebratory adornments in the city of Rome itself. Inscriptions on specially built monuments, paintings displayed in public buildings, captured booty such as columns and weapons, statues of generals in the forum – these were not just designed to reflect upon the glory of the aristocracy. They were also meant to impress the people and to instill confidence and loyalty. Songs praising the achievements of military heroes were sung at banquets and other ceremonies, and Roman writers also utilized drama and poetry to spread the fame of 'the great and the good'. Even funeral processions were used to display the achievements of a particular family before 'the whole people', as Polybius described. Death masks worn by relatives kept alive the memory of illustrious predecessors so that 'young men' were inspired 'to endure everything in the public interest, for the sake of achieving the glory that attends good men'.

Roman military organization was legendary, but military dynasts who fostered a relationship with their troops based on loyalty to themselves rather than the state were ultimately to destroy the Roman Republic. Plutarch may have insisted in his biography of Gaius Marius (d. 86 BC) that soldiers admired generals who shared their conditions more than those who merely relied on money to secure their soldiers' loyalty, but good pay and booty remained an essential way of avoiding mutinies and ensuring high morale. Great care was taken to distribute booty evenly, and thus avoid serious disputes. And it was Marius who, towards the end of the second century BC, professionalized the Roman armies by broadening their recruitment base beyond the peasantry, employing men who lived solely for the army and had no need to worry about returning to their farms for the winter. Marius also took responsibility for the welfare of his troops when they were injured or when they retired, and they, in turn, looked to him – rather than the State – for leadership and reward.

The implications of Marius' reforms are obvious. Thereafter, Roman legions consisted of professional regular soldiers whose loyalty was first and foremost to their individual paymasters, not to the State. If that individual commander was loyal to the State, well and good; if he was not, then Rome was in more danger from within than from without. Later, during the period of the Roman Empire, emperors had to ensure that propaganda among their own troops was conducted effectively as it was not always easy for them to go to war personally (leaving conspiratorial Rome was frequently more dangerous than the battlefield itself). A military oath, introduced in 216 BC, bound soldiers to defend the State by obeying their military leaders, but when Sulla used his troops to march on Rome in 88 BC the relationship became based more on personal loyalty – an ominous portent of the civil wars that occurred later in the century.

The more astute Roman sources make clear that the key to Roman military success lay in the training and organization of the armies. This very fact often gave Roman armies the psychological edge over their opponents. And nothing succeeds like success. As Rome established its reputation for military invincibility, despite such setbacks as those inflicted by Hannibal at the battles of Lake Trasmene and at Cannae, Rome was able to trade upon its reputation for occasionally losing battles but always winning the war. The very existence of Roman communications, of roads and of sea routes, and the detailed attention given to logistics and troop supplies, usually deterred all but the most committed aggressor. As the nineteenth-century French military writer, Ardant du Picq, stated: 'No army is worthy of its name without discipline ... Discipline cannot be secured or created in a day. It is an institution, a tradition.'

Discipline and morale were essential in view of the way in which the Romans waged war. Unlike the Greek phalanx, which relied upon mutual dependence in keeping the ranks together, the Romans fought in thinner lines or waves which involved all the soldiers in combat. It was a more efficient means of deploying the maximum number of men to the front line, but it also required greater attention to the details of why and how men fought. Panic usually started in the rear of the Greek phalanx, but there was no room for the faint-hearted in the Roman legions, where front-line troops were constantly reinforced during the course of battle. Moreover, given that Greek battles were usually decided by one single engagement, whereas Roman battles often required a more prolonged and complicated strategy depending upon movement and manoeuvrability of the troops, a more sustained propaganda campaign directed at the *esprit de corps* of the Roman troops was essential. Great attention, for example, was paid in Roman fortified camps to relaxing the soldier before battle and so minimizing nervous strain. These camps were an important factor in Roman military strategy, and successful fighting units were kept together rather than being broken up to strengthen weaker ones. When, in one battle during the Civil War, 200 veterans saved themselves and 220 recruits surrendered only to be massacred, Julius Caesar commented: 'here might be seen what security men derive from a resolute spirit'. The tactics employed ensured that, even when defeated, Roman troops inflicted heavy casualties upon their enemies who were invariably less well organized and less well disciplined. Indeed, discipline may have been the key to the effectiveness of

Roman war propaganda amongst their own troops. It was only when Roman troops fought one another as mercenary forces loyal to individual paymasters in the numerous civil strifes which plagued Roman history that more disorganized enemies could cross Roman frontiers with some hope of success.

Julius Caesar was, of course, one of history's greatest military commanders and, like all great commanders, he was fully aware of the role morale could play before, during, and after battle. He led by personal example, addressing his troops as 'fellow-soldiers' before battle and letting his own self-confidence filter through the ranks. He sometimes even led from the front once combat began. In his *Commentaries*, Caesar described how, following a surprise attack on his army, the commander

> had everything to do at one moment: the flag to raise as signal of a general call to arms, the trumpet to sound, the troops to recall from entrenching, the men to bring in who had gone somewhat further afield in search of material ... the line to form, the troops to harangue, the signal to give ... [the] harangue was no more than a charge to bear in mind their ancient valour, to be free from fear, and bravely to withstand the onslaught of the enemy ... He started off at once in the other direction to give a like harangue, and found them already fighting.

Caesar was a fierce disciplinarian who severely punished deserters and mutineers, and he never forgot the role which money and booty played in motivating his soldiers to fight. He was one of the first Romans to have his portrait stamped on coins during his lifetime, rather than posthumously as hitherto, under a senatorial decree in 44 BC. Payment in such coins reminded the troops of where their interests lay.

Caesar not only handed out land and money to his veterans. He also distributed food to the poor and he courted the masses by providing banquets and receptions, complete with entertainment. He also realized that the people loved a parade and elaborate triumphal processions were staged – all to boost the morale of the people whose support he counted on. He put on mock naval battles on specially constructed lakes, contests featuring gladiators from his own training school at Capua, and was even responsible for bringing the first hippopotamus from Africa – all for the purpose of winning and maintaining public favour. As for his enemies, Caesar recognized the value of clemency and leniency in winning new

friends and loyalties, and Roman citizenship came to be extended
to non-Romans as a means of attracting their support.

However, it was these very characteristics that were to be Caesar's
undoing. By courting the crowd, often by attacks on certain nobles,
he ended up alienating the aristocracy. His propaganda became too
blatant and counter-productive. The hostile Suetonius wrote:

> Not only did he accept excessive honours ... a statue placed among the
> kings and a throne in the orchestra at the theatre – he also allowed to be
> decreed to himself honours even surpassing human rank, such as a
> golden seat in the Senate house and on the tribunal, a ceremonial
> carriage and litter in the Circus processions, temples, altars, images
> next to those of the gods, a ceremonial couch ... and a month named
> after himself.

The more sympathetic Dio admitted: 'Caesar did sometimes
make a mistake by accepting some of the honours voted him, and
believing that he really deserved them, but most at fault were those
who after beginning by honouring him as he deserved, then led him
on and blamed him for what they voted to him.' The aristocratic
conspirators who assassinated him in March 44 BC were also to
learn the unpredictability of the mob in the years that followed.
Undoubtedly believing that they were acting with public support,
Brutus and his fellow-conspirators eventually became victims of the
very propaganda campaign they had directed at Caesar's power
and person.

Caesar was the historian of his own wars but, as with most
memoirs, his writings were less concerned with providing strictly
accurate information than with vindicating his actions in the eyes
of his contemporaries. In other words, they are essentially propagandistic. This does not invalidate, for example, Caesar's *Commentaries*
as historical evidence; it simply means they should be handled with
caution. Published in 51 BC, the seven books dealing with the
Gallic War (58-52 BC) often tell us as much about the political
crisis facing Caesar at that time as they do about his military
achievement. This is even more apparent from the two books
Caesar wrote about the Civil War in which, even when addressing
his troops before battle, Caesar portrays himself as a lover of peace
forced reluctantly to fight his enemies, to whom he is nonetheless
magnanimous in victory. The significance of such orations was
described by Cicero, who said that although military commanders

'may see their soldiers absolutely prepared for battle, they none-theless exhort them'.

Caesar's successor, his great-nephew Octavian, who became the Emperor Augustus, was an even more successful propagandist – in that he survived to die a natural death. As Professor Syme has written, 'the heir of Caesar at once devoted himself to Caesarian propaganda'. By praising Caesar and perpetuating his memory, Augustus was by implication reminding the people that he was the son of a god – although he was careful not to repeat Caesar's mistake of adopting divine status in his lifetime, at least in Italy. The eastern empire was otherwise; like Alexander the Great, Augustus recognized the value of different propaganda approaches for different cultures. Although not a great military commander himself (his military successes were achieved largely through his subordinates), one would never guess it from his propaganda. Nor would one guess from his idealized statues or from coin portraits that the man was ugly. His autobiographical tract, *Res Gestae Divi Augustus*, often says more by its omissions (such as military defeats), but it does provide us with a picture of what Augustus wanted to be remembered for. Adopting Caesar's reputation for clemency, he wrote: 'I fought many wars, civil and foreign, by land and sea throughout the entire world, and as victor ... such foreign peoples as it was safe to pardon I preferred to preserve rather than exterminate.' He went on to point out that he had refused many honours which the people tried to bestow on him for restoring the peace while listing all those that he did accept. Inscribed on his mausoleum, the *Res Gestae* is an unabashed exercise in propaganda, as was most of Augustus' civic architecture; but it did not end there.

During the civil war that followed Caesar's death, the principal rivals for his mantle all made use of their portraits – for example, on coins used to pay their troops. Some portraits of Pompey the Great and Mark Antony depicted them as Zeus, others as Alexander the Great. After Mark Antony had been defeated at the battle of Actium in 31 BC, Augustus reunited Rome and rigorously controlled the use of his image in order to avoid the kind of propaganda war and rumour-mongering that had preceded Caesar's death. He also avoided Caesar's more blatant excesses (for instance, he forbade his statue to be carried in religious processions) and he only allowed temples to be built to him in certain areas where popular sensitivities would not be offended. He went back to the practice of granting divine status to the dead, not the living – although Augustus did of course bask in his own genetic link to the god Caesar and he retained the practice of putting his own head on his coinage. The aim of this controlled use of his image was to establish his position as First Citizen of the restored Republic in a modest way (he even melted down eighty silver statues of himself and donated the proceeds to the temple of Apollo in Rome because silver was not considered an appropriate medium for mortals), both in war-torn Rome and Italy and in the divided provinces.

Of the numerous statues of Augustus which survive, several depict him in the role of general. It was essential for Augustus – and his successors – to identify himself with his troops, and one way of doing this was to accumulate an impressive array of titles and military honours. One of the most famous statues of Augustus is from the villa of his wife Livia at Prima Porta on the outskirts of Rome. The front of the breastplate depicts the return in 20 BC of the battle standards lost to the Parthians at the battle of Carrhae in 53 BC. But it is the idealized style that concerns us here. The cupid on a dolphin supporting Augustus' right leg refers to Venus, the divine founder of the Julian family, and the feet are bare – an image more appropriate to a Greek god than to a Roman general. But the proliferation of the image of Augustus in his numerous roles – though never as a god until after his death in AD 14 – was marked and he was perhaps the first mortal to have his image as widely disseminated as those of the Royal Family or the Pope on souvenir stalls in London or Rome today.

Augustus established an imperial tradition that was to survive for several centuries. The success of Roman military power was in itself excellent propaganda. It was used to frighten potential opponents, such as when imperial legations visited 'barbarian' courts with news or reminders of recent triumphs, and was perpetuated in a cult of invincibility as reflected in art, ceremony and games, coins (carrying the words 'Victory of ...' or 'Eternal Victory'), and even in the battle cries of the Roman troops. The troops were tradition-ally addressed by their commanders before battle. As Vegetius stated: 'A general can encourage and animate his troops by suitable exhortations and harangues ... He should employ every argument capable of exciting rage, hatred and indignation against their adversaries in the minds of his soldiers.' And once victory had been secured, its role in the mind of Roman society was celebrated and perpetuated in the form of the triumphal march through Rome.

Coins were an important medium of Roman propaganda, a valuable means of spreading visual images of Rome's triumphs all over the Empire. They were used, for instance, to publish Augustus' manifesto of 'Peace and Victory' after the civil wars and to advertise his subsequent military and diplomatic achievements (such as the capture of Armenia and the return of the Parthian standards). Yet despite the pretence of restoring the Republic, Augustus was in fact establishing an imperial dynasty, as reflected in the building of his Mausoleum in 28 BC. His building programme in Rome ('I found the city in brick and left it marble'), including his forum dedicated to Mars, the god of war, was on a grand scale and designed not only to reflect his achievements but also to link his heritage to the founders of Rome. It was in the Augustan forum that the recovered Parthian standards were displayed, and the entire monument was decorated with captured weapons, statues of distinguished Republican generals and statesmen (within whose ranks, of course, Augustus was naturally at home), and captured artefacts from all over the Empire. It was in the Temple of Mars that military commitments and treaties were debated and foreign heads of state received. It was in the Altar of Peace, completed in 9 BC, that Augustus celebrated the other side of his achievement. The altar was designed to celebrate Augustus' safe return from Spain and Gaul, but in many ways it reflects the emperor's own view of Rome – a disguised monarchy led by a man but blessed by the gods, Senate, and people. Like most of Rome's architecture, such as the triumphal arches (over fifty of which were erected in Rome) and the columns of Trajan and Marcus Aurelius, the aim was to present the splendour of Roman military achievement to as wide an audience as possible.

The climax of any Roman war propaganda campaign came with the triumphal procession through Rome following a significant military victory. Though not held too frequently, in order to protect the dignity and splendour of the occasion and to inhibit the rise of ambitious generals, their popularity with the crowds was enormous, especially during the period of the Republic. Their function, originally religious, became largely political in that they demonstrated the suitability of the emperor to govern – which was why, during the period of the Empire, only members of the Augustan dynasty were permitted to hold them. The procession, with its ceremonially clad troops, its captives and spoils, was designed to inspire the large crowds, who would already be at a high pitch of excitement by the time the emperor appeared in his golden triumphal chariot. Enemy booty was paraded along with captives, and the celebrations might last for days or even months (Trajan's second triumph in AD 106 lasted 123 days). A special breakfast for the troops was followed by an imperial speech, the procession, and perhaps the public execution of the enemy leader. The British king Caractacus was pardoned by the Emperor Claudius to demonstrate his magnanimity before all. Although there were only thirteen triumphs between 31 BC and AD 235, they were memorable occasions and an invaluable means of forging a bond between emperor and army and between emperor and people. But discipline remained an integral fact of Roman military life and Augustus, according to Suetonius, recognized this, even disbanding the tenth legion in disgrace for insubordination. Units or individuals who crumbled in battle were dismissed, deserters executed, and other offences severely punished. They were literally decimated, one in ten being killed.

Throughout the period of the Roman Empire, successive Roman Emperors perpetuated an elaborate pretence: that Rome was still ruled by the people and by the Senate when it was in fact ruled more in the style of Rome's founding kings, as a Principate. Augustus sponsored poets and writers, Virgil and Horace among them, to help him in his task. Pliny eulogized Trajan in AD 100 for not courting blatant propaganda: 'Respects are paid to you in serious poems and the eternal renown of chronicled history, not in short-lived publicity. Indeed, the greater the silence on the stage about you, the more united are the theatre audiences in rising to pay you their respects.' Such eulogies were, themselves, an ideal medium of imperial propaganda and display a recognition of the principle that it is always better to get someone else to sing your praises than to do it yourself. The eulogists were like propaganda writers working to perpetuate the cult of their imperial leaders, their statements widely heard and repeated, and even published for the benefit of the literate. This had been appreciated for some time; as Cicero requested to one of his friends: 'I should be glad if you would undertake to look after all my other interests, and most especially my reputation.' In an age when rumours and libel were rife (it is no coincidence that satire is regarded as one of Rome's major contributions to culture), a good public relations exercise was essential to political survival. This was particularly true for the army, upon which the emperor's power had come to rest by the third century. As one historian has put it: 'The emperor at first ruled through the army. In the third century the army ruled through the emperor.'

Yet it was not the pagan gods, used so cynically by the Romans for propaganda purposes, but the Christians who were ultimately to conquer the hearts and minds of the later emperors. At first, the peace established by Augustus enabled Christ's disciples to spread his teachings and the propaganda techniques they used helped what began as a cult religion to spread throughout the Empire. Perhaps it was because it was a religion for the individual, unlike most other ancient religions, which gave it its appeal.

Rome at first tolerated the cult – as it did scores of other cults; but Christianity's claim to recognize a supreme and exclusive authority higher than the State made it subversive in Roman eyes since Christians refused to participate in emperor-worship. And, like the impact of Christ's death, the more martyrs Rome created, the more people became impressed with the manner of their deaths. Rome, in other words, may have believed that it was destroying the cult in its war against the Christians, when in fact it was helping to spread its message still further by the cruelty of its persecution. The early Christian martyrs recognized that actions on the field of 'battle' – such as the manner with which they faced crucifixion and other torments – reinforced the words and the messages that had caused their death while following their Saviour's example. 'The blood of the martyr', wrote Tertullian, an early Christian writer, 'is the seed of the Church.'

Forced underground by State persecution it was not until the fourth century, when the cross became the dominant Christian symbol, that the movement could begin to boast a following wider than the slaves, aliens, and social outcasts to whom it had at first appealed. Many historians have argued that Christianity helped to destroy the Roman Empire; Christians will argue that Rome was saved by it. Constantine the Great, the first Roman emperor to be converted (in AD 312-13), recognized Christianity as the official religion of the Roman Empire and moved its capital to Byzantium (Constantinople). Constantine may be seen either as villain or hero, but in reality it was the Goths and the Vandals who destroyed the western Roman empire in the fifth century (in 476 when the last Roman emperor abdicated before Odovacar the Ostrogoth) and the Turks who destroyed the Roman empire in the east when they sacked Constantinople in 1453.

Prior to the professionalization of the Roman army, the Roman soldier returned to his land once the campaigning season was over. By the third century, Roman armies recruited non-Romans almost like mercenary armies. Soldiers motivated more by profit than by patriotism make a different set of decisions, perhaps subconsciously, in the heat of battle; they have to decide whether it is worth the risk of dying. Whereas Rome could once rely upon superior organization to fight the Goths, by the fifth century the decline in discipline and organization within legions recruited from all parts of the Empire was marked. Following the defeat at Adrianople in 378 (the worst since Cannae) and barbarian invasions such as the Visogoth attack on Rome in 410, it was clear that Roman legions no longer held the tactical advantage over their enemies. For one thing, they were frequently too busy fighting each other in the name of candidates to the imperial throne, whilst Germanic invaders took advantage of the unguarded frontiers. Despite the relative stability of Diocletian's reign (285-305), the rot had set in. What might be described as a failure of morale was a key factor in the collapse of the Roman Empire. When Attila the Hun spoke at the battle of Chalons in 451, he talked of the Romans fighting much as they had done for centuries, in close formation of lines; but what was lacking was discipline and organization. Attila was not fighting the legions of Marius, Pompey, and Caesar. He was effectively fighting against fellow barbarians, amongst whom the organization of warfare was less pronounced than it had been in the armies of Republican Rome but whose leaders, as a result of the cumulative influence of history, experience, Christianity, and 'civilization', had perhaps begun to recognize the merits of peace even more than those of war. Or, as St Jerome put it: 'It is our sins which strengthen the Barbarians, it is our vices which undermine the Roman army.' And just as the cohesion and unity had gone out of the army, so also had Roman propaganda crumbled and fragmented.

Part Two

Propaganda in the Middle Ages

Chapter 4

The 'Dark Ages' to 1066

The slow and tortuous collapse of the Roman Empire in the west at the hands of the Germanic invaders saw the disappearance of the Roman legion as the principal instrument of warfare. With it went the kind of organization and discipline that was in some ways a substitute for morale-boosting. Islam, with its light cavalry, swept west from Arabia to Spain and it was only long after the Franks stopped the 'heathen' armies at the battle of Poitiers in 732 that western Europe and Christianity were able to counter-attack in the form of the Crusades. In the meantime, the Roman art of war was replaced by the barbarians' style of fighting. It was a style characterized by speed, brutality, and improvization and motivated by the very nature of barbarian society itself.

We do in fact often have less information about war and communication in the so-called Dark Ages than we do about the Roman period, with few surviving detailed descriptions of battles. Roman sources would have us believe that chaos replaced order, and there is little testimony to provide us with an alternative view. But it would be a mistake to assume that, after the disastrous Roman defeat by the Goths at Adrianople in 378, warfare became less sophisticated and more chaotic. Many military historians see Adrianople as a turning point, a point at which light cavalry became more important than infantry (although the Romans had used cavalry to some extent for centuries before). This process was helped by the development of the stirrup in the eighth century (though it had been used in China and the East for some time before), which in turn encouraged the development of the heavy cavalry units of knights that were to dominate warfare in Christendom for the rest of the Middle Ages. The stirrup enabled heavily armed knights to stay in the saddle during combat. 'Speed could be converted into shock', Professor Howard observes, 'spears need no longer be thrown but could be couched as lances and driven home.' By the eighth century, the heavy cavalry was 'queen of battles' and the sheer expense involved meant that the wealthy landed class became the principal instrument of both warfare and, as we shall see, of feudal society as a whole. Although generalizations are dangerous, the point is that medieval warfare was not necessarily more chaotic than in Roman times but that battles were in many respects less predictable, less 'formulaic'. Seldom were wars decided by individual battles, but the manner in which they were fought and the behaviour of the soldiers on the battlefield was as much determined by social factors as they had been in Greece and Rome.

It would equally be erroneous to assume that propaganda similarly became a less significant factor, either in society or in warfare, after the fall of Rome. War remained a terrifying experience; equally, persuasion remained an essential component of recruitment, morale, and combat motivation. In many respects, propaganda became an even more important instrument of social control, of maintaining the prevailing social, political and religious order – the 'hierocratic theme' as one historian has called it – as the struggle to control not only the Church but also the successor states to Rome proceeded. Propaganda provided cohesion, a set of answers in a confusing world.

The cultural monopoly of the Church ensured that whatever ideas were spread conformed to the wishes of the religious Establishment. From the time of Pope Gregory I (590-604), the successors of the principal apostle, St Peter, began to establish their spiritual dominance over western Europe by a wide variety of means. As Gregory wrote: 'to adore a picture is wrong; to learn through the picture what is to be adored is praiseworthy.' To Gregory, statues were 'the books of the illiterate'. Popes recognized that war was often necessary to 'defend the peace', and indeed argued that war was the price of peace (as articulated by St Augustine, 354-430), especially when it was forced upon them by pagan aggressors. This was, in itself, a means of establishing their dominant position within medieval society. It was a dominance that was, remarkably, to last for more than a thousand years.

The spread of Christianity was achieved with the important aid of visual imagery. Drawing upon the vivid stories from the Old and

New Testaments, visual symbols that were instantly recognizable and beautifully simple (the cross being the most obvious example) helped to unite people from different areas and from different social backgrounds in a common faith. Christian imagery frequently blended with the pagan beliefs of the past. The earliest representations of Christ from the third century reveal that he was modelled on the clean-shaven Apollo; a century later he resembles the bearded Jupiter. Although an increasingly universal phenomenon, Christianity also catered for antiquity's yearning for local gods and cults by the creation of saints (such as St George and St Christopher) and local martyrs. The lives of the saints were written down (though for public recital) to provide role models and doctrinal lessons for converted and unconverted alike. Hymns provided a further focus of communal worship.

To ensure orthodoxy, and thus maintain the unity and position of the Church, priests and preachers held regular services in which ritual behaviour, visual imagery, and sermons helped to encourage loyalty and convert the unenlightened. Christianity was a complex doctrine whose messages had to be passed to the ignorant and illiterate in as simplistic a way as possible, and its appeal was largely due to the success of its leaders in simplifying those messages with the use of propagandist techniques. The Venerable Bede, writing in about 700, described how some twenty-five years earlier Benedict Biscop had built his church of St Peter on the River Wear in England and how he had adorned it with religious symbols

> so that everyone who entered the church, even if he could not read, wherever they turned their eyes, might have before them the benevolent face of Christ and his saints, though it were but in a picture, and with watchful minds might meditate on the benefits of Our Lord's incarnation, and having in front of their minds the perils of the Last Judgement, might the more strictly examine their consciences on that score.

It was the increasing role of the Church in European society which naturally encouraged the development of art, architecture, and what we would now call the decorative arts. Cathedrals and churches became points of communal identity and pride, attracting donations from the rich and the loyalty of the poor in return for the promise of eternal life.

In the east, however, church propaganda was causing offence to the Roman emperor at Constantinople, Leo III (717-802), who issued a decree against religious images. This precipitated the Iconoclastic ('image-breaking') Schism with the papacy. This clash irrevocably sundered the bond between the Church in Rome and Byzantium. It may seem ironic that the old Roman Empire, which had done so much to develop the use of imagery, both pagan and Christian, was finally broken in two by a dispute over the role such propaganda could play. As a consequence of the split, the papacy began to look to the successor states of the West as allies. Even as those states began to acquire new strength, their kings realized that the Church could make a powerful ally in legitimizing their regimes.

Transport affected both warfare and propaganda. But it did not mean that either went into decline. The ability of migratory tribes to move from east to west and, later, of crusading armies to travel from Western Europe to the Middle East bears witness to that. In many places in Europe, warfare was endemic, the interludes of peace being so unusual that they earned the special attention of commentators, which makes it virtually impossible to separate war propaganda from all other forms. As in antiquity, wars were brief and largely confined to the summer campaign season. Money remained important to pay the troops, but armies were comparatively small – forces of 10,000 men were unusual – and plundering campaigns were perhaps the most common type of warfare in the early Dark Ages. The Germanic hordes which wrested western Europe from Roman grasp may appear barbaric when compared to 'civilized' Rome (i.e. 'Christianized' Rome in which 'peace on earth' was regarded as a virtue), and their propaganda was certainly less well developed. But they fought in clans, alongside people they had been brought up with. This inevitably tightened the bond between them in battle. It was not just peer pressure on the battlefield that motivated them to fight effectively, but social pressure to do well amongst their friends and relatives. Their leaders in peace were the same leaders in war. As Tacitus (our best source for the Germanic peoples) wrote in the first century:

> On the field of battle it is a disgrace to the chief to be surpassed in valour by his companions, to the companions not to come up to the valour of their chief. As for leaving a battle alive after your chief has fallen, that means lifelong infamy and shame. To defend and protect him, to put down one's own acts of heroism to his credit – that is what they really mean by 'allegiance'. The chiefs fight for victory, the companions for their chief.

The psychological advantage of fighting alongside people you have known for years rather than relative strangers – despite the bonds created in training – cannot be ignored. Indeed, this factor may have provided the Goths and the Vandals with more of their psychological cohesion than simply their training and discipline. It proved to be their major contribution to the Middle Ages.

Part of the reason for this was that the German 'barbarians' who overan western Europe in a wave of migratory invasions in the fifth, sixth, and seventh centuries did not regard war as the sole reason for existence. Even the Lombards, to whom war was a great tradition, an extension of feuding and sacrifice, understood the concept and virtues of peace, or at least of non-hostility. Having said that, their record as warriors was impressive. Military service was obligatory amongst these warlike peoples; military training began early, and failure to join the army on maturity or on campaigns thereafter incurred at least a heavy fine. Soldiers supplied their own weapons (the rich would bring armour and weapons, the poor bow and arrows). Inspired by the gods, to whom pre-battle sacrifices were made, barbarian soldiers were motivated by tradition, peer-pressure, and booty. If the gods did not oblige by providing victory, they could quite easily be abandoned, as Clovis (481-511, the founder of the Frankish kingdom of Merovingian Gaul) did after the battle of Tolbiac when he became the first barbarian king to convert to Christianity. The gods thus served a propagandist function, as always.

Our principal source for the Franks in this period, Gregory of Tours (538-94), described mainly civil warfare and the feuding of kings. The royal circuit or 'wandering monarchy', which tried to keep together the different Frankish tribal groups, was aware of the importance of ceremonial and circuses, culminating in an annual assembly of kings and aristocrats known as the Marchfield. Sometimes military leaders – or their champions – would settle their differences personally in duels rather than mobilizing their troops. In more conventional fights, brutality against the vanquished was common, as in 539 when the king of the Franks threw Ostrogoth women and children into the River Po. Others became slaves and ransoms were frequently demanded to increase the hoard of booty used to pay the victorious troops. Their reputation for sheer brutality in battle was the main psychological warfare element employed by the Goths, Vandals, Franks, and

Lombards. Their tribal origins and traditions were the main ingredients of their war propaganda, at least until they began to settle in
Gaul (threatened by the western migration of the Huns under
Attila, 433-53), when they began to lose their war-like habits and
traditions, to some extent. Rome may have been partly barbarized,
but the Germans were also to become partly Romanized.

Their Christian opponents, led by the Pope, were motivated by
'higher' (that is, more sophisticated) things – in particular the
conversion, rather than the enslavement, of the heathen. Inspired
by the teachings of St Augustine, who believed that peace on earth
was impossible and that war on behalf of the True Faith was both
a consequence of and a remedy against sin, the Church employed
the war-like traditions of the conquered and converted barbarians
to spread the word, although certain 'rules' of war had to be
followed in accordance with the theory of divine mercy. If those
rules were broken and, say, an atrocity was committed (as often
happened), it was necessary to gain absolution by a system of
penitence and repentance.

If we accepted uncritically the religious sources, we would
believe that the outcome of battles was decided by miracles, the
intervention of God, or of some saint or other. But it may perhaps
be more accurate to state that those phenomena are more likely to
have got the soldier to the battlefield in the first place. What
happened thereafter was down to strategy, tactics, courage, and
luck. It was thus essential for the Church to create a mentality
which would encourage people to fight, if necessary, on its behalf.
Everlasting Life was the carrot; Eternal Damnation the stick.

Between the fourth and eight centuries, the old Roman empire –
divided between Rome in the west and Constantinople in the east –
gradually drifted further apart, not just politically as the Franks
established themselves in France, the Visogoths in Spain, the
Vandals in North Africa, the Ostrogoths and later the Lombards
and Normans in Italy, and the Lombards and Saxons in North and
North-western Europe, but also religiously between the Latin
(Catholic) Church based in Rome and the Greek (Orthodox)
church in Byzantium. In the east, the main military threat came
from Islam, inspired by Mohammed (570-632) and the concept of
'jihad' (holy war), and gradually moving into the areas once
conquered by Alexander the Great, from the northern shores of
Africa to Persia and India. The bulwark against this threat was

Constantinople, which finally fell to the Ottoman Turks in 1453. Especially under the Emperor Justinian (527-65), Constantinople became the New Rome of the East, where imperial traditions were preserved and where imperial grandeur – as epitomized by the Great Church of St Sophia – was in full view. But by the seventh century, the Byzantine empire was on a virtually permanent war-footing as military threats from all sides threatened Justinian's successors. In 626, Constantinople managed to withstand a combined assault from the Slavs, Avars, and Persians when the centuries-old Persian threat was finally eliminated. But it cannot be said that the eastern Roman empire was wholly successful, for within a generation the vacuum created by the Persian defeat was filled by the emergent Arab empire. Even after the first wave of Arab expansion (630-730) had been arrested by the successful defence of Constantinople in 717-18, the Byzantine empire lost much of its territory in Egypt and Syria.

Meanwhile in the west, the Merovingian dynasty founded by Clovis was in decline under a series of 'do-nothing' kings. The civil strife, the early stages of which are described by Gregory of Tours, reached its climax in the reign of Pepin the Short (741-68) who was crowned King of the French in 751 and founded the Carolingian dynasty. The Pope, alarmed by the Iconoclastic Schism with the Greek Orthodox Church, now turned to the west and embraced the Carolingians. After all, Pepin's father, Charles Martel (714-41), had saved western Europe from Islam by defeating the Moslem invaders who attacked his territory from Spain at the battle of Poitiers in 733. He did this with foot soldiers against cavalry, but because he was unable to pursue the enemy in flight he resolved to build up his own cavalry arm, which was paid for out of requisitioned Church money, whereupon he drove the Moslems back into Spain. Perhaps even more significant was the fact that Pepin had invaded Italy, defeated the Lombards, and given the Pope his conquered lands, thus founding the Papal States. Under Pepin, Church and State formed a mutually beneficial alliance – the first time a western secular ruler had had his legitimacy consecrated by the 'Vicar of Christ'. The Pope's power to do this was, in fact, spurious, but he claimed the right using a forged document, the infamous *Donation of Constantine*.

In 800 Pepin's son Charles, King of the Franks, was crowned Charlemagne, Holy Roman Emperor in Rome itself. Charlemagne

(768-814) stabilized the Carolingian regime and extended the
borders of the old Merovingian empire by moving further east into
Germany and south into Italy and Spain. He was an inspired leader
of men, suggesting that he understood the importance of propaganda in war, but much more than that we cannot say. We know he
was fanatical about hunting and that he waged war with similar
enthusiasm. We know also that his armies were prepared for battle
by prayers. But his major military achievement was the organization and discipline he brought to his armies, factors which had
been absent since the heyday of Rome. His vassals were bound by
tradition to turn up for the campaign season, complete with their
own arms in accordance with their economic circumstances. Non-
appearance effected a heavy – indeed crippling – fine: 'Any man
called to the army who does not arrive on time at the designated
place will be deprived of meat and wine for as many days as he has
delayed.' But as these peasants depended upon their lords for
protection in peacetime, it was advisable and socially accepted in a
feudal context that they should turn up, especially as they had
probably sworn an oath of loyalty. Deserters (of which there were
many given the impatience of peasants to return home in time for
the harvest) were executed although Charlemagne did allow some
exemptions towards the end of his reign. Although there was a
general levy of freemen, Charlemagne's armies were composed
largely of professional soldiers – chiefly the royal vassals, who
received considerable rewards.

   Campaigns were carefully prepared and planned, supply trains
organized, and pillage forbidden until enemy territory was reached.
The principal prize was booty. Subsequently, great victories were
celebrated in verse and in song, but other than this celebratory
propaganda, we know very little about Charlemagne's efforts at
morale-boosting among his own troops. They certainly composed
or recited edificatory treatises exhorting the men to behave in a
Christian manner. Although primarily intended for the aristocratic
knights, they could equally have been read to the illiterate peasant
soldiers. These 'mirrors', as they were called, advocated the virtues
of justice, courage, generosity, and fighting for God's cause and
warned of the vices that could lead to eternal damnation. They
were probably of great significance in easing the frightened minds
of men about to follow Charles into his endless wars.

   Charles first invaded Italy in 773-4 and proclaimed himself King of the Lombards. He then began the long campaign to subdue the Saxons to the north-east, which he did with a brutality character-ized by massacres, forced conversions, and mass deportations. The sympathetic Einhard, in his *Life of Charlemagne,* tends to gloss over these excesses. When Charlemagne was ready to attack the German Avars (Huns) in 791, he made his soldiers fast and pray for three days beforehand, every priest had to sing a mass, and the clerics had to sing fifty psalms a day while remaining barefooted. Fasts and prayers, in other words, prepared the men for battle, while crosses and banners were carried before them as they went into combat. To the south, Charlemagne fought a largely defensive war against the Moslems in Spain and it is these campaigns that are described in the later *Song of Roland* (written about 1100). Such poetic songs had a long tradition and demonstrate the continuing need to celebrate victory, as do contemporary murals and other court decorations.

By 800 no king since the Roman empire had ruled so vast an area. Notker the Stammerer, in his *Life of Charlemagne*, describes the emperor's appearance outside the city of Pavia in 774. The heavily-armoured Charlemagne in full military glory was insuffi-cient to intimidate the citizens, who refused to let him enter the city. Charlemagne won them over by building a church – Notker said in a single day – outside the city walls, thus demonstrating his Christian intentions. But we have few details of Charlemagne's propagandis-tic efforts from the sources. We know that he did not cultivate an imperial myth in the style of the Roman emperors and he did not have his head stamped on his coins. During his lifetime, particularly in his later years, Charlemagne was renowned for his encourage-ment of the arts, and of literature in particular, and a principal feature of the so-called Carolingian renaissance was the copying of manuscripts to enable the clergy to increase their level of education.

However, Charlemagne's reign did become the object of con-siderable propaganda after his death in 814. Within thirty years his mighty empire had been divided by his grandsons and the new public desire for literature that Charlemagne had done so much to stimulate was able to read of his glorious accomplishments – the new Christian Caesar. When the Capetians replaced the Carolin-gians as rulers of France in 987, they insisted they were merely continuing Charlemagne's work and many of them married Carolingians to legitimize their link with the past. Einhard's *Life of*

Charlemagne was written in about 850 to provide a model of how kingship should work just at the time when Louis the Pious' reign was going wrong. In fact, decentralization of government was matched by decentralization of warfare, with feudal lords levying their own armies from their own lands, which meant that armies became smaller but the aristocrats who raised them became more powerful within their own society.

The political chaos that followed Charlemagne's death merely left western Europe open to a new threat of invasions from the Vikings. Originally indiscriminate pillagers, the Vikings may be said to be the last of Europe's barbarian fighters whose purpose was 'trade and raid'. Following the departure of the Romans from Britain in 436, Britain had been successively invaded by the Jutes, Angles, Saxons, and, from 784, the Vikings. Despite the successes of Alfred, King of Wessex, against the Norse invaders, a Scandinavian monarchy was established in England in 1016. Alfred, however, had proved himself to be an able propagandist through his construction and consolidation of the idea of the English nation, as celebrated in the *Anglo-Saxon Chronicle*, and his organization of national defences against the Viking invaders.

Meanwhile, following the demise of the Carolingians, large numbers of pillaging Norsemen began to raid the towns of western and northern Europe, beginning seriously in 834, and penetrating the Rhine, Seine, and Loire rivers. Militarily and psychologically, their greatest asset was surprise, appearing without warning in their swift long-boats to plunder and pillage towns and monasteries before escaping back to their Scandinavian bases. Given that the Carolingian empire was also subjected to Moslem raids in the south – in Spain, Italy, and France – the Vikings provided Charlemagne's successors with a guerilla war on two fronts, extended to a third when the Magyars crossed the Danube at the end of the ninth century. The Vikings were not slow to take advantage of the internal disintegration of the Carolingian empire. Between 840 and 865, the Franks reacted ineffectively but thereafter more effective resistance was organized and the Vikings changed their tactics. Instead of hit-and-run raids they began to establish fortified base camps and conducted mounted raids deeper into the countryside. It was from such sites, such as in the north-east of England (the Danelaw), that more permanent settlements were established. In 911 they were granted land around Rouen which became the basis for the later Duchy of Normandy. Here they began to assimilate feudalism and Christianity, invaded England in 1066, and moved south into France and southern Italy. Armed with their unique double-handed axe and with weapons stolen from their enemies, the pagan Vikings terrorized Europe militarily and psychologically. But, like their predecessors, their success was short-lived. Such was the fate of regimes which relied heavily upon terror for their power at the expense of a sustained campaign of propaganda to accompany it.

Chapter 5

The Norman Conquest

For the Norman Conquest of England in 1066, at least, we do have a considerable record of the role of propaganda in medieval warfare, left to us by William of Poitiers. William the Conqueror portrayed his invasion as a holy war under a papal banner. Having informed the Pope of his intentions, Poitiers described how he had 'received of his benevolence a standard as a sign of the approval of St Peter, *behind which he might advance more confidently and securely against his enemy'* (my italics). In fact William, Duke of Normandy, had only a dubious claim to the throne of England following the death of Edward the Confessor (1042-66). The Norwegian King Harald Hardrada staked his claim by invading England via the Humber estuary, whereupon King Harold marched north to defeat him at the battle of Stamford Bridge near York. It was while the south coast was left unguarded that the Duke of Normandy staked *his* claim by invasion. His biographer said of William that 'in every battle he fought with his sword, either as the first man or at least among the first' and that 'armed and mounted he had no equal in all Gaul'. William of Poitiers again:

> It was a sight both delightful and terrible to see him managing his horse, girt with sword, his shield gleaming, his helmet and his lance alike gleaming. For as he looked magnificent in princely apparel or the habiliment of peace, so to be in his war-gear especially became him.

Image was clearly important for William. But then it needed to be at the forthcoming battle of Hastings.

William's spectacular cross-Channel invasion was mounted with some 7000 mercenaries and volunteers (motivated by the prospect of booty); only about half the invasion force comprised William's landed tenants, and it must have been difficult to keep such a disparate force together. William had answered his detractors with the words: 'wars are won by the courage rather than the number of soldiers'. William of Poitiers explained the psychological tricks employed by William during the invasion:

> By prayers and offerings and vows the duke committed himself with utter confidence to the will of heaven, this prince whose spirit could not be broken by delay or contrary winds, by the terrors of the deep or by the timorous desertion of those who had pledged their service. Rather, he met adversities with prudence, concealing the loss of those who were drowned as far as he could by burying them in secret, and increasing the rations every day in order to mitigate their scarcity. Thus by encouragement of all kinds he was able to restrain those who were afraid and put heart into the dismayed. He strove by prayer to obtain a favourable instead of a contrary wind, and brought out from the church in solemn procession the body of St Valery, confessor beloved of God, in which demonstration of humility all those who were to go with him on the expedition took part.

Once the weather changed, 'thanks were rendered to Heaven with hands and voice, and a tumult arose as each shouted encouragement to the other'. William then was the first to sail for England and ate a 'hearty breakfast washed down with spiced wine as though he were in his solar at home' as a further confidence-boosting gesture for his troops.

After defeating Harald Hardrada, King Harold's forces returned south to meet William at Hastings where Norman morale was again put severely to the test. King Harold had possibly received a monk-envoy from the invader spelling out William's right to the English throne, whereupon Harold is alleged to have said, 'May God this day judge the right between me and William.' Despite the ominous appearance of 'the long-haired star' (Halley's comet) as a portent for disaster, the Conqueror was taking no chances: 'He himself attended with devotion the mystery of the Mass and fortified his body and soul by partaking of the Body and Blood of the Lord. He humbly hung about his neck the relics whose protection Harold forfeited by breaking the sacred oath which he had sworn upon them ... The clergy led prayers before the battle.' William even laughed at the supposed ill-omen of putting on his tunic the wrong way round.

Despite the admiration which William of Poitiers revealed for the English defenders, the Normans with 'their eager courage' attacked up-hill against the odds to make their victory all the more impressive – and more 'just'. The Normans were in most danger when a rumour spread during the battle that William had been killed, but it would appear that William's reappearance and courage spurred on his troops at this critical moment. William rode in front of his lines with his helmet removed shouting:

> 'Look at me. I am alive and, with God's help, I shall win. What madness puts you to flight? Where do you think you can go? Those you could slaughter like cattle are driving and killing you. You are deserting victory and everlasting honour; you are running away to destruction and everlasting shame. And by flight, not one of you will avoid death'.

'At this', William of Poitiers continued, 'they recovered their morale.' He does not explain how the words of their military commander could be heard above the noise of battle. But this is only one point at which the source has to be challenged. At the next stage of the battle, William's force was in danger of being routed by the English. Here, Norman chroniclers of the battle describe how William feigned flight to draw the English out of their lines and maintained that this ploy gave the Normans victory. The English 'remembered how, a little while before, flight had been the occasion of success':

> The barbarians exulted with the hope of victory. Exhorting each other with triumphant shouts, they poured scorn upon our men and boasted that they would all be destroyed then and there. As before, some thousands of them were bold enough to launch themselves as if on wings after those they thought to be fleeing. The Normans, suddenly wheeling their horses about, cut them off, surrounded them, and slew them on all sides, leaving not one alive.

Throughout the Middle Ages, the Norman Conquest remained the subject of controversy. Modern historians, however, have doubted the testimony ot the feigned flight. It was only when Harold was hit by an arrow and his banner fell that the English melted away into the countryside. William thereafter took Canterbury and Winchester and established an army of military occupation.

Apart from William of Poitiers' invaluable, though biased account, we do of course also have a unique visual record of the battle: the Bayeux tapestry. The work (actually an embroidery) was commissioned by Bishop Odo for his new cathedral at Bayeux in or about 1017 and as such can be regarded as a near-contemporary record inspired by one who was actually present at the Battle of Hastings. Told from the Norman point of view, and especially from Odo's (the Conqueror's half-brother), the visual narrative was designed for public display and depicts the defeated Harold in a dignified light, although its purpose (apart from celebrating one of the most impressive military achievements of the medieval world – a fact fully appreciated by contemporaries and a great source of myth-making afterwards) was to demonstrate the legitimacy of William the Conqueror's claim to the throne of England to the now occupied peoples. In the build-up to the invasion, and even during the battle of Hastings itself, Bishop Odo's role is depicted as being almost as prominent as that of the Conqueror, revealing the degree to which the enterprise had both Church and family support.

But why was the tapestry made? Was it celebratory, possibly like those early cave drawings or Roman victory columns? Perhaps there was a strong element of this, although we know little about the arrangements made for its display in England or Normandy. Indeed, it would appear to have been made in England and displayed in various English towns. Can the tapestry therefore be regarded as a sort of visual epic poem? It is of course a work of art in its own right, but its content can be interpreted on a variety of different levels – one of which is entertainment (a potent medium for propaganda). Was it perhaps designed to legitimize the invasion and conquest on both sides of the Channel? The historian H. E. J. Cowdrey has pointed out that in the first portion of the tapestry the animals and fables depicted at the top and bottom of the work act as a symbolic counterpoint to the central storyline: they 'serve to call into question the fair-seeming Harold of the main story. Things are not as they seem. There is a cryptic reminder that Harold's fine appearance conceals an inner man who is flawed and false.' This may have been significant in view of the persistence of Harold's good reputation in England after his death, and the tapestry may have been designed subtly to undermine that image during the Norman occupation.

The final segment of the tapestry provides us with a vivid depiction of medieval warfare and also indicates, chiefly in the lower margin, just how crucial the Norman archers were in a battle that was, after all, a close run thing. The Norman knight who butchers

Harold's body after he has fallen victim to an arrow is certainly not behaving in a chivalrous way. It would not be unreasonable, therefore, to speculate that the tapestry was indeed intended as a propaganda device by an occupying regime attempting to establish its legitimacy in a country whose co-operation was essential if the Normans were to govern successfully (as demonstrated by the Domesday Book). It was a means of raising the morale of a defeated but proud nation and to encourage loyalty in the new Anglo-Norman society. Although Harold is depicted as a usurper to William's throne, he and his men are given due credit for their courage and military skill against an enemy whose cause was 'just' but whose behaviour was also open to self-recrimination. The tapestry was, in short, a means of winning over English hearts and minds and the affection with which it is still regarded in England today bears witness to its lasting success.

Chapter 6

The Chivalric Code

'Religion', 'war', and 'chivalry' are three words without which the late medieval mind cannot be understood. After religion, chivalry was perhaps, in the words of the great Dutch historian Johan Huizinga, 'the strongest of all the ethical conceptions which dominated the mind and the heart' of late medieval man. From the eleventh to the fifteenth centuries, the chivalric 'code' determined the way in which western nobles fought and behaved in battle. It was an ideal, a concept to which men should aspire – although whether they could actually live up to the concept was another matter. Nevertheless, the code created a mental framework for the military profession, a mentality which not only served to determine battlefield behaviour but also to justify the new-found social, political, and economic position of the knights in the medieval order of things. In the service of kings, knights were an invaluable instrument of power. Especially after Pope Gregory VII (1073-85), whose Gregorian Reform signalled the way for religious approval of warfare, the knights found that in some circumstances they could also conduct their brutal business with God's blessing.

For the most part, medieval leaders relied for their troops upon their vassals, whose military role and rank were determined by their economic circumstances, upon their ability to bring certain weapons with them, and upon their desire to fight for reasons of social standing or personal security. It was a feudal relationship. Once on the battlefield, according to one historian, 'the battle was a collection of individual combats in which the commander of the army participated as a single combatant'. What made such men fight? Often it was a negative factor: the 'shame' of not fighting, the stigma of cowardice, which could affect not just the individual but the entire family, especially if the story was picked up by some chronicler or poet. The notion that 'he who lives and runs away lives to fight another day' was alien to the medieval aristocratic mind.

But it was necessary to do more than just turn up for a battle. One had to demonstrate bravery and courage in combat. It was one of the few ways of acquiring honour and glory in society, of gaining financial reward and social promotion. The knights, as professional soldiers, fought for a living. It was their way of becoming a king or a duke or a baron. Even so, battleaxes and double-edged swords concentrate the mind wonderfully and it was necessary to take out a little insurance in the form of armour and by fighting in closely formed ranks. The Crusading knights found that their armour not only protected them in battle but also that this protection provided an enormous psychological boost: the chances of killing were higher than those of being killed. The enemy realized this, too: after his defeat at Arsuf in 1191, during the Third Crusade, Saladin refused to engage the 'iron men' under Richard I again. Elaborately decorated garments were not encouraged at first, although a later chronicler noted that 'when they march out to battle those who want to wear gold or silver may do so, so that the sun may shine upon them and fear may melt the courage of the pagans'. For the poor footsoldiers who could afford no such luxury, the religious community in which they lived had to provide a mental approach to warfare as a social, economic, and spiritual duty that could only be avoided at an unacceptable price. Those who were members of a lord's retinue owed their livelihood to that lord and their fortunes were inextricably bound up with his. Shields decorated with the lord's coat of arms, banners decorated with the cross, and uniforms (of a sort) all helped to foster the sense of common identity.

It was from such circumstances that the code of chivalry evolved, although that of course is more usually associated with wealthy knights. One chronicler wrote of the battle of Brémule in 1119, between less than a thousand knights, that 'only two were killed':

> They were all clad in mail and spared each other on both sides, out of fear of God and fellowship in arms; they were more concerned to capture than to kill the fugitives. As Christian soldiers they did not thirst for the blood of their brothers, but rejoiced in a just victory given by God for the good of holy Church and the peace of the faithful.

If a knight knew that, if captured, he would be spared rather than killed (whether out of chivalry or for a ransom) he was less likely to fight ferociously to the death. When Christian fought against heathens, however, it was quite a different story (although mercenaries employed by the counts of Flanders between 1297 and 1302 were criticized by the chroniclers for their lack of mercy towards Christian men of war, who, when they were captured, were treated 'no better than dogs'). During the Crusades, when soldiers were fighting far from home, flight was often as dangerous as battle and some sources testify to the view that it was better to die trying to defend yourself than it was attempting to flee in a hostile country. As in antiquity, panic was not uncommon.

War, as Phillipe Contamine has put it, is 'a cultural phenomenon'. The way a war is fought is invariably determined by the prevailing set of moral standards which influence the individuals involved. During the Middle Ages, once heavy cavalry became the predominant arm of warfare, military training of knights was turned into high art. As one English chronicler who described the training of Henry II's sons put it:

> No athlete can fight tenaciously who has never received any blows ... the oftener he falls, the more determinedly he must spring to his feet again. Anyone who can do that can engage in battle confidently. Strength gained by practice is invaluable ... the price of sweat is well paid where the Temples of Victory stand.

And not just in terms of glory. War was a good way of making money: 'There is going to be fighting here! Now I shall get rich!', shouted one impoverished knight before a campaign. Before the battle of Doryleum in 1097 the knights encouraged each other with the words: 'Be of one mind in your belief in Christ and in the victory of the Holy Cross, because you will become rich today, if God wills.' It is important also to remember that the knightly class was small when compared to the mass of the European population. It was therefore comparatively easy for ideas and values about the way to behave in battle or in tournaments to spread throughout a restricted educated ruling class of nobles who all spoke the same language.

In this respect, literature played an important part in determining the chivalric mentality amongst the aristocratic nobility. One noble advised his son to read classic texts to discover the meaning of honour, although 'for stronger reasons, we who are Christians should wish even more to do honourable and virtuous deeds, and preserve ourselves from vile reproaches, than those Romans who believed the soul died with the body'. But reading about war and actually fighting one are completely different things. One thing the Romans did teach the medieval knight was the virtue of discipline and, for this purpose, militaristic religious orders were created. In 1118, the Knights Templar were formed to guard the pilgrim route between Jerusalem and Jaffa. The charitable Order of the Hospital of St John of Jerusalem, which received papal sanction in 1113, became more militaristic in the 1130s, and thereafter several other secular chivalric orders were formed for laymen, such as Edward III's Order of the Garter in 1348.

The development of games and tournaments was partly for military training purposes and, 'just as in real wars, tournaments served to foster local pride and increased moral solidarity in military units' (Verbruggen, a recent Dutch scholar). Such tournaments provided a substitute for war without the killing – theoretically. 'It was a sham fight, a mock battle, but one which closely resembled "real" warfare,' writes Malcolm Vale. Casualties were inevitable and popes and kings often tried to ban tournaments, especially when they were used as a form of ritual feuding. Stricter rules and blunted weapons were introduced later to reduce casualties, but some observers claimed this was due to increasing decadence on the part of the knights and a declining chivalric code.

Tournaments were also a valuable means of social promotion. William the Marshal began life as a landless and comparatively poor minor aristocrat but rose to become Earl of Pembroke and Regent of England through the military prowess he demonstrated in tournaments. But tournaments were also useful training grounds. Jousts provided exercises for the lance and sword, simulating the sort of hand-to-hand combat that took place around a banner in real battles. 'Captured' or 'defeated' opponents and their retinues became 'brothers-in-arms'. Brotherhoods thus formed became military units on the field of battle, wearing the same coats of arms and sharing the same camps and castles, whilst their symbols and names were registered in lists for consultation by others. By the late Middle Ages, heraldry had become a flourishing art and design business, inspired by the *Tree of Battles*, having evolved from a sign of recognition to a symbol of aristocratic achievement and lineage.

The war-torn eleventh and twelfth centuries were fuelled by the chivalric code, which often led to a love of war for war's sake and a romantic glorification of fighting skills. An over-zealous admirer of the code later wrote:

> It is a joyous thing, a war. I believe that God favours those who risk their lives by their readiness to make war to bring the wicked, the oppressors, the conquerors, the proud and all those who deny true equity, to justice. You love your comrade so much in war. When you see that your quarrel is just, and your blood is fighting well, tears rise to your eyes. A great sweet feeling of loyalty and of pity fills your heart on seeing your friend so valiantly exposing his body to execute and accomplish the command of our Creator. And then you are prepared to go and die or live with him, and for love not to abandon him. And out of that, there arises such a delectation that he who has not experienced it is not fit to say what delight it is. Do you think that a man who does that fears death? Not at all, for he feels so strengthened, so elated, that he does not know where he is. Truly he is afraid of nothing [*Le Jouvencel*, written in 1466.]

Perhaps this rather romanticized view of the medieval concept of courage more accurately describes battle-rage, but it does provide us with an insight into the ideal by which men measured their own code of behaviour. It is also an example of war propaganda. In reality, military commanders had to ensure that fear and panic did not overtake their own soldiers while attempting to induce chaos amongst the enemy. The former could be achieved by training, discipline, superior numbers, and armour – which all served to enhance confidence and morale – whereas the latter might follow naturally from it.

Chivalric songs provide us with an excellent insight into what made medieval men fight. As already illustrated, religion played an important role. Mass was held before every battle at which soldiers would take communion and confession (and also perhaps make their wills). The songs themselves were recited to entertain and inspire the troops on their long marches, with the words reminding them of their religious duties and their illustrious predecessors. They were an important element of morale-boosting – for the most effective propaganda is that which entertains as well as instructs and exhorts – but they also provide us with certain insights into the chivalric code. In the *Song of Roland*, we have the portrayal of an ideal knight. Roland is said to have fought against overwhelming odds, choosing to fight rather than flee in accordance with the chivalric code, and died for his cause. In fact, he refused to summon help until it was too late, largely out of pride! Such songs, however, did help to perpetuate the qualities valued at the height of the Middle Ages and thus served as inspirational pieces – in other words, as role models.

Chapter 7

The Crusades

It is with the Crusades that the study of war propaganda is provided with the most fertile evidence to date. The knights of the first (People's) crusade, advocated by Pope Urban II in a sermon at Clermont in 1095, had little idea of their Muslim opponents, other than they were heathens. The crusade was a holy war authorized by the Pope in the name of Christ and, as such, was justified or legitimate violence. It was around this rather simplistic point that atrocity propaganda was constructed, although events such as the burning of the Church of the Holy Sepulchre some ninety years earlier were seized upon to enflame passions. But no more recent atrocity could be found to justify the expedition or Pope Urban's call for a 'great stirring of heart' against the infidel. The Turks were, it is true, threatening Byzantium by advancing further into Asia Minor. Urban preached that 'the barbarians in their frenzy have invaded and ravaged the churches of God in the eastern regions. Worse still, they have seized the Holy City of Christ, embellished by his passion and resurrection, and – it is blasphemy to say it – they have sold her and her churches into abominable slavery.' Robert the Monk, writing some years later, provides us with one version of Urban's call to arms which contains blatant atrocity propaganda. The Saracens, Urban maintained,

> have circumcized the Christians, either spreading the blood from the circumcisions on the altars or pouring it into the baptismal fonts. And they cut open the navels of those whom they choose to torment with a loathsome death, tear out most of their vital organs and tie them to a stake, drag them around and flog them before killing them as they lie prone on the ground with all their entrails out. They tie some to posts and shoot at them with arrows; they order others to bare their necks

and they attack them with drawn swords, trying to see whether they can
cut off their heads with a single stroke. What shall I say of the appalling
violation of women, of which it is more evil to speak than to keep silent?

No other surviving version of Urban's sermon contains such vivid
propaganda but they do emphasise the psychological significance
of Jerusalem in the Christian universe. Even so, none of this
explains the timing of the call. Guibert of Nogent claimed that
'there was no need for any churchman to exhort people from the
pulpit to go and fight when ... each man advertized to his neigh-
bour, no less by his advice than by his example, the vow to go on
the journey. All were on fire with eagerness.' This contemporary
source's explanation of the wave of popular enthusiasm for the
People's or Peasant's Crusade was that God had directly mobilized
the universal Christian heart.

In reality, greed and self-interest probably played a more signi
ficant role. Stirred by popular orators, many of those that went
were peasants and landless knights and this motley crew of
adventurers, led by Walter the Penniless and Peter the Hermit,
lacked both organization and discipline. Disaster and cruelty were
inevitable. It was these factors which help to explain why the first
Crusaders acted as brutally as they did: enemies were beheaded
and their heads thrown into besieged cities or impaled on their
lances to frighten the enemy. Sheer cruelty or an acute awareness
of the role of psychological warfare? Perhaps a combination of both.

The First Crusade, which began the year after the People's
Crusade had ended in slaughter at the hands of the Turks at
Civetot in Asia Minor, has to be explained in terms other than
revenge or the chivalric code. Modern historians have put forward
over-population in the west, the Church's efforts to discourage
domestic warfare between Christian peoples, and economic factors as
the reasons for the First Crusade. Certainly the Church was anxious
to persuade the knightly class to turn its aggressive energies
against non-Christians; as one version of Urban's speech has him
proclaiming: 'Let those who have once been robbers now become
soldiers of Christ, let those who have been mercenaries for a few
pennies now achieve eternal reward.' Now fuelled by real atrocity
stories committed by the Turks at Civetot, perhaps the real motivation of the knights who travelled to the Holy Land in 1096 was
their increased social status as an aristocratic profession, a process
sanctioned by the Church. They had acquired status through war

and they needed to maintain their status through war. Crusading was a lucrative business and land was the source of power. All these factors came together at the same time to provide a fertile field in which Urban's words could flourish and, through a system of remission of sins, the soldiers could conduct their profession against the infidel as brutally as they liked, in the safe knowledge that they were committing no mortal sin.

Indeed, thanks to the Gregorian Reform, war against the infidel was a more acceptable way for knights to gain salvation than the previous options of joining a monastery or a pilgrimage. As such, the crusades can be seen partly as armed pilgrimages. Later, monks and knights joined together in the Templars and the new warfare was praised by St Bernard with the words: 'Advance in confidence, you knights, and boldly drive out the enemies of the Cross of Christ, be sure that neither death nor life can separate you from the love of God.' The role of religious propaganda in launching the armed pilgrimage to Jerusalem is thus beyond dispute.

At the siege of Antioch (1097-9), the critical battle of the First Crusade, the Crusaders were heartened by reports of visions – a not unfrequent event throughout the Crusades – by the alleged discovery of the Holy Lance that had pierced Christ's side, and by the intervention of God himself. The lure of the Holy City of Jerusalem often pulled soldiers onwards against the advice of their leaders. With Antioch in their hands, in 1099 the Crusaders organized a religious procession around the besieged city of Jerusalem, described by one source in the following terms:

> When the Saracens saw this, they proceeded in the same way along the city walls carrying on a spear the image of Muhammad covered with a cloth. When the Christians had reached the church of St Stephen and had made a station there as is the custom in our processions, the Saracens stood on the walls and shouted aloud at it. They made a great din with trumpets and subjected the Christians to every kind of mockery which they could devise. But worst of all, in the sight of all the Christians they struck the most holy cross, on which merciful Christ redeemed the human race by shedding his blood, with a piece of wood and then, to distress the Christians even more, they dashed it to pieces against the wall ...

Such provocation was not uncommon in sieges and may perhaps help to explain the brutality of the Crusaders towards their captives contrasted with the Christian doctrine of mercy and forgiveness. Jerusalem fell to the invaders in 1099. The defenders were massacred.

Inspired by religious fervour, the Crusaders also recognized the financial rewards of battle in the wealthy Middle East. In the *Song of Antioch* are the words: 'Out there on the grass, we shall either lose our heads or else become so rich in fine silver and gold that we shall no longer have to beg from our comrades.' But the chivalric code also demanded that certain rules be observed, especially when Christian fought Christian. The advantages of fighting the infidel on his rich home soil soon became apparent.

The Second Crusade, proclaimed by Pope Eugenius III in 1146, attempted to capitalize upon the success of the first. The reoccupation of conquered lands, and Edessa in particular, by the infidel provided the excuse, but the real reasons are similar to those which motivated the earlier campaign. This time, however, the sons of the First Crusaders were called upon to regain the honour – and salvation – of their fathers, 'so that the dignity of the name of Christ may be enhanced in our time and your reputation for strength, which is praised throughout the world, may be kept unimpaired and unsullied'. St Bernard, the official preacher of the Second Crusade, extended the call to fight the Moslems not just in the Holy Land but also in Spain, and to take on the pagan Slavs of eastern and south-eastern Europe. In France, Bernard and King Louis VII designed an elaborate ceremony in 1147, described as follows:

> Since there was no place in the fortress which could hold such a multitude [who had gathered], a wooden platform was built for the Abbot in a field outside of Vezelay, so that he could speak from a high place to the audience standing around him. Bernard mounted the platform together with the king, who wore the cross. When the heavenly instrument had, according to his custom, poured out the Dew of the Divine Word, the people on all sides began to clamour and to demand crosses. When he had sowed, rather than passed out the crosses which had been prepared, he was forced to tear his clothing into crosses and to sow them too.

Bernard recruited throughout Europe using such propaganda devices, but his efforts were not to be rewarded with victory. Lisbon was recaptured but the war against the Slavs proved less successful. In the Holy Land, the Crusaders were driven back at Damascus and the entire venture became a débâcle. Their failure was explained by apologists with the argument that the troops had been unworthy executors of God's will.

After Saladin defeated the Crusaders at the battle of Hattin in 1187 and captured Jerusalem, the Third Crusade (1189-92) was launched to recover the Holy Land. Pope Gregory VIII called upon Christendom to avenge the victims of the 'savage barbarians'. The religious arguments now had to be even more forceful. Other than eternal salvation, the Church offered protection to property, land, and goods. Violence was justified by drawing upon the Old Testament and upon the writings of St Augustine. Hence the justification: 'we do not seek peace so that we may wage war, but we wage war so that we may attain peace.' But chivalric notions continued to motivate the knights in battle. During the Third Crusade, the Grand Master of the Templars refused to flee at the battle of Acre and was killed, but at least he died with honour. To have fled before the standards had fallen would have brought disgrace, not only upon him personally but also upon his Order, not to mention his family. Orders such as the Knights Templars were thus in many respects a development of the old Gallic tribes in which individuals fought alongside people as though they were members of the same family: 'One for all and all for one'.

Exposure to the fighting ability of the Saracens inevitably led the Crusaders to respect and admiration for their enemies. This happens in most wars when soldiers realize that the image of the enemy they have had painted for them by propagandists rarely conforms to the reality. Fighting men admire fighting men if they display qualities in battle that they can respect and relate to by virtue of their own training and experience. Of the battle of Dorylaeum in 1097, one source has testified that if the Turks had been inspired by the Holy Spirit 'it would have been impossible to find a people more powerful, more courageous, or more skilled in the art of war'. In other words, the Christian God provided the difference in morale between the two sides. Their motivation to fight an enemy they respected – and this usually meant an enemy they feared – was derived from the Crusaders' religious zeal and from the belief that they were securing divine redemption by attempting to destroy the anti-Christ. By the late twelfth century, the crusading ethos was being used to justify wars elsewhere than in the Holy Land – in the Baltic, for example, or within Christendom itself in campaigns against heresy. Anyone who threatened the Church found themselves the object of a crusading call.

An important psychological factor in late medieval warfare, and of the Crusades in particular, when the knights were usually outnumbered by the Saracens, was the tightly-packed formations of heavily armoured knights. During the Third Crusade in 1190 one chronicler described how the Crusaders, having seen Saladin's camp, were 'terrified because they looked so powerful', but then 'began to draw closer together, as they had been trained to do'. The enemy found it impossible to break the formation and were fought off, whereupon the knights relieved the fortress of Darum. Such tactics enabled men to overcome their fear, relatively safe in the knowledge that their comrades and their armour would protect their lives. Should the formation be broken, the men would attempt to reform in a compact unit around the banner or standard. The banner was thus not just a means of signalling the troops to advance in battle. It was also a symbol of resistance in adversity. As the Rules of the Templars stated: 'If the troops lose their banner, they are shocked, and this can lead to a terrible defeat.'

The Crusades also demonstrate the psychological significance of an able military commander. During the disaster at Damascus in the Second Crusade, one source relates how the Holy Roman Emperor severed in one blow virtually the entire side of an armour-protected Saracen. 'At this deed the citizens, both those who witnessed it and those who learned it from others, were thrown into such a fright that they despaired of resisting and even of life itself.' Richard I of England (the 'Lionheart') is another excellent example. A strict disciplinarian, he was a man who took care not to march his men too hard or too far, ensured that they were well supplied, and personally supervised the execution of his orders. Richard's personal guard formed one of the main strike forces in the battle of Arsuf, men who were supplied and armed by the king himself and whose loyalty to him he could depend upon. But he was not averse to brutality, ordering the decapitation of 2700 Turks at Acre when Saladin delayed in returning the Holy Cross. Tancred, one of the leaders of the First Crusade, according to his biographer, always took his turn at guard duty and even replaced the wounded or the exhausted. When a crusade was not led by one of the European kings, the military leader was elected by his fellow military leaders or by the Pope.

The climax of Crusade propaganda came in 1213 when Pope Innocent III proclaimed the Fifth Crusade. Distributed throughout

Christendom, the Pope's letter was widely copied and provided a set of guidelines for preaching this latest campaign to *all* members of Christendom, regardless of class or status:

> For how can a man be said to love his neighbour as himself, in obedience to God's command, when, knowing that his brothers, who are Christians in faith and in name, are held in the hands of the perfidious Saracens in dire imprisonment and are weighed down by the yoke of most heavy slavery, he does not do something effective to liberate them, thereby transgressing the command of that natural law which the Lord gave in the gospel, 'Whatsoever you would that men should do to you, do you also to them'? Or perhaps you do not know that many thousands of Christians are being held in slavery and imprisonment in their hands, tortured by countless torments?

The Pope pointed out, perhaps anticipating criticism from a war-weary populace, that the Holy Land had been in Christian hands before Islam's seizure, before Muhammad (the 'false prophet who has seduced many men from the truth by world enticements and the pleasures of the flesh'):

> So rouse yourselves, most beloved sons, transforming your quarrels and rivalries, brother against brother, into associations of peace and affection; gird yourselves for the service of the Crucified One, not hesitating to risk your possessions and your persons for Him who laid down his life and shed his blood for you, equally certain and sure that if you are truly penitent you will achieve eternal rest as a profit for this temporal labour.

Even those who did not physically join the Crusade but contributed towards it were to be granted remission of their sins. Anyone who hindered the war (Jews and pirates were cited as examples) was to be excommunicated and cast into slavery. 'We order sentence of this kind to be read out publicly each Sunday and feastday in all maritime cities.' Monthly prayer processions were to be held 'with this wise proviso that during the procession the preaching of the cross which brings salvation should always be offered to the people in a way that is assiduous and encouraging'. During daily mass, 'everyone, men and women alike, must humbly prostrate themselves on the ground and the psalm 'Oh God, the heathens are come into thy inheritance' should be sung loudly by the clergy.' Churches were to have contribution chests for everyone to donate alms for the Crusade. Priests 'should devote themselves conscientiously to prayer and exhortation, teaching the crusaders both by word and example' and the clergy were to donate one-twentieth of their income for three years. The Pope also ordered an end to civil strife within Christendom for four years.

Such was the thoroughness of the propaganda campaign orchestrated on behalf of the Fifth Crusade that the Pope also appointed special officials to preach 'with great care and attention to detail' the messages in the guidelines: 'You must promote the cause of Christ with such zeal and vigilance that you will share in the many and great benefits we believe will result from it.'

Yet the Fifth Crusade took place amidst great changes in medieval warfare. Improvements in State administration and increased centralization enabled kings to raise armies on a more regular basis, permanent professional armies whose pay and recruitment were organized througkh indentures. A distinction was now being made between 'private war', waged between individuals with as little damage as possible to the general community, and 'public war' in which prisoners could be taken and held for ransom, enemy property seized as booty, and reparations exacted from the local population. The emerging nation-states of western Europe began to utilize more effectively a peasantry that could be brought to the battlefield at a reasonably low cost, thanks to the crossbow and longbow, although the aristocratic knights initially resented this development which placed more emphasis upon collective rather than individual combat. But the Normans and the Saracens had demonstrated the value of archers and the value of defence over attack. Stone castles and fortified towns built by the Normans throughout Europe in the eleventh and twelfth centuries demanded the development of siege warfare and tactics and the introduction of gunpowder in the late fourteenth and fifteenth centuries helped to inaugurate a new era for both warfare and propaganda, symbolized by the concept of *guerre mortelle* in which both the property and the lives of the conquered lay at the mercy of the conqueror.

Chapter 8

The Hundred Years War

The Hundred Years War, which in fact lasted intermittently from about 1337 to 1453, was a struggle between the English and French kings. It was but one of a number of conflicts which plagued Europe in the thirteenth, fourteenth, and fifteenth centuries, such as the advance of the Ottoman Turks, the Hussite wars in Germany, the campaigns of Philip the Good and Charles the Bold, and the wars in Italy. But it is a conflict which illustrates well many of the changes in warfare that are relevant to this study. It saw the reappearance of armies of foot-soldiers, of the type that had triumphed over mounted knights in the battles of Courtrai in 1302, Bannockburn in 1314, Morgarten in 1315, and Crécy in 1346. Previously a secondary and less well-trained arm of warfare since later Roman times (or perhaps it was simply a less-glamorous arm which attracted insufficient attention from the chroniclers), it was the Swiss who reminded Europe of the value of foot-soldiers, but the English also used them effectively – especially after the introduction of the longbow by Edward I and by the use of pikemen. Even when the cavalry dismounted to fight, as at Poitiers in 1356 or Agincourt in 1415, it proved an inadequate tactic. Despite this, however, the Hundred Years War saw medieval rulers cling to the now outdated use of heavy cavalry. Old habits died hard amongst conservative aristocratic élites, whilst the chivalric tradition acted as a reminder of past notions of single combat. The old view that a hundred knights were worth a thousand infantrymen persisted.

Even so, mounted knights continued to fulfil an invaluable military role. As Malcolm Vale has written:

> Throughout his long history of European deployment the heavy cavalry-man's function has been as much psychological as physical, and it was

essentially this aspect of his role which was strengthened in the course of the fifteenth century. Pitted against footsoldiers, heavy cavalry charge relied largely upon the 'shock' principle for its effect.

John Keegan confirms this, stating that the impact of a cavalry charge on the morale of enemy infantry was greater than its physical effect. The objective was to induce fear, panic, and flight and it took iron discipline not to succumb, especially after morale had already been lowered by archery fire. Hence the significance of the development of full plate armour, which replaced chain mail in the second half of the fourteenth century and offered some measure of protection against arrows, thus aiding morale. And the cavalry retained an essential function of the immediate aftermath of a battle by their capacity to pursue the fleeing enemy.

It has to be remembered that the Normans who invaded England in 1066 retained family lands in France, and indeed after the accession of Henry Plantagenet to the throne of England in 1154, the English ruled a third of France, occupying virtually the whole of the west side of the country. Much of this was lost in the early years of the thirteenth century. Political struggles between the kings of France and England-Normandy to extend their territory had exploded into open war in 1294 and 1324, but the issue which was to cause lasting conflict was the death of the last Capetian king, Charles IV, in 1328.

After the great French defeat at the battle of Poitiers in 1356, French public opinion felt that too many knights had fled and had thus brought disgrace upon France and upon the nobility as a whole. They were accused of treason and the king was advised to mobilize the peasantry: 'The peasantry will not flee to save their lives, as the knights did in Poitiers.' The peasants who constituted the new armies of foot-soldiers had for centuries endured the maraudings of knights; now it was their turn to 'enjoy' the benefits of medieval warfare. However, the advent of gunpowder at the end of the fourteenth century was to change the face of battle in a profound way. Don Quixote, Cervantes' famous hero, looked back to the good old days before artillery:

> Blessed be those happy ages that were strangers to the dreadful fury of these devlish instruments of artillery, whose inventor I am satisfied is now in Hell receiving the reward of his cursed invention, which is the cause that very often a cowardly base hand takes away the life of the

bravest gentleman; and that in the midst of that vigour and resolution which animates and inflames the bold, a chance bullet (shot perhaps by one who fled, and was frighted by the very flash the mischievous piece gave when it went off) coming nobody knows, or from where, in a moment puts a period to the brave designs and the life of one that deserved to have survived many years.

In other words, the advent of gunpowder made war cold and impersonal, the antithesis of the chivalric ethic that had dominated European warfare for at least 400 years. Developed initially as part of the Anglo-French arms race in the Hundred Years War to improve and speed up siege warfare (which had remained essentially static since antiquity), artillery and later hand weapons became increasingly common in warfare from the late fourteenth century onwards.

Perhaps gunpowder initially revolutionized the conduct, but not the outcome, of wars. Because early cannon were slow to fire, unwieldy, and inaccurate, their main purpose may have been psychological or symbolic (as suggested by their nicknames: 'Mad Margaret' and 'Mons Meg'). At the battle of Crécy in 1346, as various sources attest, the English used cannon 'to frighten' the enemy, but it was not until the middle of the fifteenth century that gunpowder was affecting the outcome of battles. For the first time in centuries, the initiative now lay with attack rather than defence. The gun was nonetheless regarded as an instrument of the devil, imported from eastern infidels like the Turks and Chinese, and developed by magicians, a 'cowardly' weapon which killed from afar. This did not however prevent even chivalric armies from employing it. Its use could be justified as a modern version of the crossbow manned by lower-class types who would never know the meaning of chivalric combat. This kind of class interpretation and snobbery is evident in contemporary sources, notably Philippe de Commynes who testified to the panic caused by a besieging army when cannon were fired. The gun had come to stay and was even given its own patron saint – St Barbara.

From a psychological point of view, the essential point to bear in mind about the gun was that it increased the distance between soldier and enemy even further than arrows had done earlier. As a result, it reduced the need to bolster the morale of troops who previously only expected to fight in hand-to-hand combat and whose physical and psychological courage could determine the outcome of battle. The possibility of hand-to-hand combat remained a contingency – the bayonet survives even to this day – but effective artillery fire diminished its likelihood. On the other hand, the need to bolster the morale of troops likely to be on the receiving end of artillery fire correspondingly increased, especially as death could now strike like a bolt from the blue. Not even military commanders, princes, or kings were safe from the new danger. With the arrival of the cannon, therefore, it was essential for both sides to possess it; this led to a technological race to make better and more efficient weapons, which in turn increased the frequency of their use.

Perhaps the most celebrated English victory was the battle of Agincourt (1415), immortalized for centuries by Shakespeare's *Henry V*. The English king's invasion of France was designed to reclaim lands lost during the previous fifty years. The battle illustrates the persistence of various themes of medieval war propaganda. Religion, superstition, and omens remained important psychological factors. Before the battle, every English soldier put soil to his mouth and 'fell to their knees and kissed the earth three times'. The battlefield was blessed (useful for those who were about to die and who would at least be buried in hallowed ground) and a cross erected. During the battle, the priests constantly said prayers while the soldiers pumped up their adrenalin with battle cries. John Keegan's masterly re-enactment of the battle points out that the long periods of waiting during the various stages of the battle were the critical moments from the point of view of morale. Both sides would have been drinking to provide 'false' courage and the English would have been further fortified by the physical presence of the King: 'Though the late medieval soldier's immediate loyalty lay towards his captain, the presence on the field of his own and his captain's anointed king, visible to all and ostentatiously risking his life in the heart of the mêlée, must have greatly strengthened his resolve.'

Other than religion and drink, Keegan continues, and 'more important still for the common soldier than the man-at-arms, was the prospect of enrichment': 'It is the gold-strike and gold-fever character of medieval battle which we should keep foremost in mind when seeking to understand it.' Combining with the element of compulsion – there was nowhere to run for the English soldiers – and the medieval mentality which accepted war not merely as 'natural' but 'just' in the eyes of God and glorious in the eyes of chivalric society, war propagandists in the Middle Ages knew exactly how to make men fight.

Part Three

Propaganda in the Age of Gunpowder and Printing

Chapter 9

The Gutenberg Galaxy

No historian likes rigid chronological divisions that separate historical periods like fixed iron gates. Human history is like the process of evolution: growth, development, adaptation. These are not words implying cataclysmic or sudden change. We have already seen how the ancient world did not suddenly end with the collapse of Rome and how certain features of antiquity persisted into the medieval period. Historians writing for the purpose of convenience and clarity may well fix upon certain key dates in human history as their start and end points, but human development is not so easily compartmentalized or simplified. The Middle Ages did not stop suddenly, giving way to the modern world with entirely new and quite distinct characteristics. Besides, in Britain the most convenient date of 1485 (the battle of Bosworth) and the advent of the Tudors would be challenged by European historians who prefer 1494 and the French invasion of Italy as their 'turning point'. For our purposes here, the advent of the printing press in the middle of the fifteenth century (though it had appeared in China some time earlier) may well serve as an even more appro-priate dividing line – not least because reading and writing now became an important means by which a man could make his way in the world and rise up through society other than the time-honoured method of warfare. The shift from script to print, writes Professor Eisenstein, also led to an intensification of propaganda wars, 'exacerbating traditional friction between crown and estates, court and country, church and state, laying the basis for the formation of political parties as distinct from the mere "factions" of an earlier age'.

With the growth of universities as recognized centres of learning in the thirteenth and fourteenth centuries and, perhaps more significantly, with the production of cheap paper replacing expensive parchment in the first half of the fifteenth century, the way was open to capitalize upon printing as a means of catering for the increasingly literate population of Europe. By 1500, printing presses had been set up in more than 250 places. But Johann Gutenberg's invention of the printing press some fifty years earlier also opened up the floodgates for a massive growth in literary persuasion of all kinds, not the least significant of which was war propaganda. Thus, the phenomenon with which we are familiar today begins to assume shape during the Renaissance and the Reformation. Indeed, it is difficult to overstate the significance of printing as an instrument of change. Thanks to books, for example, the 'realities' of war – or rather literary representations of those realities – become more accessible to people who were unused to its actuality. Literary images of warfare disseminated to a wide readership played on the collective imagination in a way that monuments and paintings, fixed in time and place, could never do. Moreover, visual images could now be reproduced to communicate ideas to a wider audience than ever before. The publication of maps and the advances made in cartography (not least after Columbus 'discovered' America in 1492) further stretched the imagination of rulers and ruled alike and served to bring distant places more within their reach.

Chapter 10

Renaissance Warfare

The advent of the printing press coincided with other significant developments in human activity, especially in the conduct of warfare. We have already noted the arrival of gunpowder by the late Middle Ages, although its initial impact had been more psychological than military. By the late fifteenth century, its military use was being perfected in the form of cannon and hand-held weapons. This in turn, as we have seen, tended to depersonalize combat. It increased the physical distance between opposing forces and thus reduced the need to bolster up the courage of men for the type of hand-to-hand fighting characteristic of previous periods. Armies grew in size, new tactics emerged in battle and in siege warfare (such as the introduction of fortified bastions to resist artillery fire more effectively), in which the gap between soldier and civilian grew narrower. By 1598, one English writer noted that 'it is rarely seen in our days that men come often to hand blows as in old times they did'.

The siege warfare so characteristic of the final stages of the Hundred Years War served to involve civilian populations to an unprecedented degree in the rigours of battle. The people of besieged cities, hammered by artillery fire, also had to have their morale catered for, as did local populations which found themselves subject to foreign armies of occupation. Renaissance cities in Italy, for all their self-conscious cultural development in the arts and philosophy, remained deeply affected by the military ethic. In Florence, for example, the Medici staged mock battles and sieges and even imitation Roman triumphs to amuse their subjects – and, of course, to remind them of who was in charge. The Italian city-states in which the Renaissance flowered in the fifteenth century may well be better remembered for their artistic achievements, but a glance at much of that art will serve to remind us that the ethos of war and violence was alive and well. In art, as in writing, the purpose of images was to entertain and convince. Plausibility, as ever, was essential to success. Hence the Renaissance preoccupation with style (such as perspective) and historical legitimacy (which provided the mind with less realistic but more credible views of the past). The art of rhetoric was perfected and, in cities such as papal Rome, vast building schemes were launched in praise of man's achievement through God, especially after the Peace of Lodi in 1454 which brought a semblance of tranquillity to Italy for nearly half a century. Drawing on the traditions of devotional religious images, shrines, and relics, civic authorities used the bodies of the saints and the heroes of antiquity for their own purposes (Michelangelo's statue of David in Florence being one well-known example), protecting towns and warding off enemies and evil, thus providing a psychological rallying point in times of crisis. The rewriting of history was used to stimulate imitation of the glories of the Roman past; statues were commissioned depicting commanders on horseback in the style of Caesar, while the less glamorous infantryman also began to make an appearance in art, most notably in the work of the German woodcarver Albrecht Dürer.

In 1471, a veteran of the Hundred Years War wrote:

> War has become very different. In those days, when you had eight or ten thousand men, you reckoned that a very large army; today, it is quite another matter. One has never seen a more numerous army than that of my lord of Burgundy, both in artillery and in munitions of all sorts... I am not accustomed to see so many troops together. How do you prevent disorder and confusion among such a mass?

The increased size of armies was prompted by the example of the French who created Europe's first standing army in 1445-8 – a permanent, professional body in the direct employment of the king where status no longer qualified automatically for command. The example was followed by Burgundy in 1465-6. Again, this development undermined chivalric notions and led to increased specialization in the new non-aristocratic armies. This was further aided by the increased use of mercenaries, especially the Swiss and Germans who brought with them specialized fighting skills and weapons such as the arquebus and the pike.

When the French king Charles VIII invaded Italy in 1494, thereby launching the Italian wars, which spread across Europe through the Hapsburg-Valois rivalry and lasted until 1559, his army consisted not just of Frenchmen but also mercenaries from Switzerland, Scotland, and even Italy itself. The best mercenary troops came from countries that were torn apart by internal chaos, men who had no sense of 'national' pride but who were accustomed to violence and were thus prepared to sell their skills to the highest bidder. Money was the major motivation in such men, and their employers directed their propaganda towards them around the promise of financial reward. It didn't always work. When the risks outweighed the reward, mercenaries demonstrated the fickleness of their loyalty – as in 1525 when Swiss troops deserted the French before the battle of Pavia because they were not paid. Better to rely on the more predictable loyalty of men recruited from the emerging nation-states, men with at least a modicum of what we would now call nationalism or patriotism. However, despite Machiavelli's call for a citizen militia, there remained a clear distinction between the solider whose job was to fight and the civilian whose duty was to finance and support his efforts.

As for our veteran's question, a variety of methods were used to prevent 'disorder and confusion' – in other words, to sustain morale. Standards and ensigns were allocated to the new professional captains, around which smaller units of men would fight. As the military treatise, *Le Rozier des Guerres*, put it, 'there is nothing so profitable for achieving a victory than obeying the orders of the ensigns'. Quartermasters ensured better supplies, although their very existence would suggest that morale was a big problem, especially when it came to billeting. Uniforms were introduced to increase the sense of communal identity, and to serve as a reassurance to soldiers that they would not be hacked to death by their own side in the confusion of battle (although uniforms also served to identify soldiers to the enemy as well). With so many men in the field, new methods of issuing instructions were required. The aural therefore replaced the visual (especially as vision was now obscured by gunpowder smoke) with the increased use of drummers, fifers, and trumpeters – apparently an innovation of the German and Swiss mercenaries. As one sixteenth-century source stated:

> The noise of all the ... instruments serves as a signal and warning to the
> soldiers to strike camp, to advance and to withdraw; and to give them

heart, boldness and courage to attack the enemy on sight; and to defend themselves manfully and vigorously. For soldiers can march in confusion and disorder, so that they would be in danger of being overthrown and defeated.

Military musicians thus became an integral part of combat morale, much as they had been in some ancient armies. As Professor Hale has argued, this military music – criticized at the time as being 'too effective in arousing bloodlust' – formed part of the conditioning and environment that was as important as uniforms, pageantry, or training in inducing the recruit to fight. Another morale-boosting feature adopted from antiquity was the pre-battle exhortation to the troops. Machiavelli, like many of his contemporaries, looked back to Greece and Rome for examples. He wrote:

> Many things may prove the ruin of an army if the general does not frequently harangue his men: for by that he may dispel their fear, inflame their courage, confirm their resolutions, point out the snares that are laid for them, promise them rewards, inform them of danger and the way to escape it, rebuke, entreat, threaten, reproach and encourage.

How this was to be done with larger multi-national armies of troops is not explained, but the lessons of Caesar were clearly not lost on one commander who shouted in 1544:

> Fellow soldiers, let us now fight bravely, and if we win the battle we gain a greater renown than any of our men ever did before. History records that up to now, every time the French fought the Germans hand to hand, the Germans got the victory. To prove that we are better men than our own ancestors we must fight with double courage to overcome them, or to die – and to make them recognise the kind of men we are!

And just in case the enemy did not recognize them in their uniforms, he gave them a quick lesson in how to hold the Swiss pike before rushing them 'and you will see how staggered they will be'. That such speeches worked is rarely doubted by contemporary sources. Claude de Seysell testified to their effectiveness, writing that they put 'great heart into a whole army, to the point of making them courageous as lions where hitherto they had been frightened as sheep'.

Such exhortations, however effective, had become an essential medium of propaganda if men were to risk their lives for the dynastic aspirations of kings. The old concept of the 'just war' no longer commanded respect, especially when Christian fought Christian. Charles VIII tried to justify his invasion of Italy as the prelude to a new crusade against the Turks following the collapse of Constantinople in 1452. But this was merely propaganda: his real aim was conquest, wrapped in the disguise of his dynastic claim to Naples.

But the idea of the 'just war' persisted. So did chivalric notions of battle. Charles VIII's successors, Louis XII and Francis I (1515-47), inherited his dynastic claims. Francis I was actually captured by the Emperor Charles V (1519-56) at the battle of Pavia in 1525, ransomed, and released a year later by his arch enemy. As late as 1535, Charles V was still challenging his rival to single combat. But such practices were in decline, as indeed was the decisive battle, which virtually disappeared from Europe for nearly a century. The images remained, however, as Titian's famous portrait of Charles V in 1547 shows; although by then the emperor was too fat to sit on his horse, he is depicted on horseback as an armoured and conquering medieval knight.

Before then, despite the influence of Humanist philosophers who glorified the dignity and less violent achievements of man, warfare remained an acceptable means of resolving disputes and an endless source of fascination even to the Humanists. To some, war was regarded as a useful means of diverting domestic unrest into the 'healthier' practice of foreign adventure and for strengthening the moral fibre of a population. Others felt a yearning for alternative methods of settling international disputes, and the ideal of European Concord and Universal Peace became a device that kings utilized for their own purposes, accompanied by a growth in the use of diplomacy. This in turn gave rise to the view that defensive wars were the only legitimate type, although what constituted a 'defensive' action was open to debate and certainly the source of much justificatory propaganda. As one English writer put it in 1539:

> I know right well that the office and part of all good men is to desire peace, concord and earnest amity between nation and nation, and yet if an enemy assault us, it might well be accounted extreme madness, and we more than mad, not to avoid our own slaughter, yea, though it were with the slaughter of many other. God gave not the sword unto kings only to punish their subjects when they transgress, but to defend them from the violent power of their enemies, to keep them from rapine, spoil and force or foreign powers.

But, as always, such arguments cut both ways.

Printing certainly perpetuated war's glorification, as Professor Hale has pointed out:

> From a manuscript dribble, treatises on war became a printed flood... Word by word, woodblock by woodblock, diagram by diagram, from tourneying dolls to full formations of lead soldiers, 'war' was studied and discussed throughout the west.

But the savagery unleashed by the Italian wars, especially on civilian populations, gave many cause for concern. Thomas More, for example, described the brutal sack of Rome in 1527 in the following graphic terms:

> And old ancient honourable men, those fierce heretics letted not to hang up by the privy members [private parts], and from many they pulled them off and cast them in the streets. And some brought out [one Roman] naked with his hands bound behind him, and a cord tied fast around his privy members. Then would they set before him in his way other of those tyrants with their moorish pikes... and draw the poor souls by the members towards them. Now was all their cruel sport and laughter, either to see the silly naked men in shrinking from the pikes to tear off their members, or for the pain of that pulling, to run their naked bodies in deep upon the pikes.

Atrocity stories such as this helped to fuel the growing anti-war feeling of many intellectuals. Erasmus, for example, decried the use of religious justification for war, 'because in war there is nothing either good or beautiful'. He recognized the folly of using the idea of a religious just war in an age of growing secular power because 'who does not think his own cause just?' A more pragmatic Machiavelli believed that 'war is just when it is necessary' and indeed we see the transformation of the idea of the 'just war', with its religious connotations, into the concept of the 'just cause' with its secular justifications, although the whole issue became confused during the religious wars sparked off by the Reformation.

Assaults on the validity and dignity of warfare were met with a concerted and vigorous reaction, 'a deliberate re-inflation of the military virtues and splendours, which amounted to a positive cult of war'. This is revealed not just in printed literature, which included military manuals and treatises, but also in art, the decoration of rich households, on tombs, and in statues. The sixteenth century also saw the first military academies, a renewal of interest in knightly orders, and the popularity of such plays as Shakespeare's *Henry V.*

But there is a large difference between theory and practice. The gap between theoretician and military practitioner is the difference between reading about courage and experiencing panic, chaos, and courage on the battlefield. Experienced military commanders realized that the key to battlefield morale was discipline and training. This was no easy matter with armies from such divergent backgrounds. It was not just the language problems with multi-national mercenary units: domestically recruited troops were no more likely to inspire the confidence of their leaders in their morale. Often recruited from illiterate, poor, and violence-ridden rural communities, the sixteenth-century soldier was notoriously difficult to train. Desertion and indiscipline were rife. In the 1540s printed hand-outs notified troops of fines for gambling, hanging for desertion, and imprisonment for failing to bury their excrement. For those who could not read (probably the majority) the rules would be read out to them. Morale was obviously affected by supplies, long marches, disease, and non-payment. Not that the attitude of their commanders helped. When, for example, Charles V discovered that none of his noblemen was among the disease-ridden fatalities at the siege of Metz in 1552, he is alleged to have said that 'it makes no matter' if his men died since they were 'caterpillars and grasshoppers which eat the buds of the earth'.

So again, we have to ask the question: what motivated men to fight in this period? Professor Hale, whose thesis is that sixteenth-century armies formed military communities which were distinct from the societies around them by virtue of their rules, behaviour and attitudes, writes:

> Army service followed a separation from civilian society that generated its own risky brand of defiance. It is only from this assumption that we can understand why large numbers of men, not only individual dare-devils, attained the morale that enabled them to fight, and fight again.

If we continue to regard war as a 'cultural phenomenon', this becomes easier to understand. There have always been volunteers, men who wish to fight regardless of the publicity given to the horrors of war or the disincentives. They need not concern us here. Nor need those who were forced into military service by the remnants of feudalism or the new indentures of states. Recruits, however, have different motivations and are inspired by different factors – amongst them the opportunity to travel, an ideological or religious cause, patriotism, and unemployment. It was these people – perhaps the majority – who were most prone to recruitment propaganda. These were the people, 'the great unwashed', who, denied even a fundamental education that could have taught them how to think for themselves, were most affected by prevailing social and cultural values, by superstition and by authority. As such, they provided a fertile field for propagandists.

Chapter 11

The Reformation and the War of Religious Ideas

Printing, wrote Francis Bacon, together with gunpowder and the compass, 'changed the appearance and state of the whole world'. The printing press certainly provided the artillery that enabled the lines to be drawn up in an unprecedented religious war of ideas. 'The Reformation', writes one historian, 'was the first religious movement which had the aid of the printing press.' When Martin Luther pinned his 95 Theses to the door of the church of the castle at Witenburg in 1517 calling for the reform of the Catholic Church, he was acting like any other normal medieval polemicist but his action was to launch a war for the hearts and minds of Europe and beyond that utilized all the available media of persuasion. As Professor A.G. Dickens has written:

> Between 1517 and 1520, Luther's thirty publications probably sold well over 300,000 copies ... Altogether in relation to the spread of religious ideas it seems difficult to exaggerate the significance of the Press, without which a revolution of this magnitude could scarcely have been consummated ... For the first time in human history a great reading public judged the validity of revolutionary ideas through a mass medium which used the vernacular languages together with the arts of the journalist and the cartoonist.

Indeed, it is difficult to overstate the significance of the printing press as a medium of Reformation propaganda. Luther regarded Gutenberg's invention as 'God's highest act of grace whereby the business of the Gospel is driven forward'. This is not to suggest that the principal medium of medieval propaganda – the pulpit – went into decline; quite the reverse happened in fact, and during the sixteenth century there was a resurgence of pulpit propaganda as sermons were thumped out from Catholic and Protestant apologists alike.

The difference now was that the clergy had access to printed works that served as guidebooks for their ideological messages. Previously, papal letters copied meticulously by a select band of monks had served this function. Thanks to printing, messages could be controlled at source and distributed to a much wider audience. It has to be remembered that sermons did not just serve a religious purpose; they were an important means by which local, national, and international news could be transmitted to the population, laws and decrees announced, taxes justified, wars announced, and so on. Most early books were heavily illustrated to provide visual aids for the text, thus widening their readership beyond the literate. They also served to transmit ideas beyond linguistic frontiers, while the need to read Latin was becoming less significant as Protestant reformers pioneered the use of printing, particularly of the Bible, in local languages. While this facility was open to much abuse, such as in the dissemination of pornography, its value in supplying a more uniform set of rules and ideas to preachers who could then pass on the messages to congregations from Peru to Padua ensured that this became a universal struggle not just a series of local battles. But, once again, this cut both ways, and what one side could do the other could attempt to match. The Reformation, Professor Eisenstein again writes,

> was the first movement of any kind, religious or secular, to use the new presses for overt propaganda and agitation against an established institution. By pamphleteering directed at arousing popular support and aimed at readers who were unversed in Latin, the reformers unwittingly pioneered as revolutionaries and rabble rousers.

Luther himself, initially surprised at the degree to which academic theses designed for internal Church debate were commanding such widespread interest, came to regard printing as the medium by which God, through Gutenberg, chose to liberate the German people from the corruption of Rome. Protestants seized upon the pen as a weapon that really was to challenge the might of the sword.

Between 1517 and 1520, Luther produced thirty major pamphlets which, together with his translations of the Bible, became best-sellers. His attacks upon papal corruption, the wealth and complacency of the monasteries, the myth of clerical celibacy, and the buying and selling of religious positions, sparked off a reaction that was to spread with phenomenal speed throughout European society. Luther's beliefs centred around his view that God spoke to man directly rather than through a priesthood. All men were priests and should not have their religious ceremonies thrust upon them by a papacy that had become corrupt. The Catholic Church was thus exposed as a tyrant, an instrument of social control that denied man his direct access to his Maker. Though initially an unintentional revolutionary, Luther appealed to an age of transformation in which individuals were beginning to rethink their physical and spiritual relationship with the world around them. Luther quickly revealed his skills as a publicist of the first order, especially following his excommunication in 1520. Luther the propagandist publicly and ceremoniously burned his excommunication document together with papal laws and the works of his opponents in 1520. The speed with which his own publications were selling merely served to reinforce his view that his teachings had the backing of God himself. Those princes and kings, particularly in Germany, who began to convert to Protestantism saw in Luther's writings a means by which they could seize control over their own subjects from a foreign pope.

Following the Diet of Worms in 1521, which denounced Lutheran heresy, both Pope and Emperor were committed to fight Protestantism by every means open to them, including persecution and violence. That the Emperor Charles V was not always able to give the heresy his undivided attention was due to the sheer geographical extent of his empire and the troubles he faced on various fronts, from France in the west to the Ottoman empire in the east. Meanwhile, Luther took refuge in the Word. As Professor Elton has written:

> If there is a single thread running through the whole story of the Reformation, it is the explosive and renovating and often disintegrating effect of the Bible, put into the hands of the communality, and interpreted no longer by the well-conditioned learned, but by the faith and delusion, the common sense and the uncommon nonsense of all sorts of men.

The Reformation, in other words, was taken out of Luther's hands and others, less reluctant to take up the sword than he, such as the German princes and radical reformers, challenged the Pope and Emperor. Bloodshed was inevitable, from the Peasants Revolt of

1525 to the excesses of the Inquisition in Spain and the French king's ruthless persecutions in France.

One commentator wrote from Paris in 1520 of Luther's publications: 'No books are more eagerly bought up... One bookshop has sold 1,400 copies... Everywhere people speak highly of Luther. But the chain of the monks is long...' Despite measures to stem the tide, even in this most Catholic of countries Lutheran works continued to be smuggled in, although it was not always possible for the Protestants to control the mounting battle of the books. In 1534, an anti-Catholic broadsheet by a renegade pastor, *True articles on the vile, grave and intolerable abuses of the Papal Mass, invented in direct contravention of the Holy Supper of Our Lord, sole Mediator and Saviour, Jesus Christ*, was posted throughout Paris, including the door of the royal bedchamber. King Francis I was furious and this 'Affair of the Placards' unleashed a violent reaction: heretics were burned at the stake and all printing was temporarily banned. As with Rome and the early Christians, the Catholic reaction merely created Protestant martyrs whose piety and bravery in the face of appalling torments invoked admiration and respect – and a whole host of publications perpetuating their courage. Even Catholics admired their courage, especially as so many continued to preach while the flames consumed them:

> We wept in our colleges on our return from his execution and pleaded his cause after his death, cursing the unjust judges who had justly condemned him. His sermon from the tumbril and at the stake did more harm than a hundred ministers could have done.

Such persecution, which reached its notorious climax with the Inquisition, merely served to force many Protestants underground and books ('silent ministers for those deprived of sermons') enabled them to sustain their faith in secret. Easily hidden, these works penetrated widely to all classes of society, aided by the evangelical nature of fearless Protestants who put psalms to music and who preached at every available opportunity. Of one Geneva publisher who transported and sold his books in France, it has been written:

> Many believers have told how, as he went through the countryside, he would often watch for the hour when the men in the field took their meal, sitting under a tree or in the shade of a hedge, as is their wont. And there, pretending to rest alongside them, he would take the opportunity, by simple and gradual means, to teach them to fear God

and to pray to Him before and after their meals... whereupon he would ask the poor peasants if they would not like him to pray to God for them. Some were greatly comforted and edified by this, others were astounded at hearing unfamiliar things; some molested him, because he showed them that they were on the path to damnation if they did not believe in the Gospel.

Such activities helped to spread the 'Lutheran contagion' out from such centres as Lyon and Paris throughout France and which manifested itself in the smashing of religious statues, the spoiling of church icons, and finally in the French wars of religion (1559-98).

The Catholic reaction, spearheaded by such propagandists as John Eck and Frederick Nausea, was backed up with a degree of reform that ultimately became the Counter-Reformation. But the papacy was not content to rely solely upon positive methods of propaganda. It also recognized the value of censorship. Many individual books were condemned and in 1527, Pope Clement VII issued a bull attacking heretical works and their readers. The first list of prohibited books in England was issued in 1529, to be followed a year later by a licensing system (whilst still a Catholic, Henry VIII burned Luther's works in 1531). In 1559 the Papacy issued an Index of Prohibited Books. As John Foxe wrote, 'either the pope must abolish knowledge and printing or printing must at length root him out'. But prohibition and repression failed to stem the Protestant tide; actions tend to speak louder than words (provided they can be publicized sufficiently) and it was only with the reforms laid down by the Council of Trent (1545-63) that the Catholic Church was able to lay the foundations for an attempt to regain its supremacy.

Chapter 12

Tudor Propaganda

In England, where indeed the Catholic Church had been rooted out by the Henrician reformation of the 1530s, Henry VIII's minister Thomas Cromwell is said to have launched 'the first campaign ever mounted by any government in any state of Europe' to exploit the propaganda potential of the printing press. Henry VII, the founder of the Tudor dynasty, had always been acutely aware of the importance of propaganda as a means of consolidating his power. Henry was determined to legitimize his dynasty in the eyes of God, the Pope, and Europe, not to mention the English people, and he did this with the aid of a judicious marriage, ceremonial, and propaganda. He presented his Bosworth standards to St Paul's cathedral, the white and red roses of the Houses of York and Lancaster were combined into a united two-coloured rose, papal recognition of his dynasty was published with the aid of the printing press introduced to England in 1476 by William Caxton (Henry appointed a royal printer in 1504), and he went on a 'progress' to various English cities, including York. The progress was an established method of royal propaganda and the forerunner of today's royal 'walkabout'. By the time his son, Henry VIII, came to the throne in 1509, the pattern for Tudor royal propaganda had been well and truly set.

Henry VIII, inspired perhaps by the magnificent propaganda of the Holy Roman Emperor, was determined to impress his continental peers. Elaborate ceremonies, sumptuous court life, the Tudor coinage, mock battles, jousts and tournaments, in which the young athletic king himself excelled, all gave the impression of Henry as a warrior king in true chivalric fashion. And it seems to have worked, if the testimony of one Italian visitor in 1517 was anything to go by:

The wealth and civilization of the world are here; and those who call the English barbarians appear to me to render themselves such. I here perceive very elegant manners, extreme decorum, and very great politeness; and amongst other things there is the most invincible King, whose acquirements and qualities are so many and excellent that I consider him to excel all who ever wore a crown.

Despite the fiasco of the French war of 1512-14, Henry's propaganda efforts managed to give an impression of England as a much more significant European power that it actually was. Perhaps the climax of his propaganda achievement came in the period 1518-20 with the signing of the Treaty of Universal Peace and the spectacular meeting with the French king, Francis I, on the Field of the Cloth of Gold (1520).

The Treaty of Universal Peace (1518), signed by virtually all the Christian powers of Europe, was really more a statement of intent in the vein of the twentieth-century Kellogg-Briand pact outlawing war than an effective attempt to rid Europe of the scourge of war. Yet this brief moment of European unity in the face of the Turkish threat (or so it was presented) set the scene for an Anglo-French rapprochement and a meeting in a field near Calais that was described by one contemporary as the eighth wonder of the world. This rare expression of Anglo-French brotherly love took months to plan and a fortune to stage. As Sydney Anglo has noted:

> The display and propaganda of 1520 seem, amidst the political machin-ations of the great powers, like some colossal anachronistic game which all the monarchs, all their ministers, and all their retinues had decided to play... The whole affair – with its romantic palaces and pavilions [specially erected for the occasion], its costly tournaments and sumptuous banquets – seems a late flowering of the most extravagant medieval chivalry...But the reality was far removed from this... Europe had been treated to a display of simulated affection which scarcely veiled the antagonism between the Kings of England and France.

One such reality was Luther's Reformation, already spreading rapidly throughout Europe. While Wolsey burned his books in ostentatious public displays and officially sponsored sermons were delivered by people such as John Fisher, Bishop of Rochester, Henry wrote a tract condemning Luther's teachings, whereupon the Pope gave Henry the title 'Defender of the Faith', still borne by the monarch today. However, even as Francis I and Charles V were fighting out their old rivalry at the Battle of Pavia in 1525, ominous storm clouds were forming as Henry's wife, Catherine of Aragon, failed to produce an heir for the dynasty Henry's father had fought so hard to create and which he had done so much to consolidate.

Henry's propaganda efforts at home, aided by Cardinal Wolsey, served to pave the way for public acceptance of the forthcoming break with Rome. With Francis the prisoner of Charles, Wolsey tried to whip up popular support for war against France. One of his officials informed him that in Norwich he had 'appointed fires to be made in every town in the Shire on Sunday night, and in every town discreet persons to declare to the people the great overthrow of the French king, and to do the most they can to encourage them to this invasion this summer'.

The war did not materialize. Nor did a son for Henry, and Wolsey's successor, Thomas Cromwell, had to follow through the break with Rome precipitated by the king's divorce from Catherine and his marriage to Anne Boleyn. During the build-up to the divorce, Henry had launched a pamphlet debate arguing the merits of his case, although the reformist publications of William Tyndale had in many respects already paved the way, despite the counter-efforts of Sir Thomas More.

The Act of Supremacy (1534), which placed Henry at the head of the Church in England, led to a massive intensification of the propaganda struggle. The task Henry gave Cromwell was enormous: to change a thousand years of English thinking. If one remembers the deep-rooted influence the Catholic Church had been able to exercise upon the medieval mind in helping to explain people's relationship with their environment, this task becomes even more enormous. Perhaps, thanks to the arrival of printing, it was just possible. Luther had, after all, recently demonstrated that the influence of the Church upon European society could be challenged with some success and printing was regarded by contemporaries as a major instrument of change. When, therefore, Henry's proven concern with dynastic consolidation threatened to clash with the authority of the Pope it was perhaps inevitable for him to turn to propaganda as a means of persuading his subjects that a thousand years of history could be overturned, that he was right and the Pope was wrong.

Cromwell proved to be more than equal to the task. Foxe described him as 'This valiant soldier and captain of Christ... by whose industry and ingenious labours divers excellent ballads and books were contrived and set abroad, concerning the suppression of the pope and all popish idolatry.' Once Sir Thomas More's objections to the king's divorce made the issue public, Cromwell embarked upon promoting a 'right view' of events in the Henrician revolution, both at home and abroad. He did this by positive and negative means. Avoiding the papal mistake of publishing an index of prohibited books for fear that it would only draw attention to them, Cromwell attempted to censor dissenting works and to control the output of official propaganda from the king's printer, Thomas Berthelet. In 1536 a proclamation ordered the surrender of any publication spread abroad 'in derogation and diminution of the dignity and authority royal of the King's majesty and his imperial crown'. However, it proved impossible to suppress completely the spread of heretical works so a campaign was started to question the Pope's right to dispense the law of the scriptures in England.

The debate started in a somewhat academic style with the publication of *The Determination of the most famous and excellent Universities of Italy and France, that it is unlawful for a man to marry his brother's wife and that the pope hath no power to dispense therewith* (1531). This provoked a response from the opposition, the *Invicta Veritas,* censorship was intensified, and the debate widened to a popular audience. *The Glass of Truth,* published in 1532, written partly by the king himself, was a short, readable, and lively tract which argued the case in the form of a discussion between a theologian and a canon lawyer. The stress placed upon the need for a male heir to save the realm from disaster reduced the issue to a nationalistic one and began the argument for the transfer of power from Rome to throne. Then came the *Nine Articles devised by the whole consent of the King's most honourable Council,* a blatantly official pamphlet designed 'not only to exhort but also to inform his loving subjects of the truth'. In this, the Pope is reduced to the 'bishop of Rome', but there was little debate about the issues. These were statements of fact, guidelines to be followed, published in English and designed to eradicate dissent.

While Edwarde Foxe and Richard Sampson championed the king's cause in academic and theological Latin texts designed for the learned, Cromwell was aware that material had to be produced for the masses, 'though they forbear to speak at large, for fear of punishment, yet they mutter together secretly'. Some sources testify to a distinct chill among the people as they witnessed the king's marriage, even though the ceremony had been designed to legitimize his action. A *Little Treatise against the muttering of some papists in corners* was printed as a sort of handbook for priests to tackle the problem via the pulpit. But many priests themselves remained disaffected. In 1536, therefore, one of Cromwell's chief writers, Richard Morison, advocated a more intensive anti-papal propaganda drive. In his *A Persuasion to the King that the laws of the realm should be in Latin,* Morison advocated an annual triumph with bonfires, feasts, and processions to serve as a permanent reminder to the common people of their deliverance by the king from the bondage of Rome. Morison's view was 'into the common people things sooner enter by the eyes than by the ears', which was why he placed so much emphasis upon spectacle – such as plays and processions – as a means of countering the sermons of the hostile clergy.

Despite Morison's programme, Cromwell continued to place his faith in printed propaganda. Stephen Gardiner's *De Vera Obedientia,* printed by Berthelet in 1535, achieved considerable fame since it was written by a man who had at first opposed the king's action but who had now 'seen the light'. Official sermons were published at crown expense and distributed to the clergy. Yet when popular discontent erupted in open rebellion in the north after 1536, it was essential to print works linking domestic treason with the threat of foreign invasion – a classic propaganda device designed to pinpoint the enemy within. Papists now became part of a conspiracy to overthrow the crown engineered from abroad, especially when Cardinal Pole threatened invasion at the end of the decade. Morison wrote *An Exhortation to stir all Englishmen to the defence of their country* in which he urged the need to support the king in his efforts to defeat external and internal enemies. Printed statutes, distributed throughout the country for public display, were perhaps less effective than the instructions issued to the clergy but even here there was too great a risk that old views would surface. Accordingly, Cromwell appointed 'official' preachers who worked hard to replace opponents of the government in the pulpits and attempted to enforce popular support by the swearing of oaths. It was Thomas More's refusal of the oath of succession 'without the jeopardizing of my soul to external damnation' that caused his political downfall and execution.

References to the Pope vanished from all official Church books while the king's new title of supreme head of the Church appeared everywhere. School teachers were instructed to follow the same course. Repeated offenders, however, demanded strict measures and Cromwell soon realized the need to reinforce propaganda with punishment. Magistrates were charged with watching over the bishops and were instructed to prosecute dissidents with announcements of why they had broken the laws of the land. The bench thus also became a pulpit for Henrician propaganda. As Professor Elton says:

> Changes in doctrine, changes in ceremonies, attacks on monasteries and purgatory and superstitions, the promotion of the English Bible, positive moves towards a better education for laity and clergy alike, the institution of parish registers – these and other manifestations of Cromwell's relentless reforming zeal brought real disturbance to the people at large. Never content merely to decree, always conscious of the need to apply and make real, Cromwell continued to bombard the country with exhortations to act.

How far all this was a success cannot be determined, but it is clear that the policy and propaganda concerning the Tudor revolution of the 1530s implemented enormous changes in the behaviour and thought of Englishmen. Despite Cromwell's execution in 1540, Henry VIII had launched a revolution in the hearts and minds of his subjects that was to be completed by his daughter, Elizabeth I, when she ascended the throne in 1558.

The virulence of Cromwell's anti papal propaganda campaign did not survive his death. The Tudor dynasty did – at least for another forty-five years. That this was so was due, in no small part, to the role which the Tudors continued to place on propaganda as an agent for the development of an English national consciousness. An Englishman's duty was now to his monarch, the head of both Church and State. Thus, both the chief influences that shaped thought and behaviour resided in the crown, and the pomp, pageantry, and ceremony of Elizabeth's reign reflected this new national consciousness. External threats, especially Catholic ones such as those posed by France and Spain, were used by the Tudors to consolidate their position and justify their actions. The glorious propaganda of the Elizabethan age helped to make the Protestant monarch master of her own house in a way that only the German princes could rival. Militarily, England remained a relatively inconsequential continental power, especially after the loss of Calais in 1558. But the new national distinctness ushered in by the Tudor revolution took refuge in the development of a naval tradition that suited England's geographic position perfectly. However, the carefully controlled images of the monarchy – such as the flattering portraits in paint and pen of the Faeiry Queen – provided an illusion of unity. This was the lasting propaganda triumph of the Tudors.

Chapter 13

The Thirty Years War (1618-48)

Since the Treaty of Cateau-Cambrésis in 1559, which ended the Hapsburg-Valois struggle between France and Spain, France had been subsumed by religious wars which were only partly resolved by the Edict of Nantes (1598). Spain had had to deal with the revolt of the Netherlands, together with a renewed Turkish threat in the Mediterranean, not stemmed even by the spectacular naval victory at Lepanto in 1571. Although the Turkish threat had provided a uniting rallying cry for Europe since the Crusades, it no longer served such a purpose except as propaganda. All this took place against the background of Reformation – now inspired by Calvin – and Counter-Reformation, championed by Philip II of Spain, now in full flow following the Council of Trent in 1563. In England, the death of Elizabeth I in 1603 saw the accession of the Stuart dynasty with James I (r. 1603-25) and the end of the twenty-year struggle with Spain. The exposure of the Gunpowder Plot in 1605 ensured that England would continue to persecute Catholics, and every Englishman over eighteen years of age became obliged to swear that 'I do, from my heart, abhor, detest and abjure, as impious and heretical, this damnable doctrine and position', under penalty of imprisonment. Catholicism, in other words, was treason; an Englishman's loyalty was to his sovereign, not the Pope. Propagandists such as Robert Cotton, however, argued against religious executions as they only created martyrs that impressed public opinion ('temporal armies are remedies serving for a time, but the spiritual sword is permanent in operation'), and the second half of James I's reign was marked by a greater degree of toleration.

At the start of the seventeenth century, therefore, most of the conflicts of the previous century were still in full swing. Yet Europe was also in the throes of a military revolution. Medieval concepts of warfare had all but disappeared with the advent of gunpowder and the increased role of the artilleryman and the musketeer. This, together with the decline in the frequency of decisive battles and the corresponding growth of wars of attrition, the rise of Dutch and English seapower, and military reforms which introduced new tactical methods and concepts, were all accompanied by a marked increase in the destructive capability of warfare. The 'professional-ization' of armies, with improved methods of recruitment, training, drill, and pay, was under way (though it was late to establish itself in England), the costs of implementation being to some extent offset by riches acquired from the New World. And although the Dutch had demonstrated in their Eighty-Year War (1567-1648) with their imperial Spanish overlords that well-organized forces of patriotically-inspired and highly-disciplined men could resist even the mightiest opponent, the title 'Father of Modern War' (at least on land) must go to Gustavus Adolphus of Sweden.

When Ferdinand II was elected Holy Roman Emperor in 1619 and attempted to consolidate Hapsburg power in Bohemia, a Protestant reaction sparked off a series of religious conflicts which attracted the intervention of foreign powers such as Denmark, Spain, and Sweden and devastated Europe for the next thirty years. Essentially, a German civil war became a continental struggle between the great powers. From some points of view a series of separate wars, the Thirty Years War (1618-48) was as much a European-wide struggle for religious and secular loyalty as any-thing else, and its role in the development of nationalism and the emergence of the nation-state cannot be over-estimated. Neither can its destructive impact upon Europe, with perhaps a quarter of the population being killed from battle, famine, or disease. Contemporaries noted how armies seemed more willing to attack peasants in occupied areas than confront their enemies on the field of battle, and devastation and despair scarred the physical and mental landscape of Europe. It is against this background that the 'professionalization' of propaganda techniques, particularly using the printing press, needs to be seen.

Indeed, this period also gave the word 'propaganda' to the world. During the Counter-Reformation, the Society of Jesus (the Jesuits), founded by Ignatius Loyola in 1534, had proved an effective instrument in combating Lutheranism and Calvinism, restoring

Catholics to Austria, converting most of Poland, and extending its mission to South America and China. The Jesuits fully recognized the importance of discipline and of educating their recruits from an early age. Loyola was made a saint in 1622. It was also in that year that Pope Gregory XV decided to extend the methods of the Jesuits by creating a new papal department – the 'Sacra Congregatio de Propaganda Fide', the Congregation for the Propagation of the Faith. This body was charged with the task of reviving Catholicism in Reformation Europe and strengthening it in the New World. Five years later, in 1627, Pope Urban VIII founded the Collegium Urbanum to serve as a training ground for a new generation of Catholic propagandists who were given a remarkable amount of discretion concerning the methods to be employed in the field. In the context of the Thirty Years War, this often involved secrecy, whether of production or distribution of material, and these characteristics have left a cloud of suspicion over the word 'propaganda' ever since, especially in north European Protestant countries.

Despite this 'modernization' of propaganda, many of the old methods were still in evidence, although they were refined in accordance with scientific and technological discoveries. Astrology, for example, was given further credence in the eyes of a superstitious public by the writings of such respected scientists as Johann Kepler (1571-1630) and Galileo (1564-1642) who were commissioned to produce astrological charts for leaders. If favourable, they were published as propaganda tracts to indicate predestined success. The appearance of a comet in 1618 at the outset of the Thirty Years War was subject to a wide variety of propaganda interpretations, much as Halley's comet had been in 1066. Similarly, heretics and undesirables were easily branded with the stigma of witchcraft and numerous pamphlets were printed on demonology, describing in graphic detail with explicit instructions the 'symptoms' and 'evidence' as extracted under torture. The *Malleus Maleficarum* – the Catholic handbook on the right qualifications for burning, first published in 1486, had been reprinted more than thirty times by 1669. The mere threat of being burned at the stake was an invaluable aid to any attempt to bring lost souls back to the true faith, although many Jesuits opposed this style of terror campaign at the expense of their preferred method of indoctrination and education. Even so, actual executions by fire reached epidemic proportions in Germany in the 1620s.

Misery also appeared in a soldier's uniform. In his *Art of War on Foot* (1615), Johann Wallhausen listed the qualifications required by a good soldier, including discipline and having 'God in his heart'. The brutality of European armies as they crossed backwards and forwards across the countryside was one of the main characteristics of the Thirty Years War. Soldiers could hardly argue that they had not been warned of the miserable conditions they faced. One widely printed poem went:

You must help God and Fatherland
   For protection and honour
And often duck, hump your load and crawl
Often sleep but little, lie uncomfortably,
   Often hunger, thirst, sweat and shiver
And anywhere to be ready for your fate or fortune.

Mercenary troops, as we have seen, were notoriously indisciplined and unreliable, despite the attempts of articles of war and oaths of loyalty to restrain them. They often preferred to spend their initial pay and travelling expenses on wine, women and song rather than on uniforms or weapons. Unless the prospect of booty was sufficiently attractive to keep them in the field, desertion and mutiny were rife. But increased attempts were made to drill and train them into some form of coherent fighting unit, most notably by Gustavus Adolphus of Sweden. Pay and training were regularized and the king himself led his men into battle amidst a colourful array of flags and banners. Morale increased accordingly and it was said of Swedish troops that they 'preferred to die chivalrously rather than flee'. When the Swedish army entered the war in 1630, its superior discipline, morale, and tactics were illustrated at the victories of Breitenfeld, Rain, and Lützen (1631-2) and the lesson of using indigenous troops rather than mercenaries was not lost on many of its opponents. However, with the drain on Scandinavian manpower, together with the death in battle of Gustavus Adolphus himself at Lützen in 1632, even the patriotic troops of Sweden began to assume the lawless characteristics of other European armies.

Too one sided a picture must not be painted. Discipline and morale of a sort were maintained by time-honoured devices, such as stirring music and flying flags, which were used to control the line of battle and issue orders. Drums and trumpets were also useful in drowning battlefield cries of fear. Psalms and hymns soothed the men before battle while rousing poems served to inspire them. As Herbert Langer has written:

> Fear of supernatural beings, of mysterious forces, of the barbarous punishments employed by the officers and of death at any moment and the prospects of booty and the easy acquisition of goods of any kind were obviously the most powerful factors which guaranteed a certain degree of combat efficiency on the part of the mercenaries. Military drill, customs and traditions also helped to maintain discipline and resolution in battle despite the tendency to disintegrate which affected many mercenary formations.

Plundering armies living off the land forced terrified peasants to flee into the fortified towns and gave rise to a large literature on the savagery of military barbarism and atrocities. Soldiers speaking in unknown foreign languages and wearing unfamiliar clothing became the Devil in Disguise and in areas peasants organized themselves to rid themselves of the parasitic troops, as in Bavaria or in the 'Peasants' War' of Upper Austria. Defending commanders accordingly found themselves aided by local populations and peasant units were particularly useful in guerilla warfare, skirmishes, and ambushes.

It is against this background that the war propaganda of the Thirty Years War must be seen. If war aims were presented in the age old disguise of religion, then much of the 'credit' for this must go to the poets, songwriters, pamphleteers, and painters whose work reached just about every class of society. This was greatly aided, for example, by the development of copper plate, which enabled posters to be printed more efficiently than from woodcuts. As Professor Kamen has written: 'short, well phrased tracts with a clear argument and simple language became the staple fare of the ideological conflict... [and] came closest to providing some sort of propaganda for the masses.' Professional publicists emerged; painters such as Van Dyck produced portraits of generals, Vrancx specialized in battle scenes, and Velasquez glorified the Spanish monarchy. But it was the copperplate engravings and etchings that achieved mass circulation and their propaganda significance becomes obvious when one considers that the viewpoint they take invariably reflected the viewpoint of the people who commissioned them – the ruling élite.

But it was not just illustrated books and posters that benefited from the new technology. News-sheets, distributed locally in the sixteenth century, now achieved a much wider circulation. Fast-moving events required a rapid turnover in news and information, and weekly news-sheets printed from copperplate could now be distributed more rapidly through an improving – though still rudimentary – postal system. Newspaper historians generally point to the monthly Strassburg *Relation,* first published in 1609, as the first true 'newspaper', and the first weekly newspaper was probably the *Frankfurter Zeitung* in 1615. The first English newspaper appeared in 1620, though published in Amsterdam, giving news reports on the Thirty Years War. Appearing perhaps once or twice a week, these early newspapers were published in a variety of languages. Between 1636 and 1646, weekly newspapers were founded in six Italian cities. The first daily newspaper appeared in Leipzig in 1660 and indicates the degree to which news communications were improving during the course of the first half of the seventeenth century.

As for the war itself, the principal medium of propaganda was the small-format publication: the poster, the single-page news-sheet, the leaflet, and the pamphlet. The 'war of the pens' reflected the degree to which ordinary people were becoming increasingly involved in warfare. The popularity of such publications has been described by Langer in the following terms:

> Apart from the familiar Biblical matter and religious questions, moralizing warnings, prophecies, admonitions to repent and return to a life of modesty acceptable to God, they dealt with subjects which had their origin in the realm of world experience: death and ruination, violence, power, gluttony, avarice, deceit in coinage and weights, litigious dispositions, crime, miracles, the quarrelsome nature of women, the annoyance of matrimony, social injustice, wealth and poverty, fortune and ill-luck, the latest fashions, the decline in moral and linguistic standards, state events – and especially the persons, parties, events and vicissitudes of the war, such as the guilty and the victims, those really and supposedly responsible, news from the theatres of war, of negotiations and treaties.

Merciless caricatures – an effective means of communicating pointed ideas to the illiterate – were directed at leaders in the pay of foreign regimes and played upon the direct experience of people who needed some explanation for the misery that engulfed them.

Attempts at censorship were sporadic but failed to stem the rising tide of invective, sponsored in the main by warring factions, especially when captured documents fell into the hands of one side or the other. The most celebrated occasion of this happening took place after the Battle of White Mountain in 1620 when King Frederick V of Bohemia was defeated by the Catholic League and Spanish and Imperial troops. Letters written by the Emperor to Spain concerning the transfer of Protestant lands were intercepted by supporters of Frederick, published, and distributed to demonstrate the Spanish-Imperial Catholic conspiracy.

The intervention of Sweden on the side of the Protestant forces in 1630 was the occasion of a renewed propaganda campaign. Gustavus Adolphus' *War Manifesto,* justifying his involvement to the German people as an act of religious liberation, was widely circulated, together with other justificatory leaflets. Swedish propaganda played on words, using *Sued* spelled backwards as 'deus' as a trick to present Gustavus as a Homeric heroic figure. Such support as may have initially greeted the Swedish 'liberators' dwindled as his opponents launched a wave of terror that was accompanied by a propaganda campaign with the theme 'Where was your liberator when you needed him most?' Following Gustavus Adolphus' death, Germanic enthusiasm dwindled as the 'liberators' came increasingly to resemble 'invaders' who had merely made conditions worse for the peasantry by their intervention. However, it would be inaccurate to suggest coherence on the part of the propagandists; even the Protestants waged paper war against one another – to the delight of the Catholic Church – as the Lutheran stronghold of Saxony launched a psychological war against the Calvinist forces in the Palatinate. Changing military fortunes demanded changing propaganda explanations and exhortations. As one writer put it, 'the pen and the sword can do great things. They can both make war and peace again. It is true that the pen precedes the sword, but sometimes progress is quicker with the sword.' After thirty years of conflict, however, the pen and the sword had forged a formidable alliance in which the one was now recognized to be invaluable to the other for its success. Although there was nothing new about this combination of warfare and propaganda, it was the scale on which the alliance was formed, and the extent to which the material was distributed, which marks this period as a genuine turning point in the history of war propaganda.

'For sheer volume of publicity, the seventeenth century was one of innovation,' concluded Professor Kamen. For the sheer internationalization of propaganda, the Thirty Years War was a watershed.

Chapter 14

The English Civil War (1642-6)

The increasing involvement of the public in both politics and warfare since the Reformation partly reflected and partly caused the growth of propaganda. In England in the 1640s it exploded into full scale civil war, or the Great Rebellion as it was known. Professor Kamen again:

> The situation had to be faced: revolutionary propaganda was more than an exercise in persuasion; it frequently reflected genuine popular attitudes, it was committed not to the support of established parties but to the questioning of all authority. As soon as the floodgates of censorship had been opened, the sentiments of all sections of the people burst through.

The printing press enabled people to involve themselves in politics to an unprecedented degree. As one man commented in 1641, 'the art of printing will so spread knowledge that the common people, knowing their own rights and liberties, will not be governed by way of oppression'. When, therefore, the opponents of Charles I (r. 1625-49) launched a massive propaganda assault against the king, whom they believed was trying to destroy their constitutional position, they were not only defending their rights as 'freeborn Englishmen', they were also developing the idea of propaganda as a liberating force. From the Reformation and the Dutch Revolt onwards, printing provided a means by which oppressed could attack oppressor, a medium of liberation and revolution of such power that it inevitably demanded the twin response of counter-propaganda and censorship from the authorities.

Although both James I and Charles I had tried to continue Elizabeth's censorship system, they were unable to stem the rising influence of the Puritans, a dissident Calvinistic movement within

England's state Church, and of the growing Parliamentary criticism of their policies. By the late 1620s the political and religious opponents of the Stuarts had forged an alliance in an attempt to prevent the king's extravagant spending and his High Church innovations. Charles I dissolved Parliament and ruled without it throughout the 1630s. He also got the Star Chamber to pass a decree prohibiting the import of books from abroad unless a catalogue was submitted to him or to the Bishop of London in advance.

Without a standing army, however, Charles was unable to suppress the Scottish rebellion that occurred in 1638. When the Scots invaded England, Charles had no option but to summon Parliament. It was during this Long Parliament, from 1640 to 1653, that all the ideological issues (merchants v. aristocrats, Puritans v. Anglicans, parliament v. royal absolutism) came to a head. Though it was initially successful in dismantling the king's personal government of the previous decade (including the abolition of the Star Chamber and the dismantling of other agents of royal absolutism), the Long Parliament quickly divided into royalist and parliamentary factions, and when the king attempted a military-style coup against the latter, mob pressure forced Charles to leave London and the opposing sides began to raise troops.

During the civil war that followed from 1642-6, the breakdown of the censorship and licensing system established by the Tudors and Stuarts led to a massive flow of news-sheet propaganda. Royalists ('Cavaliers') and Parliamentarians ('Roundheads') also produced their own newspapers, the former's principal organ being the *Mercurius Aulicus* and the latter's the *Mercurius Britannicus*. Motivated by Puritan zeal, and with the advantage of holding London and the southeast with its abundance of printing presses, the Roundheads were also able to gain the military advantage over the king's northern-based forces. Mass demonstrations were held to maintain public morale while a huge torrent of pamphlets poured forth from Puritan and Parliamentary presses. The bookseller George Thomason collected 15,000 pamphlets between 1640 and 1663 and his collection in the British Library lists 2000 for the year 1642 alone. Newspapers likewise increased in number; Thomason's collection contains only 4 for 1641 but 167 for 1642 and a staggering 722 for 1645. But the Long Parliament grew alarmed at the vehemence of opposing viewpoints and reintroduced censorship by licensing in 1643.

Among the most successful propagandists were the Levellers,

who managed to circumvent the renewed censorship and licensing laws with particular skill. They made extensive use of the printing press and had publications smuggled in from the continental publishing centre of Amsterdam. In 1647, John Lilburne declared that he was determined 'to appeal to the whole kingdom and Army' against the Presbyterians and he did this through the newspaper, the *Moderate*. The risks were considerable, with severe penalties for sedition, including dismemberment. But freedom of speech, within the confines of national security, was one of those rights for which 'free-born Englishmen' were prepared to fight. Censorship, wrote the Puritan John Goodwin, prevented the Holy Ghost from coming forth by way of the press. The Puritan poet John Milton echoed this demand in his famous work *Areopagitica,* published in 1644. But it was for political reasons that the Levellers protested against the reintroduction of censorship; as one of their leaders demanded in 1644, the press must 'be free for any man that writes nothing highly scandalous or dangerous to the state'. The Stationers Company, they argued, now had powers 'to suppress everything which hath any true declaration for the just rights and liberties of the freeborn of the nation', while at the same time could 'print, divulge and disperse whatsoever books, pamphlets and libels they please, though they be full of lies and tend to the poisoning of the kingdom with unjust and tyrannical principles'. But it was the definition of what constituted a danger to the State which then, as now, caused most controversy. Not even Milton trusted purely to unfettered truth and recognized in *Areopagitica* the need for control of that 'which is impious or evil absolutely against faith or manners'. However, it was from demands for religious freedom of speech and conscience that demands for political freedom of expression emerged.

Older Roundhead generals were reluctant to fight their anointed king. In civil war, the image of the enemy presents a much more difficult task for the propagandists, especially in one which began so reluctantly as in England. But Oliver Cromwell, whose Ironside regiment was characterized by a high degree of religious fervour and zeal and motivated by a genuine conviction that his cause was the right one, had no such qualms. Winning every engagement it fought, Cromwell's New Model Army finally defeated the Royalists at Naseby in 1645. 'God made them as stubble to our swords,' wrote Cromwell of his enemies. Thus, with strict discipline and high morale (singing psalms as they went into battle), Cromwell's troops captured the king in 1646 and imprisoned him for two years. With the war over, the various political factions began to jostle for power. But the king refused to accommodate Puritan demands and, once the Presbyterian and Cavalier opponents of Cromwell's Independents had been prevented from entering parliament by military force in 1648, the 'rump' parliament decided to execute the king in 1649 and Britain became a Puritan republic. Cromwell's ruthless suppression of Ireland, his conquest of Scotland, and his war with the Dutch and Spanish all took place against the establishment of a personal dictatorship at home by which he became Lord Protector.

Foreign wars and the establishment of a new regime that had to consolidate its position necessarily led to a controlled propaganda campaign employing both positive and negative means. Neither seems to have been particularly effective, despite the justificatory works of Milton and Andrew Marvell. In 1651 Cromwell published his *First Defence of the People of England* in order to sell the idea of the Commonwealth; a *Second Defence* in 1654 portrayed him as a biblical figure come to restore liberty to England. But these titles reveal a key flaw: Cromwell was indeed on the defensive, and increasingly so by the later 1650s when projected coins and published broadsheets began to show him wearing an imperial laurel, even a crown. With his position at home resting upon the support of a 50,000-strong standing army, public opinion came to resent not only his military dictatorship and his expensive and belligerent foreign policy, but also a range of powers that would have been the envy of the late King Charles. Despite censorship regulations romanticized images were able to maintain the offensive (literally, in view of the satirical broadsides levelled at 'Copper Nose' Cromwell) with such publications as England's *New Chains Discovered*. The political crisis that followed Cromwell's death in 1658 demonstrated that centuries of monarchical propaganda could not be eradicated from the English psyche by a ten-year experiment in republicanism. The Tudors had done their work well. England wanted a legitimate king, and Charles I's son was crowned Charles II in 1660. Although the crisis was by no means over, the English monarch now realized that his (or her) government would in future be dependent for its position upon public support rather than divine right. And with the advent of party politics, attempts to appeal to that public were bound to increase.

Chapter 15

Louis XIV (1661-1715)

If the case of England in the mid-seventeenth century provides an example of how Cromwell, despite the use of propaganda, failed to make his regime generally acceptable, the case of France is an even more glaring example of the dangers of shadow without the substance. France under the Bourbons also reveals the dangers of denying constitutional outlets to public opinion. The concept of the press as a liberating force, by which public opinion could influence political change, was inimical to the concept of absolutist monarchy. However, the monarchical ostentation that character-ized the first half of Louis XIV's reign was revealed as nothing more than propaganda when finally exposed in the second half to the challenge of a crippling war.

Louis XIII (r. 1610-43) and his chief minister Cardinal Richelieu plunged into the Thirty Years War on the side of the Protestant Dutch and Swedes in order to break the encirclement of France by the Catholic Hapsburg rulers of Spain. According to the French historian Jean-Pierre Seguin, sixteenth-century French kings had already established a propaganda system designed to 'win the psy-chological war which prepared and accompanied [their] military operations'. Richelieu died in 1642 and Louis followed him a year later, to be replaced by the 5-year-old Louis XIV (r. 1643-1715). But by the time the Treaty of Westphalia, which ended the Thirty Years War, was signed in 1648, France was being administered by Cardinal Mazarin and the 'general crisis' which afflicted all European societies, and which had exploded into civil war in England, also threatened to undermine the French monarchy during the period of the Fronde (1648-53).

Richelieu had inspired the founding of an official newspaper,

Théophraste Renaudot's *La Gazette de France,* in 1631. Designed as a weekly four-page journal 'for kings and the powers that be' to advertize their policies and viewpoints, it also supplied news of a more general character so that 'the merchant will no longer trade in a besieged and ruined town, nor the soldier seek employment in a country where there is no war; nor to speak of the comfort for those writing to their friends who were formerly forced to give news that was either invented or based on hearsay'.

This precedent was quickly followed by other European governments that were experiencing the enormous growth in printed political propaganda. During the Fronde, which started as an aristocratic protest against the erosion of privileges but which rapidly included the Paris mob and the newly demobilized French army, some 5000 pamphlets and news-sheets attacking Mazarin were published. Written in a simple style and sold at a low cost, these pamphlets were known as *mazarinades* after the best-known assault on the king's minister, *La Mazarinade,* published in March 1651. We know their number from a catalogue compiled by Moreau, although it seems likely that the pamphlet war produced many more publications than those listed – all the more remarkable in view of rigorous censorship restrictions. The *Gazette de France* was used as the chief government mouthpiece and, as one source has it:

> From the great to the small, everyone discusses what is going on only through the *Gazette.* Those who can afford it buy copies and collect them. Others are satisfied to pay in order to borrow and read it, or else they group together so as to buy a copy.

It has to be remembered that we are still talking about a relatively small number of literate people in a Christian Europe that accepted an orthodox view of man's nature in relationship to God. But, as we shall see, the forces of change required more outlets than those provided by the *Gazette.* Just as it had been the duty of the Church to direct opinion in order to protect and guide man, so now the State was assuming responsibility for disseminating 'the truth'. Printing aided this process for the literate whose responsibility it was to recite aloud the Truth to the illiterate. It was a measurement of their loyalty. But the State was soon to discover that too restricted a view of 'the truth' was counter-productive.

But no amount of censorship could prevent 'untruths' from being printed clandestinely or smuggled in from abroad. Richelieu and

Mazarin attempted to use censorship as a means of controlling public opinion (the Code Michaud of 1629 made writers of illegal works subject to arrest and trial), but they were never able to prevent illicit publications from entering France, especially the French language political periodicals produced by Huguenot *émigrés* in Holland following the Revocation of the Edict of Nantes in 1685. Instead, they relied heavily upon positive means of persuasion. As one French minister wrote, the king needed to employ 'skilled pens, have *them* write clandestine pamphlets, manifestos, artfully composed apologies and declarations in order to lead [his people] by the nose'. Or, as one of Richelieu's 'skilled pens' wrote: 'Arms uphold the cause of princes, but well-tempered books publicize their equity and orient public affections to regard them as epiphanies of justice.'

The young boy king had been deeply affected by the experience of the Fronde when rioters had even burst into his palace bedchamber in 1651. When, therefore, Mazarin died in 1661 and the 22-year-old Louis XIV assumed personal charge of France, he resolved to transfer his court away from Paris and its mob to Versailles. The new palace was to symbolize the glory and grandeur of Louis XIV's reign over a France that was (at that time) incontestably the pre-eminent power in Europe. Devoting half of his working day to court life as a means of ensuring the continued loyalty and unity of the aristocracy through the dispensation of privileges and honours (with the chief nobles living in, where Louis could keep an eye on them), the king allowed ministers such as Colbert and Le Tellier to administer his absolute monarchy and create the finest army in Europe. To Louis, prestige was the essence of his power. His palace at Versailles was not designed simply to impress friend and foe alike; it was the tangible expression of his absolute power. As the historian of his propaganda, Joseph Klaits, has written:

> The man who wore the crown had to play the part of a demigod, and Louis XIV fulfilled the role brilliantly. As virtuoso performer in the elaborate piece of baroque stagecraft that was his reign, he wanted Europe to believe that he also had composed the script, built the set, designed the costumes, and directed the action. By identifying himself totally with his role of monarch, Louis gave dynamic life to absolutist ideology.

Portraits, invaluable in providing us with insights into the aspirations, ideals, pretensions, and self images of rulers, had been employed since antiquity as devices for the consolidation of power, and in this Louis XIV was no exception. The theme of the ruler as a great war leader is illustrated in the Hall of Mirrors at the palace of Versailles, which is decorated entirely with depictions of Louis' victories in the Dutch War (1672-8). Artists portrayed Louis as the Most Christian King, the Sun King whose initial was placed on buildings and textiles alike, and whose glory was celebrated in countless ceremonies. The historian John Stoye has added:

> The literate classes in France matched this by an increasing tendency to refer to the king in language not only of submission; their formulae of adulation were wrought into a fixed habit of mind. Conceivably, this might have been checked by real military set backs in the 1670s, but instead the triumph of 1678 [over the Dutch] was exploited to place the person of the monarch above criticism.

Literary works reinforced the visual eulogies, with Racine maintaining that 'every word in the language, every syllable, is precious to us because we consider them as the instruments which must serve the glory of our august protector'. Bossuet likewise believed that in Louis 'is the will of the whole people'. For their efforts, artists, scientists, and writers received about 100,000 livres per year from the government. In short, all aspects of French life were dedicated to the concept of Louis' absolute monarchy, and for a while it worked: during the first half of his reign, the cult of Louis XIV effectively disarmed all opposition.

War was to challenge the effectiveness of this propaganda. Louis regarded war in much the same way as his ornamental court, not merely as a luxury but as a means by which his glory could be displayed and extended. However, the disastrous effects of war upon his subjects, especially in the second half of his reign with the War of the League of Augsburg (1688-97) and the War of the Spanish Succession (1701-14), required a sustained campaign to boost sagging morale, civic as well as military. This was all the more essential in view of the growing number of propaganda attacks against the Sun King from both his domestic critics and his foreign opponents, attacks which centred upon the accusation that Louis was attempting to create a universal monarchy. The most influential exponent of this view was François de Lisola whose *Le Bouclier d'état et de justice* (1688) was sponsored by the Emperor Leopold I. Such claims were met by Louis' later foreign minister Colbert de Torcy who placed great emphasis on external propaganda directed at people who were not personally exposed to the Bourbon cult of kingship within France. Internally, Torcy was able to control the Parisian press reasonably well with the aid of the police, although, as Chancellor Ponchartrain lamented, 'printing of bad books goes on at Rouen with greater liberty than ever' and 'Paris is often flooded with these editions'. Abroad, however, Torcy attempted to encourage the suppression of offending works by diplomatic appeals to foreign governments, by controlling more effectively the French postal system, through which much printed propaganda was distributed, and by a positive campaign in Louis' favour.

One of the reasons why foreign publications became so popular in France was the shortage of news and alternative views in such official publications as the *Gazette*. Largely a vehicle for the personal glorification of the king rather than a news-sheet, readers began to look to French-language newspapers published abroad, especially Holland. The problem for Torcy was that such newspapers often contained anti-monarchical values and sentiments amidst their spicy news of foreign wars. And because he felt he could not use the *Gazette* more effectively, since it was a recognized official mouthpiece of the French government (and, as such, might jeopardize diplomatic negotiations if it embraced propaganda assaults on foreign governments), he had to look to other outlets. Torcy's problem was a classical propaganda dilemma: how to boost domestic morale by disseminating one set of anti-foreign sentiments while taking due account of the sensitivities of foreign governments to such domestic attacks that might hinder the path to better diplomatic relations. No nation in the age of communications is an island, sealed off from the outside world and its attitudes. During the final stages of the War of the Spanish Succession, when France was in great difficulties both militarily and economically, Torcy had to balance the need on the one hand to sustain loyalty and morale at home while avoiding offence amongst his Austrian, English and Dutch enemies.

He did this by the only course open to him: by adopting a policy of secret official connections with pro-French publications. The academic *Journal des savans,* founded in 1665, with its international learned readership, became a vehicle for clandestine royalist propaganda, while 'hired pens' also tackled the religious issues of war against the Protestant English and Dutch through the *Mémoires de Trévoux,* another secretly sponsored official journal.

La Clef du cabinet des Princes de l'Europe reached a wider audience by combining political and literary news and Torcy was able to insert pro-French articles into this publication, which also carried anti-French pieces (thus enhancing their credibility and their disguise). French pamphlet propaganda, which had gone into decline in the last quarter of the seventeenth century, was revived as a means of debating the validity of Hapsburg and Bourbon claims to the Spanish throne on the death of Charles II in 1700. The accession of Louis' grandson, Philip V, and the Sun King's recognition on the death of James II of his Catholic son as rightful heir to the English throne, had revived fears of a universal monarchy, and the outbreak of a new Europe-wide war had prompted a renewed burst of ideological propaganda in which the pamphlet played a significant role.

As one contemporary noted, 'when a pamphlet goes unanswered, people are persuaded that it is a sign that one agrees with what is contained therein'; or, as another claimed, 'silence is taken as evidence of the accused party's guilt and acquiescence'. The need for counter-propaganda was thus paramount. The charge of universal monarchy was answered by reasoned denials and by pointing to the political rather than the religious machinations of France's enemies: how else could Catholic Austria ally itself with Protestant England and Holland? Or was it because the morally corrupt Austrian regime had become the willing dupe of an Anglo-Dutch attempt to establish a Protestant Europe? Was it not France's duty to God and true Christendom to prevent this? That was why France had to uphold the claims of the Bourbons to the Spanish throne and of the Stuart Pretender to the English at the expense of the House of Orange. France was the last bastion of the Counter-Reformation, an unwilling and reluctant victim of Protestant-Lutheran-Calvinist-Huguenot conspiracy. All these points were made with the utmost objectivity, as befitted the emerging intellectual climate known as the Enlightenment. An increased awareness in the eighteenth century of the existence of a public that needed to be addressed in the interests of the State, whether at home or abroad, was not, however, matched by a corresponding ability on the part of French propagandists to forge any bond of unity between rulers and ruled. Torcy and his successors failed to learn the lessons of the Cromwellian experience in England and this failure was a major reason why absolutist monarchy in France was eventually to fall victim to the French revolutionaries of 1789.

Part Four

Propaganda in the Age of Revolutionary Warfare

Chapter 16

The Press as an Agent of Liberty

Like an ascending curve on a graph, the eighteenth century witnessed both an expansion in the role of public opinion in affairs of state and an increase in the degree to which the Press was accordingly utilized as a political instrument. Many governments were quick to recognize this and, drawing upon early modern precedents, established rigorous censorship systems to regulate the flow of ideas. In England, the emergence of parliamentary liberty and religious toleration following the 'Glorious Revolution' of 1688 provided a safety valve for ideological dissent. The Press became an essential part of the English political process. In France under the *ancien régime,* despite the flowering of the Enlightenment following the death of Louis XIV in 1715, no such comparable outlet for popular expression was tolerated – with cataclysmic consequences. Indeed, the liberating qualities which many ascribed to printing can perhaps first be seen in the emergence of British party politics and constitutional democracy. Small wonder that Horace Walpole was to call the press 'a third House of Parliament'.

A century earlier, following the foundation of more than a dozen news-books and weekly news-magazines, Oliver Cromwell's measures had attempted to create a State monopoly of news controlled by a government censor. With the restoration of the monarchy, the 1662 Printing Act placed the Press under strict parliamentary control. Following the revolutionary settlement of 1688, government showed itself less inclined to censor, but in 1695 the old Long Parliament's Licensing Act expired. This meant that the Press was now free from official censorship prior to publication; freedom of the press as we understand it today can therefore be said to have begun in 1695. It was a system which allowed for the publication of any news and views within the confines of national security and for criminal prosecution of offending items only *after* publication. A massive growth in the number of newspapers followed, both in London and the provinces. This is not to suggest that the English Parliament had suddenly embraced the notion of unfettered Press freedom. Indeed, in 1712 a new means of controlling the press was found with the introduction of the Stamp Act, which imposed a tax on all publications containing public news, intelligence, or notice of occurrences. The tax increased in direct proportion to the size of the publication, which now, by law, had to include the place and the name of the publisher. What had happened was that the old system of pre-censorship had been recognized as unworkable – a lesson that many European governments subsequently had to learn the hard way. The Stamp Act was a means by which government could control the Press by imposing financial burdens that limited the number of printing presses; at the same time new revenue was generated as a result of conceding the principle of Press freedom. Jonathan Swift commented shortly afterwards: 'The Observator is fallen, the Medleys are jumbled together with the Flying Post; the Examiner is deadly sick; the Spectator keeps up, and doubles its price.' Fears that the Press would die were compounded by the advent of European peace and the corresponding drop in war news with the 1713 Treaty of Utrecht, which ended the war of the Spanish Succession, and the 1721 Peace of Nystadt, ending the Great Northern War.

The effects of the Stamp Act were, however, short-lived. The demand for European news continued after the accession of the Hanoverian George I to the British throne in 1714, while at home parliamentary democracy and party politics continued unabated. Ways were found by some propagandist publications to avoid paying stamp duty and such journals, wrote one observer, 'being industriously calculated for the taste of the mob, contribute perhaps more than all other artifices to poison the minds of the common people against his Majesty, to vilify his ministers, and disturb the public peace, to the scandal of all good government'. New Stamp Act legislation was introduced in 1725 and again in 1757; the very fact that such legislation was required is indicative of the growth of the press in the eighteenth century. The Stamp Acts might have forced up the price of newspapers, but they did not reduce either their number or their circulation. Nor did they check the growth of newspapers as the principle medium of eighteenth century propaganda.

Perhaps the best known example is *The Craftsman,* the principal organ of the opposition to Robert Walpole, the popularity of which in the 1720s and 1730s was unrivalled. One contemporary said that this paper distributed '12-13,000 copies every week for undeceiving the good people of Great Britain'. Less well known, but almost as popular, was the *Weekly Journal* founded by Nathaniel Mist in 1716 and described by one contemporary as 'a scandal shop ready to receive and vend sedition in, and will never be laid down while there is an enemy to the British constitution capable of writing scandal in English'. Denied the weapon of pre-censorship, the government resorted to prosecutions under the libel laws and even bully-boy tactics of sending in the King's Messengers to smash printing presses. And of course it established its own newspapers, such as that founded by Robert Harley in 1704, the *Review.*

Harley has recently been described as a pioneer of British government propaganda and counter-propaganda and he used both Swift and Daniel Defoe as writers on his paper, which attempted to serve as the voice of moderation in a period of extreme viewpoints. Indeed Defoe, the greatest English journalist of the age, was used secretly by the Whig government to write for the opposition (including Mist's *Weekly Journal*) so that criticism would be moderated and toned down. When Defoe's real position was exposed, destroying his reputation, the government attempted other tactics, such as buying opposition newspapers (the *London Journal* being one example) and transforming them into effective official organs. Robert Walpole in the 1730s and 1740s also took particular care to manipulate public opinion through the press; during the last decade of his administration, the secret service paid £50,000 to pamphleteers and Treasury-run newspapers. Walpole circulated free newspapers and pamphlets such as the *London Gazette* to influential sections of the community, distributed through the Post Office, which in turn attempted to block the distribution of opposition propaganda. The *London Gazette* was in the privileged position of enjoying a monopoly on the reporting of official news, such as royal proclamations and the resolutions of the privy council, and it was run directly by the government. Yet it was not a popular success and went into decline after the fall of Walpole in 1742.

Nothing encourages newspaper circulation more than war, and in England sales increased dramatically during the Seven Years War (1756-63). Although expensive (prices were not helped by increases in the Stamp Tax), newspapers were widely shared and read aloud in public places such as coffee houses, barber shops, and pubs. As early as 1711, it was calculated that one newspaper was seen or heard by a minimum of twenty readers. Edmund Burke (1729-97), the editor of the *Annual Register,* wrote that 'newspapers are a more important instrument than is generally imagined; they are part of the reading of all; they are the whole of the reading of the far greater number'. Even so, newspapers in England printed virtually anything they wanted, with the result that Lord Camden could comment with some authority that 'the newspapers are so poisoned with falsehood, that I find it utterly impossible to distinguish the truth'. As Professor Levy has written, 'the press, once the object of censorship, placed the government under its censureship... [the government] manipulated the press, subsidized it, and prosecuted it, but could not control it.' The degree to which politicians such as John Wilkes (1727-97) used his newspaper, the *North Briton,* for his own political purposes says more about his criticisms of the period than it does about the period itself. Eighteenth-century historians must therefore approach such newspaper sources with extreme care, despite Macaulay's claim that 'the true history of a nation is to be found in its newspapers'. In England, the press provided an outlet for dissent and criticism of constitutional government, a liberating force without recourse to violent change.

Chapter 17

The American Revolution

From the beginning, the American colonists who debated the 'unwise, unjust and ruinous policy' of their British imperial overlords were only too conscious of the importance of public opinion and propaganda in supporting their cause. Following their victory over the French in the Seven Years War, the British had tried to protect the Indians by controlling colonial expansion west of the Appalachians and by passing the Quebec Act in 1774, which was intended to serve as a Magna Carta for French Canadians. Both actions greatly alarmed the American colonists, who were worried that they would prevent profitable westward expansion. The cost of garrisoning troops to implement these measures, and to protect the Americans themselves from Indian and French attacks, was to be met from the Stamp Act of 1763. American resentment was immediate, especially as they were being forced to meet the costs of measures passed on their behalf but in which they had no say: 'no taxation without representation' began the slogan war that was backed up by a boycott of British goods. After the repeal of the Stamp Act in 1766, the British government attempted to raise money by trade levies but colonial resistance became increasingly militant. By 1773, the year of the Boston Tea Party, the British government was less prepared to back down, although, once again, its insensitivity to the North American situation proved its undoing. The Quebec Act, combined with the Intolerable and Quartering Acts of 1774 which attempted to regain control of Massachusetts, exacerbated tension by turning economic grievances into political issues; as King George III commented: 'The die is cast'.

Boston proved to be the Revolution's propaganda nerve-centre. It was the scene of the Boston Massacre in 1770, when British troops fired on rioters, killing four of them. This event was blown up out of all proportion to its significance by colonial propagandists who wished to illustrate British tyranny and oppression. Paul Revere's romanticized cartoons of the massacre were widely circulated. Samuel Adams, 'master of the puppets', manipulated and inflamed anti-British opinion through the *Boston Gazette*. The presentation of the Boston Tea Party, again an event of more symbolic than actual significance, was a triumph for Adams. Boston became a city of martyrs when British troops occupied it in 1773. Great believers in propaganda by committee, American politicians turned to Adams' Boston Committee of Correspondence as its chief agency of persuasion. It directed its attention to influencing both Canadian and British public opinion. To the former, for example, American printed propaganda appealed for a combined effort to resist tyrannical oppression, despite linguistic and religious differences with the French Canadians. The British colonial secretary received complaints by the early 1770s that unrest in Canada was growing with 'the minds of the people poisoned by the same hypocrisy and lies practised with so much success in the other provinces, and which their emissaries and friends here have spread abroad with great art and diligence'. But the American colonists who organized the First Continental Congress in 1774 (Sam Adams, John Hancock, and George Washington among them) and issued their Declaration of Rights and Grievances were not yet revolutionaries; they merely demanded their rights as Englishmen. Their propaganda campaign, however, fostered calls for independence. Minutemen were appointed to deliver short, sharp lectures explaining Congress' demands, newspapers debated the issues, and 'sedition flowed openly from the pulpits'. Following the attempt by British redcoats to arrest Sam Adams and John Hancock, the first shots were fired at Lexington and Concord in 1775. British troops found that they were also the target of propaganda broadsides, including *To the regular Soldiery of Great-Britain now on Service in the British American Colonies,* which incited them to desert King George III's tyrannical cause. The second Continental Congress in Philadelphia appointed Washington as commander of the American forces, and after huge British losses at Bunker Hill encouraged American confidence, plans were made for an American invasion of Canada, complete with propaganda appeals. Demands for the redress of grievances turned into calls for independence from an occupying power that was proving itself incapable of governing and for the 'natural rights' of men described by Tom Paine in his best selling tract *Common Sense.*

All these events were accompanied by a barrage of propaganda, with the American colonists recognizing the importance of securing public support for their cause from the outset. Shortly after the flight of British troops from Lexington and Concord, for example, four engravings by Amos Doolittle appeared depicting the scene in a fairly objective manner but were used to illustrate more subjective accounts in newspapers of how simple farmers had forced 1800 British regular troops to flight. One poem went:

> How brave you went out with muskets all bright,
> And thought to befrighten the folks with the sight;
> But when you got there how they powder'd your pums,
> And all the way home how they pepper'd your bums,
> And is it not, honies, a comical farce,
> To be proud in the face, and be shot in the a—se.

On a policy level, George Washington wrote his address *To the Inhabitants of Canada,* distributed by Benedict Arnold's army during the ill-fated expedition to Quebec in 1775-6. The American forces that besieged Quebec attempted to encourage its surrender by firing further appeals to the inhabitants tied to Indian arrows. When that tactic failed and the Americans proved unable to take the city militarily, propaganda was used to try and counter the effects of defeat. Congress' appeal was the epitome of reason:

> The best of causes are subject to vicissitudes; and disappointments have ever been inevitable. Such is the lot of human nature. But generous souls, enlightened and warmed with the sacred fire of liberty, become more resolute as difficulties increase; and surmount, with irresistible ardour, every obstacle that stands between them and the favourite object of their wishes. We will never abandon you to the unrelenting fury of your and our enemies.

Despite the establishment of French printing presses in Canada and the recruitment of Catholic priests to explain their cause, the Americans were forced to abandon their Canadian invasion and concentrate their efforts on domestic and British opinion. Yet it would appear that American propaganda played some role in neutralizing Canadian opinion in the War of Independence. General Burgoyne, for example, attributed the difficulties he experienced in recruiting Canadians to his regiment partly 'to the poison which the emissaries of the rebels have thrown into their mind'.

With the die cast, American revolutionary propaganda blossomed, from Liberty Songs to ballads, from paintings and poetry to printed caricatures, from plays to pamphlets. 'Yankee Doodle', originally a British army tune to deride the disorganized enemy, was adopted by the colonial troops as a means of taunting the redcoats in retreat and defeat, and it became an American rallying song. As one British soldier commented: 'After our rapid successes, we held the Yankees in great contempt; but it was not a little mortifying to hear them play this tune.' Plays such as *The Battle of Bunker's Hill* and *The Fall of British Tyranny, Or, American Liberty Triumphant: The First Campaign* were written to spread the merits of the American cause through the medium of entertainment. Poets also placed their services behind the cause; as one wrote, 'this is not the proper time for poetry unless it be such as Tyrtaeus wrote' – by which he meant the kind of rousing verse used to inspire the Spartans to victory. Another poet, John Trumbull who was later arrested, asserted:

> The same ardour of ambition, the same greatness of thought, which inspires the Warrior to brave danger in the conquering field, when diffused among a people will call forth Genius in every station to life, fire the imagination of the Artist, and raise to sublimity the aspiring Muse.

American propagandists were undoubtedly among the most eloquent in history, as the extract from Washington's leaflet has already illustrated. In the Age of Reason, their appeal on behalf of the Rights of Man struck a chord in the minds of all freedom-loving people and retains its resonance even today. The Declaration of Independence, proclaimed on 4 July 1776, is a classic illustration of the fusion of ideology and propagandistic appeal and, although well-known, is worthy of reiteration:

> We hold these truths to be self-evident, that all men are created equal; that they are endowed by their creator with certain unalienable rights; that among these are life, liberty and the pursuit of happiness. That to secure these rights, governments are instituted among men, deriving their just powers from the consent of the governed; that, whenever any form of government becomes destructive of these ends, it is the right of the people to alter or to abolish it, and to institute new government, laying

its foundation on such principles, organizing its powers in such form, as to them shall seem most likely to effect their safety and happiness.

Although also a list of grievances, the declaration is best remembered for this, the second, paragraph and the propagandistic effect of such sentiments could only be enhanced by its widespread circulation.

Despite the efforts of the British, in the words of one historian, to erect a 'voice-proof wall on the frontier', the power of such words was unstoppable at least amongst the North American colonists. As for the indigenous Indian population, they must have had a somewhat hollow ring and British propagandists were certainly able to play upon such facts as the Quebec Act, the colonists' encroachments upon Indian territories, and the long-established power of monarchical images and militaristic display. Both sides competed for the hearts and minds of the Indians, with the Americans appealing for their neutrality; but it was their portrayal by the British as 'scalp-hunting savages' that provided American propagandists with yet another outlet for their eloquence – with disastrous long-term consequences for certain tribes. By attempting to terrorize the colonists with Indian troops, the British merely provoked stiffer colonial resistance and a desire for revenge, as in the celebrated case of Miss Jane M'Crea. What began as an isolated, and not uncommon, murder and scalping by an Indian scouting party, which could not be punished by the British for fear of mass Indian desertion, became a highly successful atrocity story of American purity defiled and a focus of colonial resistance (even though Jane M'Crea was a Tory sympathizer and the girlfriend of a loyalist soldier).

The defeat of Burgoyne's army at Saratoga in 1777 provided a major boost to American morale, which had been demoralized by the loss of New York to the British. American hopes had already been raised by Washington's daring crossing of the Delaware to attack Britain's German forces at Trenton on Christmas night 1776 (immortalized by Leutze's famous painting of seventy years later) and by his driving out of the British at Princeton. But the surrender of 'Gentleman Johnny Burgoyne' (or 'Sir Jack Bragg', as he was known to the American troops) in October 1777 proved to be a real turning point. The French, eager to recover their prestige after the Seven Years War, were brought into the war, and with them their Spanish allies, eager to regain Gibraltar. Congress issued the

Articles of Confederation and by 1780 the newly formed United States of America were at war with Britain, alongside France, Spain, the Dutch, and the League of Armed Neutrality (eventually consisting of Russia, Denmark, Sweden, Portugal, Prussia, and Austria, all of whom wanted to protect their rights to trade with the colonists). With Britain now preoccupied with a front that stretched from America to India, the War of Independence was all but won. With the aid of French seapower, money, and men, the Americans fought the British to a standstill, besieged General Cornwallis' forces at Yorktown, and captured 7000 men in October 1781 as a military band played 'The world turned upside-down'. Independence was granted in 1783.

Propaganda played a major role in the American revolution. Of long term significance were the writings of John Locke (1632-1704), especially his *Treatises on Government,* published in 1690, which refuted the divine right of kings and absolutist government. Of more immediate significance were the works of Richard Price, whose *On Civil Liberty* (1776) sold nearly 200,000 copies, and, of course, Tom Paine *(Common Sense* and *Rights of Man),* who also edited the *Pennsylvania Journal.* Washington even had Paine's writings read out to his troops, recognizing in his words the power and emotion of inspirational propaganda. In the *American Crisis* for example, Paine wrote:

> These are the times that try men's souls. The summer soldier and the sunshine patriot will, in this crisis, shrink from the service of his country ... Tyranny, like hell, is not easily conquered; yet we have this consolation with us, that the harder the conflict the more glorious the triumph.

Such readings were, wrote one observer, 'as wine to the weary patriots'. The victory at Trenton occurred a week later and the image of British military invincibility lay in ruins.

Propagandists also exploited the British employment of German troops – the Hessians – to indicate that reconciliation with the imperial mother-country was impossible. The British, they maintained, had enlisted the help of 'certain foreign princes who are in the habit of selling the blood of their people for money' and appeals were made to the mercenaries to accept 'lands, liberty, safety and a communication of good laws and mild government, in a country where many of their friends and relations are already happily settled'. Incitements to desert in return for land and the freedoms embodied in the Declaration of Independence were translated into German and distributed through agents. Once they had been shown the error of their ways, German deserters and prisoners were sent back into the British ranks to spread the word still wider. As Professor Berger has concluded, 'the American psychological warfare campaign against the mercenaries was the most successful one of the Revolution'.

Against the well trained regular British soldiers, American propagandists were less successful. Although stories of legendary frontier riflemen were circulated in an attempt to frighten the British, the American marksmen actually lacked discipline in battle and tended to flee before advancing columns of redcoats and their bayonets. The Continental Army only began to use the bayonet in 1778, but propaganda broadsides had long been a feature of its activities. Atrocity stories were used to rally local support while Congress published its case in such leaflets as *To the Inhabitants of the United States* (1777), which warned of 'the secret arts and machinations of emissaries' who 'dismayed' the timid and 'misinformed and misled' the unsuspecting. The British responded by using similar tactics and by promising land in return for desertion; General Howe described how he attempted 'to quiet the minds of the people at large...[and] disunite their army'. While Washington's forces endured the harsh winter of 1777-8 at Valley Forge (losing 2500 men in the process), Howe's propagandists moved in with their promises and persuasions while morale was at its lowest. Washington grew alarmed at the rising number of desertions: 'Our enemies, finding themselves unable to reduce us by the force of their arms, are now practising every insidious art to gain time and disunite us.' One such effort was the leaflet *To the Soldiers in the Continental Army* (1780), which Washington believed had a 'considerable effect' upon the soldiers. The desertion of Benedict Arnold to the British side was likewise given widespread coverage in an attempt to demonstrate that the Americans were fighting a lost cause. Arnold himself wrote appeals for the British, although their impact can only have been limited given the way in which his defection was presented by the Americans as the ultimate act of treachery. Effigies of this 'vile, treacherous, and leagued with Satan' figure were burned throughout the colonies. Equally, the publicity afforded to Britain's first real martyr of the war, Major John André, executed as a spy by the Americans, helped stiffen British resolve.

General Clinton reported that the André affair created 'such a rage for revenge' amongst his troops that he was finding it difficult to restrain them. However, successive British defeats, combined with news of Britain's growing international predicament, meant that the Americans invariably retained the propaganda initiative.

The wide-ranging propaganda campaign launched by Congress extended not only to Canada, but also to England and France. In charge of wooing the French was Benjamin Franklin who, together with Silas Deane and Arthur Lee, proved highly effective in winning sympathizers in Paris. Exploiting anti-British feeling left over from the Seven Years War (and indeed dating back centuries), Franklin's popularity in France manifested itself in the reproduction of his image in portraits and prints, in statues and on snuffboxes. In fact, to the French, Franklin *was* the American Revolution, and the ageing philosopher-scientist appeared as an American Voltaire, although the anti-monarchical elements of revolutionary ideology had to be watered down for fear of offending Louis XVI. Yet as Franklin realized:

> Now, by the press, we can speak to nations; and good books and well written pamphlets have great and general influence. The facility with which the same truths may be repeatedly enforced by placing them daily in different lights in newspapers, which are everywhere read, gives a great chance of establishing them. And we now find that it is not only right to strike while the iron is hot but that it may be very practicable to heat it by continually striking.

As in so many other areas, these words reveal just how great a pioneer of propaganda Franklin was. He recognized that it was much better to speak to foreigners through foreigners, that peoples resented being told what to think by outsiders; and so Franklin worked through the French Press and through the official publication *Affaires de l'Angleterre et de l'Amérique,* which reprinted many of his own essays and American newspaper articles supplied by him.

Franklin may also lay claim to being one of the first modern practitioners of black propaganda – that is, propaganda which appears to come from one source but in fact comes from somewhere else. When *The Sale of the Hessians,* a document purportedly written by a German prince to the German commander of the Hessian troops in America, appeared in France in 1777 it caused a sensation. In this letter, the ruthlessness of German princes (both names were in fact fakes) in their dealings with the British government was exposed (it stated, for instance, that surgeons had been advised to let the injured die). The letter had in fact been written by Franklin. Franklin was also one of the first American propagandists to exploit the Irish issue as a means of attacking Britain with his address *To the Good People of Ireland*, published in 1778. His European-wide campaign, reinforced by Charles Dumas working from Holland, received a further boost in 1780 when John Adams joined the team. Adams wrote to Franklin from Amsterdam:

> It is necessary for America to have agents in different parts of Europe, to give some information concerning our affairs, and to refute the abominable lies that the hired emissaries of Great Britain circulate in every corner of Europe, by which they keep up their own credit and ruin ours.

Adams' personal knowledge of recent events in America proved a great asset in refuting much of the disinformation circulating about the American revolution, and his work in Holland did much to secure public sympathy – and Dutch recognition – for the United States of America. Franklin can equally lay claim to a similar achievement in France, but his activities also extended into Britain itself.

Franklin cultivated his pro-American contacts in England, organized in such societies as 'The Society of 13' and 'The Deistic Society of 1774', and distinguished figures such as Josiah Wedgwood and Joseph Priestley corresponded with him. Franklin's supporters had the enormous advantage of a press that was dominated by opponents of George III and the ministry of Lord North (1770-82). The king took little notice of public opinion, which left the field open to opposition ministers such as Charles James Fox whose press manager, Dennis O'Brien, operated through the *General Advertiser*. The government tried to respond through the official *London Gazette* and by employing the by now time-honoured system of paying printers and authors for the publication of anti-American tracts and royalist propaganda. Most notable among its employees was the professional propagandist Dr Jon Shebbeare and the playwright Hugh Kelly. The *General Evening Post*, *Lloyd's Evening Post*, and latterly the Revd Henry Bates's *Morning Post* were the only newspapers to support the Tory cause. Yet, out of the

25,000 or so newspapers that were calculated to have been circulated in London every day, the circulation of supportive papers was small by comparison – although of these the *Morning Post* was by far the most popular paper of its day. Even so, the *General Advertiser* accused the government of subsidising views which 'deceived, duped, and seduced [Englishmen] into an opinion that this unhappy, wicked, and self-destroying war against America was the right measure'. The Americans, many argued, were merely fighting for those same Whig principles for which Englishmen had fought in 1688.

After the British defeat at Saratoga, the war became even more unpopular in Britain, especially as it began to drag the country into a European-wide conflict. Few could understand why disenchanted Englishmen could team up with Britain's traditional – and Catholic – arch enemy. Blame in the press was fixed squarely upon North's government, which found it impossible to ignore the calls for negotiation and conciliation with the Americans whilst being faced with the real menace closer to home in the form of France, Spain, and Holland. The Gordon Riots in London in 1780 revealed genuine domestic discontent. It was in this atmosphere that Franklin's activities in Paris began to bear fruit. The opposition press was far better informed of events in America than government-sponsored publications and this was due, in no small part, to the information it received from men such as Franklin. With the defeat at Yorktown and the fall of the North government, the way was open to the conclusion of a war which the vast majority of newspapers had maintained all along could never be won.

John Adams maintained that the American Revolution was essentially a struggle for the hearts and minds of the people even before the war began. Perhaps so, but the war itself was a severe test of loyalty. Without an effective propaganda campaign to explain away setbacks and defeats and glorify (sometimes out of all proportion) victories, the idea that independence was an achievable goal might have remained confined to the members of Congress. Without the aid of the press, the publicity-conscious architects of the United States of America might never have achieved their goals. While Adams and Jefferson worked on American opinion and Franklin worked on French, Washington worked on the morale of his troops. Washington became a true American icon, a commander to rank amongst the greatest. Professor Bowman has written that 'a message from him could stir an entire corps to enthusiasm. His appearance in camp would produce general jubilation.'

The 1760s and 1770s had also pointed the way to new developments in warfare. Frederick II (the Great, r.1740-86) of Prussia had initiated far-reaching military reforms that enabled a relatively small power to assume wider significance. Frederick's armies were light and fast; mobility and discipline were the key to their success. Rigorous training and drilling in marching and re-loading ensured that his armies arrived at the battlefield in good order and maintained their line and discipline throughout. With parade-ground precision, Frederick's armies felt safe in the knowledge that their king had devoted himself to every detail, including morale. In his *Military Instructions Written by the King of Prussia for the Generals of his Army* (1763), Frederick wrote:

> It is our interest to carry on our wars with great spirit and alacrity, to prevent their continuing too long; because a tedious war must relax our excellent discipline, depopulate our country, and exhaust our finances: therefore it is the duty of every Prussian general to endeavour to the utmost of his abilities to bring matters to a speedy issue.

Leading by example, Frederick's boldness to commit his troops brought spectacular successes, such as his defeat of the Austrians at Rossbach in 1757 when the Prussian forces were outnumbered 2-1. Addressing his troops before the battle, the king said:

> You all know that you have suffered no fatigue, no hunger, no cold, no watching, no danger that I have not shared with you, and you now see me ready to sacrifice my life with you and for you. All I desire of you is the return of that affection and fidelity, which you may be assured of on my side. I will now only add, not as an encouragement to you, but as proof of my gratitude for your past services, that from this hour, to the day you get into your winter quarters, your pay shall be doubled. Now! fight like brave men, and trust for success in God.

Before long, Frederick's innovations and reforms were being adopted in other countries, though Prussian discipline was not so easily recreated elsewhere. Clockwork efficiency was not always the most human way of ensuring discipline and, in the Age of the Enlightenment, in which Man's relationship with the Nation was being re-examined in favour of the former, the views of even enlightened despots such as Frederick the Great were considered flawed. The American Revolution had demonstrated that men were also motivated by ideology, patriotism, and nationalism. In France, Jacques de Guibert's *Essai Général de Tactique* (1772) had already foreshadowed popular involvement in national wars. No longer would wars be fought between professional armies but between entire peoples, and such conflicts would change the face of the earth. The idea of a nation-in-arms was to reach its full potential during the era of the French Revolution.

Chapter 18

The French Revolution and the Napoleonic Wars

We have already seen from the case of Louis XIV that official censorship, by itself, is insufficient to prevent the flow of subversive ideas, especially from outside. In the Age of the Enlightenment, the very existence of a rigorous censorship system in France was used as a further focus of criticism of the *ancien régime*. In England, the press may have been comparatively free to criticize, and thus became a nuisance and an irritant to government; but it did provide an outlet for dissenting views, the frustration of which might other-wise have provoked more extreme action. It used to be thought that the absence of such 'democratization' in France contributed to the outbreak of the French Revolution in 1789, but recent research has shown that, despite censorship, the eighteenth-century French press was more active in communicating political ideas than had been previously realized. Challenges to royal authority were much in evidence in books, periodicals, and journals of the period. Official censorship prevented distribution and circulation on the scale seen in England, but underground or tolerated publications certainly did cater for an élite literary audience drawn from the educated bour-geoisie and aristocracy. And, as the Jansenists demonstrated after 1750, critics of royal authority were able to disseminate notions of constitutionalism and the need for representative institutions to a wider public. The government responded in the only way it knew: by repression and by clinging to an increasingly hollow propa-ganda line of insisting that absolute monarchy knew what was best for its citizens and that there should be no further debate.

A royal declaration of 1764 outlawed 'memoirs and projects formed by persons without standing, who take the liberty of making public instead of submitting them to those persons destined by their position to judge them'. In the same year, however, Voltaire played down the impact of books in the famous *Philosophical Dictionary* – a sort of handbook of the Enlightenment. In an entry entitled 'Freedom of the Press', he defended the need for censorship by the State, derided the press freedom of Britain and Holland that had plunged them into 'horrible decadence', and insisted that most books were boring and had little impact:

> Oh, you say to me, the books of Luther and Calvin destroyed the Roman religion and part of Europe...No, Rome was not conquered by books. It was because it drove Europe to revolt by its plundering, by the public sale of indulgences, by degrading men, by wishing to govern them like domestic animals, by abusing its power so excessively that it is astonishing that it preserved a single village.

Although there was a lesson here for Louis XVI, Voltaire's essay was curiously contradictory. In the same piece he admitted that Britain and Holland controlled 'the trade of the whole world' and pointed to the danger of Spinoza's writings. With such advice, it is small wonder that Louis XVI's government failed to put its own house in order. Attempts at reform, especially of financial issues, failed miserably. In short, the failure of the Old Regime's censorship and propaganda system was matched only by the failure of its government.

As Madame d'Epinay prophesied in 1771, 'The knowledge the people acquire must, a little sooner, a little later, produce revolutions'. The growth in anti-monarchy propaganda that introduced the 'theology of administration' to the people received a further boost during the American Revolution when government propagandists allowed their traditional hatred of the English to blind them to the dangers of promoting the American republican cause. In other words, the *ancien régime* contributed unwittingly to the arguments of its opponents, and thus to its own demise. As Montesquieu wrote in his *L'Esprit des Lois* (1748), with the example of England in mind:

> In a free nation it is very often a matter of indifference whether individuals reason well or badly; it is enough that they reason: from this ensues liberty, which guarantees the effects of this reasoning. Similarly, in a despotic government, it is equally pernicious to reason well or badly; that one reasons is enough for the principle of government to be shaken.

This was an accurate diagnosis. Democratic governments must tolerate a free press, regardless of criticism. It is a measure of their democracy. Despotic governments must not; press freedom is a sign of weakness. You must either have a total media control, enforced by terror, or as little as possible within the confines of national security. The only way a despotic government can allow criticism and debate is if it is accompanied by reform. *Perestroika* is the handmaiden of *Glasnost*. The failure of the *ancien régime* in France was its failure to realize this – or at least to act decisively.

Although certain concessions had been made to the various discontented parties in France in the 1780s, such as increased parliamentary representation, power still remained ultimately in the hands of the government, now increasingly troubled by financial scandals. When, therefore, the Estates-General was summoned for the first time since 1614 and convened in May 1789 with the representation of the Third Estate (commoners) doubled to equal the combined strength of the First (aristocrats) and Second (clergy) Estates, reform quickly turned into revolution. The economic debate exploded into a torrent of ideological political propaganda. In that month over a hundred pamphlets appeared, the most famous of which was Siéyès' *What is the Third Estate?*, and the figure rose to 300 in June. By the end of the year over sixty new newspapers had appeared to cater for a public that needed 'educating' on the various issues in these exciting and fast-moving times. As an English traveller in France at the time observed:

> The business going forward at present in the pamphlet shops in Paris is incredible ... The spirit of reading political tracts, they say, spreads into the provinces so that all the presses of France are equally employed. Nineteen twentieths of these productions are in favour of liberty, and commonly violent against the clergy and nobility ... Is it not wonderful, that while the press teems with the most levelling or even seditious principles, that if put into execution would over-turn the monarchy, nothing in reply appears, and not the least step is taken by the court to restrain this extreme licentiousness of publication?

The traveller went on to describe, with even more astonishment, the coffeehouses of Paris: 'they are not only crowded within, but other expectant crowds are at the doors and windows, listening ... to certain orators, who from chairs or tables, harangue each his little audience.'

The French revolutionaries were not just crude mob orators. They were great believers in the use of symbols as a means of transmitting complicated ideas in a simple form; one symbol was capable of arousing passions and loyalties that needed no explanation, just obedience. The red, white, and blue tricolour came to represent the various revolutionary factions and was also worn as a sash, while other garments and symbols came to represent the calls for 'Liberty, Equality, and Fraternity'. Right from the start, the revolutionaries recognized the importance of symbols as propaganda: the Phrygian cup was worn as a symbol of equality, the Fasces emerged as a symbol of fraternity, and the female figure of Marianne as a symbol of liberty. A female figure was chosen partly to reflect the growing role of women in politics and partly to represent an idea to be nurtured and protected, the mother of a new kind of political child. The Bastille became a symbol of monarchical oppression, while its storming in 1789 became a symbolic gesture of defiance – even though it was largely empty of prisoners. Professor Rudé has examined the way in which crowds were manipulated by the revolutionaries with orchestrated demonstrations, fireworks, burning of effigies, and mob orators chanting 'Long Live the Third Estate!'

As revolutionary change gathered momentum the crowds got out of hand. One orator tried to reinject an element of reason:

> Frenchmen, you destroy tyrants; your hate is frightening; it is shocking...like you, I am seized to the quick by such events; but think how ignominious it is to live and be a slave; think with what torments one should punish crimes against humanity; think finally of what good, what satisfaction, what happiness awaits you, you and your children and your descendants, when august and blessed liberty will have set its temple amongst you! Yet do not forget that these proscriptions outrage humanity and make nature tremble.

It proved difficult for the revolutionaries to regain control of the crowd, drunk with its own success as an instrument of change. However, gradually, after the Declaration of the Rights of Man was proclaimed in October 1789, after the three Estates merged into one under the Constituent Assembly, as aristocrats and clergy fled with the establishment of the Constitution in 1791 and, finally, after Louis XVI was arrested, the revolutionaries were able to restore a measure of law and order, although they remained vulnerable to the whims of the mob.

Of the numerous new newspapers founded during this period, two in particular deserve mention by virtue of their founders. The first was the *Friend of the People,* founded by the mob orator and journalist Marat. Here was a propagandist who clearly recognized the necessity of translating the ideas of the Enlightenment and of the revolution into language the masses could understand. The other newspaper was *The Defence of the Constitution,* founded by Robespierre. Both men developed clubs to instil and debate the ideas of freedom and liberty and to create an alternative to religion, complete with rituals, hymns, and symbolism. The problem, however, was that several revolutionary factions were now competing for control and their various publications reflected their differing views of what direction events should now take. A new constitution was clearly necessary. Meanwhile, the Girondins were able to assume power by virtue of adopting the patriotic stance and attempted to unite the country behind them under the banner of war. By 1793, this approach had failed and the Jacobins – with their clearer view of domestic solutions and their greater ideological coherence – assumed control under Robespierre. His brief reign, helped by the murder of Marat and by the organization of the Terror to purge his opponents, was to end in the same way for him as for so many of his hated aristocrats: at the guillotine.

With the establishment of a republic to replace the monarchy in 1792, the revolutionaries found that they now had to assume the propaganda techniques of the ruler rather than those of the discontented ruled. The very existence of a Committee of Public Instruction bears witness to the central role the French revolutionaries ascribed to propaganda. Their task was greatly aided by the declaration of war on France by European powers alarmed at the republican regime and further shocked by the execution of the king in 1793. Nothing unites a nation so much as a foreign war, and the War of the First Coalition against France helped to consolidate popular support for the new revolutionary National Assembly. Equally, however, nothing united Europe so much as common opposition to the French Revolution, especially when it called for 'a new crusade, a crusade for universal freedom'. But first, the consolidation of the revolution at home required the skilled attention of the propagandists. When debating the symbols of the new regime, the French looked to the American Revolution for inspiration. Marianne as the symbol of Liberty was chosen 'so that our emblem, circulating all over the globe, should present to all peoples the beloved image of Republican liberty and pride'. A new calendar was introduced to underline a new beginning, with 1792 becoming Year One. Lafayette, the French hero of the American Revolution, now became the hero of French liberty as the old monarchial propaganda was replaced by new republican imagery. Statues of liberty, busts of heroes old and new, and festivals of freedom and other ceremonies all helped to consolidate the republican idea in a society familiar only with monarchical government.

What of the effect of all this upon the French army? In effect, what was happening in French society as a whole was reflected in the French armed forces. In 1789, the French army could have suppressed the revolution; instead the vast majority of the soldiers joined it, thus forging a formidable alliance with the people. One appeal of July 1789 went: 'Brave soldiers, mingle with your brothers, receive their embraces. You are no longer satellites of the despot, the jailers of your brothers. You are our friends, our fellow citizens, and soldiers of the Patrie.' As a result, one foreign observer noted in 1793:

> A force appeared that beggared all imagination. Suddenly war again became the business of the people – a people of thirty millions, all of whom considered themselves to be citizens...The people became a participant in war; instead of governments and armies as heretofore, the full weight of the nation was thrown into the balance. The resources and efforts now available for use surpassed all conventional limits: nothing now impeded the vigour with which war could be waged.

Inspired by revolutionary fervour – and of course propaganda – the French rapidly became a nation-in-arms, a military force of unprecedented size and intensity. Heartened by the victory over the invading Austro-Prussian army at Valmy in 1792, the revolutionary regime reorganized its troops during the Reign of Terror (1793-5) in which anti-republican elements (and political opponents of Robespierre such as Danton) were brutally removed. Every Frenchman capable of carrying arms was levied to defend the principles of the revolution, every woman and child was likewise instructed to work in hospitals, or to make uniforms and bandages, while 'the old men shall go out into the public squares to boost the soldiers' courage and to preach the unity of the Republic and the hatred of kings and the unity of the Republic'. But it did not end there. The revolution adopted a crusading zeal; forced to defend Liberty against the forces of foreign absolutism, the revolution now assumed the offensive in the name of 'Universal Republicanism'.

The victory at Valmy was in many respects a lucky one. The revolution, with its egalitarian ideals, had greatly weakened the French army by eroding discipline and structured command (60 per cent of officers joined the aristocratic emigration). But the entry of Britain into the war in 1793 turned the conflict into a pan-European struggle in which revolutionary fervour was not, by itself, sufficient to motivate the ordinary men and women who were now involved in continuing the struggle. Discipline and training were increased, tactics developed, and strategy improved. Even so, the French revolutionary armies were very different from previous armies in their psychological motivation. For the first time, the interests of the individual were recognized to be bound up with those of the nation. These citizen-armies fought, not for money or because they were forced to: they fought for a cause, a common cause in which their individual interests were recognized to be the same as those of their country: 'every citizen ought to be a soldier, and every soldier a citizen'. Payment was a reward, not an incentive; discipline was self-imposed, not enforced; obedience a duty rather than a sign of submission. The identification of the army as an instrument of the people, rather than as something separate from the society as a whole, was a major departure – or rather, a return to classical antiquity. The difference now was scale, as wave after wave of new levies joined the new Grand Army.

With this forged unity between a nation and its army, military propaganda fused with civic propaganda. Municipal celebrations or *fêtes,* marriages, and even baptisms always included soldiers, because everyone was a soldier of the revolution. *Fêtes* were an essential means of raising troops and celebrating their departure as a means of enhancing collective identification with the revolutionary-patriotic cause. However, given the uncertainty of many army units in the immediate aftermath of 1789, specific campaigns were launched. One such campaign involved the publicizing of the new Constitution in 1793 and the swearing of a new oath of allegiance. The commanding general in Cambrai described the event as follows:

> It is necessary to be a republican to fully grasp the effect which was produced by the entrance of the cortège into the centre of the troops drawn up in the square. One could see that during the reading these

brave soldiers could hardly contain themselves from interrupting the reading to applaud. How touching it was to see these warriors hold themselves back out of respect, desiring the moment when they would be able to burst with their satisfaction. And how happier still it was to be a witness to the shouts and cries of 'Vive la République', one and indivisible, 'Vive la Constitution' which rang out at the end of this proclamation. On the spot I began to sing the 'Marseillaise'; I can think of nothing to compare with the rapidity with which the song could be heard on all sides, with an electrifying effect. All the songs, all the patriotic airs, then followed; and it was only after two hours of the republican joy that the troops' enthusiasm gave way.

On a more sustained basis, the Committee of Public Safety organized special clubs or societies and printed special journals for the army in an attempt to retain loyalty and reiterate the principles of the revolution. As one of its propaganda agents was instructed:

> One of the principal objects of your mission is the distribution of patriotic journals and the maintenance among our brothers in arms of the love of liberty which has made them win so many victories, to warn them against the manoeuvres of the aristocracy, and to unmask the false patriots who only want to win their confidence in order to betray the Republic.

Where suitable journals were not available, the Committee of Public Safety launched its own, the *Soirée de camp,* 29,000 copies of which were circulated to military units in one day, whilst the *Bulletin* served as an official record of events, to be posted in public places or read aloud 'in such a manner that everyone can hear, and it ends with Bravos'. Small wonder when soldiers were depicted as brave, heroic warriors, fighting for their country in all the printed propaganda of the period. They were, moreover, the heroes of some 3000 revolutionary songs written between 1789 and 1799, printed in song books, and freely distributed to the troops so that they could revel in their new-found status. One recruit, describing the rather sombre mood of his first march, described how 'suddenly the smallest man in the battalion began to sing…The whole battalion repeated the chorus and great joy replaced the sadness in our ranks.' The popularity of songs 'to excite … the courage of the defenders of the Patrie' was fully appreciated by the Committee of Public Safety, as was political theatre with such plays as *Fraud and Liberty* and *Democracy.*

All this indoctrination was one thing, but when it came to the heat of battle, would morale hold up? This has been one of our recurring questions and, as in previous wars, we must not discount the social climate that affected battle morale. During the revolutionary wars, many of the same pressures that have influenced men to acts of courage on the battlefield throughout history still applied. As one father reminded his son, 'When you march into combat, never forget that it is for your father, your mother, your brothers and your sisters, and know how to prefer even death to disgrace.' What was different now was that everyone had sons or relatives in the field; cowardice was no longer merely a family disgrace but a national one. And the propaganda reflected this: 'Life is nothing without liberty!' Only victory could secure the life and liberty of a revolutionary society. The alternative was the restoration of the old tyranny.

All this suggests a monumental propaganda success, and to a large extent it was. Though battles, not words, are ultimately decisive in warfare, it is difficult not to be impressed by the degree to which revolutionary propaganda fuelled the morale of the nation at-arms in this period. With French armies consisting perhaps of a million men, who took the revolution to virtually every corner of Europe, one can only marvel at their success. They overwhelmed their enemies with sheer numbers, lived off the land, moved quickly, and travelled light. The mobilization of French society to back up this effort was the nearest thing to total war prior to the twentieth century. But the war took its toll, as one domestic crisis followed another. In the army, desertion and indiscipline were far from eradicated, losses remained high, and by 1798 it was necessary to introduce full-blown conscription with compulsory military service for five years. Yet despite desperate measures introduced by the governing Directory, it was during this period that Napoleon Bonaparte was to emerge as leader both of a revolution that had lost its way and of the revolutionary army.

For Napoleon, good morale was the essence of success: 'In war, morale counts for three quarters, the balance of material force only makes up the remaining quarter.' Appointed to command the Army of Italy in 1796 at the age of 36, Napoleon emerged from his subsequent Egyptian campaign as a formidable military propagandist, playing up his victories and playing down his defeats. On his return to France in 1799 he was acclaimed as a conquering hero and by the end of the year was appointed First Consul. In 1802 he became Consul for life and in 1804 he was proclaimed Emperor. Napoleon was conscious of the similarities in his rapid rise to power to the career of Caesar and, like Caesar, he wrote self-congratulatory accounts of his military campaigns. The artist David, who had fallen out of favour at the fall of Robespierre, was restored to the position of chief visual propagandist in order to provide paintings and statues of Napoleon in the style of the Roman Caesars, while triumphal arches and other monuments were erected throughout Paris and the provinces. With his crowning as Emperor, Napoleon began the process of creating an imperial propaganda that was to help sustain his political position for a decade but which was to affect European life long after his death.

Under Napoleon, France became the first truly modern propaganda-based State. An example of the degree to which his propagandists orchestrated every aspect of French life followed the assassination of French delegates by the Austrians in 1799. A national day of mourning was announced and local authorities were informed that the theme was to be Vengeance:

> Miss no opportunity to give the ceremonies a solemn, inspirational character. On urns, mausoleums, pyramids and funerary columns let artists place broken olive trees stained with blood, Nature veiled, Humanity in tears...Show Despotism gathering their blood in a goblet. Depict all the evils which come in its train: famine, fire, war and death; depict Republicans rushing to arms to withstand the monster...Let funeral music of desolating sadness be followed by a period of silence and then – suddenly – let it be broken by the cry: Vengeance!

With such attention to detail (including instructions to report back on the public reaction), it is obvious that we are dealing here with something quite new in the history of propaganda: total propaganda. Napoleon believed that 'three hostile newspapers are more to be feared than a thousand bayonets' and he accordingly closed down 64 out of the 73 French newspapers in 1800-1. His censorship system would succeed where Louis XIV's had failed: by its sheer thoroughness.

Napoleon had suffered at the hands of hostile journalists working for the massively expanded revolutionary press during his campaign in Italy. Although the press had served his military campaigns well, by refusing to publish *news* that might prove of value to the enemy, it was its *views* that he feared most. Close supervision was therefore called for, and he and his ministers contributed regularly to the surviving papers and to the many 'non political' publications he encouraged. The *Moniteur* became the official government mouthpiece and was distributed free to the army. His image appeared on coins, medals, statues, and paintings. The letter 'N' was everywhere as a massive wave of public building works refashioned the architecture of Paris between 1804 and 1813. When Napoleon was offended by a newspaper article, as in 1807 when the poet Chateaubriand criticized the government in the *Mercure de la France,* he closed it down, and by 1810 there were only four newspapers left in France. 'If I had a free press', he wrote, 'I wouldn't last more than three months.' In 1812, the British view of Napoleon's press control was that 'it is a mortifying truth that he has done more mischief by means of the *Moniteur of Paris* than he has ever effected by the united efforts of the cannon and the sword'.

Napoleon's control over French thought affected all aspects of French life. In 1810, he established the 'Direction Général de l'Imprimerie et de la Librairie' to direct all cultural activity while artists and writers were mobilized to serve the glorification of his rule. Working through his police chief, he required all authors to submit two copies of every book for examination prior to publication; similar demands were made of plays, lectures and even posters. Publishers were licensed and made to swear an oath. History, especially the history of his own campaigns, was rewritten, inspired by Napoleon's belief that 'history is a myth which people choose to believe'. And Napoleon himself became a legend in which people chose to believe. He spent an average of £16,000 a year on pictures and sculpture; he commissioned buildings that were notable for their scale rather than their style, and he reformed the educational system. He used conspiracies against the state to strengthen his position (sometimes invented for the purpose), and elections to demonstrate his popularity. In short, from rigorous censorship to positive image projection and black propaganda, Napoleon was a master, one of the greatest propagandists in history.

An essential ingredient of Napoleon's power was his cultivated image of the soldier-emperor. While national festivals and public ceremonies continued to abound, they now came to be dominated by the military theme as Napoleon turned France into a militarized state. As the First Coalition crumbled, with Prussia making peace

in 1795 and Austria in 1797, Britain stood virtually alone in the
war against France. A second Coalition was formed in 1798, but
this too was characterized more by disunity than harmony. As Clive
Emsley has written: 'Pitt's government was faced with the problems
of maintaining and boosting morale and, as ever, raising money and
men for the conflict.' The aggressively loyal *Anti-Jacobin* was
founded in 1797 to aid this task and to combat the anti-war faction
of Charles Fox. A new 'British War Song' was published which ran:

> Let France in savage accents sing
> Her bloody revolution;
> We prize our Country, love our King,
> Adore our Constitution;
> For these we'll every danger face,
> And quit our rustic labours;
> Our ploughs to firelocks shall give place,
> Our scythes be changed to sabres.
> And clad in arms our Song shall be,
> 'O give us Death – or Victory!'

As fears of a French invasion mounted, a surge of patriotism
gripped the English as the *Anti-Jacobin* and other publications
summoned the spirit of Crécy and Agincourt, recalled the Spanish
Armada, and found a new national hero in Horatio Nelson, who
destroyed the French fleet in Aboukir Bay in 1798. James Gillray's
famous political cartoons attacking the French and the Foxites were
widely reprinted, especially his series depicting the 'Consequences
of a Successful French Invasion'. Riding this upsurge, the government persecuted the anti-war factions, suspended the Habeas
Corpus Act, and arrested conspirators and hostile publicists; but
the rising cost of the war, poor harvests, and growing popular
discontent at home was accompanied by Russian and Austrian
withdrawal from the Second Coalition and the peace of Amiens
was signed in 1802.

The peace was short-lived – just fourteen months in fact. The
renewal of hostilities between France and England saw continued
invasion scares, but while Napoleon remained superior on land
Nelson's victory at Trafalgar in 1805 was a reminder of British
superiority at sea. A Third Coalition was constructed, coastal
fortifications built, and patriotic propaganda promoted. The poet
William Wordsworth praised the 'Men of Kent', now in the front

line against invasion: 'In Britain is one breath/We are all with you now from shore to shore/Ye men of Kent, 'tis victory or death!' Gillray created his 'Little Boney' cartoons lampooning Napoleon, anti-French plays (including the old faithful *Henry V)* were performed, patriotic songs praised the efforts and character of John Bull, and even sermons against the French emperor rang out from the pulpits. The press and pamphlets pointed to Napoleon's barbarous armies, their cruel treatment of prisoners and civilians and other atrocities. Children were 'soothed' with such rhymes as:

> Baby, baby, naughty baby
> Hush, you squalling thing I say;
> Hush your squalling or it may be
> Bonaparte may pass this way.

The possible involvement of the entire population in resisting a French invasion meant that propaganda was directed to all classes of men, women, and children. Once that threat had subsided the war still dragged on, and mounting economic distress and popular discontent served as a counterbalance to any amount of patriotic propaganda. By 1812, however, Napoleon had been driven back from Moscow and the Duke of Wellington was preparing to march against France from Spain. In April 1814, surrounded by British, Austrian, Prussian, and Russian forces, Napoleon threw in the towel and abdicated. Within a year, however, Napoleon was back in Paris and the euphoria that had greeted his flight to Elba had to be suspended until his final defeat at the Battle of Waterloo.

Waterloo, despite Wellington's subsequent attempt to 'leave the battle as it is', became the focus of enormous national pride and the object of endless eulogies and myth-making. On both sides of the Channel, romanticized accounts (including epic poems by Byron and Victor Hugo) and monumental paintings served to promote Waterloo as one of the most decisive battles in history. For our purposes here, the significance of Waterloo lies in the degree to which it demonstrated the loyalty of the French troops to their emperor and the extent to which the outcome was used to promote a view that revolutionary tyranny had finally been defeated.

Chapter 19

War and Public Opinion in the Nineteenth Century

With Napoleon finally defeated and safely out of harm's way in exile, Europe breathed a huge sigh of relief that peace had at last returned after a generation of war. It is sobering to think that a 25-year-old in 1815 would not be able to remember a time when Europe had not been at war. This experience, together with the ideas unleashed by Napoleon and the French Revolution, did not suddenly disappear with the defeat of France. Quite the reverse happened, in fact, as Europe began to reconcile itself to the forces of change the wars had accelerated, not the least significant of which was the continued development of public opinion and propaganda. The extent to which the ordinary people of Europe for a generation had been affected by, and involved in, the Napoleonic wars narrowed the gap between ruler and ruled still further than ever before. The nineteenth century saw attempts to widen that gap again, notably in Victorian Britain. But the forces of change could not be stemmed and, as a result of technological innovations, the century saw a steady rise in the role of public opinion and in the use of propaganda by governing élites to influence it. In the words of Professor Qualter:

> Even those whose attitude towards public opinion in politics did not change found that of necessity they had to learn the mechanics of peaceful persuasion by propaganda. With an extended franchise and an increasing population it was becoming too expensive to do anything else. Where at one time voters could be bought, they now had to be persuaded. Politicians had, therefore, to become interested in propaganda.

This was greatly aided by major advances in the speed with which newspapers could be produced, by the invention of photography, by improved transport systems such as railways and, later in the century, by the advent of electricity and flight. Asa Briggs was right when he described such nineteenth-century developments as constituting a genuine 'Communications Revolution'.

It is something of a myth that the hundred years separating the end of the Napoleonic wars and the outbreak of the First World War was a 'century of peace'. One need only recall the Crimean War, the American Civil War, the Opium Wars, the Franco-Prussian War, and the wars of imperialism to dispel that myth. But if wars between the great powers were comparatively scarce, smaller conflicts began to receive widespread publicity by virtue of developments in communications. Even so, in the generation after Waterloo a war-weary Europe tried to heal its scars by political rather than military means as industrialization and population increased, as nationalist movements emerged to challenge the established order, and as revolutionary ideas began to secure a wider audience. If the century was to be remembered as a 'century of revolutions', the role of the media in society also underwent revolutionary change. In the 1830s, the first mass newspapers appeared. With the founding of the *New York Sun* in 1833, the era of the 'penny press' began and, according to one authority, 'ushered in a new order, a shared social universe in which 'public' and 'private' would be redefined'.

In Britain, newspapers catering for a particular class of people began to appear and, following a reduction in the Stamp Duty from 4d. to ld. in 1836, cheap popular weeklies building on the tradition of broadsheets emerged and were put to good use by such movements as the Chartists. The *Northern Star* was the principal Chartist propaganda paper, committed to educating the working class. Rising circulations and the numbers of newspapers reflected improving standards of literacy. Whereas there had been 76 newspapers and periodicals published in England and Wales in 1781, the figure had risen to 563 in 1851. Between 1840 and 1852 the circulation of *The Times* (founded as the *Daily Universal Register* in 1785) quadrupled from 10,000 to 40,000 copies per issue. With the advent of Koenig's steam press at the start of the century, 1000 issues an hour could be produced, a rate that was increased to 8-10,000 by 1848 when the type was fixed on to a cylindrical rather than a flat bed. The growth of the railways in the 1830s greatly speeded up the distribution of newspapers, while the development of the electric telegraph in the 1840s meant that the transmission of news could now be done more rapidly than the older methods of pigeon and semaphore. The development of a global cable network and the emergence of the great news agencies such as Reuters greatly accelerated the speed of international communication and improved the coverage of news from all around the world. By the end of the century, with the advent of cinema and radio, this communications revolution – which we are still undergoing today – was in full flight.

Examples mainly from the British experience have been chosen because, even though one could repeat the exercise for any other nation, Britain was the country that emerged as the unrivalled leader in the field of political propaganda and, in the twentieth century, the undisputed master of war propaganda. This will be a startling claim to those (mainly British people, it must be said) who believe that, of all the nations, Britain was, and remains, the most reluctant of the world's propagandists. In Britain, propaganda is something that other people do, an 'un-English' activity associated with subverting freedom of speech, action, and thought. Yet in the nineteenth century, Britain's unique position enabled her to develop a system of media manipulation both at home and abroad that was to serve her well in the century that followed. As the cradle of the industrial revolution comparatively free from the internal up-heavals threatening other powers, and as the creator of a genuinely world-wide empire, this small group of islands off the north-western coast of Europe was able to develop a position of power and influence within the world communications system that was matched only by her position as the world's leading power. Her far-flung empire, from Scotland to Singapore, was maintained as much by effective communications as by the efficiency of the British Army and the Royal Navy. The development of the 'all red' cable network enabled London to communicate its decisions and ideas to those scattered points on the world map shaded in the appropriate imperial colour. If British power was to be sustained it was vital for the Empire to 'think British'.

At home, more and more people were beginning to think politics. The expansion in the size of the electorate by the 1832 and 1867 Reform Acts – though more modest than implied in most school textbooks – broadened the base of political power and helped to diffuse political unrest. Newspapers became an intermediary between government and people – the Fourth Estate – especially when the Stamp Duty was finally abolished in 1855 and the tax on paper (the 'tax on knowledge') abandoned in 1861. Not only did the press communicate political ideas to the people, it also conveyed public opinion to the politicians. This two-way process can be seen in the propaganda campaigns of the Chartists and of the Anti-Corn Law League, though both also employed other techniques such as demonstrations and slogans, banners, badges, and bands. The press began increasingly to use pictures, especially after the founding of the *Illustrated London News* in 1842 which capitalized on Louis Daguerre's invention of photography (1839) and W.H. Fox Talbot's development of the Calotype printing process (1841). Politicians became more and more concerned with the importance of public speaking, not just in Parliament, where their speeches were reported freely in the press from the 1780s onwards, but also in public meetings to audiences of increasingly politicized voters upon whose support many of them now depended for their position. All these developments increased even more markedly in the second half of the century, with Gladstone, Disraeli, and others perfecting the art of political propaganda pioneered in Britain by Canning and Palmerston, and they deserve more attention than can be given here. But they do provide the essential background to any understanding of a major innovation in war propaganda: the arrival of the war correspondent.

In 1815, *Cobbett's Weekly Political Register* was furious that the defeat of the British by the Americans at the battle of New Orleans in the Anglo-American War (1812-15) had received scant attention in the British press:

> The country people in England, and a great many of the townspeople, never know anything of such defeats. The London newspapers, which alone have a very wide circulation are employed in the spreading of falsehood and the suppressing of the truth.

Although the press at this time was inevitably more concerned with the victory at Waterloo, much nearer to home, the point was well made. As the press came to rely less on government subsidies and more on income obtained on a commercial basis from sales and advertising, newspapers began to employ special correspondents to gather exciting news that was often designed more to entertain than to inform. They had to use a variety of disguises and ruses since army commanders (including Wellington) would not allow any civilians near the battlefields. But military news, often in great detail, did manage to get back to the London press, prompting complaints from Wellington and Napoleon's celebrated remark that 'English papers make my best spies'. The dangers of providing information that would be of value to the enemy were to result in rigorous military censorship later in the century but, for the moment, the authorities attempted to control leaks by issuing dull official communiqués and forbidding serving officers from publishing their letters. Yet even after the return of peace, newspapers continued to send special correspondents to the small wars and on military expeditions, in China and India, for example, in order to cater for an increasingly news-hungry readership. And as virtually the whole of Europe reeled from the shock of the 1848 revolutions, the growing involvement of ordinary people in politics was reflected in a press that could now report events from afar faster than ever before.

In 1851, as Europe recovered from its recent political upheavals, Britain basked in the glory and prestige of its imperial achievements at the Great Exhibition held in the Crystal Palace. Such displays of national self-advertisement had become increasingly commonplace, but Victorian London provided the setting for the most spectacular propaganda exhibition of the nineteenth century. It was both a national and an international exercise in propaganda. As Paul Greenhalgh has commented:

> The Great Exhibition can... be viewed as a giant counter revolutionary measure; indeed, from its earliest days it was conceived of as an event to foster fear as well as pride in the minds of the British public, an immense show of strength designed to intimidate potential insurrectionists.

This might seem startling, yet the fact remains that despite the progress that had been made in the political representation of the English people, much remained to be done. It is no coincidence that *The Communist Manifesto* was published in London in 1848 and that historians have been grappling ever since with the question of why, uniquely, no revolution occurred in England in that year. But, as the Great Exhibition revealed, the Victorians were perhaps the most effective English myth-makers since the Tudors. One of their most important myths was that the British Army, with its tradition dating back from Waterloo of recent memory to Agincourt and

Crécy, remained the 'finest, most powerful army in the world'. Within three years of the Great Exhibition, the gap between that myth and reality was to be exposed in graphic terms by the Crimean War, and in particular by the writings of the most famous of all war correspondents, William Howard Russell of *The Times*. As Phillip Knightly has written, 'Russell's coverage of the Crimean War marked the beginning of an organised effort to report a war to the civilian population at home using the services of a civilian reporter.'

Of the many complex reasons for the outbreak of war between Britain, France, and the 'sick man of Europe', Turkey, on the one side, and Russia on the other, the one that captured the public imagination most was the struggle for the holy places in the Near East. Popular enthusiasm, however, quickly gave way to concern as the 34-year-old Russell, appalled by the lack of preparations and the poor conditions he everywhere observed, started sending home his critical despatches from the front. *The Times*, at the height of its popularity, published his letters, together with hard-hitting editorials by its editor, John Delane, and quickly earned the hostility of both the government and the military authorities. Despite official efforts to frustrate his ability to report what he saw, Russell continued to send home vivid descriptions that alarmed his readers. From the Crimea he wrote:

> Few of those who were with the expedition will forget the night of the 14th September [1854]. Seldom or never were 27,000 Englishmen more miserable... No tents had been sent on shore... the showers increased about midnight and early in the morning dew in drenching sheets... pierced through the blankets and great coats.

Russell placed the blame squarely on an inefficient and outdated military system, yet it was ironically that very inefficiency that enabled his reports to evade the censors. French correspondents found their censorship restrictions much tougher, which was one reason why French newspapers were more supportive of their Emperor Napoleon III's efforts (although it has to be admitted that conditions in the French army were better than those in the British). Russell and his Fleet Street colleagues, including the war artists who provided visual images to reinforce the critical words, were unrelenting in their attacks, prompting a public outcry during which Florence Nightingale volunteered her services and which eventually toppled the government.

Now the press had an 'angel of mercy' to praise as a new form of British war hero. However, it had also begun to destroy some old ones. Lord Raglan, military secretary to Wellington at Waterloo and leader of the British forces in the Crimea, became a major target after the heroic but futile Charge of the Light Brigade at the Battle of Balaclava. Here was yet more substance to the accusations of incompetence. Russell informed Delane:

> I am convinced from what I see that Lord Raglan is utterly incompetent to lead an army through any arduous task... But the most serious disadvantage under which he labours is that he does not go amongst the troops. He does not visit the camp, he does not cheer them and speak to them.

Such were Russell's observations of war minus the battles. At first he could only witness the action from afar and his skill lay in recreating the battle from (often contradictory) eyewitness accounts by those soldiers who would talk to him. But, under pressure from The Times, he was able to secure a more privileged position and he witnessed Balaclava from the overlooking plateau, 'as the stage and those upon it are seen from the box of a theatre'.

Russell's feelings as he watched Lord Cardigan's 673 cavalrymen charging the Russian guns with appalling losses in the 'valley of death' immortalized by Tennyson's poem (1854) were a mixture of pride and horror. They provide us with an insight into the eternal dilemma of the war correspondent: when to criticize and when to praise. No patriotic journalist (as distinct from a neutral one) wishes to appear over critical of his country's efforts, but in the Crimean War – as happened later in Vietnam – journalists felt they had no choice but to publicize what they saw as a national scandal. The authorities tried to retaliate by accusing Russell of providing valuable information to the enemy – a charge that was now possible given the speed with which his despatches could reach London even before a battle had started and which could be relayed back to Russia almost as quickly by her agents. Eventually, in 1856, too late to be effective in the Crimean War but establishing a precedent for future conflicts, the army issued a general order – the origins of modern British military censorship – which forbade the publication of information which might help the enemy. It also allowed for the expulsion of correspondents. Before then, counter-propaganda was also tried when the royal photographer, Roger Fenton, was despatched to record a clean, ordered war in which the troops looked happy and healthy. Comparing Fenton's photographs with the overwhelming body of critical press coverage should raise alarm bells about that old axiom that the camera never lies. It depends where you point it, and Fenton did not even bother to unpack his camera on the battlesite of Balaclava, which was riddled with half-dug graves and the rotting corpses of the 'heroic six hundred'.

The significance of Russell's work lies in the fact that it brought the horrors of war before a public that now had more say than ever before in the policies and conduct of the government which had declared it. War was no longer the business of sovereigns, statesmen and the professional soldiers; it was the business of the people in whose name it was being fought. The press saw to that. And if the government was to ensure that the right sort of public attitudes and support were forthcoming, it would have to take the business of official propaganda and censorship seriously. It took another half century for this to filter through properly, but the Crimea was a true watershed.

Official recognition – perhaps over-estimation – of the power of the independent press was evident in the Indian Mutiny of 1857 when the authorities closed down the five principal Indian newspapers. The new breed of war correspondents to which Russell had given birth flocked to the sub-continent to report the massacres conducted by both sides. The British Empire was being portrayed to the British public as never before, and the public thrilled at the exotic tales of imperial campaigns in India, China, and Africa. Military success appeared to prove British racial superiority over inferior peoples, and this myth was perpetuated in a variety of media, from newspapers to novels, from parades to postcards, from school textbooks to societies, from board-games to biscuit tins. As John Mackenzie has written, this wide-ranging imperial propaganda campaign 'was concerned to glorify the combination of military adventure and aggressive expansionist Christian culture'.

Propaganda as an instrument of social control, of ensuring that the masses thought and behaved as the ruling élite wanted them to, found an ideal expression in imperialism. It had all the right ingredients: military adventure, racial superiority, and exotic locations. But it was risky and depended for its success upon military (and naval) superiority and sensitive colonial government. When British forces suffered at the hands of supposedly racially inferior troops – as they did in the Zulu and Boer wars – it was because they had been overwhelmed by sheer weight of numbers and savagery, the 'white man's burden' that had to be borne. The Victoria Cross emerged as the highest symbol of military courage and the glorification of the imperial achievement was evident throughout Britain, with its statues of Queen *and* Empress Victoria, its Pomp and Circumstance, and its celebrations of military heroes such as Gordon of Khartoum. Other European nations were equally impressed and scrambled for bits of Africa and China to demonstrate their status as great powers. Like Britain, countries such as France and, after 1870, a united Germany, recognized the domestic advantages of an overseas empire and of the importance of news communications within it. Havas of France and the Wolff Bureau in Berlin were officially subsidized news agencies and governments in both countries were quick to recognize the importance of controlling images through official newspapers, public architecture, and the arts. By comparison, British propaganda occurred perhaps more by accident and private enterprise than by government design, but the imperial mentality created by various groups, organizations, and publications provided a valuable unifying role for any government contemplating overseas wars.

In the United States, a distinct lack of unity was more in evidence as the country plunged into civil war in 1861. Over 500 American war correspondents joined the northern side and found their work greatly aided by the telegraph. They were less well served by photography since no American newspaper at that time possessed the technology for making half-tone blocks, and although there is a photographic record of the conflict (especially Mathew Brady's work) it is more profitable to study the visual impact of the war artists who worked for such illustrated weeklies as *Harper's*. As popular interest in the war increased, America became a nation of newspaper readers dependent upon reports from war correspondents who saw their business more in terms of morale than objectivity. Harper's, for example, published an engraving of a totally fictitious account of Confederate soldiers bayoneting wounded Union troops, while Horace Greeley's *New York Tribune* spear headed the northern propaganda cause in words. As in the Crimea, troops did all they could to hamper hostile journalists and ease the lot of friendly ones, such as letting them pitch their tents near the military telegraph wagon. But the gap between the soldier about to risk death and the civilian about to witness it for the edification and entertainment of his readers remained wide, especially as journalists began to compete more ferociously for scoops and exclusives in a war initially short of decisive battles.

Gettysburg, July 1863, changed that. Yet the ultimate failure of correspondents to report the civil war adequately was also revealed after this battle when one of the finest speeches ever delivered, Lincoln's Gettysburg Address, received wholly inadequate coverage, with one newspaper account merely reporting: 'The President also spoke.' The propaganda value of Lincoln's eloquence was exploited only subsequently and had more impact in the First and Second World Wars than it did in the Civil War. The instructions of the editor of the *Chicago Times* for his staff to 'telegraph fully all news you can and when there is no news send rumours' give the game away: the soldier would fight the battle, the journalist would fight the truth. Criticism of the northern cause or of the appalling conditions in the army would anyway be stamped out by censorship, and about twenty Union newspapers were suppressed during the course of the war. Bull Run, the first skirmish of the conflict, was reported as a glorious Union victory rather than a spectacular defeat, while military authorities reduced casualty figures and Secretary of War Stanton began issuing daily war bulletins that can best be said to have been economical with the truth. General Sherman, who believed that journalists caused 'infinite mischief', did all he could to deny them access to information and found, as a result, that the press afforded more coverage to the less significant victories of a more publicity-conscious General Grant.

The southern cause, served by about a hundred war correspondents working for low circulation, old fashioned weeklies, was severely hampered by its previous dependence on the north for newsprint, staff, and equipment. Rather, the older system of relying upon letters and reports from serving officers furnished a deeply-partisan propagandist press that progressively diminished both in numbers and circulation. Retreats became strategic withdrawals, defeats became temporary setbacks or simply didn't happen, losses became insignificant. Dependence upon letters from the front was not the most reliable method of reporting the war, given that any one soldier could not possibly be expected to see the battle as a whole. Besides, his mind would have been understandably on other things. If there was a correspondent watching, he may have been conscious of the need to be seen doing his duty bravely, and thus serve as a boost to courage. Letters and journals written by soldiers after the event served as a form of exorcism of the demons experienced during combat: fear, courage, killing. They were a rationalization and an explanation of behaviour considered in hindsight. Private letters home might contain admissions of fear; public letters to the press contained no such admissions, only tales of courage and uncommon valour – the very stuff of propaganda designed for proud but perhaps demoralized civilians. As one soldier commented, 'we fought with the feeling that we were under the straining eyes of those who loved us and had sent us forth.' The role of the press as an interpreter of soldiers' actions to civilian thoughts, and thus as a morale booster to both, cannot be overlooked.

Discipline was, however, a major problem in Civil War armies. After the First Bull Run, General Sherman complained that 'each private thinks for himself' and 'I doubt if our democratic form of government admits of that organization and discipline without which an army is a mob'. This was an interesting observation, and one which was to be put severely to the test in the twentieth century. If democracies cherish the notion of freedom of thought, how was a democratic army to become effective? Discipline and training were time-honoured means of providing cohesion, but, as nations became more and more democratic, could their war needs be met by more and more training and discipline? Patriotism born of nationalism is perhaps one solution; but in a civil war this proves difficult. For this reason northern propaganda depicted the Confederates as traitors or, as one soldier wrote, 'they war for a lie, they are enemies of morals, of government and of man. In them, we fight against a great wrong.' The Confederates, for their part, depicted the Union as being un-American, an assembly of immigrants who were the scum of the earth come to plunder the genteel south. In a mass society, propaganda can serve a unifying role, but the United States in the 1860s was far from being a mass society. In many respects, it was the actual experience of ordinary Americans in the battles of the Civil War, where soldiers shared with the enemy common qualities and characteristics and witnessed each other's courage, that served to move the United States further down that road. The war propaganda conducted by both sides – as in any civil war – served as a barrier.

But the war also had international dimensions, as both sides realized when they embarked on an overseas propaganda campaign aimed mainly at Britain. Lincoln appealed to English northern textile industrialists, whose sympathies naturally lay more with the cotton producing Confederacy, by writing directly to them and both sides organized lecture tours and inserted sympathetic articles in the British press. But the North found it had a formidable enemy in The Times. Russell was sent from London to cover the war and although his own sympathies were against slavery he deeply alienated the Union by reporting accurately the outcome of Bull Run. Unable to secure permission to report the Union cause from the front, and despite his pro-Northern disposition that urged restraint on a warmongering *Times* following the *Trent* affair (when a British steamer was boarded and two Confederate delegates to Europe arrested), Russell's dispatches were at odds with his paper's views and his influence began to decline. Other correspondents fared little better when their pro-Southern line, though welcomed in London, conflicted with actual events. Following the Confederate defeat and Lincoln's assassination, *The Times* sacked Charles Mackay, Russell's successor, because his reportage had been 'one sided and every remark spiteful'. But the damage had been done, with the victorious North resenting the hostile role of the British press for years to come.

If the experience of the Crimean War and American Civil War had taught authorities that they must begin seriously to address the question of military censorship as a weapon of war propaganda, it also taught the press that it must observe more professional standards in its coverage of wars. Both felt they were serving the nation, but the major concern was to ensure that their respective sense of responsibility coincided rather than clashed. To the military authorities war correspondents were 'newly-invented curses to armies' and it took time for them to realize that newspapers could make valuable allies. In other words, both government and press had to learn to unite in support of the same cause if a national propaganda campaign in wartime was to be effective. This became all the more important in Britain, for example, as newspaper circulations continued to grow with improving standards of literacy following the Elementary Education Act of 1870 and further acts in 1881, 1891, and 1902. The same was true elsewhere. The press, aided by the speed with which news could now be transmitted by telegraph from all parts of the globe, was able to increase its coverage of foreign wars and a measure of objectivity was possible only when correspondents reported conflicts that did not involve their own countries. Most, however, glorified war and helped to perpetuate its image as the sport of gentlemen.

f military authorities were slow to appreciate the role the press could serve in glorifing their 'sport', politicians, mindful of the need for public support of their policies, were not. Bismarck, for example, recognized the value of a friendly press and went to great lengths to orchestrate the domestic German newspapers and to cultivate the foreign press, especially during the Franco-Prussian war of 1870-1; his deliberate leaking of the Ems telegram, deliberately doctored to give the impression that French demands were unreasonable, provoked the war. In Italy, the leaders of unification were outstanding propagandists: Cavour was a former editor of the *Risorgimento*, Mazzini was a skilled pamphleteer, and Garibaldi a master of public demonstration and crowd manipulation. Disraeli, the author of a propagandist novel *Sybil*, was quick to exploit swings in popular mood and cultivated images of monarchy, imperialism, religion, and race as political tools. Politicians of the late nineteenth century, in other words, recognized that they were operating in a new kind of world, a world in which public opinion across a wide spectrum was becoming increasingly important in a mass industrialized society. This recognition was accompanied by a concerted effort to influence that opinion through the intermediary forces that shaped public attitudes. Politics had indeed become public, and neither politics nor warfare would ever be quite the same again.

Part Five

Propaganda in the Age of
Total War and Cold War

Chapter 20

War and the Communications Revolution

The twentieth century saw the arrival of a fundamentally different kind of warfare: 'Total War'. Although the Napoleonic wars and the American War of Independence had foreshadowed this phenomenon by their level of popular involvement, the world wars of the twentieth century differed markedly from previous conflicts, not just in their scale but also in the degree to which civilians were affected by, and contributed directly to, events in the front line. War now became a matter for every member of the population, a struggle for national survival in which the entire resources of the nation – military, economic, industrial, human, and psychological – had to be mobilized in order to secure victory or avoid defeat. Failure to mobilize on a maximum scale, as the experience of the Russian Revolution of 1917 demonstrated, might result not simply in defeat but in the very destruction of the old order.

The new warfare brought battle closer to the lives of ordinary citizens than ever before, whether in the form of women being recruited into factories or in the form of civilian bombing. Conscription, air raid precautions, and rationing all became vital factors. Ordinary men and women who had previously been largely unaffected by the impact of wars fought by professional soldiers in far-off lands now found themselves directly affected by events at the front. In fact, the people themselves became the new front line; men, women, and children formed the new armies and their morale, their will to fight and resist on a mass scale, accordingly became a significant military asset. Indeed, such was the nature of the 1914-18 and 1939-45 conflicts, such was their scale in a national, global, and psychological sense, and such was their cost in terms of human destruction and material devastation, that war could never again be regarded as the sport of kings and nobles. It had even become, as the French Prime Minister Clemenceau said, 'too serious a business to be left to the generals'.

The twentieth century, however, also saw the arrival of the modern mass media. The year 1896 was a truly momentous one that saw three significant developments. First, Lord Northcliffe founded in Britain the world's first mass circulation daily newspaper, *The Daily Mail,* to cater for the new generation of educated and literate working people. Following the Education Acts of the 1870s, and subsequent social improvements, ordinary working people were not only becoming increasingly literate but were also enjoying the benefits of liberal Victorian reforms that provided them increasingly with more pay and more leisure time. Newspapers previously had catered for a comparatively small and educated section of the community. *The Daily Mail* broke the mould and imitations rapidly followed throughout the industrialized world. In America, Randolph Hearst pioneered the phenomenon known as 'Yellow Journalism'. But for those who did not wish to take advantage of their new found literacy – the majority, one suspects – 1896 also saw the first commercial screening of the cinematograph by the Lumière brothers in Paris (although claims about the real inventors and timing of the event remain the subject of much historical debate). Originally springing from scientific curiosity about the movement of wildlife (scientists wishing, for example, to investigate birds in flight so that man might imitate the process), world-wide and often separately conducted research finally transformed the cinematograph into the most potent means of mass communication in the first half of the twentieth century. In 1896, a third significant event took place when Guglielmo Marconi demonstrated the practicability of wireless telegraphy on Salisbury Plain. In one remarkable year, therefore, the principal means of mass communication – press, radio, and film – came into their own and the communications revolution made a quantum leap. It was the convergence of total war and the mass media that gave modern war propaganda its significance and impact in the twentieth century.

At first the impact of the new media in the conduct of war propaganda was comparatively small. Certainly, in the Boer War (1899-1902), the popular press became increasingly jingoistic while the masses also enjoyed their war through music hall songs.

But that war and its horrors were still physically distant, despite the coverage given to it by the fledgling newsreel companies. In America, Hearst had proved just as capable of jingoistic slogans in the Spanish-American War (1898) with his cry to 'Remember the Maine' (an American warship sunk by the Spanish at the outset of the war). But it was the Russo-Japanese war of 1905 that was watched with particular interest by political and military authorities alike to ascertain the role of the modern media in determining the outcome of a conflict between major powers. Within a decade, the lessons learned from that conflict were to be put to the test in the bloodiest struggle yet experienced by mankind.

Chapter 21

The First World War

The locomotive of historical change was set in full flight in 1914 for both warfare and propaganda. The war that began with dancing in the streets throughout Europe's capitals ended four years later with an armistice signed in the Compiègne Forest amid sorrow, tragedy, and recrimination. It was a war that began with traditional volunteer armies and ended with all the belligerents having introduced conscription. It saw the destruction of four European empires – the Russian, German, Austro-Hungarian, and Ottoman – and the creation of new, independent but insecure states – Rumania, Yugoslavia, Czechoslovakia, Poland – that were to sow the seeds of future conflict. Untold dead and maimed, poison gas, trench warfare, tanks, aeroplanes, blockades and starvation, mutinies, revolution – all seemed inconceivable in that innocent summer of 1914 when the Germans unleashed their Schleiffen Plan amidst a cultivated illusion that fostered the belief that it would all be over by Christmas.

The very fact, of course, that Germany had invaded Belgium and France in August 1914, and was to remain fighting on their soil for the rest of the war, forfeited the moral high ground the German government had hoped to secure by its pre-war propaganda. No matter how much propaganda material the Germans poured out in an attempt to justify their actions, 'Poor Little Belgium' remained a rallying cry for their enemies throughout the war. War could no longer be regarded as a sport fought between gentlemen playing the game by the correct rules. Instead, it became a bloody and relentless struggle in which sustaining morale became just as essential for both sides as sustaining the military effort. It was not just a battle between troops, guns, submarines, ships, and aeroplanes but a battle between entire peoples. It was a battle that, despite better pre-war planning, the Germans were to lose, with dramatic effects for Europe and the world as a whole.

Within hours of the expiry of the British ultimatum to Germany, the British cable ship *Telconia* cut the direct subterranean cables linking Germany with the United States. Thanks to this prompt and premeditated action, the British were able to seize the initiative in what was perhaps the most vital of all the propaganda battles: the struggle for the sympathy of the American people. In 1914, Britain and Germany were each other's best trading partners. On the outbreak of war it became essential for both to compensate for their mutual loss by increasing their trade with the rapidly expanding markets of the United States or, better still, to entice the Americans into joining their cause. Britain, at the head of the Allied Powers, was of course better placed than Germany to direct this campaign against American neutrality by virtue of her common language and heritage. Even so, great caution was required; no nation likes to be told where its duties lie, least of all by foreigners with foreign accents. This was a mistake that was to be made by the German government, which promptly and blatantly poured propaganda material into neutral America, using the German-American societies or bunds as their distribution agents. All the evidence available to the British government suggested that this approach was counter-productive.

To wage this highly delicate campaign for securing American sympathies, the British government set up a secret war propaganda bureau at Wellington House under the direction of Charles Masterman. This department was the single most important branch of the British propaganda organization between 1914 and 1917 and its work was so secret that even most Members of Parliament were unaware of it. It was essential to disguise from the American people the fact that the massive bulk of paper material they were receiving from Britain about the war – pamphlets, leaflets, cartoons, and even the news itself – was emanating from Wellington House under Foreign Office guidance. Several other important – and ultimately successful – principles of operation were also established. For example, the British campaign adopted a low-key and highly selective approach based upon persuasion rather than exhortation. It was also decided that the best propagandists for the Allied cause were sympathetic Americans, particularly those in influential positions in government, business, education, and the media. The principle here, as one document put it, was 'that it is better to influence those who can influence others than attempt a direct appeal to the mass of the population'. Thanks to their control of the direct cable communications between Europe and North America, the British also monopolized the news, and news was to be the basis of the British propaganda campaign – all of it carefully censored and selected, of course. The factual approach had the advantage not only of credibility; it also left American editors with the freedom to present the news in their customary style so that their readers could make up their own minds about the issues reported. But it must always be remembered that the British controlled the source of that news; even the American correspondents working behind the German lines relied on the direct cables – the indirect cables running through neutral Scandinavia and Portugal were slower and more expensive, and the newspaper business, then as now, relied upon speed and economy. Indeed, censorship was the source of much friction between Britain and America between 1914 and 1917, but it was an essential element of the successful British propaganda campaign.

The British campaign was greatly aided by several spectacular German mistakes, the best known being the sinking of the *Lusitania* in 1915 and the Zimmermann Telegram in 1917. These incidents enabled the British to punctuate their softly-softly approach with the occasional rabbit punch. The evidence discovered by marine archaeologists and salvage experts in the mid-1980s suggests strongly that the passenger liner holed by a German U-boat in May 1915 was in fact carrying illegal armaments. However, to contemporaries, the act was presented as a blatant atrocity, another example of Prussian barbarism at the expense of innocent civilians. The Germans insisted that the sinking was a justifiable act of war but, combined with the publication of the *Report of the Committee on Alleged German Outrages* in Belgium, better known as the Bryce Report, within a few days of the *Lusitania* incident, it served to reinforce precisely the stereotype of the Hun that British propaganda had been trying to create. But the real German mistake came a year later when a bronze medal was struck by the German artist Goetz to commemorate the sinking of the liner. The Foreign Office managed to obtain one of the limited editions, photographed it, and sent it to the United States, where it was published in *The New York Tribune* on the anniversary of the sinking. The photographs caused so much excitement that the British decided to exploit further the resulting anti-German feeling by producing virtually an exact replica in a presentation box, together with an 'explanatory' leaflet. The medal was reproduced in hundreds of thousands. What was originally an attempt by a private German artist working on his own initiative to justify the submarine campaign to his own people became a *cause célèbre* of Hunnish barbarism and one of the most dramatic British propaganda coups of the war.

The publication in America of the *Lusitania* medal photographs came at an opportune moment for Britain. Following the abortive Easter Rising in Ireland and the subsequent execution of its leaders, pro-Irish sympathy in America was hampering the British cause and forcing British propagandists back onto the defensive. They responded by launching an attack on the moral reputation of the rebel leaders, particularly Sir Roger Casement, whose alleged diaries – in fact forgeries – contained lurid details of homosexual activities. What is most significant about the Irish question, together with other sources of Anglo-American friction such as the Blockade of the Central Powers and the censorship, is that the Germans singularly failed to exploit these issues in America. Combined with their own mistakes, these lost opportunities stand out in marked contrast to the successful British initiatives. Take for example the case of Nurse Edith Cavell. Her execution in 1915 appeared to confirm the brutality of the Germans so well 'documented' in the Bryce Report. The Germans may well indeed have been justified in this action as a legitimate punishment for someone aiding the escape of Allied soldiers, but the wave of world-wide indignation her execution caused was another serious blow for the German cause. It was not just that she was a woman that created the outcry; the execution on spying charges of Mata Hari by the French in 1917 caused no such wave of sympathy (partly because, again, the Germans failed to exploit her death). Cavell was presented as an 'angel of mercy' whose tragic murder was set against the background of Belgian violation. By rigidly adhering to military justice the Germans were merely conforming to the stereotype created for them by British propagandists of Teutonic brutality and ruthless inhumanity.

Atrocity stories were, of course, a time-honoured technique of war propagandists. The First World War was no exception. Images of the bloated 'Prussian Ogre', proudly sporting his pickelhaube, the 'Beastly Hun' with his sabre-belt barely surrounding his enormous girth, busily crucifying soldiers, violating women, mutilating babies, desecrating and looting churches, are deeply implanted in the twentieth century's gallery of popular images. Evoked repeatedly by Allied propagandists during the Great War, the British stereotype of the Hun and the French image of the 'Boche' provided them with the essential focus they needed to launch their moral offensive against the enemy, at home and abroad. They personified and pictorialized a German society based upon militarist principles in order to bring home to soldiers and civilians alike the terrifying consequences of defeat. Neutral countries were also left in no doubt as to where their sympathies should rest. During the early stage of the war, it was important for the propagandists to cast blame on the enemy for starting the conflict and to prove that he had deliberately let loose the dogs of war upon peace-loving nations. The very fact that Germany admitted violating international law by attacking France and Belgium provided the British with the moral foundation they required to justify intervention to the ordinary men whom they now required to enlist 'For King and Country'. Atrocity stories, as ever, helped to sustain the moral condemnation of the enemy.

Perhaps the most infamous atrocity story of the Great War concerned the alleged German 'Corpse-Conversion Factory'. On 10 April 1917 – barely four days after the United States had entered the war on the Allied side – a German newspaper carried a story of a factory being used to convert corpses *(kadavers)* into war commodities. A week later, the British press – for which atrocity stories were frequently good copy – accused the German government of boiling down *human* corpses to make soap. An official investigation was launched to ascertain the origins of the story. A Berlin newspaper had indeed reported the discovery in Holland of a railway carriage loaded with dead German soldiers. The train had been destined for Liège but had been diverted to Holland by mistake. A Belgian newspaper had picked up the story, claiming that the bodies were destined for soap bars. No further substantiating evidence could be found, save the testimony of a British army officer who reported that he had seen the Germans removing their dead from Vimy Ridge where there was a noticeable absence of German war graves. That, however, was enough for the British press who had a field-day with the story. Many members of the government who thought it was more likely that the word *kadaver* referred to horse flesh were none the less prepared to allow the publicity given to the story. The Foreign Secretary, Balfour, even went so far as to claim that, however flimsy the evidence, 'there does not, in view of the many atrocious actions of which the Germans have been guilty, appear to be any reason why it should not be true'! Had the British government swallowed its own propaganda? Perhaps it would be fairer to say that such was the success of the image of Hunnish brutality that 'facts' were frequently interpreted more in accordance with the stereotype than in light of the real evidence.

This was one reason why the greatest single propaganda coup of the war had to be treated with great caution and delicacy. The publication of the Zimmermann telegram was undoubtedly the crowning achievement of the British propaganda campaign in the United States and helped to bring the Americans firmly into the war on the Allied side. The story is also a classic example of the relationship between propaganda, censorship, and secret intelligence in the modern world.

Shortly after the outbreak of war, the British enjoyed three remarkable strokes of luck that gave them all three of the major German naval codes. The first, the HVB code used by the German Admiralty and warships to communicate with merchant vessels and each other, was seized by the Royal Australian Navy off Melbourne from a German steamship whose captain was still unaware that war had been declared. The second, the SKM code, which, once cracked, eventually yielded high grade German naval signals, was found by a Russian vessel on the body of a dead German sailor from the *Magdeburg*, sunk in the Baltic. The third remaining code, the VB code, was found in a chest by a British fishing vessel in November 1914. Courage, and luck again, was at work in securing the diplomatic codes used by the Germans. The courage belonged to a British-born Austrian wireless engineer, Alexander Szek, who worked on repairing the Brussels wireless station now in German hands. Szek managed to copy down much of the German diplomatic ciphers and handed them over to the British in the late summer of 1915. For his efforts, he was shot shortly afterwards – probably not by the Germans but by the British, who were afraid that he might inform the enemy of what he had done, thereby jeopardizing the code breaking operation. Good fortune, also in the summer of 1915, revealed the whereabouts of a complete German diplomatic codebook – in the basement of the India Office where it had been left as part of the abandoned luggage of a German vice consul who had been forced to flee Persia! As a result the British were able to monitor the cable traffic in and out of Germany; by the end of 1915 they could also decipher most of it.

All this was carried out in Room 40 at the Admiralty. When, therefore, in the early hours of the morning of 16 January 1917, the night duty officers in Room 40 intercepted a telegram from the German foreign minister, Zimmermann, to the German ambassador in Washington, Count Bernstorff, proposing to introduce unrestricted submarine warfare from 1 February and suggesting an alliance with Mexico in the event of American intervention, they knew immediately that they had a propaganda bombshell on their hands. Most of the message was deciphered immediately; enough at least to grasp its meaning and significance. But two major problems remained: first, how to convince the Americans that it was authentic, especially since American code-breakers could not crack the ciphers and thereby verify the telegram; and, second, whether to risk publicizing it and thereby inform the enemy that their codes had been broken. Moreover, the telegram had been sent via the American cables, which the British were reluctant to admit they had also been tapping for fear of antagonizing Washington. While Room 40 and its flamboyant chief 'Blinker' Hall pondered the problems, the Germans, right on schedule, launched their unrestricted U-boat campaign to starve Britain into submission. A copy of the telegram was obtained from the Mexican end and duly deciphered using the India Office fluke; this eased the worry about revealing to the Americans the degree to which Britain's codebreaking activities extended to neutrals. On 23 February, Balfour handed the telegram over to the American ambassador in London, Walter Page, and it was published in the United States on 1 March. Not unnaturally, it caused a sensation. The Germans were actually threatening to bring the Old World's war into America's back garden; Mexico had been offered their lost territories of Texas and Arizona in return for offering a springboard to invasion. Remember the Alamo!

In fact, President Wilson, who barely six months earlier had fought and won a presidential election on a 'Keep America out of the War' ticket, had already made up his mind to intervene on the Allied side before he heard of the Zimmermann telegram from Walter Page. The growing economic dependence of the Allies upon American money, the unrestricted U-boat campaign itself, the memories of the *Lusitania*, the numerous other passenger liners sunk by the Germans, the Bryce report, all combined with the quietly persistent and skilfully handled secret British propaganda campaign to help Americans 'take the right view' of the issues, and the USA duly declared war on Germany on 6 April 1917. But the Zimmermann telegram undoubtedly helped to smooth Wilson's path with the powerful anti-interventionist lobby. And any lingering doubts as to the authenticity of the Zimmermann telegram were, in an astonishing fit of stupidity, dispelled by the German foreign minister himself on 3 March when he admitted that he had sent it. Room 40 had also been able to disguise the fact that their code had been broken from the Germans, who assumed that a decoded copy of the telegram had been stolen in Mexico. Even better was the fact the American codebreakers, who had been given nothing of worth but enough to convince them that the telegram was genuine, got most of the credit for deciphering it.

Once the Americans had entered the war, there was obviously less need for the British to concentrate so much of their propaganda in their direction and Wellington House declined in importance. A week after declaring war, the Americans set up their own propaganda organization, the Committee on Public Information (CPI), under the direction of George Creel, a journalist and supporter of the president. This body was responsible for censorship and propaganda, although Creel was more interested in 'expression rather than suppression'. He later described its work as 'a plain publicity proposition, a vast enterprise in salesmanship, the world's greatest adventure in advertising'. The Creel Committee was divided into two sections, the Domestic, which attempted to mobilize America for war, and the Foreign, subdivided into the Foreign Press Bureau, the Wireless and Cables Service, and the Foreign Film Service. The Foreign section supervised offices in more than thirty overseas countries. More than twenty further subdivisions handled the specialized aspects of the work. Like Wellington House before it, this body was staffed with writers and journalists but, unlike the British body, it operated in full view of the public. These men poured out millions of pamphlets, often dealing with issues of personal concern to their liberal, reform-minded intellectual authors who often seemed more determined to reaffirm the ideals of the American republic than to combat Prussian militarism. In other words, many of the CPI's staff saw their appointment as an ideal opportunity to promote an ideology of American democracy at a time when America itself was undergoing significant social transformations, such as the growth of cities and the closing of the frontier (which in turn affected immigration). Such an ideology could therefore provide a unifying cohesion for a country as diverse as America at a time of war and social change.

A major concern of the Creel Committee was how to bring home to ordinary Americans why they were now involved in a war being fought over 4000 miles away. Despite the U-boats, and given that the first trans-Atlantic flight did not take place until 1919, the American homeland was not itself directly threatened. Making it appear so was done in a variety of ways. Firstly, official speeches suggested that America was fighting a war for peace, freedom, and justice for *all* peoples. Even ordinary Germans deserved the benefits of democracy rather than the oppression of autocrats and ruthless military regimes. As President Wilson stated in 1917: 'We have no quarrel with the German people. We have no feeling towards them but one of sympathy and friendship. It is not upon their impulse that their government acted in entering this war.' This kind of tone was to set an example to the other Allies, whose major propaganda theme against the enemy for the rest of the war was to divide the German people from their leaders. But it also served to warn Americans that their enemy was a regime, not a people, an ideology rather than an army, and that if such an autocratic regime triumphed, democracy everywhere would be endangered.

The CPI had an established source of anti-German propaganda in the atrocity stories already circulating in Allied countries. These were duly drawn upon to demonstrate the nature of the Kaiser's regime and its incompatibility with democratic ideals. The Kaiser was portrayed as a devil in a spiked helmet, German soldiers as violators of innocent women (nurses and nuns being favourite targets of their lust) and child murderers. Germany's record in Belgium, Mexico, and in the Atlantic was also exploited as an illustration of German *kultur*. British propagandists were only too happy to help in supplying material, such as the cartoons of Louis

Raemakers, which by October 1917 had been reproduced in more than 2000 American newspapers with a combined circulation of just under 250 million readers. A captured German U-boat was even sent to America on loan for public display. But the British had to be particularly careful not to antagonize American opinion and were now happy to let the Americans themselves take the lead. The CPI attempted to promote an internationalist mentality to justify intervention as an American mission to bring democracy to the Old World. The message was taken into the schools, for instance through the CPI's publication *The National School Service,* into the factories, and indeed into all public places including the motion picture theatres which now became centres for overt jingoism.

With radio still largely at the stage of morse-code transmissions, a network of speakers was formed known as the Four Minute Men who gave a million four-minute speeches to perhaps 400 million people. They were highly successful in stirring up emotions, increasing the level of popular involvement in the war, promoting the sale of war bonds, and aiding recruitment. America was also bombarded with posters, photographs, and exhibitions, while American advertising companies, which had done so much pre-war to pioneer modern sales techniques, were also employed to bring their professional expertise to the campaign. The American motion picture industry was rapidly emerging as the most powerful in the world as a result of the effects of the war on European film production. Having moved in large part from New York to Hollywood, it was only too happy to help the government through the War Co-operation Committee of the Motion Picture Industry whose chairman was D. W. Griffith, the renowned director of *Birth of a Nation* (1915), a film which symbolized the transformation of the cinema into a serious art form and an instrument of mass persuasion. Stars like Charlie Chaplin, Douglas Fairbanks, Mary Pickford, and William Hart appeared in such films as *The Great Liberty Bond Hold-up* (1917), a short trailer which exploited the screen images of its stars for war bond ('liberty bonds') sales, and the feature *The Little American* (1917), directed by Cecil B. De Mille, about a young girl (Mary Pickford) who travels to France to visit her sick aunt. *En route* her ship is torpedoed (no prizes for guessing by whom). Arriving in France she witnesses German atrocities, supplies information to the French about German positions, is arrested by the Germans but is rescued just before she is due to be executed by firing squad. At home, spy films brought the German threat to American soil itself, whilst films such as *The Hun Within* (1918), *The Kaiser, the Beast of Berlin* (1918) and *The Claws of the Hun* (1918) also helped to maintain the overall climate of anti-German sentiment.

With such a willing partner, the American government might be forgiven for leaving film propaganda solely to Hollywood, but the CPI was not always happy with the dream factory's more zealous wartime products. After a slow start, the CPI's Films Division itself produced over sixty official films, ranging from feature films like *Pershing's Crusaders* to a weekly newsreel, *The Official War Review*. The US Army Signal Corps was designated as an official film unit in July 1917, and although it was perhaps to achieve greater fame in the Second World War, when top Hollywood professionals were recruited to serve in it, the initially inexperienced army cameramen of 1917-18 were able to produce some impressive combat footage that was included in many CPI compilation films such as *America's Answer* (1918) and *Our Colored Fighters* (1918). The official films were less overtly propagandistic than the commercial industry's productions. They were designed to serve military needs (recruitment and morale), to inform and educate, and to serve as historical 'records'. In other words, they represented part of the CPI's philosophy that it was its duty to engage in patriotic education for a modern democracy.

With an average weekly audience of 80 million, together with a growing appreciation of the role of the cinema's power to persuade and inform, the CPI could ill afford to ignore the movies as an instrument of propaganda. And just in case the Hollywood products were not serving national interests in the movie theatres, Four Minute Men would turn up to deliver their oration between reel changes. All means of communication were therefore used to enhance the sense of American nationalism, but the CPI was felt by some to be a threat to the very democracy in whose name America was fighting. By arguing that the needs of the government outweighed the needs of the individual, the CPI was felt to be flying in the face of an American philosophical institution. In fact, Creel and his colleagues felt that the war had brought out certain issues concerning the role of the State and its relationship with its people in the modern world that America needed to confront. But all that would be irrelevant unless Germany could be defeated.

The Creel Committee's major preoccupation was with the domestic front, but the Americans could only join in the work already begun by their allies in the campaign against enemy morale. Here again, the leading practitioners were the British. The French did have a substantial propaganda organization, the Maison de la Press, but it was the constant subject of political suspicion and infighting. Its most useful work was done in the German occupied areas of France where it attempted to keep its citizens in touch with Paris's conduct of the war. But the French modelled their propaganda organization on the British and, by 1918, the British organization was at its most complex. Wellington House had gone into decline, its task done. A Ministry of Information was created under Lord Beaverbrook to deal with all propaganda in allied and neutral countries while the Department of Enemy Propaganda was formed at Crewe House under Lord Northcliffe. This was the work of Lloyd George, Prime Minister since 1916, who was passionately interested in propaganda and who disliked the career diplomats who had been doing such sterling work in America. Lloyd George wanted to see the target audience of Britain's propaganda widened beyond opinion-making élites. For this, he wanted to recruit the services of Fleet Street (Northcliffe owned many newspapers, including *The Times* and the *Daily Mail*; Beaverbrook owned the *Daily Express*). Besides, by harnessing the energies of the newspaper barons into the service of government, it might also disincline them to criticize his government. But there was a danger in the eyes of many critics that this type of propaganda machinery might be used for political purposes at home by helping to sustain an unscrupulous government in power.

It is too often thought that British propaganda directed against the enemy began with the creation of Crewe House. In fact, the campaign predated Northcliffe. One veteran German soldier recalled:

In the year 1915, the enemy started his propaganda among our soldiers. From 1916 it steadily became more intensive and at the beginning of 1918, it had swollen into a storm cloud. One could now see the effects of this gradual seduction. Our soldiers learned to think the way the enemy wanted them to think.

The man who wrote this was none other than Adolf Hitler. In *Mein Kampf*, the future German leader devoted two chapters to the subject of propaganda that reflect his admiration for the British campaign as well as his appreciation of its finer points, such as the importance of timing, cumulative effects, and repetition. They were lessons he himself was to put to formidable use later.

More senior German figures, such as General Ludendorff, were also impressed with the work of 'The Ministry for the Destruction of the German Confidence'. He said that 'we were hypnotized by the enemy propaganda as a rabbit is by a snake'. All this enemy testimony to the effectiveness of the Allied campaign has to be treated carefully: would, for example, they have been so complimentary if the Germans had won the war? In other words, many figures in defeated Germany used propaganda as an excuse for defeat. But there was an ominous conclusion to the explanation. The argument ran as follows: the German armies were not defeated on the field of battle; Germany had not been invaded; indeed Germany had been victorious in the East with the Treaty of Brest-Litovsk (1918). How then did Germany lose the war? Because she was betrayed from within; Allied propaganda had caused a collapse of morale at home; the German armies had therefore been 'stabbed in the back'. This thesis was, of course, used by right-wing elements in the Weimar Germany of the 1920s to 'prove' a Jewish-Bolshevik conspiracy that was to help Hitler to power in 1933.

But how valid was the thesis? It was certainly true that the British began practising psychological warfare early in 1915. At first the military authorities were reluctant; as General Wilson stated, propaganda was 'a minor matter – the thing was to kill Germans'. But after the Germans began dropping leaflets over Allied lines around Nancy during the battle of Grande-Couronne in September 1914, even producing the *Gazette des Ardennes* for the benefit of French troops, the British decided to respond through the Director of Special Intelligence and the department known as MI7. By March 1915, a full scale 'paper war' had developed between the German airforce and the Royal Flying Corps. Six months later, the French established their own Service de la Propagande Aerienne, dropping *La Voix du Pays* over the occupied areas. But these types of operations were obviously directed at the troops; German civilians were a long way out of range of Allied aircraft. The leaflets would contain news denied the other side, maps showing the way home, descriptions of how well prisoners were being treated, and so on. As the Allied blockade of Germany began to bite, menus from London restaurants were reproduced to illustrate the futility of the German submarine campaign to starve Britain into submission. Other methods used included loudspeakers placed along the trenches which would announce the futility of the enemy's plight. In Basle in neutral Switzerland, the British Consul even had as one of his tasks the placing of propaganda messages in bottles which he then floated down the Rhine into Germany. It is hardly credible that such methods fuelled the German revolution and brought about the abdication of the Kaiser in 1918.

Moreover, for most of 1918, the principal method of distributing enemy propaganda was by balloon, not aeroplane. This was because, at the end of 1917, four captured British airmen were tried by a German court martial 'for having distributed pamphlets containing insults against the German army and Government among German troops in the Western Theatre of War'. Although two of the accused were acquitted due to lack of evidence, and although the court itself questioned the ruling about whether this act was a violation of international law, two officers were sentenced to ten years' imprisonment. When news of this punishment reached the War Office in January 1918, all leaflet dropping by aeroplane was suspended. Reprisals were threatened resulting in the pardoning of the two officers, who were returned to their camps and treated as normal prisoners of war. But the Air Ministry remained reluctant to commit its men and machines to leaflet raids and the suspension order remained in force until October 1918, barely a month before the end of the war. Instead the British relied on distribution by balloon over the Western Front, but given that the absolute maximum range of most balloons was about fifty miles, only occasional freak conditions allowed German civilians to be reached until the crucial days of early November 1918 when aircraft resumed distribution. But given the cumulative nature of propaganda – and the treatment meted out to the two British officers in late 1917 would suggest a long-standing fear of Allied propaganda on the part of the German High Command – explanation for the 'stab-in-the-back' thesis must lie elsewhere.

In fact, Crewe House had initially chosen to target Germany's ally Austria-Hungary. Following the Bolshevik revolution and the subsequent Russian withdrawal from the war, the situation in Germany appeared to offer less prospect of a propaganda success than conditions in the Hapsburg empire, where crippling mass strikes broke out in January 1918. The multi-national nature of Austria-Hungary provided scope for separatist propaganda. President Wilson led the way on 8 January 1918 with perhaps the most significant propaganda speech of the war when he proclaimed his Fourteen Points calling, amongst other things, for a readjustment of Italy's frontiers along lines of nationality, autonomy for the peoples of Austria-Hungary, including the establishment of self-governing states for the Yugoslavs, Poles, Rumanians, and Serbians. This declaration of policy – the most substantial of the war to date – provided Crewe House with the green light to foster the disintegration of the Dual Monarchy through the promotion of internal disaffection and even insurrection amongst the 'oppressed nationalities' which, in turn, would weaken Germany's capacity to sustain the fight. An additional bonus was the fact that, unlike the Germans, the Austrians had made no threats concerning captured pilots distributing propaganda by aeroplane.

Between May and October 1918, some 60 million copies of 643 different leaflets in eight languages, together with 10 million copies of 112 different newspapers in four languages, were distributed by the Allies in Austria-Hungary. By the end of the period, desertions were taking place on a massive scale. One source claims that hundreds of thousands of Slavs surrendered without a fight, and many were found to be carrying Allied propaganda material – despite the penalty of death if they had been caught doing so by the Austro-Hungarian authorities. Eight hundred leaflets were found on 350 prisoners of war on a single day. When on 16 October, the Emperor Charles, in anticipation of certain defeat, conceded to the nationalities the right to form their own separate states, thus taking Austria-Hungary out of the war as an effective ally, Germany could have made some claim to have been stabbed in the back – but by her own ally.

Part of Germany's problem was the inadequacy of her own propaganda machinery. From the outset, despite being prepared in advance, Germany's war propaganda was poorly organized and co-ordinated. The Kriegspresseamt, the German Press Bureau, had the dual function of supplying war news to the German press and co-ordinating the maintenance of morale at home and among the troops. Unlike the British, who had separate departments for these specialized areas, the German body was thus overburdened and its work diluted. It chose to concentrate on war news rather than on morale, with the result that, when Allied propaganda began to escalate in 1917 and 1918, morale was revealed to have been seriously neglected. German attempts at counter-propaganda therefore came too late. The Army High Command began a programme of patriotic instruction among the troops using films, army newspapers, and lectures; but, as previously, this work was conducted by the military authorities whose first priority – not unnaturally – was waging war. They appreciated too late that modern warfare required as much attention to the munitions of the mind as to the planning of battles. Even the German army's own news-sheet, *Nachrichtenblatt der 18 Armee,* admitted on the eve of defeat:

> In the sphere of leaflet propaganda the enemy has defeated us. Shooting poison darts from a secure hiding place was never a German art. We realized, however, that this struggle is a life-and death matter, and that one has to fight the enemy with his own weapons. Yet the spirit of the enemy leaflets skulks around and refuses to be killed.

Despite rewards for handing in enemy leaflets, and severe punishments for not, the German military authorities were simply unable to provide the victories necessary to dislodge the seeds of discontent sown by earlier Allied propaganda and exploited with ruthless efficiency by Crewe House both in and behind the German lines.

Propaganda, by itself, could not of course have defeated the Germans. After four years of stalemate and the failure of the last great German offensive in July, the preconditions of Germany's internal collapse were rapidly becoming evident. Despite the momentary triumph over Russia, the unrestricted U-boat campaign that had done so much to provoke America's entry into the war ultimately failed to force the Allies into submission. Food shortages caused by the Allied blockade, socialist-pacifist propaganda inspired by Bolshevik Russia, and the arrival of the American troops on the Western Front all seriously affected the German will to fight, let alone win. The collapse of Austria-Hungary was a further blow. Thus when Crewe House began to concentrate its attention on German morale in the summer of 1918, having already contributed materially to the Hapsburg collapse, the internal cohesion of the German Empire was already beginning to disintegrate. But the question remains: how far did Allied propaganda actually contribute to the final collapse of German morale, and was it civilian or military morale that collapsed, or both?

In 1918, the War Office began to compile information as to whether interrogated German prisoners claimed that they had been influenced by propaganda. These were rudimentary investigations and they are far from conclusive. Even so, many prisoners were found to possess propaganda material when they were captured. Of the 48 reports compiled between 13 May and 17 October on the effectiveness of balloon propaganda, only one contained an adverse comment by a German prisoner of war. Deserters in particular spoke of the propaganda leaflets with great enthusiasm, stating that at times they had even been exchanged for money and had indeed contributed towards their eventual decision to surrender. One American source claims that 80 per cent of captured prisoners were found to be carrying leaflets. Of course, statements made by captured prisoners are often suspect; often they would say merely what they thought their interrogators wanted to hear. But the millions of leaflets dropped over German lines in the final months of war were clearly getting through and were being read. Whether or not they actually produced a general collapse of morale among the German troops is, however, unlikely. There was certainly no large-scale military uprising on a par with the experience of troops in Russia. Yet where British propaganda may have had a significant effect was in those rest areas and readjustment camps just behind the lines where soldiers tried to relax after the exhilaration of battle and where they had time to read the leaflets, as well as letters from home that talked of the deprivations and hardships of German family life under the Blockade. It was here, and on leave, that most soldier-civilian interaction was most likely to occur, and it was here that British propagandists were at their most effective.

The German Army argued consistently that insufficient attention had been paid to civilian morale by the German propaganda organization. In Britain, this was not quite the case. There were no post-war debates about whether British morale had cracked and thereby affected the final outcome. However, patriotism was not by itself enough. Certainly, during the first eighteen months of the war, the British government had tended to rely on this factor alone. On the outbreak of war, the British Regular Army totalled 160,000 men – large enough, as Bismarck had once quipped, for the German police force to arrest. Although it was far from being the 'contemptible little army' many Germans believed it to be, this highly professional volunteer force was clearly not large enough to make any decisive impact on the course of this new struggle. Accordingly, Lord Kitchener, who was rare among soldiers and politicians at that time in believing that the war would not be a short one, launched on 8 August 1914 his appeal for men to take up the sword of justice and fight for King and Country. At first, there was no shortage of volunteers; within a month, the figures had reached 30,000 a day. Recruitment stands set up by the War Office throughout the nation found it difficult to cope with the sheer weight of volunteers who rushed forward to sign up in response to Kitchener's outstretched index finger inviting them to enlist simply because 'Your King and Country Needs You'. The initial flood, however, soon dwindled into a stream and then into a trickle as enthusiasm began to fade. Because of the horrendous casualties on the Western Front, the shortage of volunteers was so alarming that conscription became inevitable. In the meantime, however, the early attempt by the Parliamentary Recruiting Committee (PRC) to raise a volunteer force marked the first modern systematic official propaganda campaign in Britain directed at the mass of the civilian population. Recruitment was to remain the dominant theme of domestic propaganda until the introduction of conscription in January 1916 and was to serve as the principal focal point of the individual citizen's commitment to the national war effort.

The methods employed at the start of the war were largely variations on the famous Kitchener appeal. They were generally straightforward in their imagery and messages, depicting a Union Jack or a popular military hero calling for volunteers. Amateur and unofficial propagandists were in abundance, and there was also the enormously jingoistic influence of the press. Once recruitment began to dwindle, the campaign adopted a more threatening tone by depicting those who were already fighting and thus, by implication, suggesting that there were those who were not doing their fair share. Hence the message: 'Who's absent – is it You?' with John Bull pointing an accusing finger. Pressure was thereby exerted not just directly on potential recruits who had not yet joined up, but also indirectly on their families, who were also expected to make the sacrifice. Hence 'Women of Britain Say Go' and 'What did you do in the Great War, Daddy?' Posters, cigarette cards, lectures, films, and recruitment rallies all made the same point: it was more patriotic and socially acceptable to go rather than stay.

This pressure became more difficult to exert as casualty figures from France continued to rise. In January 1916 compulsion rather than patriotism became the key element in recruitment. But pacifism was also on the increase, especially after the battles of Verdun, the Somme, and Ancre. Clearly, more concerted efforts to sustain the will to fight among the civilian population were required and in 1917 the National War Aims Committee (NWAC) was set up to concentrate upon domestic propaganda. The NWAC continued many of the methods used by the PRC to maintain the level of popular commitment to the war. Films, in particular, were effective among the working classes who were becoming increasingly attracted to the pacifist Labour Party. Films such as the highly popular *Britain Prepared* (1915), *The Battle of the Somme* (1916), and *Battle of the Ancre and the advance of the Tanks* (1917) capitalized on the growing popularity of the cinema as a mass form of entertainment by injecting patriotic themes that were all the more effective for being transmitted in the context of entertainment. The British government even commissioned D. W. Griffith to make *Hearts of the World* (1918), a propaganda film about a small French village under German occupation, which was portrayed with great brutality. Another aggressively anti-German film was *The Leopard's Spots* (1918), barely $2\frac{1}{2}$ minutes long, which was actually discussed in Parliament under the erroneous title *Once a Hun, Always a Hun*. This film depicted two German soldiers in a ruined French town who attack a woman and her baby; the same two characters then appear as commercial travellers in an English village after the war trying to sell their wares. An English shopkeeper is impressed by a pan they show him until his wife appears and finds the words 'Made in Germany' on the underside. They are promptly thrown out of the shop and a caption appears (films still being silent) declaring: 'There must be no trading with these people after the war'.

The effect of this kind of hate-inspired war propaganda was to be felt on the return of peace when calls to 'Hang the Kaiser' and 'Make Germany Pay' were heard during the immediate post-war general election. If the First World War was really to be the 'War to end all Wars', then wartime recriminations would need to be quickly forgotten – not least so that Britain and Germany could resume their formerly lucrative trade links – essential if Germany was to pay her reparations and Britain her war-debts. The 'same old Hun' was, however, a resilient popular theme, the legacy of which was not even removed by the appeasement of the 1930s.

The wartime propaganda experience had four further consequences that were to prove just as damaging to future peace. The
first has already been discussed – namely, the use to which the likes
of Adolf Hitler manipulated the alleged role of propaganda in
wartime to serve their own political purposes. Less well appreciated
is the role played by propaganda in the creation of those new states
in central and eastern Europe. When President Wilson announced
his Fourteen Points in January 1918 he was making the most
detailed statement of war aims of any Allied leader to that date.
But they nonetheless remained somewhat generalized and when the
subject nationalities of central and eastern Europe pressed for more
details, they were not exactly forthcoming. However, even general
promises about national self-determination provided Allied propagandists with their best opportunity yet to offer real incentives to
the 'oppressed nationalities' and the newly created Crewe House
seized upon them with great vigour. The problem was that, in the
process, they often made promises about the post-war settlement
that were yet to be agreed by the Allied governments. This broke
one of the fundamental tenets of effective war propaganda: that
policy and propaganda should be conducted hand-in-hand. Lord
Northcliffe was quite willing to force the British government's
hand by propaganda promises about policies that had yet to be
decided in anything other than in terms of general principle. These
particular chickens came home to roost in the Paris Peace Conference
of 1919, when the Poles, Slavs, Czechs, Rumanians, and so on all
turned up expecting those promises to be fulfilled. The result was
the creation of a series of independent central and eastern
European states created in accordance with the principle of self-
determination on ethnographic, rather than strategic or economic,
lines. The Italians in particular were furious. They had entered the
war on the Allied side in 1915 under the secret Treaty of London in
return for post-war territorial gains in south-eastern Europe that
were now being denied them by the principle of self-determination.
They left Paris disappointed and disillusioned, seized Fiume
(Trieste) in a clash with newly-created Yugoslavia and, in a wave of
nationalist euphoria, began the swing to the right that saw
Mussolini appointed Prime Minister in 1922. Wartime propaganda
had played a significant part in Mussolini's rise and he himself was
to convert the lessons of the wartime experience into peacetime use.
There was a third legacy of the wartime propaganda experiment

that was to have serious peacetime consequences, this time concerning the United States. Following the decision of the American Senate in late 1919 not to ratify the Versailles Treaty with Germany, a series of investigations was launched into the reasons for American entry into the war. During the course of these enquiries, many of the details concerning the nature and scope of Britain's propaganda campaign in America between 1914 and 1917 came to light. The conclusion was that the United States had indeed been duped into becoming involved on the Allied side, particularly by secret British propaganda emanating from Wellington House. A series of historical investigations by learned scholars reinforced what was fast becoming a legendary belief in the power of propaganda. The debate was, however, seized upon by isolationist elements in American politics who now argued for non-involvement in European affairs and for Americans to be on their guard against devious foreign propaganda. Indeed, such was the degree of American sensitivity to foreign propaganda that in 1938 the Foreign Agents Registration Act was passed by Senate requiring the registration with the US government of all foreign propagandists operating on American soil. The act remains in force to this day. During the 1930s, when American support might have strengthened the hand of the European democracies in their dealings with the dictatorships, the use of propaganda as a means of gaining that support was largely denied the very countries who had pioneered its wartime use.

As it turned out, the British chose to dismantle their wartime propaganda machinery on the return of peace. It had never been an activity with which the British had felt comfortable. True, it had played an invaluable role in wartime, both in helping to bring America into the war and in contributing to the defeat of the enemy. But there was felt to be no function for it in peacetime. The whole business left a bad taste in the mouths of the English gentlemen who presided over a British Empire that appeared to be at the height of its power and prestige. Never before had so many parts of the map been shaded red; the wartime achievement of the British was plain for all to see. Where was the need for further propaganda? Lord Ponsonby reflected the mood of many when he wrote in 1926 that 'the injection of the poison of hatred into men's minds by means of falsehood is a greater evil in wartime than the actual loss of life. The defilement of the human soul is worse than the destruction of the human body.' That an activity which attempted to persuade a soldier to lay down his arms and stop fighting was somehow morally worse than actually killing him might seem peculiar today. But it was quite common in Britain after the First World War and reflected how much the meaning of the word 'propaganda' had changed since 1911 when the *Encyclopaedia Britannica* had described it as an activity relating largely to religious persuasion. But the popularity and virulence of wartime atrocity propaganda in particular led to a different meaning being assigned to the term and to the British abandoning their initiatives in this field. The British had demonstrated to the world the enormous power of propaganda in war but had abandoned it in peacetime; Soviet Russia and, later, Nazi Germany now took up where the British had left off.

But there was a fourth, and perhaps even more tragic, consequence. Lord Ponsonby had written his opinion following a postwar investigation into the accuracy of wartime atrocity stories. This and other enquiries could find little or no evidence that any of them had been true. The effect of this atrocity propaganda, however, led to a general disinclination on the part of the public in the 1930s and 1940s to believe real atrocity stories that began to come out of Nazi Germany. In this respect, the distortions of the First World War merely served to obscure the realities of the Second.

Chapter 22

The Bolshevik Revolution and the War of Ideologies (1917-39)

The 'war to end all wars' did not live up to its name. Neither did the peace treaties that concluded it herald a return of world peace. As the Chief of the Imperial General Staff noted in 1919 after counting 44 wars in progress, 'this peace treaty has resulted in wars everywhere'. The year 1918 may have seen the end of the Great War but international conflict none the less remained. Most notably, there was an intensification of a struggle that had begun with the Bolshevik seizure of power in Russia in 1917 and which raged intermittently for the next 70 years, sometimes as open war, sometimes postponed, and mostly, since 1945, as Cold War. It was essentially a struggle between two diametrically opposed ideologies in which propaganda has always played a central role. The Bolshevik Revolution may well have taken Russia out of the First World War, but it also led to a new and significant development in the conduct of international affairs. After 1917, propaganda became a fact of everyday life. For Lenin and his successors, who owed so much to the successful employment of propaganda in securing power at the expense of the tsars, propaganda also became an essential ingredient in the ideological war against capitalism and the struggle for world revolution. But it also had to be used to spread the word internally to the vast majority of peasants initially untouched by the actual events of the revolution in St Petersburg but whose lives were to be changed radically by them, particularly during the crucial days of the Civil War (1918-21).

The crusading element in Marxist ideology, to bring the essential 'truth' to the peasants and working classes of both Russia and the wider world, combined with the experience of underground struggle and covert resistance, led to great emphasis being placed by

Lenin and his supporters on the role of propaganda in helping to secure power and to maintain it. The Russian revolutionaries were, of course, great publicists. Working from underground presses, frequently from abroad, they began to distribute their ideas long before the revolution itself through such publications as *Iskra* ('The Spark') and *Pravda* ('Truth'). Yet despite the reputation of *Iskra* for lighting the spark that fuelled the revolution, its importance as a propaganda newspaper was never matched by its popularity. It was printed in Munich, edited by Plekhanov, and smuggled into Russia via Switzerland under the supervision of Lenin's wife Krupskaya, but its somewhat doctrinaire and intellectual style made it rather heavy reading and its circulation never reached more than 40,000. Following the 1904 split between the Bolsheviks and the Mensheviks, *Iskra* passed into the latter's hands, whereupon the Bolsheviks founded other papers. Trotsky was responsible for founding *Pravda* in 1912 and its circulation rose steadily thanks to its simpler and more readable style. During its first two years, the paper was closed down nine times by the authorities.

The Great War gave impetus to the Bolshevik cause, particularly when, following the abdication of the tsar in February 1917, Russia continued its involvement. The Germans even helped the Bolsheviks produce a version of *Pravda* for the trenches that helped to foster pacifist agitation and the paper reopened in Petrograd. *Izvestia* ('News') was founded. Also at home, the Bolsheviks were able to play upon growing war-weariness with their ideological messages through the use of such masterly slogans as 'Peace, Land and Bread' and 'All Power to the Soviets'. And, of course, there was the oratorical skill of Lenin himself. From his position in exile before 1917 he also had every opportunity to study the propaganda battles being waged on the various military and civilian fronts; he returned to Russia as an expert in the role which indoctrination and mass persuasion could play both at home and abroad. Perhaps this, ironically, was the greatest German propaganda achievement of the First World War.

A major obstacle to Lenin was the illiteracy of the mass of the Russian people and thus the relatively limited role which newspapers could play. *Izvestia* had the largest circulation with 400,000 copies at its highest point; *Pravda*'s was barely a third of that – tiny figures given the size of the Russian population. Yet the masses *were* historically and culturally receptive to icons, which had formed a central role in their daily and spiritual life for centuries. If that tradition could be adapted to transmit political images through modern means of communication, then the Bolsheviks stood a good chance of getting their message across. This meant using posters, and before long the Bolsheviks were producing posters of such design and imagination that they have often been regarded as works of art. Indeed posters of the Civil War period are regarded as being among the most impressive contributions to pictorial art ever made by the Soviet Union. The poster, like the icon, could present symbols in a simple and easily identifiable way, even to barely literate peasants. A style of visual story-board poster – not unlike the modern cartoon strip – emerged that is still popular today. Experimentation in this new form led men with no formal artistic training, such as D. S. Orlov and V. Deni, to emerge as the principal exponents of poster art. But it was Mikhail Cheremnykh who originated the most distinctive posters of the Civil War period – the 'Satire Window' format, sometimes known as the ROSTA windows. ROSTA were the initials of the Bolsheviks' Telegraph Agency, set up in September 1918, and this organization published its own newspapers. Because of severe paper shortages, however, Cheremnykh devised the idea of wall newspapers to be pasted in busy parts of Moscow and in shop windows. Posters soon followed and the idea quickly spread to other cities. By the end of the Civil War, ROSTA had nearly fifty agencies around the country using these methods, the window posters of the poet Mayakovsky being especially successful. But their success was limited to the Civil War period. They often attracted more artistic than political attention, and the avant-garde movement which pioneered them accordingly went into decline after 1921.

The Allied invasion of Russia in support of the White counter-revolutionaries began before the First World War ended. While Britain, France, and Germany slugged it out on the Western Front, the fighting being intensified by the release of German troops from the east following the Russo-German Treaty of Brest-Litovsk in March 1918, Allied troops (principally Japanese) landed at Vladivostok on the Pacific coast of Russia in the following month. But the western powers at this stage were not motivated by ideo-logical considerations. Alarmed at Russia's departure from the war, the move was designed to keep Germany distracted in the east. Hence the British occupation of Murmansk in March 1918 and of

Archangel on 1 August. Even so, from Siberia, the Civil War spread to the Cossack territories and the Caucasus, but it was only after the defeat of Germany that the European Powers could afford to intervene more intensively. This gave time for Trotsky to build up the new Red Army and for the Cheka, the secret police, to establish its grip on the domestic population.

Following the Armistice with Germany, Allied intervention increased dramatically. The French landed at Odessa in the south in December, while the British and Japanese reinforced their detachments in northern Russia and in the Far East, the latter being joined by American forces. But, after four years of bloody war, public support for Allied intervention declined, particularly after the failure of the White generals Kolchak and Denikin to make substantial progress in their offensives of 1919. Poland took up the cause and attacked Russia in 1920 but, despite the help of the Ukrainians, suffered a series of defeats at the hands of the Red Army. The Treaty of Riga was signed in March 1921. By that time, most Allied troops had been withdrawn, with the Japanese finally evacuating completely in 1925. The White cause had collapsed. The Bolsheviks had survived.

The role of propaganda in all this chaos and confusion is difficult to evaluate. The Whites, to be sure, were less skilled in this as in most other areas, particularly in their failure to capture the support of the peasants. Their ideology also lacked the cohesion of their opponents. The presence of foreign troops on Russian soil in support of the Whites helped the Reds to play on nationalistic desires to drive the invaders out of Mother Russia but, as will be seen, this was not without its irony given the international aspirations of the Bolsheviks. But Russia was far from being a unified country; separatist elements exploited by the Whites in various republics made disintegration a very real possibility. The Bolsheviks for their part seized upon the disunity of their opponents while themselves unifying the towns and countryside behind their own party organization. This was done through a combination of agitation, terror, and propaganda. Lenin's land decree – his first act in power – was itself a masterstroke of propaganda and served to provide the basis by which the peasants could be won over. Activists went out into the countryside to take the news to the peasants that they now owned the land, to organize them, and to agitate.

However, as the Civil War dragged on, food shortages in the cities led to requisitioning, and this merely alienated the peasantry. The Bolsheviks responded with increased 'education' (i.e. propaganda) and the Commissariat of Enlightenment was formed to supervise public readings for the illiterate peasants, workers, and soldiers. The young – always a primary target for any aspiring propaganda state – were organized and indoctrinated through the Komsomol. Agit-ships went down rivers and agit-trains went into the countryside to take the message to the people. Agitational outposts, *agitpunkty*, were set up at railway stations complete with libraries and lecture halls for the purpose of establishing links 'between the localities and the centre, to agitate, to carry out propaganda, to bring information, and to supply literature'. Even the names of the agit-trains and agit-ships had a propaganda purpose: *V.I. Lenin*, *The October Revolution*, and *Red Star*. Each of these were highly decorated mobile propaganda units, covered in posters, flags, and slogans. They carried about a hundred people (including Cheka officers and representatives of all the leading Bolshevik committees) to organize selected local officials, a complaints section (always busy), its own press, a wireless transmitter, and, most important of all, a film projector.

Lenin's often quoted view that 'for us the most important of all arts is the cinema' reflected an appreciation of the role which the new mass media could play in the revolutionary context. Although the situation varied from city to city and from town to countryside, on average only two out of five adults were literate in the Russia of 1920. The most effective means of reaching the majority of uneducated Russians was by using film. For Lenin, the cinema was primarily an educational device – for political education, that is. For the audiences, it was primarily a medium of entertainment (Charlie Chaplin being particularly popular). For many peasants, who had never seen a film until the agit-trains brought one to them, it was a miracle. The fact that films at this time were silent helped to overcome the problem of communicating to the numerous different nationalities with their different languages. Foreign films, often portraying ideas that were incompatible with Bolshevik ideology, were popular and had to be countered by a domestic film industry that was not yet capable of meeting the needs of the revolution. Indeed, the Civil War momentarily destroyed the Russian film industry. It was not until 1927, after a period of reconstruction, that Soviet films earned more at the box-office than imported products. Lenin had nationalized the Russian film industry in August 1919 but, starved of film stock and equipment from abroad, not to mention the shortages of electricity and of those many technicians, actors, and directors who had fled the revolution, it was unlikely that film propaganda itself played a significant role in determining the final outcome of the revolution. What the available films did in the countryside was to attract a curious audience, whereupon the officials from the agit-trains would disembark to deliver their message using classic techniques of crowd manipulation.

From this disastrous beginning, however, the Soviet film industry soon began to produce one of the most acclaimed bodies of work in the history of world cinema. A national production company, Sovkino, was established in 1925 and new studios were set up in Moscow, Leningrad, Kiev, and Odessa; thirteen were functioning across the nation by 1928 producing 123 films in that year, each reaching an average audience of $2^{1}/_{2}$ million people. Virtually all the films were made to serve the State. *Battleship Potemkin* (1926), made by Sergei Eisenstein, portrayed the 1905 mutiny at Odessa but its message had more to do with propaganda than with history. Eisenstein's next film, *October* (1927), made to commemorate the tenth anniversary of the revolution, fell into a similar category. They had the feel of documentaries but concentrated on events rather than individuals. As a result, they are often mistaken even today as being film 'records' of what actually happened in the 1905 and 1917 revolutions rather than re-enactments designed to serve the interests of the Soviet state in the 1920s. Pudovkin's *End of St Petersburg* (1927), another anniversary classic, paid more attention to the human elements of the revolutionary struggle, but here again its message was symbolic and propagandistic rather than historical. Such films legitimized the revolution and thereby the regime that inherited it. They appear, however, to have created a greater impression abroad than they did at home.

Although the Soviets pioneered new methods of domestic propaganda that were watched with great interest by other countries, it was their foreign propaganda that caused most concern abroad. The Bolshevik leadership was certainly quick to appreciate the role propaganda could play in undermining the position of the 'capitalist-imperialist' powers and spreading its ideas about world revolution. In October 1917, for example, the Bolsheviks published various secret treaties that had been negotiated by the tsarist regime with the Allies, notably the 1915 Treaty of London. The embarrassment this caused the Allies – at a time when President Wilson was calling for national self-determination – was to contribute towards Italian disillusionment with the Paris Peace Settlement. Moreover, influenced by Trotsky's theories of world revolution, the role of propaganda in spreading an international class-based ideology that recognized no national frontiers was a serious threat to established regimes suffering from the intense socio-economic and political chaos caused by the First World War. Great hopes that the theories were about to become a reality with the revolution in Germany, followed by the establishment of a short-lived communist regime in Hungary, were reflected in the foundation of the Third International, or Comintern, in March 1919. Comintern agents were included in the staff of Soviet diplomatic missions; indeed, in the years immediately following the revolution, Soviet foreign policy and Soviet propaganda became virtually indistinguishable.

For Russia's former allies, the replacement of 'Prussian militarism' by Bolshevism as the principal perceived threat to civilization as they knew it was clearly a matter requiring urgent countermeasures. The British Empire, in particular, was a primary target for the Comintern and was identified as the main bastion of the world 'capitalist-imperialist' order. Troubles in Ireland, India, and Palestine provided ideal opportunities to stir up revolutionary activity. But Britain had also largely dismantled its efficient wartime propaganda machinery and had to rely on military intervention in the Civil War as its best means of stopping Comintern activities. Following the Red victory, the Communist International continued its activities, but the chance for world revolution seemed to have passed. Aid was given to the Chinese communists until Russian advisers were expelled in 1928. And the chance seemingly provided by the General Strike in Britain in 1926 also seemed to have faded. Following the death of Lenin in 1924 and the internal struggle for power which followed, resulting in Trotsky's expulsion and Stalin's accession, the economic chaos that the Civil War had created in Russia required urgent attention. With the adoption of the first Five Year Plan and of the policy of Socialism in One Country by the end of the 1920s, the Comintern went into decline.

Fear of Bolshevism in the western democracies, however,

remained. The formation of 'Little Moscows' in 1919 throughout Europe and America had rocked the established order. The Red Flag had even been hoisted over Glasgow Town Hall! Calls for the workers of the world to unite were made with the aid of the new medium of radio. For Lenin, radio was 'a newspaper without paper... and without boundaries'. When Radio Moscow began transmissions in 1922, it was the most powerful transmitter in the world. In 1925, it added the world's first short-wave transmitter. In the following year, when the General Strike in Britain conjured up memories of 'Red Clyde' and the widespread strikes of 1919, Radio Moscow tried to fuel the agitation until the British government jammed its broadcasts. Despite the Russian promise in the 1921 Anglo-Soviet Trade Agreement not to attack Britain by propaganda, violations continued throughout the next ten years, although by the end of the decade, with a more introspective Stalin in charge, the threat was felt to have subsided. Democracy in Britain, France, and America had survived its immediate post-war crises. Counter-measures (such as the banning of *The Battleship Potemkin* and other Soviet classics) seemed to have prevented the spreading of the Bolshevik word, and the powers looked forward to the restoration of peace amidst hopes for world disarmament.

The new spirit of optimism in the late 1920s saw important developments in the communications revolution: 1927 in fact was almost as momentous a year as 1896. That was the year of Charles Lindbergh's historic solo trans-Atlantic flight, which heralded the beginning of the end of North America's geographic isolation from Europe. With the rapid development of international civil aviation routes, the world was becoming more like a global village. The telephone also contributed to the feeling of a shrinking world, and in 1927 communication was established across the Atlantic by radio telephone. In the same year, the British Broadcasting Company became the British Broadcasting Corporation with the motto 'Nation shall speak peace unto Nation' and, within five years, the BBC had initiated its Empire Service designed to enable the far-flung peoples of the British Empire to remain in constant touch with the mother country. Australian broadcasts were heard in Britain for the first time in 1927. That year also witnessed the arrival of the first commercially successful talking picture, *The Jazz Singer*. Radio and the cinema, both in their infancy during the First World War, were the first true mass media and their implications for politics, propaganda, and warfare were to be far-reaching. In Glasgow, Baird demonstrated the transmission of colour television pictures in 1927 (the Russians had demonstrated the technology of television before even the First World War), although this particular medium was not to receive its real significance as a propaganda medium until the late 1940s.

The World Economic Depression that resulted from the collapse of the American stock market in 1929 quickly dashed the short-lived optimism of the late 1920s. In Germany, Hitler began his rapid rise to power and was appointed Chancellor in 1933. He then began to dismantle the Weimar democracy and establish the Nazi totalitarian state using many of the propaganda methods pioneered by the British and the Soviets. Meanwhile, the Japanese, also badly hit by the Depression, decided to abandon any notion of international collective security and attacked Manchuria in late 1931. World opinion was shocked by the first newsreel footage of military operations against civilians with the Japanese bombing of Chinese towns. The League of Nations, established in 1919 to safeguard a lasting peace, did nothing to punish the aggressor or protect the small power involved. Hitler walked out of both the World Disarmament Conference and the League of Nations and began rearming Germany. Mussolini attacked Abyssinia in 1935. Again the League was unable to prevent aggression. The Americans, never a League member, passed Neutrality Acts and tried to isolate themselves from mounting European aggression. France was in the middle of a political and economic crisis and was rocked by a series of scandals and riots. Britain, the only true world power with interests stretching from Europe through the Mediterranean to the Far East, found herself confronted by three potential enemies but totally unprepared to meet force with force. Russia, which could have helped by virtue of both her European and Far Eastern interests, decided to abandon her isolation and entered the League in 1934. A pact with France followed the next year. Whatever unfinished business Stalin had at home, the advent of a regime in Germany dedicated to the overthrow of communism was a threat he could not ignore. By the mid-1930s Europe was once again becoming increasingly polarized into two opposing camps and the ideological conflict between the forces of the left and the right was to become even more acute when the Spanish Civil War broke out in July 1936.

Coming as it did so rapidly after the crises in Europe, the Far East, and Africa, many observers felt that the Spanish Civil War could quite easily develop into a second world war. As in the case of the Russian Civil War, the European powers became involved in affairs that might at first appear to have had little to do with them. But although the Second World War broke out in 1939, Poland, not Spain, was the immediate cause. This was to some extent due to the fact that Britain and France, at least, tried desperately to limit the effects of the Spanish Civil War and prevent it from spreading into a wider conflict by a non-intervention agreement. Russia, Germany, and Italy, however, honoured the agreement more in the breach. They exploited the conflict for their own purposes and it became a major battleground in the international propaganda war of the 1930s – a dress rehearsal for things to come. By the late 1930s, in other words, propaganda had become an established fact of everyday life. International broadcasting, State-controlled cinemas and newspapers, public opinion polls, mass rallies: all these were new features of an age characterized by an ideological struggle with world-wide dimensions thanks to the technology of the communications revolution. As such, truth was a major casualty long before the actual fighting began.

Chapter 23

The Second World War

The Second World War witnessed the greatest propaganda battle in the history of warfare. For six years, all the participants employed propaganda on a scale that dwarfed all other conflicts, including even the First World War. There were several reasons why this was so. In the first place, this was a war between entire nations, even more so than in 1914-18. In the totalitarian nations, coercion had replaced consultation in the political process, democracy had been dismantled and the masses subjugated to the will of one party regimes. In many ways, 1939-45 was a battle between two new types of regime struggling for supremacy with one another in a battle for the future. Modern democracy and totalitarian dictatorship had both emerged from the First World War and 1939 was a testimony to their mutual incompatibility. There followed a struggle between mass societies, a war of political ideologies in which propaganda was merely one, albeit a significant, weapon. Moreover, the continued development of the communications revolution had, since the advent of sound cinema and radio, provided a direct link between government and those they governed, and between the government of one nation and the people of another. Propaganda was in this respect the alternative to diplomacy. The old rule that governments did not interfere with the internal affairs of others had been swept away by the Russian revolution. In addition, there was also the impact of modern technology on warfare, particularly the advent of the bomber which, for the first time, brought war 'into the front garden'.

Fear of the devastation that German bombers, attempting a sudden knock-out blow from the air, might cause, closed all British cinemas on the outbreak of the Second World War. However, significantly for the propaganda battle to come, the war began for most Britons on the radio. The Prime Minister's speech announcing the start of hostilities against Nazi Germany, broadcast by the BBC on that Sunday morning of 3 September 1939, established the moral high ground for democratic principles. Chamberlain informed his listeners:

> We have a clear conscience. We have done all that any country could do to establish peace, but a situation in which no word given by Germany's ruler could be trusted, and no people or country could feel themselves safe, had become intolerable... Now may God bless you all and may He defend the right. For it is evil things that we shall be fighting against: brute force, bad faith, injustice, oppression and persecution. And against them I am certain that the right will prevail.

This was not the sentiment of a tired old man who had seen the policy of appeasement – in which he had placed so much faith to preserve the peace so dearly won in 1918 – now in tatters following the German invasion of Poland. It was a brilliant propaganda speech by a skilled politician whose popular image as the 'Guilty Man of Munich' is not matched by the historical evidence. It was, in other words, a speech that established the essential moral justification for why Britain was fighting, for why (together with France) she had declared war on Germany rather than vice versa, and why the British people should now brace themselves for an onslaught of German bombers.

Chamberlain was right to point out that the British had declared war for just reasons. At Munich, twelve months previously, he and Hitler had signed an agreement whereby 3½ million Germans living unwillingly under Czechoslovakian rule in the Sudetenland would be transferred to the Third Reich. In other words, Munich was essentially about the application of the Wilsonian principle of national self-determination that had been denied Germany by the Versailles Treaty of 1919. The redressing of that mistake had been behind the British acceptance of the German reoccupation of the Rhineland in 1936 and the *Anschluss* with Austria in 1938. It was also fundamental to the Sudeten crisis, which almost boiled over into a war that nobody either wanted and or was prepared for. Too often it is forgotten that Munich was extremely popular at the time, both in Britain and Germany, and that Chamberlain was hailed all over the world as 'The Peacemaker', the 'Man of the Hour' who had brought Europe back from the brink of catastrophe.

Barely twelve months later, Chamberlain declared war on Germany believing that Armageddon might erupt a mere generation after the 'war to end war'. Poland, however, was the reason for war, but not the cause. The events of March 1939, not September 1938, demonstrated that Hitler could not be trusted, that he represented 'brute force, bad faith, injustice, oppression and persecution' – 'evil things' which no decent, peace-loving nation could tolerate, even at the risk of destroying civilization as the world had known it. For it was only when Hitler seized the rump of Czechoslovakia in March 1939 that the majority of people began to realize that Hitler could not be trusted, that he was intent upon war. Some reservations may have been felt after *Kristallnacht* (the 'Night of the Broken Glass') in November 1938, the biggest anti-Jewish pogrom to date. But Bohemia and Moravia were not Germany's backyard and, for the first time, non-Germans were compulsorily forced to join the Third Reich. No longer could Hitler legitimately argue that he was merely redressing German grievances against the Versailles Treaty. Chamberlain dropped appeasement overnight when that happened and immediately began to issue guarantees to the small states of central and south-eastern Europe next threatened by Hitler: Poland, Greece, Rumania, and Turkey. And too often it is forgotten that Britain had been rearming for a war against Germany since 1935. But she was far from ready in March 1939. Munich had provided a breathing-space, but shortages of money and skilled labour hindered the rearmament programme. Britain was hardly ready in September 1939 either, and it was only thanks to the extra year provided by Munich and the six month period of the 'Phoney War' that she could build enough Spitfires and Hurricanes to stave off the Luftwaffe in the Battle of Britain.

The war that began with a cavalry charge in Poland and ended six years later with the dropping of atomic bombs on Hiroshima and Nagasaki only became a World War in the real sense in 1941, when the Germans invaded Russia and the Japanese bombed the American fleet at Pearl Harbor. But the British people entered the war in 1939 against Germany with a unity and resignation to the inevitable that belied the fears and anxieties of the 1930s, when fear of the bomber had fuelled the tide of pacifism. They did not turn out in the streets to dance and cheer as they had done in August 1914, nor did they believe that it would all be over by

Christmas. But neither did they succumb to panic or despair. If anything, those feelings were more evident in government circles, where it was believed that, if only the knock-out blow could be survived, the British Empire might – just might – win a long war of attrition against the German military phoenix. This First World War type of thinking, with its emphasis on blockade, was matched by the government's attitude towards propaganda which placed initial emphasis on separating the German people from their leaders, as in 1918, but which soon developed into a much more sophisticated and even dirtier war of words.

The Luftwaffe did not arrive in hordes over British cities in that first winter. While the Germans fought the courageous Poles in the East, and divided the spoils with Stalin's Russia in accordance with the terms of the Nazi-Soviet Pact, war seemed a long way off for the majority of the British people. Britain prepared and took advantage of the time bought for it by the Poles. The cinemas were reopened by the end of September to cater for the increasing boredom caused by the absence of any war action in the West. In the meantime, the propaganda machinery was primed for the crisis to come. Whether through civilian bombing or through a war of attrition, morale would obviously be a crucial factor and the Ministry of Information, set up on the outbreak of war, would have to compete with a German propaganda machine under Joseph Goebbels that had already had six years of experience. Planning for the Ministry of Information (MOI) had in fact begun as early as 1935, but it was far from complete by 1939. Again, the time provided by the 'Phoney War' allowed the MOI an invaluable opportunity to prepare itself adequately for the tasks to come.

Most attention had been devoted, perhaps typically for the British, to the question of censorship. Censorship as negative propaganda, designed not only to prevent valuable information from reaching the enemy but also to prevent news that might damage morale, had long been recognized as invaluable in the manipulation of opinion. If the term 'Total War' can first be applied to the First World War, it became even more appropriate a description of the 1939-45 struggle. Indeed, this was the first British war in which enfranchized men and women were called upon to determine its outcome, a genuine People's War. The bomber attacked civilians as well as military targets, and just as peacetime involvement in mass politics had increased, so now would the entire population become involved in Total War. Elected British politicians and their unelected civil servants had realized this since the Representation of the People Act of 1918 and the Equal Franchise Act of ten years later. But they remained suspicious of the new working-class electorate, despite the fact that it had not succumbed to anarchy and revolution during the strikes of 1919, the General Strike of 1926, and the Depression of the 1930s. The bomber, however, was felt to be the latest potential harbinger of civil insurrection and civilian chaos. Hence the emphasis on social control and its chief instrument, censorship.

So keen were the authorities at the start of the war on censoring virtually all news of interest that film cameramen were not allowed to accompany the British Expeditionary Force to France. Even in 1914, film crews had been allowed initially to accompany the troops before having their permits revoked by the War Office following the British retreat from Mons. The 1939 story was the victim of a total news blackout that was only lifted after a Paris radio announcement that the BEF had actually arrived in France; it was then reimposed after the newspapers had actually gone to press – a farce which saw Fleet Street offices occupied by Scotland Yard and the offending newspapers seized from startled early morning commuters before the ban was lifted again shortly afterwards. This kind of behaviour reflected the initial chaos of the MOI and served merely to antagonize the media through which it needed to operate. Most of the censors were retired naval officers – the real villains of these early bungles. The military authorities were supposed to supply the MOI with information but they did not, tending to operate instead on the principle that no news is good news. But it was the MOI, not the War Office or the Admiralty, that attracted the criticism of the press. The MOI was ridiculed for having 999 staff who were labelled 'Cooper's Snoopers' (after the Minister then involved, Duff Cooper). One journalist who asked for the text of a leaflet that had been dropped by the millions over Germany was even told: 'We are not allowed to disclose information which might be of value to the enemy.' By May 1940, the MOI had seen two ministers come and go: Lord Macmillan and Lord Reith. The latter lasted only four months, but at least he had some interest and knowledge of propaganda after fifteen years of service as Director General of the BBC, and it was he who put the MOI on a more efficient footing. Reith's axiom was simple and effective. News, he argued, was 'the shocktroops of propaganda' and, before long, the MOI's motto became: 'The truth, nothing but the truth and, as near as possible, the whole truth'.

By the middle of 1940 the censorship problems had largely been resolved and the system was to operate remarkably effectively for the remainder of the war. It formed the basis of the domestic propaganda campaign, but how did it work? The essential point was that all quick (or 'hot') news was censored at source. The British news media – the press, BBC, newsreels – relied upon the news agencies for most of their information. Before the First World War, the Post Office had re-routed Britain's world-wide cable network so that all commercial cables came together at a single point. The London headquarters of the Press Association (which supplied the domestic press) was also in the same building as Reuters (which supplied the overseas press). It was here that the censors controlled the bulk of news passing to the media *before* it actually reached them. It was, in other words, pre-censorship (newsreels were also subject to post-censorship). Once the censored news left the MOI, editors and journalists were allowed to do with it what they liked in accordance with their own house style. Their *opinions* were not censored, which gave the impression that little censorship was being imposed. It also gave the impression of a voluntary system, and this provided an effective disguise for official propaganda and a clearer conscience for a liberal democracy at war. Slow (or 'cold') news, such as that found in books, magazines, and the mail, could be dealt with at a more leisurely pace. This system operated so effectively on a day-to-day basis that many observers were unaware that a compulsory pre-censorship system was in fact operating and it helps to explain why Britain's wartime propaganda gained its reputation for telling the truth when, in reality, the truth was rarely being told whole.

The remarkable feature about Britain's wartime censorship after 1940 was how few clashes there were with the media. It is important to stress that those clashes that occurred were so few in number that they bear testimony to the routine efficiency of the censorship system. That there should be no more than half a dozen serious clashes with the press in six years of war (and most of these were in the difficult days of 1940, when the MOI was only just finding its feet) was an impressive achievement for a liberal democracy at war. The MOI brought only four prosecutions against the press in the entire war. And when all is said and done, and in spite of the wartime anxieties of the press concerning censorship, it was not so much what the MOI actually did but rather what it might do which most frightened journalists. The essential realization that government and the media had the same objectives as far as winning the war was concerned, and that their partnership in shaping morale might help to determine its outcome, led to a mutual appreciation of the limits to which either side could and could not go.

In May 1940, the government banned the export of communist journals. Stalin had signed a non-aggression pact with Hitler in August 1939 and Russia had to be treated as unfriendly, if not as an enemy, until June 1941 when the Germans attacked them. The ban was only lifted after the battle of Stalingrad. In July 1940, the *Daily Worker* was warned that its pacifist line contravened Defence Regulation 2D, which made it an offence under the Defence of the Realm Act 'systematically to publish matter calculated to foment opposition to the prosecution of the war'. The warning was ignored, and in January 1941 the Home Secretary, Herbert Morrison, ordered Scotland Yard into the offices of the *Daily Worker,* together with those of *The Week*, to stop the presses. They were only allowed to resume publication in August 1942 when a comprehensive re-education campaign about 'Our Soviet Friends' was in full flight. Far more serious, due to the size and nature of its circulation, was the constant sniping of the *Daily Mirror*. The circulation of this newspaper rose from 1.75 million in 1939 to 3 million in 1946 and was particularly popular among the troops – no doubt attracted by the charms of its erotic comic strip heroine 'Jane'. Even when Churchill replaced Chamberlain as Prime Minister in May 1940, the paper conducted its acrimonious campaign against the 'Guilty Men of Munich' to the point where even Churchill was embarrassed. In January 1941, Churchill summoned its owners and virtually ordered them to desist. His inclination to suppress the paper was tempered by the Home Secretary and the MOI who did not wish to suppress opinion or indulge in post-censorship. A personal interview was sufficient to abate the paper's attacks on that occasion.

The period between February and November 1942 was as bleak for Britain in terms of morale – public as well as private – as at any time in the war. Barely had the country recovered from the shock of the news that German battleships had passed undetected through the English Channel when the bastion of Britain's Far Eastern Empire, Singapore, surrendered to the Japanese with the loss of 60,000 prisoners. German successes in the Battle of the Atlantic continued, oil prices increased, and the press, starved of good news, launched an attack on the military conduct of the war by 'bonehead generals'. So when, on 6 March 1942, the *Daily Mirror* carried Philip Zec's famous cartoon depicting a half-drowned, oil-smeared merchant seaman clinging to a raft in a barren ocean with the caption 'The price of petrol has been increased by one penny (official)', it was bound to cause trouble. The implication was that heroic sailors were risking their lives for the benefit of black market-eers and higher profits with government connivance. Churchill was furious and Morrison, who thought the cartoon 'worthy of Goebbels at his best', warned the *Daily Mirror* that Defence Regulation 2D might be invoked. Fleet Street rallied to the *Mirror* behind its age-old battlecry of freedom of speech. Parliament rallied behind the government. The storm subsided, although the warning was sufficient to tone down the Mirror's criticism. Post-censorship had thus been avoided, but the episode served to place the British press on its guard for the rest of the war.

Another celebrated censorship attempt, this time concerning a film, also took place in this period. The eminent film-making team of Michael Powell and Emeric Pressburger planned to make a film based upon David Low's cartoon character 'Colonel Blimp' entitled *The Life and Death of Colonel Blimp*. Churchill, now extremely sensitive about charges of 'Blimpery', heard of the project and was furious. The MOI refused to extend its co-operation, even prevent-ing Laurence Olivier from leaving the Fleet Air Arm to play the title role (Roger Livesey played 'Blimp' instead). Churchill, now with the bit between his teeth, tried to prevent the film being made at all, raging 'I am not prepared to allow propaganda detrimental to the army'. The storm continued throughout the summer of 1942 with the MOI again extremely reluctant to see opinion censored. The censors saw the film prior to its release and concluded that it was harmless enough. But the storm surrounding it continued when Churchill's attempt to prevent the film going abroad attracted considerable media attention. When the film was released the public flocked to 'see the banned film'. The entire episode was something of a storm in a teacup and said more about Churchill's sensitivity to criticism than anything else.

Churchill, like other war leaders such as Roosevelt, Stalin, Mussolini and Hitler, was a great film fan and he fully recognized the power of film as propaganda. He was less appreciative of the degree to which allowing public criticism of the government's conduct of the war served the interests of the domestic propaganda campaign. It reinforced the illusion that no censorship was taking place, which was an excellent propaganda line to adopt with former neutrals like the United States, enemies like Nazi Germany, and new-found allies like the Soviet Union. If Churchill had been allowed to have his way over the *Daily Mirror* and *Colonel Blimp* episodes, it would have constituted post-censorship which would only have undermined the moral posture of a liberal democracy at war (as occurred in France before its fall in 1940). But it would also have given the propaganda game away in exposing the degree to which pre-censorship was already being practised.

Propaganda, therefore, is as much about what is not said as about overt expression. But what about the more positive aspects of Britain's war propaganda? Here again, the MOI began disastrously. At first, it adopted a stance of exhortation that was reflected in the poster '*Your* Courage, *Your* Cheerfulness, *Your* Resolution Will Bring *Us* Victory'. And although posters were less important in 1939 than they had been in 1914, the country was nonetheless littered with examples that adopted this old-fashioned approach. This merely served to create an 'us and them' attitude, the folly of which was soon realized. This was, after all, to be the People's War in which the previous gap between soldier and civilian and between politician and public was to be narrowed almost to the point of invisibility. The MOI quickly learned its mistake; hence the Churchill posters, 'Let Us Go Forward Together' and 'We're Going to See It Through'.

Posters were also used to convey information ('Coughs and Sneezes Spread Diseases'), suggest economies ('Make Do And Mend' and 'A Clean Plate Means a Clear Conscience'), prevent rumours ('Careless Talk Costs Lives', 'Keep it under your Hat', 'Tittle Tattle Lost the Battle', and 'Keep Mum – She's Not So Dumb'), and reinforce the will to persevere and sacrifice, ('Women of Britain, Come into the Factories' and 'Back Them Up'). After 1940, the MOI produced posters whose design could stand favourable comparison with any in the world. Cyril Bird, better known as Fougasse, the creator of the 'Careless Talk Costs Lives' posters, stated that propaganda posters had to overcome three obstacles:

> Firstly, a general aversion to reading any notice of any sort, secondly a general disinclination to believe that any notice, even if it was read, can possibly be addressed to oneself; thirdly, a general unwillingness, even so, to remember the message long enough to do anything about it.

It was for these reasons that the spoken word, as conveyed by radio and, in conjunction with images, film was far more potent an instrument of propaganda.

The MOI was at first slow to act in the case of film propaganda. The first propaganda film of the war, *The Lion Has Wings* (1939), was made independently of MOI influence by Alexander Korda. But by 1940 the MOI had drawn up a programme for film propaganda and it had taken over the old GPO Film Unit, renaming it the Crown Film Unit, to produce its own official films. Going to the pictures remained what it had become in the 1930s – a normal part of most people's life, an 'essential social habit', by far the most popular form of entertainment, particularly for the working classes who were now being called upon to fight the People's War. In 1939, 19 million people went to the cinema in Britain every week and by 1945 the figure had risen to 30 million – half the population. After November 1939, there were no less than 4000 cinemas in operation at any given time, even during air raids. Although the long-established Hollywood dominance of screen fare was never really challenged by the British film industry during the war, British cinema none the less enjoyed something of a golden age between 1939 and 1945, both in terms of popularity and of critical acclaim. Whereas Hollywood produced an average of about 400 feature films per year during the war years, the British output was never more than a fifth of that figure. Although most of these were escapist entertainment, with the comedy films of Gracie Fields and George Formby being particularly popular, British films did begin to compete favourably at the box office with their American rivals. Some were even awarded Oscars by the American Academy of Motion Picture Arts and Sciences: Noël Coward's *In Which We Serve* (1942) and Olivier's *Henry V* (1944) were awarded special Academy Awards, and Roy Boulting's *Desert Victory* (1943) won the Oscar for Best Documentary. By the end of the war, despite the fact that 80 per cent of the films seen weekly by those 30 million

cinema-goers were American, British films were enjoying an unprecedented degree of popularity and success.

One of the reasons for this was that British films were now
portraying ordinary working people – the bulk of their audiences –
in a serious light. Before the war, the working man and woman had
been largely caricature figures of fun. The People's War, however,
demanded that they were now taken seriously and in many respects
the strict censorship of the pre-war years, as exercised by the
British Board of Film Censors (BBFC), was now relaxed in its
treatment of social issues. Walter Greenwood's novel *Love on the
Dole*, for example, banned pre-war by the BBFC, was allowed to
be made into a film in 1940. Much of this was due to the influence
of the documentary film-makers who had made major contributions
to British cinema in the 1930s and whose services, after 1940, were
eagerly sought by the MOI. Initially ignored due to the emphasis
placed by the government on newsreel propaganda, these docu-
mentarists were recruited to make films of record and to portray
the British at war for purposes of morale, not least because the
audiences now demanded them. The artist-writer poet-director
Humphrey Jennings produced an exceptional body of work in this
period, notably *Listen to Britain* (1941), *Fires Were Started* (1943),
and *A Diary for Timothy* (1945). These films remain a moving
record of the British people at war; they also bear witness to the way
the war acted as a creative catalyst for the British film industry.

The work of Jennings and others brought new vitality to the
British film industry. During the war, the MOI's Crown Film Unit
made nearly 2000 'official' short films, while the MOI itself was
responsible for approving (or otherwise) over 3000 newsreel issues
and nearly 400 British-made feature films. In a sense, all films shown
in Britain were 'official' in that none could appear on the screen
without MOI approval or a BBFC certificate. Moreover, due to the
fact that film stock (i.e. celluloid) was classified as a vital war
material and was rigorously controlled by the Board of Trade, no
film could actually have been made without government approval.
The government gave priority to the five leading newsreel companies
(Pathé, Universal, Gaumont-British, British Movietone, and Paramount) who were in the frontline of the British film propaganda
war. But the newsreels were the most stridently aggressive in their
presentation of the issues and were obviously propagandist. The
'official' films produced by the Crown Film Unit were less strident

in tone and were produced at a far more leisurely pace than the newsreels whose business was 'hot' news. The official films were more like documentaries, short informational films explaining how to plant potatoes, how and when to wear a gas mask, how fires were extinguished, how tanks were built, and so on. They might not appear to be propagandist but they were designed to serve the war effort in its widest sense. The effective founder of the British documentary film movement, John Grierson, had already defined documentary as 'the creative treatment of actuality'. Like the newsreels, therefore, the official films presented, not reality but an illusion of reality, an illusion determined by the cameraman and where he pointed his camera, the director and where he placed his subjects (more often actors than 'real people'), the editor and where he cut his footage, and by the exhibitor and where and when he showed the final film.

The MOI recognized that 'for the film to be good propaganda, it must also be good entertainment'. Most people who went to the cinema would expect to find a newsreel and an official short film or two, as well as a supporting film, but these were not the main attractions. People went to the cinema to see the main feature, and it was there that propaganda, if skilfully handled, could most effectively be insinuated, while the audience was relaxed and thus off its guard. Feature films with war themes were comparatively few in number – most people went to their dream palaces to escape from the realities of war – and in fact declined in number as the war progressed. Romantic melodramas and films such as *The Wicked Lady* (1945), starring James Mason and Margaret Lockwood, were what the public wanted to see and studios such as Gainsborough duly obliged. The number of studios in operation, however, dropped from the pre-war figure of 22 to 9 as technicians were called up, taxes affecting the industry were increased (and seat prices as a result). Under such conditions, the achievement of the native film industry was extraordinary and the production of recognized 'classics' nothing short of miraculous.

This is not a history of the wartime cinema, but no discussion of Britain's war propaganda between 1939 and 1945 can fail to mention several examples of classic film propaganda. The films of Powell and Pressburger (*Contraband* [1940], *49th Parallel* [1941], *One of Our Aircraft is Missing* [1942], *The Life and Death of Colonel Blimp* [1943], *A Canterbury Tale* [1944], and *A Matter of Life and Death* [1946]) made a notable contribution, as did those of Carol Reed (*The Young Mr Pitt* [1942], *The Way Ahead* [1944], and *The True Glory* [1945]), Charles Frend (*The Big Blockade* [1942], *The Foreman Went to France* [1942], and *San Demetrio, London* [1943]), and Anthony Asquith (*Freedom Radio* [1940], *We Dive at Dawn* [1943], and *The Demi-Paradise* [1943]). The propaganda content of such films is not always obvious but most dealt with themes that were the object of MOI attention, such as the German Fifth Column, and would therefore have been more familiar to contemporary audiences.

The notion that Germany's dramatic military successes in the west, leading to the Dunkirk evacuation and the fall of France in 1940, had to be explained in terms other than Anglo-French incompetence gave rise to the belief that a Fifth Column had been operating as an advance guard for the German army. The notion of 'the enemy within', or, as Churchill called it, the 'malignancy in our midst', was behind the MOI's 'Careless Talk Costs Lives' campaign and it appeared in numerous films. In *The Foreman Went to France* (1942), a film about the recovery of vital pieces of machinery during the fall of France, fifth columnists are everywhere causing chaos and going about their treacherous deeds. The example of France was thus presented as a warning to all. With German forces lined up along the French coast, the campaign was stepped up in expectation of an imminent invasion. Official films such as *Miss Grant Goes to the Door* (1940) warned of fifth columnists and German paratroopers, whereas major feature films such as Thorold Dickinson's *The Next of Kin* (1941) and Cavalcanti's *Went the Day Well?* (1942), both made at Ealing Studios, dealt with the same theme. The latter was about a fictional English village overrun by German paratroopers disguised as British soldiers in preparation for a full-scale invasion and the means by which they were found out and finally defeated by the local villagers. It was the war in miniature, and the lesson that everyone had to pull together to defeat the enemy and their treacherous agents was plain for all to see. Spy films were naturally ideal for such propaganda purposes. They were also used to depict the enemy in a certain light, mostly unfavourably and Germans were portrayed as cruel, ruthless, and hateful – the 'same old hun'. It was rare for British wartime films to portray the idea of a 'good German'; if they did, they would have been out of step with a public opinion heavily influenced by the phenomenon known as 'Vansittartism'.

In a series of broadcasts made on the BBC's overseas service in late 1940 by Lord Vansittart, former Permanent Under Secretary at the Foreign Office, the Germans were portrayed as historically violent and aggressive, with Nazism being merely the latest manifestation of this national characteristic. The broadcasts proved extremely popular, as did the pamphlet that followed them, *Black Record: Germans Past and Present*. Taking up Chamberlain's 'evil things' theme, Vansittart argued that Hitler was no accident but the logical climax of German history. Nor was he alone, for his ideas suited well the MOI's notions of an Anger Campaign in which it was pointed out that 'The Hun is at the gate. He will rage and destroy. He will slaughter the women and the children.' A persistent stream of pamphlets, mostly written by political refugees, with titles such as *Werewolves* (by Siegbert Kahn, 1945) and *300 million slaves and serfs* (1943) by Jurgen Kuczynski, put forward supposedly rational explanations for German barbarity. At a more basic level, music hall songs reinforced the same stereotype, usually with the aid of Britain's secret weapon, its sense of humour, with titles such as 'The Jap and the Wop and the Hun' by Ronald Frankau and Monte Crick, which began:

> Whose foully cruel behaviour, to Czechs, Poles and Yugoslavia,
> And in Athens and in Hong Kong and the East,
> Has compelled us to determine that to say they're beasts and vermin
> Is an insult to the vermin and the beast?

People such as Anthony Eden, the Foreign Secretary, held views that were not so far removed from this type of attitude. He wrote: 'I have no confidence in our ability to make decent Europeans of the Germans and I believe that the Nazi system represents the mentality of the great majority of the German people.' Many other members of the government, however, were concerned at the sheer vindictiveness of this propaganda, not least because it would make a settlement with Germany after the war all the more difficult. Noël Coward parodied those critics in his song 'Don't Let's Be Beastly to the Germans', which ended with the lines:

> Let's let them feel they're swell again
> And bomb us all to hell again
> But don't let's be beastly to the Hun.

But after the policy of unconditional surrender was announced at the Casablanca conference of January 1943, it was no longer easy to distinguish between Germans and Nazis. Atrocity propaganda was never used on the same scale as in the First World War: that had long been discredited. But the underlying message of all this material was that Nazism itself was an atrocity and all Germans were guilty of it. If any further 'proof' was required, newsreel footage of Belsen and the other concentration camps was to provide it at the end of the war.

Thus far, we have been dealing with 'white' propaganda, namely propaganda emanating from a clearly identifiable source. The most potent source of white propaganda in Britain during the entire war was the BBC. The significance of radio depended not just upon its universality or its immediacy; like the other news media, its potency as a medium of news communication and of propaganda rested on the entertainment context in which it operated. The BBC's wartime role extended even further, from monitoring to overt and covert broadcasting and even to the air defence of Great Britain. But the first round of the radio war went to the Germans, partly due to the lack of preparedness with which the BBC went to war but also, of course, due to the facts of the military situation. The only ingredient present was a philosophy: 'no permanent propaganda policy can in the modern world be based upon untruthfulness'.

The outbreak of war was greeted by a virtual news blackout, producing a bleakness and dullness in radio broadcasting that was, before long, to prove counter-productive in terms of morale. In the BBC's case, this was not due solely to the reluctance of the censors to release news. Great caution was exercised by the Air Ministry, which was worried that radio beams would act as navigational aids for enemy bombers. In the event of an imminent air raid, Fighter Command would order the BBC by direct telephone to close down any transmitter serving as a beacon, whereupon the BBC would synchronize the introduction of another transmitter outside the target area, with a slight reduction in volume and quality. The result was that the BBC was permitted a single programme on two wavelengths (the Home Service) on which to serve up its reduced diet of news amidst an endless stream of pep-talks and pre-recorded gramophone music. It was not long, however, before the advantages of allowing the BBC to function as independently as possible became apparent. The MOI soon learned that it was better to leave news communications to the experienced professionals and that the credibility and integrity of their coverage could only be enhanced by an outward appearance of independence. And in 1940, the BBC was provided with an additional two wavelengths for its Armed Forces Programme. Just in case, a switch censor sat with his finger poised in the radio studio.

As western governments collapsed before the Nazi Blitzkrieg, the BBC increased its external broadcasting and provided exiles with free access to its microphones, the Dutch Radio Orange being the first of what was to become a legendary source of morale-boosting and intelligence-serving news services amongst the occupied nations of Europe. When the Battle of Britain and the Blitz began, the BBC was subordinated to the Air Defence of Great Britain. It was also during this period that special facilities were provided by the BBC for American broadcasters such as Ed Murrow, who did so much to bring the war into neutral American homes distant from the bombing and, with it, stimulated significant sympathy for the British during their finest hour. Films were also used for the same purpose. The MOI produced *London Can Take It* and Christmas Under Fire (both 1940) with American audiences in mind while people such as Alfred Hitchcock went to Hollywood to make pro-British films and combat American isolation with the help of the sizeable British Hollywood community already there (*Foreign Correspondent* [1940] was the result). Powell and Pressburger's *Forty Ninth Parallel* (1941) portrayed the Nazi menace to Americans through its plot of a German submarine crew stranded in Canada. At home, the broadcasts of J. B. Priestley, particularly his *Postscripts*, became almost as popular as the speeches of that brilliant radio orator, Winston Churchill. As the BBC began to come into its own during the Battle of Britain, the popularity of 'Lord Haw Haw' (William Joyce) declined, and thereafter the BBC proved itself to be an essential – perhaps the single most important – element in the maintenance of morale. Apart from its news bulletins, light entertainment programmes such as 'ITMA', 'Music While You Work', and 'The Brains Trust' became just as essential a part of the domestic propaganda campaign. Indeed, such was the role of the BBC in the 'war of words' that films often took their titles from radio bulletins: *One of Our Aircraft is Missing* and *Fires Were Started* are examples.

White broadcasts to Europe proved just as popular, as was demonstrated by the famous 'V for Victory' campaign. This was unwittingly launched in January 1941 following an unplanned reference in a BBC Belgian programme. Before long, resistance fighters were daubing the 'V' sign on walls throughout Belgium, Holland, and France. The Germans tried to claim the 'V' for themselves and began broadcasting as their station identification the opening bars of Beethoven's *Fifth Symphony*, which matched the Morse code for the letter 'V'. But the British government was concerned that the campaign was encouraging premature hopes for victory and ordered an end to it in May 1942. Even so, the campaign had demonstrated the influence of radio and the role it could play in fostering resistance amongst the peoples of a continent dominated by Nazi news broadcasts.

It is within this context that the work of the Political Warfare Executive (PWE) is significant. The PWE formally came into being in September 1941 to take charge of propaganda directed at the enemy and enemy-occupied countries. It evolved from the early wartime enemy propaganda department known as Department EH, which was absorbed into the Special Operations Executive (SOE) in the summer of 1940. SOE's task was, in Churchill's famous phrase, 'to set Europe ablaze' and was divided into two sections: S01, which handled propaganda, and S02, which handled sabotage and subversion. PWE was set up following a series of rows between S01 and the MOI over the control of overseas propaganda, whereupon S01 and the enemy sections of the MOI were merged into the PWE. Its brief was simple: 'to deliver a decisive blow at the heart of the enemy's morale' by any means possible. This, in effect, meant leaflets and radio broadcasts, and it was quite prepared to use both white and black propaganda techniques. PWE was initially hampered by the war situation into which it was born, but it was to have two major advantages: the reputation that the BBC was building up in Europe, and, later, the entry into the war of the United States with its huge arsenal of leaflet delivery systems, better known as bombers.

PWE's white propaganda was initially delivered either by the RAF in its leaflet-bombing raids over Germany or by the BBC in its European broadcasts. For BBC transmissions to be credible they needed to be news based; objectivity and 'the truth' (but never the whole truth) were axiomatic. At times, even good news was withheld for fear of alienating a disbelieving audience heavily influenced by a Nazi regime whose control over the news would have been total had it not been for the BBC. In so far as leaflets were concerned, PWE developed two types: 'timeless', for distribution over a prolonged period of time, and 'ad hoc', which dealt with immediate issues (here again was the distinction made between 'hot' and 'cold' news). But in practice, the work was not always satisfactory. PWE was situated at Woburn Abbey, thirty miles from London, and this physical separation from Bush House, the BBC's headquarters, did not help matters. Moreover, PWE's first head, Hugh Dalton, did not get on with Duff Cooper or with his successor as Minister of Information, Brendan Bracken, and tension between the PWE and the BBC and between PWE and the MOI often suggested that political warfare was more active on the home front than against the enemy. Equally 'Bomber' Harris, head of Bomber Command, was not keen to risk his valuable men and machines in dropping 'bits of bumph', as he called the leaflets. Gradually, however, PWE came into its own, its headquarters moved back to London, and personality clashes were ironed out following Dalton's departure. By 1942, the BBC was broadcasting in 23 languages.

PWE's black propaganda was a much more dangerous game if the credibility of the BBC was to be preserved. Black propaganda describes material emanating from an undisclosed source, so that the receiver either has no idea where it is coming from or incorrectly identifies the source. British black propaganda purported to originate in Europe when it in fact came from England, and because of its secret origin, much greater leeway could be made with the truth. But the BBC would have none of this and PWE accordingly established its own black radio stations known as Research Units (RUs), the most notorious being *Gustav Siegfried Eins*, known as GS1. The genius behind these black stations was Sefton Delmer, formerly foreign correspondent of the *Daily Express* and an expert on the German mind. The RUs initially directed their attention to the German armed forces or at submarine crews using short wave transmissions. By this means, PWE was able to spread rumours ('Sibs') and discontent and it was greatly aided by the acquisition of the *Hellschreiber*, a machine which transmitted the German wireless teleprinter service throughout Europe. This meant that PWE could monitor German news at the same time that it was being received by Nazi newspapers and radio stations; the acquisition of the *Hellschreiber* was as important to the propagandists as Enigma was to the intelligence war.

This was psychological warfare at its most sophisticated, working hand in hand with military operations. For example, captured submarine crews would be interrogated for details about the brothels in Brest and Kiel, where upon any incriminating information was broadcast by the RUs to discredit military personnel of influence or distinction. Suicides are known to have resulted after Delmer had transmitted such information. One less Hun in a war with the gloves off. Once the Americans entered the war, PWE was able to acquire a powerful medium wave transmitter code-named Aspidistra. This enabled PWE to reach the more popular medium wave sets of the bulk of the German civilian population – despite serious penalties for those caught listening to foreign broadcasts. Aspidistra broadcasts attempted to undermine loyalty to the Nazi regime by slowing down civilian contributions to the war effort. Unlike much white propaganda, the black variety depended on separating the German people from their Nazi leadership, but because it was unattributable PWE could get away with this divergence from government policy. It was more difficult after the Casablanca call for unconditional surrender, but the thrust of PWE's work was aimed primarily at the armed forces anyway. Thus, in the words of a PWE official: 'The fighting services attack the body, we attack the mind.'

With the entry of the Americans into the war, thousands of bombers became available both for striking physical blows at the heart of industrial Germany and for attacking the minds of German civilians. The Anglo-American propaganda relationship was not without its tensions, but equally it was not without its successes. The Americans also distinguished between black and white propaganda. For this purpose, they set up two separate organizations, black material being dealt with by the Office of Strategic Services (OSS) and white by the Office of War Information (OWI). (Clearly the Americans disliked the word 'propaganda' as much as the British.) The Americans also set aside a special squadron of Flying Fortresses whose sole task was to carry out leaflet raids, and by the end of the war the Americans were dropping over seven million leaflets a week over occupied Europe. Leaflets paved the way for the invasions of Sicily and Italy and they were used extensively in France, together with an aerial newspaper produced by the OWI, *L'Amérique en Guerre*. German cities received *Sternebanner* ('The Star-Spangled Banner'). Distribution was greatly aided by the invention of the Monroe bomb, a device which carried up to 80,000 leaflets released after the bomb had descended to 1000 feet. The leaflets and newspapers were largely factual, although some contained safe conduct passes to encourage surrender and desertion.

The other great achievement of the American wartime propaganda effort lay in the contribution to both American and Allied morale played by Hollywood, or rather the American motion picture industry, as it should more accurately be described. The world-wide influence and sheer propaganda potential of Hollywood at war can be simply illustrated by the following statistics. By the end of the First World War, the United States owned over half of the world's cinemas. In 1923, 85 per cent of films shown in France, for example, were American; and whereas in 1914, 25 per cent of films shown in Britain were actually British, by 1925 the figure was only 2 per cent. Even by 1939, after years of attempts by foreign governments to combat the Americanization of their national film industries, the USA owned about 40 per cent of the world-wide total of cinemas. During the war itself, more than 80 million Americans went to the cinema every week, whilst the world-wide audience for American films was measured in hundreds of millions. What has been described as the classic Hollywood style proved to be a universal formula with universal appeal.

The role that British films played in attempting to overcome American isolationism, 1939-41, was nothing compared to several key American films made in the neutral period that were pro-Allied, anti-Nazi productions. The best-known example is *Confessions of a Nazi Spy* (1939) about a German spy ring operating in America and starring Edward G. Robinson. The film was made by Warner Brothers, whose track record in dealing with foreign policy themes was second to none, demonstrated by its extraordinary love affair with the British Empire as reflected in a series of films: *Captain Blood* (1935), *The Charge of the Light Brigade* (1936), *The Adventures of Robin Hood* (1938), *Elizabeth and Essex* (1939), and *The Sea Hawk* (1940). All these films were directed by the same man, Michael Curtiz, a Hungarian *émigré* who was also to make *Casablanca* (1942). *Confessions of a Nazi Spy*, however, was explicitly anti-Nazi with its exposure of Fifth Column activities, its quasi-documentary style, and its skilled use of montage. It was also the first American feature film to mention Hitler by name. Newsreels had, of course, been presenting stories about Nazi Germany for many years, but the most explicitly anti-Nazi series, *The March of Time*, whose exposé of Nazi brutality in 'Inside Nazi Germany' (1938) was banned in Britain pre-war, used a combination of actuality footage and staged material. In other words, the American film industry was more prepared to criticize the Nazis than the British were before 1939, although after the invasion of Poland American anti-Nazi films reinforced the British propaganda effort.

So explicitly propagandist were some Hollywood products at a time when the United States was, theoretically at least, supposed to be neutral that they were banned by some American movie houses, particularly in towns and cities where German-American bunds were present. One example was *Beasts of Berlin* (1939, originally entitled *Hitler, Beast of Berlin* and subsequently released as *Goose Step* and *Hell's Devils*), which was denied a certificate by the Motion Picture Producers and Distributors Association, the American equivalent of the British Board of Film Censors. Shot in less than a week by a small production company (PRC), *Beasts of Berlin* attempted to capitalize on the success of *Confessions*, but it was in fact the forerunner of many classic wartime propaganda films. In the summer of 1941, Warner Brothers released two further pro-Allied films, *International Squadron*, a tribute to the RAF, and *Sergeant York*. Although the latter was set in the First World War, the moral and religious agonizing of its lead character, played by Gary Cooper, over whether or not to take up arms is a metaphor of the debate between isolationism versus intervention that was raging in America at the time. Indeed, this film, together with MGM's exposé of anti-Semitism, *The Mortal Storm* (1940), 20th Century-Fox's *The Man I Married* (1940, originally entitled *I Married a Nazi*), Charlie Chaplin's 1940 satirical masterpiece, *The Great Dictator*, and many others, prompted two isolationist senators, Nye and Clark, to take action. On 1 August 1941 they called for 'a thorough and complete investigation of any propaganda disseminated by motion pictures and radio and any other activity of the motion-picture industry to influence public sentiment in the direction of participation by the United States in the present European war'. This Senate Resolution 152 was not just an attempt to break the monopoly in movie-making by the eight major studios (Paramount, MGM, RKO, Warner Brothers, 20th Century-Fox, Columbia, Universal, and United Artists) that were felt by Nye to be riddled with pro-Allied foreign propagandists. It also reflected the sensitivity of many Americans to the type of propaganda campaign that was felt to have duped America into war in 1917. Nye and Clark had not seen most of the films they were accusing and the hearings that took place in September 1941 were largely a farce. And although the Japanese attack on Pearl Harbor three months later made the investigation somewhat redundant, it is difficult to avoid the conclusion that Resolution 152 was not without foundation, even if its proponents lacked the detailed knowledge to see it through.

Japan and Germany were to place the American government firmly on the Allied side by their actions in December 1941. Hollywood was quick to mobilize and in the next four years kept up a relentless pace of film production that was to serve the national propaganda effort well. As Roosevelt stated: 'The motion picture industry could be the most powerful instrument of propaganda in the world, whether it tries to be or not.'

The Bureau of Motion Pictures was right to consider that every film enhanced or diminished the national reputation abroad. And film could help to overcome the sheer distance of a war fought on the other side of the Pacific and Atlantic oceans. Characters such as Tarzan (*Tarzan Triumphs* [1943] and *Tarzan's Desert Mystery* [1943]), Sherlock Holmes (*Sherlock Holmes and the Voice of Terror* [1942]), and cartoon characters such as Batman, the Masked Marvel, and Secret Agent X-9, were recruited into the service of the propaganda war to fight Nazi agents around the world. Africa was a popular setting for such plots and served to reinforce the 'Europe First' policy of the American government, which had decided to knock out Germany before seeking revenge for Pearl Harbor. The war in the Pacific was, of course, covered by Hollywood in such films as *Wake Island* (1942), *Guadalcanal Diary* (1943), *Bataan* (1943), *Corregidor* (1943), *Destination Tokyo* (1943), and *Objective Burma!* (1945). The last of these caused such a storm of protest in Britain, due to its suggestion that the Americans were bearing the brunt of the war in Burma, that the studio withdrew its exhibition in the UK. Most of the films contained some form of 'Yellow Peril' propaganda, although it is interesting to note by way of contrast that anti-Italian stereotypes are rare in the films about the European war. The Germans, on the other hand, were portrayed as gangsters and thugs, abusers of women and the innocent (*Hitler's Children* [1943], *Women in*

Bondage [1943], and *Enemy of Women* [1944]). This was the new form of atrocity propaganda, more subtle perhaps, but with the same message: the Germans were the enemies of civilization and democracy. There were attempts to lampoon the Nazis (as in *To Be or Not To Be* and *Once Upon a Honeymoon*, both 1942), but on the whole the Nazis were too formidable an enemy to be taken lightly. Chaplin had shown how to do it in *The Great Dictator* but even he said later that if he had known what the Nazis were actually doing he would not have attempted such a treatment. Even the propaganda cartoons in which Bugs Bunny and Donald Duck were called up to fight Hitler dealt nervously with such a serious topic.

Once the Office of War Information had been set up in June 1942, the US government issued a manual to Hollywood listing the kind of themes that would serve the national effort. Classified as 'an essential war industry', Roosevelt stated: 'I want no restrictions placed thereon which will impair the usefulness of the film other than those very necessary restrictions which the dictates of safety make imperative.' Five themes were identified as needing priority: (1) to explain why the Americans were fighting; (2) to portray the United Nations and their peoples; (3) to encourage work and production; (4) to boost morale on the home front; (5) to depict the heroics of the armed forces. Though jealously protective of its independence, the American film industry duly obliged by making films about the 'people's war', such as *Mrs Miniver* (1942) (popular in the US but mocked in Britain due to its rose-tinted Hollywood view of the Blitz), and about heroic resistance in such countries as Norway and France, such as *Joan of Paris* (1942) and *Edge of Darkness* (1943). Other themes included the heroism and suffering of America's allies, including the Soviet Union (*Song of Russia* [1943], *North Star* [1943], *Mission to Moscow* [1943], and *Days of Glory* [1944]) and China (*China* [1943] and *China Sky* [1945]). The people's war theme also required that difficult subjects, such as the role of blacks and anti-Semitism, should also be dealt with, which they duly were in *The Negro Soldier* (1944) and *Mr Skeffington* (1943); but the ambiguities in many wartime films dealing with these topics often made the American melting pot boil over. Clearly a public education campaign was necessary, and there was no better way of reaching the public than through film. But this required a documentary approach that was anathema to many Hollywood studios. However, if the studios were not prepared to stray into these potentially uncommercial waters, many of their most creative members were quite willing to co-operate with the government, including John Ford (December 7th [1943] and *The Battle of Midway* [1942]), John Huston (*Report from the Aleutians* [1943] and *The Battle of San Pietro* [1945]), William Wyler (*The Memphis Belle* [1944] and *Thunderbolt* [1945]), and, most famous of all, Frank Capra.

These men all made films for the US Armed Forces, which had their own film units for training and indoctrination purposes. The OWI at first concentrated on the civilian front, but although its Motion Picture Bureau (the equivalent of the British MOI's Films Division) did make short informational films for domestic purposes (for instance meat rationing), it had to tread warily under the watchful and suspicous eye of Congress. Hollywood would look after domestic morale, with a little guidance from the OWI. But there was still a need to target Americans joining the armed forces. The US War Department, for example, spent more than $50 million annually on film production during the war with the purpose of forging, training, and welding together an army capable of defeating the war machines of the enemy. Frank Capra, winner of Academy Awards pre-war for such feature films as *It Happened One Night* (1934), *Mr Deeds Goes To Town* (1936), and *Mr Smith Goes to Washington* (1939), became Major Frank Capra and was charged personally by Army Chief of Staff George C. Marshall to make the famous *Why We Fight* series. The story goes that Capra protested to Marshall that he had never made a documentary film before, to which the General replied: 'I have never been Chief of Staff before. Boys are commanding ships today who a year ago had never seen the ocean before', whereupon Capra said: 'I'm sorry, sir. I'll make you the best damned documentary films ever made.' Few would disagree that the seven films that followed (*Prelude to War, The Nazis Strike, Divide and Conquer, The Battle of Britain, The Battle of Russia, The Battle of China* and *War Comes to America*) were indeed masterpieces of film propaganda. The first in the series, designed to explain the background to American involvement, has been described as 'the greatest gangster movie ever made'. So pleased was the War Department with the series that it became compulsory viewing for all recruits. President Roosevelt was so delighted with the way the films tackled residual isolationist sentiment that he ordered them to be released commercially to the

American public at large. Churchill filmed a special introduction for their British release and Stalin allowed *The Battle of Russia* to be shown in some parts of the Soviet Union.

Like Churchill, Roosevelt was a highly skilled radio broadcaster whose 'fireside chats' had done much to make the American public believe that their president was pursuing policies that were of concern to every citizen. With isolationism virtually eliminated by 1943, the OWI found its domestic budget drastically reduced. Thereafter, its main emphasis was on overseas propaganda. For this purpose, it produced its own newsreel series, *United Newsreels*, in sixteen languages and a bi-monthly *Army-Navy Screen Magazine* for the armed forces serving abroad. In the autumn of 1942, General Eisenhower formed a Psychological Warfare Branch in his North African invasion force to deal with leaflets and other forms of propaganda designed to aid the course of military operations. This largely American-dominated unit was upgraded for the invasion of France into the Psychological Warfare Division of Supreme Headquarters Allied Expeditionary Force (PWD, SHAEF), which had a greater British involvement, and a special OWI-PWE committee was established in London to ensure that what the military were saying coincided with civilian propaganda. When the powerful transmitter of Radio Luxembourg was captured, the Allies began beaming propaganda into the heart of Germany. But by that time, the propagandists needed more guidance on what the policy-makers planned to do with Germany after the war if their propaganda was to be really effective. It was not forthcoming. Churchill and Roosevelt were reluctant to make any statements or promises that might detract from the policy of unconditional surrender. As a result, the propagandists were severely hampered in their appeals to the German population as a whole for the final eight months of the war. Instead they had to resort to statements about the inevitability of Germany's defeat, the prolonging of German agony by continued resistance, and the corruption of the Nazi regime by way of contrast to the democratic and increasingly victorious Allies.

Following the British lead, the Americans developed their 'Strategy of Truth' as a fundamental principle of their propaganda but, when all is said and done, even in their psychological warfare, the absence of any policies that could offer the German people any hope that they would be treated differently from Nazi war criminals hindered their efficiency. The influence of years of anti-German propaganda became evident in two films dealing with the treatment of Germany in defeat, one British, the other American. The British film, *A Defeated People* (1946), directed by Humphrey Jennings for the Crown Film Unit, began: 'They asked for it, they got it!' but then went on to argue that the need was to 're-educate the Germans' so that the 'next generation will grow up a sane and Christian people'. It was far more conciliatory than the American *Your Job in Germany* (1945), made by Capra's *Why We Fight* team.

This type of vindictiveness was nothing compared to the treatment the Soviets were to mete out to defeated Germany. And if the German people had good reason to fear the western Allies, they were terrified of the Soviets. After fifteen years or more of anti-communist propaganda, halted temporarily during the period of the Nazi-Soviet Pact (1939-41), their image of the Russians was of demonic proportions. It was a reputation that was not only promoted by Nazi domestic propaganda but also encouraged by the Soviets in their own propaganda. Right from the outset, a spirit of hatred was fostered by the Soviet propaganda authorities, as in this early newsreel statement.

> Our rage is mighty and terrible. For the blood we shed we will pay back in crushing blows without mercy ... the German fascist gangs do not have the means to overcome the unconquerable, freedom loving Soviet people. All our help, our feelings, blood and life itself are dedicated to the orders of our wise government, to great Stalin in defence of our dear country. By this and this alone we will live. The Soviet army, workers, intelligentsia, all are committed to smash the fascist brigands and robbers.

As the Germans advanced towards Moscow, the newsreels shouted out their defiance: 'It is 1917 again. O.K... Come On... For every Moscow wound we will repay with shells and bayonets by the million.' By the end of the war, with 20 million Russian dead and the Red Army advancing towards Berlin, the Germans were about to discover whether there was any substance to such claims.

One of the great unanswered questions of the war is why the Soviets were so surprised by the German invasion of Russia in June 1941. Since August 1939 they had had a non-aggression pact with the Nazis that had required a major reversal of their previous propaganda policy. The pact was explained by both sides as a measure designed to keep the peace of Europe. But when the Germans invaded Poland on 1 September, and the Russians followed suit two and a half weeks later in accordance with secret clauses, this convinced no one. In Russia, all anti-German propaganda abruptly came to an end. Eisenstein's *Alexander Nevsky*, a film made in 1938 to portray the historic struggle between Teutons and Slavs, was suddenly withdrawn from circulation, as indeed were all films attacking Hitler's regime. The Russian invasion of Finland at the end of November 1939 and the subsequent 'Winter War' was, in Stalin's terms, a defensive action designed to put as much territory between Russia and Germany when the inevitable attack occurred. In the meantime, Russia prepared while the capitalist democracies slugged it out with the fascists in the west. There was much to prepare. Over 90 per cent of the Soviet High Command had been wiped out in the purges of the 1930s and the Japanese constantly menaced Russia's eastern borders. But why Stalin was caught off guard in June 1941, militarily as well as psychologically, remains a mystery. More is known, however, about the Soviet propaganda war.

The Soviets to this day describe the Second World War as 'The Great Patriotic War'. In many respects, patriotism was more significant than propaganda, and certainly the propaganda was directed at patriotic resistance rather than ideological or revolutionary change. Churchill's immediate announcement of solidarity with the Soviets was welcome, particularly as it came from the man who had done so much to champion counter-revolutionary intervention during the Civil War. But until it manifested itself in the form of aid, by which Stalin meant a Second Front, Russia was effectively on its own. (Despite this, anti-British films were withdrawn.) A non-aggression pact was signed with the Japanese to avoid a war on two Russian fronts (a pact which survived the attack on Pearl Harbor in December 1941, despite lining up the United States with Britain and Russia). Rather, Stalin looked to the defence of Russia itself and it was to the Russian population that most of the official propaganda was directed. Lenin had, after all, stated that 'a revolution is worth its name only when it can defend itself'. In his 'Holy Russia' speech of November 1941, Stalin conjured up figures from Russia's glorious past, military and cultural, and compared Nazi

Germany with tsarist Russia. He was clearly at pains to undo the effects of his own propaganda during the period of the Nazi-Soviet pact but, most significantly, he made a distinction between the Nazis and the German people. Unlike his new-found allies, Stalin felt that the propaganda possibilities of dividing the German people from their Nazi leaders were too great to miss. But here he was also at odds with his own Soviet propaganda machine. It is possible that, in Stalin's paranoid mind, he was still afraid of the western powers coming to terms with a future German regime in an anti-communist crusade. By making distinction between Germans and Nazis, he vowed to destroy the latter but hoped to win over the former.

Soviet propaganda was determined by the Council of People's Commisars and the Political Bureau of the All Union Communist Party. It was supervised by the Directorate of Propaganda and Agitation of the Central Committee under A. S. Shcherbakov and administered by the newly-established Soviet Information Bureau. These bodies, too, were caught by surprise when the Germans invaded in June 1941. Only a week before the Soviet news agency Tass had dismissed German troop movements in the east as 'nothing but clumsy propaganda by forces hostile to the USSR and Germany and interested in an extension of the war'. The rapid German advance, often greeted with enthusiasm in such places as Latvia, Estonia, and Lithuania, together with the ease with which demoralized Russian troops capitulated (there were 5 million Russian prisoners of war by the end of 1941), suggested that a great deal had to be done in terms of morale. Hence Stalin's call for a great patriotic struggle on the 24th anniversary of the revolution, the re-release of anti-German films like Alexander Nevsky, and the mobilization of the Soviet media for total war. As Pravda stated:

> Let playwrights, composers, poets, novelists and artists glorify the heroic effort of the Red Army and the entire Soviet people because, in these days of the Patriotic War, their work for the Red Army will help bring nearer our victory over the enemy.

The problem was that the German advance had seriously jeopardized the capacity of the government to achieve this. For example, the number of newspapers dropped from 8,806 in 1940 to 4,561 in 1942, whilst the number of cinemas fell, from 28,000 in 1940 (with a weekly audience of 17 million), by about a third (to a weekly audience of only 8 million).

None the less, Soviet newsreel cameramen were able to produce items within two weeks of the invasion. Before long, there were more than 250 of them filming at various fronts. Between 1941 and 1945 over 500 newsreels, together with 120 documentaries, were made with their material. The most widely seen was *The Defeat of the German Armies Near Moscow* (1942), released in America as *Moscow Strikes Back*. *Kinosborinik* (Fighting Film Collections) were popular because of their compilation of short films each based on a separate story. The production of entertainment films with flippant themes stopped and feature films relevant to wartime concerns began appearing after late 1942. There was to be no role for film as escapist entertainment in the Russian war. About twenty full-length features were produced annually throughout the war years, the most notable being *District Party Secretary* (1942), *She Defends Her Motherland* (1943), *Zoya* (1944), *Rainbow* (1944), *Invasion* (1945), and *Girl No. 217* (1945). This was all the more remarkable given the decision of the Soviet government in the first winter of the war to move all the feature film studios eastwards as the Germans advanced on Moscow. The operation was completed in 24 hours. (The newsreel and documentary studios stayed behind.) The film studios were thus scattered throughout the Soviet Union, with Mosfilm and Lenfilm being transplanted to Alma-Ata and the Kiev studio to Ashkhabad and Tashkent. From such outposts, the Soviet film industry continued to pour out films that agitated and organized the masses. The war was presented as a conflict between two ideologies. The brutality of the Nazi invaders was never avoided; indeed, the hellish reality of war was a distinctive feature of Soviet wartime cinema, particularly in the feature-length documentaries, and Soviet film makers, unlike their western counterparts, did not shrink from showing death with all its horror on the screen.

Films with historical themes were particularly valuable. All the belligerents used history as a vehicle for film propaganda but none more so than Russia. Indeed, the first major feature film production of the war was *Defence of Tsaritsin* (1942) about the Civil War period, and just as Stalin had conjured up great resistance and military heroes of the past, so too did the film industry with Eisenstein's *Ivan the Terrible* (1942-6). But it was the newsreel and the documentary film 'records' of combat that were to have the greatest effect in bringing the war to the civilian population outside the danger zones. *Stalingrad* (1943), released less than six weeks after the German surrender, was one such seven-reel example with its stunning combat footage, realistic portrayal of street fighting, maps and diagrams, and the surrender of the German commander, von Paulus. With this vital turning point in the war Soviet propaganda had more to shout about, but film remained a largely urban phenomenon. The agit-trains accordingly once again took the message to the rural peasants. In the towns, posters took on a new lease of life. The old Civil War format of ROSTA (now TASS) windows was repeated with cartoon and caricatures being both popular and effective. Relations with the Russian Orthodox Church were patched up to help the domestic campaign and provide the patriotic cause with a 'holy' theme, while Soviet radio stations kept up the stream of State controlled information and exhortation. In order to smooth external relations, the Comintern was closed down although anti-Nazi groups and resistance movements were fostered with the aid of radio. All in all, Soviet wartime propaganda proved remarkably adept at improvisation and flexibility, but then this was necessary if the difficult problem of the subject nationalities was to be glossed over in favour of patriotic resistance. Ideology and internal dissent were therefore subordinated to the business of national survival. Once the tide had turned, and the battle lines of post-war conflict were beginning to be drawn up, the Soviet propaganda machinery had, once again, to make an about turn that would make the 1939-41 period look tame by comparison.

The Russians declared war on Japan after the first American atomic bomb had been dropped on Hiroshima. With the war in Europe over, the time had come to ensure that Soviets were in at the kill in any Far Eastern settlement. Before then, however, the decision of the Japanese government to attack the United States in 1941 rather than the Soviet Union had not only enabled the Russians to concentrate solely on the defence of their western frontier, it had also allowed them to focus their efforts on the propaganda front against the Hitlerite menace. The attack on Japan in August 1945 came as a surprise to most of the Russian population; they had not been psychologically prepared for it. The Japanese, on the other hand, must have thought that their pre-Pearl Harbor fears about the communist menace had been justified. But it had been some time since the menace of communism had been given priority;

instead, the Japanese had been concentrating their propaganda efforts since 1941 against the British Empire and the Americans. The Nazi-Soviet Pact had shocked the Japanese government, who felt betrayed by Hitler after three years of German-Japanese alignment under the anti-Comintern pact. Suddenly, the Japanese redefined their foreign policy into an anti-American direction and, with it, the thrust of their propaganda. Following the attack on Pearl Harbor, which was synchronized with other attacks on Hawaii and British Malaya, Hong Kong surrendered. In January 1942, the Japanese invaded Burma and the Dutch East Indies and in the following month Singapore fell into their hands. It was not until the Americans managed to drive the Japanese from Guadalcanal in January 1943 – the same month as the German surrender at Stalingrad – that the spectacular initial Japanese success was halted.

The very fact that the Americans were caught by surprise at Pearl Harbor was a tribute to the disinformation campaign the Japanese had been conducting between 1939 and 1941. Japanese propaganda, or the 'Thought War' as they preferred to call it, was carried out by a variety of organizations (not unlike those in Britain, Russia, and the USA). A 'Bureau of Thought Supervision' in the Ministry of Education had been in existence since 1932, but the fully-fledged Government Information Bureau (Naikaku Johobu) was not established until 1941, the day before Pearl Harbor. This body was served by an Advisory Committee consisting of ten figures from the armed forces and the media, such as the President of the Japanese News Agency, Domei, and the President of the National Broadcasting Corporation, NHK. In addition there was the Greater East Asia Ministry for dealing with the countries subjugated by Japan (Manchuria, China, and the Pacific islands) but also neighbouring states (Indo-China, Thailand) and whose brief extended to overt and covert propaganda. Imperial Headquarters in Tokyo also had branches for propaganda directed at the army, navy, and air force. The sheer geographical extent of the Japanese 'Greater East Asian Co-Prosperity Sphere', spreading as it did from Burma to the mid-Pacific, meant that radio was to provide a principal instrument of the Japanese 'Thought War'.

Short-wave radio sets were banned in Japan itself. Yet although the civilian population at home were thus to be denied access to foreign broadcasts, the longer ranges of short-wave broadcasting proved an ideal means for the government to spread its message throughout the area it wished to control – but only once the wireless sets had been adjusted to receive only Japanese transmissions. Listening to foreign radio propaganda was forbidden. The Japanese themselves broadcast in more than twenty-two foreign languages from transmitters in Batavia, Singapore, and Saigon, with Australasia and India being prime targets for their attention. The most famous Japanese broadcaster was 'Tokyo Rose', a Japanese-born American-educated woman who played on the homesickness of American troops serving in the Pacific by her suggestive voice and choice of American swing music. Much more explicit were the pornographic postcards and leaflets directed at Australian troops depicting their wives and sweethearts in various embraces with drunken British or American troops stationed in their homeland. The Japanese also used a method favoured by the Russians, namely the prisoner of war broadcast in which captured soldiers made unscheduled statements over the air about how well they were being treated. Anxious relatives were thus forced to listen to the entire programme in the hope that their son or husband might appear before the microphone at some point. Yet it is unlikely that such methods had any real impact; the fact of the matter was that the Japanese had started the Pacific war by attacking Pearl Harbor and no amount of justification or explanation could erase the memory of that.

Like the radio, film was rigorously controlled by the Japanese authorities. Again, strict censorship controls prevented the portrayal of images or messages that might have a critical or detrimental effect upon the regime or its emperor. Control was tightened by a 1939 Motion Picture Law that required the submission of scripts prior to filming, and production was dominated by two combines: the Shochiku company (producing about 85 per cent of all Japanese films) and the Toho company. Newsreels were produced mainly by the Nippon Eigasha, which had a budget of 7 million yen in 1943. Newsreels were produced depicting Japanese successes, often incorporating captured Allied footage, such as *Capture of Burma and Occupation of Sumatra*. In so far as feature films were concerned, historical themes were used to spread anti-British sentiment, such as *The Day England Fell* (1942), about the brutal and racist attitudes of the British in Hong Kong, and *The Opium War* (1943), in which the British are alleged to have subdued the Chinese by turning them into drug addicts. A brief revolt by film makers about the degree of government control resulted in a fall in production in 1943, but they were quickly brought to heel. Before long, such films as *General Kato's Falcon Fighters* (1943), made by Japan's leading wartime film director, Kajiro Yamamoto, and *Forward! Flag of Independence* (1943), designed to encourage Indian independence from Britain, were released. But in 1944, increasing numbers of American B-29 bombers forced many Japanese cinemas to close. Their payloads in the end were to prove mightier than the Japanese movie camera.

The rivalry that existed between the Japanese army and navy meant that, both armed forces had their own propaganda organizations. The military control of the government also meant that all national propaganda was subject to the same control, and consequently was a victim of the same rivalry. Japanese overseas propaganda was also hampered by the shortage of broadcasters with appropriate accents and understanding of western civilization and it was too quick to invent unlikely victories and atrocities that once exposed, critically devalued future propaganda efforts. The absence of any clear philosophy concerning a 'strategy of truth' or a 'propaganda with facts' was to be a major weakness, as one Japanese writer subsequently realized:

> Japan was hopelessly beaten in psychological warfare, not because of any particular adroitness on the part of the Allies, but because the Allies based their propaganda on truth – whereas Japan was unwilling to deal in truth, almost from the outset.

Even so, during the first eighteen months of the war, the military initiative was with the Japanese and with it the propaganda initiative. Words cannot win wars, but they can smooth the path of victory. Nor can they disguise defeat. After the Battle of Midway, the tide was clearly turning in favour of the Americans although the strict censorship of the Japanese military government disguised this fact from the majority of soldiers and civilians. It was the fanaticism of those people, largely protected from outside influences until the Americans began dropping leaflets, let alone bombs, over Japanese cities, that was to be the real triumph of Japanese propaganda.

It took two atomic bombs to defeat Japan, but it is significant that morale did not crack after the first bomb was dropped. Clearly Japanese domestic propaganda had been effective. The same was true in Nazi Germany where the civilian population had been subjected to the most comprehensive propaganda campaign the world has ever witnessed, a campaign that has even been described as 'the war that Hitler won'. However, as in the case of Japan, it is difficult to distinguish between the role of patriotism and the role of propaganda in making people fight to the bitter end. Those teenage members of the Hitler Youth who defended the streets of Berlin against crack Soviet troops in April 1945 were undoubtedly indoctrinated with Nazi ideas to such a degree that propaganda cannot be discounted. Young people were a prime target of propagandists in all totalitarian countries, particularly in one which was to last 1000 years. (It might be added that the youth of democratic systems were also susceptible to all forms of propaganda; in British wartime cinemas, children cheered at newsreels of Churchill, Roosevelt, and Stalin and booed when Hitler or Mussolini appeared on the screen.) German youth had been wooed by the Nazis in the 1920s and after Hitler came into power in 1933 they were educated, organized, trained, and regimented by a Nazi education system that subordinated scholarship to ideology. Members of the *Hitlerjunge* (Hitler Youth) and *Bund deutscher Mädchen* (German Girls' League) enjoyed a military education (*Wehrerziehung*), in which uniforms, bands, parades, rallies, and films played on their emotions, rather than cultivating their intellect. The teenagers defending the streets of Berlin in 1945 knew nothing else. They were indeed 'Hitler's children'.

In 1923, after the failure of his Munich *Putsch*, Hitler had declared: 'Propaganda, propaganda, propaganda. All that matters is propaganda.' The whole thrust of Nazi propaganda thereafter was directed at man's baser instincts. In *Mein Kampf* he had written:

> The psyche of the masses is not receptive to anything that is weak. They are like a woman, whose psychic state has been determined less by abstract reason than by an emotional longing for a strong force which will complement her nature. Likewise, the masses love a commander, and despise a petitioner.

Propaganda, therefore, consisted of 'attracting the crowd, and not in educating those who are already educated'. And for Hitler, the crowd was brutal, violent, emotional, corrupt, and corruptible. Propaganda was designed to attract followers from this broad mass of the population, organization was designed to attract members of the party. But the party must not grow too large lest its strength become diluted. Rather, its role through propaganda was 'the rape of the masses'. Once that had been achieved by the election of Hitler to power in 1933, its role became even more important. Simplicity, repetition, and blind obedience became the watchwords of the ultimate propaganda state. The 'evil genius' behind this was, of course, Dr Paul Josef Goebbels. A cynical, vain, insecure man, an embittered idealist and a quasi-intellectual, he was devoted to Hitler, with whom he shared a fundamental contempt for the masses. Hitler, indeed, seems to have been the only person whom Goebbels did not regard as corruptible and he created the *Führer-prinzip* (the Hitler legend) around the man about whom he said 'never does one word of falsehood or baseness pass his lips'. It was only towards the end of the war that doubts began to enter his mind concerning the infallibility of the Führer myth that he himself had created.

Goebbels became head of the newly created Ministry for Propaganda and Public Enlightenment (RMVP) in March 1933. For the next six years, he orchestrated a propaganda campaign against the German people that was to prepare them for a single goal: the restoration of Germany's 'rightful' place in the world. Towards this end, the RMVP's tentacles spread into every aspect of German life, with twelve departments dealing with press, radio, film, culture, education, theatre, and so on, with the aim of supervising 'all tasks of spiritual direction of the nation'. The media were placed under State control, but all this was not quite as monolithic as it appears. Joachim von Ribbentrop, Hitler's wartime foreign secretary, was also interested in propaganda and in 1939 even had his responsibilities extended by Hitler (whose policy, after all, was divide and conquer) to include foreign propaganda. Much more seriously from Goebbels' point of view, especially during the war, was the existence of the Reich Press Chief, Otto Dietrich, speaking from Hitler's own office. Even so, control of propaganda in Nazi Germany was far more centralized than in any other belligerent power.

Before moving on to Nazi wartime propaganda, it is necessary to mention briefly one of the most spectacular of pre-war German propaganda techniques, namely the *Parteitag* or mass rally. In a sense, all pre-war propaganda was geared towards the psychological rearmament of the German people, but the rallies held in Nuremberg held a special place in the annual calendar of the party itself. With the help of Albert Speer, Hitler's favourite architect and later Minister for Arms Production, these spectacular stage-managed events provided an annual ritual for the party faithful to re-dedicate themselves to the Führer. Half a million or more members congregated from all parts of Germany to have their banners blessed by the Führer, to pay their respects to the party martyrs (such as Horst Wessel), and to hear speeches in a regimented yet highly emotionally-charged open-air atmosphere that was enhanced at night by searchlights pointing vertically to the sky which one observer likened to a 'cathedral of ice'. The awesome nature of these occasions was captured on film by Leni Reifensthal in her film *Triumph of the Will* (1935) about the 1934 rally. This rally was particularly important to Hitler in light of his recent purge of his brown-shirted stormtroopers in the 'Night of the Long Knives'. Reifensthal's 'record' is not only a testimony to the brilliance of Nazi propaganda techniques, but also to the extent to which Hitler had taken control of Germany within two years of coming to power. As his deputy, Rudolph Hess, shrieked at the rally: 'The Party is Hitler. Hitler is Germany and Germany is Hitler.'

Despite six years of preparation, however, the RMVP entered the war in chaos and confusion. Goebbels had been out of favour with Hitler due to his affair with an actress and the German people hardly seemed enthusiastic for the war. Indeed, according to Speer, they seemed 'depressed'. This soon changed as victory in Poland was followed by a lightning series of victories over Belgium, Holland, Denmark, Norway, and France. Nothing succeeds like success, and nothing benefits more from success than propaganda. Propaganda lubricated the wheels of victory, particularly in persuading any remaining German dissenters that the Führer had indeed been sent by God and Destiny to save the German people from their enemies. Never mind the Nazi-Soviet pact, presented as a pact of peace then quickly 'forgotten' by the Nazi propaganda apparatus. That had been a means to an end. Never mind the fact that Japan and Italy, partners in the anti-Comintern pact since 1936-7, did not enter the war against Poland in September 1939. That war was a just German war designed to redress the injustice of the 1919 Versailles Settlement. Never mind the fact that Britain and France had declared war on Germany. They had done so because of their innate hostility to National Socialism and out of their imperialistic corruption and decadence. Never mind the years of appeasement. That had been caused by weakness and fear. Destiny resided with the Führer. Victory would belong to Germany!

Of all the media, Hitler and Goebbels were most interested in film, and it was the newsreels that served to drive home the German cause and the glory of German military supremacy in the early years of the war. The *Deutsche Wochenschau* (German Weekly Newsreel) was particularly important, being compulsory viewing for all German cinema-goers. Combat footage was taken by cameramen organized in PK Units, appointed by the RMVP but under the immediate orders of the German High Command, the OKW. Their material was then sent back to Berlin and because they were in the thick of the fighting their footage was often so realistic that skilful editing was required to make it serve a constructive propaganda purpose. The success of this combination of actuality footage and propagandistic editing was evident in such early newsreel productions as *Feuertaufe* (1940) ('Baptism of Fire') and *Sieg im Westen* ('Victory in the West') (1941). These films were self-congratulatory and presented German victories in almost sporting terms. As Roger Manvell has written, 'Nazi newsreels were not informative, they were impressionist, emotive, all-conquering – a blitz in themselves of sound and image.' Their message was clear: German military superiority was plain for all to see and the ease with which victory was achieved was testimony to the superiority of the German race and the will of the Führer. Abroad, these *Wochenschau* merely demonstrated that resistance to the German military machine was pointless.

War on film is exciting and cathartic. The Nazis used newsreels and documentaries to involve the German people in the war effort and to terrorize potential opponents. And it seems to have worked. The Gestapo monitored public opinion and responses to individual films. Following the screening of a newsreel depicting German successes in Denmark and Norway, the security forces reported that it had 'undoubtedly increased confidence in victory... total silence in the cinemas – people had to pull themselves together afterwards'. The four pre-war newsreels were merged into a single product and the topicality and authenticity of the medium actually seems to have been a major reason behind the increase in wartime German audiences. By 1940 cinema audiences had almost doubled, and newsreels were also taken into the countryside and shown in schools. Lasting about forty minutes, they used music to great effect and commentary was kept to a minimum; but after 1941 they tended to decline in popularity and began to lose touch with the reality of war. Besides, after Stalingrad, the PK cameramen were filming fewer German advances and more German retreats. In other words, because of their association with early German military success, the popularity of the *Wochenschau* suffered equally when defeat became more common. And by the end of the war, the emphasis had shifted completely to the slogan 'Victory in Death'.

The major themes of the early propaganda campaigns had been directed against Germany's military enemies, particularly Britain. Attempts were made to sow discord between the Allies, with such accusations as 'Britain will fight to the last Frenchman', and throughout 1940 the broadcasts of 'Lord Haw-Haw' made some impression on British listeners, though no real impact. Anti-British feature films were produced, such as *Aufruhr in Damascus* (1939), dealing with the relief of Germans from Lawrence of Arabia's tyranny in Jordan, *Mein Leben für Irland* ('My Life for Ireland') (1941), about historical British oppression, and *Ohm Kruger* ('Uncle Kruger') (1941), about the Boer War. In posters, newspaper articles, and broadcasts, Churchill was lampooned as a drunkard, the Royal Family as decadent, and the British ruling élite as tired old imperialists who had had their day. Britain had been overtaken by the Jews, one of many explanations for the slums, unemployment, and social inequality caused by a corrupt, Jew-ridden plutocracy. Even the title of The Times was reversed to spell SEMIT[E] to 'prove' the point. The tone of this propaganda ebbed and flowed according to German hopes for an early peace settlement with Britain, but anti-British propaganda suffered a major setback when Rudolf Hess parachuted into Scotland in May 1941. Whatever the reasons for his mission, it threw Goebbels into confusion. For the first time he seemed at a loss for words and the propaganda line, that Hess was mentally ill, was worked out by his rivals Dietrich and Bormann with Hitler's approval.

With the invasion of Russia, anti-Russian films once more began to appear. Beginning with GPU (1942), about the brutality of the Soviet secret police, the anti-communist theme reached its climax with *Der Grosse König* (1942), about Frederick the Great's performance against the Russians in the Seven Years War. After Stalingrad, however, official German feature film production dropped dramatically: only four were made in 1943, three in 1944 and one – *Kolberg*, about the merits of resistance – in 1945. But the *Wochenschau* continued to portray the Russians as demonic beasts, even though the Nazis had failed to exploit those secessionist national groups who had offered to fight for the Germans against the Bolsheviks. Blinded by his own ideology, Hitler would not tolerate the idea of Germans fighting alongside these 'subhuman scum' and 'rats', and while the Germans went about systematically wiping them out, Nazi propaganda concentrated on Soviet atrocities and the torture of the GPU. Goebbels had strong reservations about statements concerning the German exploitation of the eastern lands for fear that it would merely stiffen enemy resistance. There was little of the 'Slavic subhuman' in his RMVP propaganda, which concentrated instead on the 'Jewish-Bolshevik Murder System'. But this divergence reflects the multiplicity of voices coming out of the Third Reich. For example, Robert Ley, head of the German Labour Front, carried out much party training and education so that his propagandists could take the ideology of war into the factories. Alfred Rosenberg, who had been appointed in 1934 as 'Commissioner of the Führer for Supervision of the Entire Intellectual and Doctrinal Training and Education of the NSDAP', was appointed in 1941 as a minister for the occupied eastern territories. Rosenberg provided the pseudo-intellectual justification for the anti-Semitic propaganda. He did not get on with Goebbels, or with Ribbentrop for that matter, who also despised Goebbels. Then there was Dietrich in the Führer's office, with whom Goebbels was in constant conflict throughout the war, the army propaganda branch (which produced *Signal*, the most highly circulated German magazine of the war), and the propagandists of the SS. All these men felt that the propaganda activities of the others infringed upon their exclusive territory.

For Goebbels, the most important instrument of Nazi wartime propaganda was the radio, over which he exercised more direct control than the press (if not quite as much as the *Wochenschau*). For Goebbels, radio was 'the first and most influential intermediary between movement and nation, between idea and man'. The German radio network consisted of 26 stations and was managed by the Reich Radio Society and, after 1942, supervised by Hans Fritzsche, who was also the most important German broadcaster of the war years. Foreign broadcasts were monitored so that rumours could be countered. All announcers and radio news editors were required to attend Fritzsche's regular ministerial conferences so that they clearly understood the propaganda line, from which they

were not allowed to deviate. A dramatic feature of German radio
was the special announcement or *Sondermeldung*, which inter-
rupted all programmes with a blast of trumpets to broadcast the
latest communiqué about another military triumph. Popular during
the years 1940-1 for obvious reasons, the announcement would be
followed by a stirring marching song, usually 'We're Marching
Against England'. For the attack on Russia, martial music was
accompanied by artillery fire and screaming Stukas. (The British
realized just how important music was to the Nazis when they
claimed the opening bars of Beethoven's *Fifth Symphony* as their
own.)

On 18 February 1943, Goebbels made the greatest speech of his
life and one of the most important by any war leader anywhere.
This was his famous 'Total War' speech made at the Berlin
Sportpalast. Germany had achieved its military successes between
1939 and 1941 without the kind of total war mobilization the
British had drawn upon to survive in that period. *Blitzkrieg* had
worked even beyond the wildest dreams of its creators. There had,
for example, been no need to call German women into the
factories. But after Stalingrad, with the Americans now firmly in
the war and Italy on the way out, with increasing numbers of
Allied air raids on German cities, Goebbels called upon the people
to make greater sacrifices, to work harder, to increase production.
His skill lay in not presenting these measures as desperate but as
essential to victory. He ended: 'Now, Nation, arise and let the
storm break loose!' This was Goebbels' finest hour and his visits to
bombed cities and their victims made him for a time the most
popular Nazi figure, his high profile standing in marked contrast
to Hitler's continued withdrawal from the public eye. But although
German production increased, reaching its wartime peak in 1944,
the success of the total war campaign ultimately depended upon
Hitler's willingness to grant Goebbels more authority. And although
Goebbels became an advisor on total war mobilization, he was
given no specific powers to cut through the rivalries and the red
tape that was such a characteristic of the Third Reich. By the time
he was made Plenipotentiary for waging total war in July 1944, it
was too late. By then, with the Normandy Landings and the
invasion of Europe in the west, Russian advances in the east, the
destruction of German cities by Allied air raids, and assassination
attempts on Hitler's life, Goebbels' total war drive lay in ruins.

Even his last great propaganda campaign – 'The hour of retaliation has come' – sounded hollow. How could the V1s and V2s be destroying Britain when Allied troops were marching on Berlin?

The German people entered the Second World War seemingly unconcerned about the implications of the attack on Poland. They were stunned when Britain and France declared war on them. Britain's subsequent rejection of German 'peace offers' reinforced Goebbels' assertion that Germany was fighting a defensive war against plutocratic aggressors who were attempting to encircle and destroy the German people. It seems to have worked, although initial victory in the west undoubtedly played a substantial role in heightening enthusiasm for the war. But neither the German people nor the Nazi government were prepared for a long war; shortages and early British air raids, combined with the failure to win the Battle of Britain, caused the return of doubts that reached their high point when Hess flew to Britain in May 1941. The initial success of German armies in Russia in the summer of 1941 raised morale again, which was only to be undermined as the Russian winter set in and the advance on Moscow, Leningrad, and Stalingrad halted. But the Russian campaign in many ways provided Nazi propaganda with its greatest wartime opportunity. For the first time, the German people were being called upon to make sacrifices to help the army. The gap between army and nation, so wide in 1939-41, was narrowed substantially after 1942. Now the entire German nation was involved in total war, and civilians too began to suffer at the hands of Allied air raids. It was this development that provided Nazi propaganda with its chance to unite the nation. The Allies, with their call for unconditional surrender, identified the German people with the Nazi party to an extent that Goebbels had never been able to do. They were all in the same boat now, as the total war drive confirmed. It was this nationalism that was often confused with propaganda. Nazi propaganda identified patriotism with propaganda to such an extent that, once the Allies had reached Berlin, they knew they would have to embark upon a comprehensive post-war programme of de-Nazification.

Chapter 24

Propaganda, Cold War and the Advent of the Television Age

The 'political re-education' of Germany and her former wartime allies became but one element in the post-war struggle between east and west. Yet the notion that these hostile militaristic societies could be cleansed of their aggressive leanings did in a way reflect a new faith in the power of propaganda under another label. Denazification was propaganda to eradicate propaganda, an entire psychological programme to eliminate totalitarianism and militarism. One American propaganda film described as a documentary (winning an Academy Award under that category in 1946) was *Your Job in Germany.* This film was originally designed to instruct American soldiers why they needed to occupy the American zone of Germany but was stridently propagandist in its advocacy of non-fraternization ('You'll be offered the hand of friendship. Don't take it. It is the hand that heiled Hitler'). It also described Nazi propaganda as the 'greatest educational crime in history'. For the British, however, *re-education* was designed, in Lord Vansittart's words, to 'rescue the world from Germany, and Germany from herself'. Not only were the constitutions of the defeated nations re-written to benefit the victors as well as, it was felt, the vanquished, but so also were their educational curricula re-written in an attempt to avoid the catastrophe of another major war caused by a future generation of fanatical militarists inspired by hate propaganda. So, from school lessons to the printed press, domestic radio stations and the cinema, allied representatives set about 'democratizing' the defeated peoples so that they would never wage aggressive war again.

In the democracies, the war had been presented in terms of a struggle between the 'free world' and the 'slave world'. Democracy had survived – but it had been a close run thing. Yet the very fact that it had triumphed in the end despite the Battle of Britain and Pearl Harbour was itself presented as an indicator of its inherent moral supremacy. Democracies, after all, tend not to wage open war against other democracies. The democratic aspirations of peace, equality, liberty and fraternity were embedded in important new international documents such as the Charter of the United Nations and the 1948 Declaration of Human Rights. The problem, of course, was that the war had not just been won by Britain and the United States. Victory had only been achieved with considerable help from an ally in the form of the Soviet Union whose soldiers may have fought heroically but whose rulers were more than willing to deny their people the kind of freedoms in the name of which the war had been justified in the West. Freedom of movement, freedom of thought, freedom of religion and freedom to vote lay at the heart of the Atlantic Charter from which the Russians had been excluded. And so, with the defeat of the Axis powers, the cement that had bound together the Anglo-American-Soviet alliance crumbled. And with the removal of the common enemy, Churchill's 'pact with the devil' became redundant. In the years following the Potsdam and Yalta conferences at the end of the war, deep-rooted ideological differences resurfaced following from the occupation and suppression of Eastern Europe by the Red Army and the Americanization of Western Europe through the Marshall Plan. Worse still was to come with the victory of Mao's Communist forces in the Chinese civil war by 1949, the year in which the Soviets first tested their own atomic bomb.

With the rapid deterioration of wartime allegiances into what came to be known as the Cold War, a new type of conflict emerged. This was a war on the mind, a contest of ideologies, a battle of nerves which, for the next forty years or so, was to divide the planet into a bi-polar competition that was characterized more by a war of words and the threatened use of nuclear weapons rather than their actual use. It was a conflict in which the idea of nuclear war was constantly on the mind of international public opinion. Periodically threatening to erupt into 'Hot War', as in 1948-9 with the Berlin Blockade or in 1962 with the Cuban Missile Crisis, Soviet-American relations became the focal point around which post-war thoughts of war and peace came to revolve. The erection of the Berlin Wall in 1961 was to become the perfect symbol of a divided world separated by the 'Iron Curtain' described by Churchill fifteen years earlier. Yet despite dangerous regional clashes all around the globe, most notably in Korea (1950-3), the Middle East (1967 and 1973), Vietnam (*c.*1963-75) and Afghanistan (1979-88), the superpowers did manage to avoid launching a Third World War that would have threatened the destruction of the entire planet. Now the Cold War is said to be over, we have to ask the question: how real was that threat?

The arrival of nuclear weapons was real enough. But they created an entirely new dimension in international affairs in which the risks of launching a war could no longer be matched by clear potential gains. Their actual use beggared the imagination. The acronym for one of the principal strategies – Mutual Assured Destruction – summed up the realities of likely conflict; quite simply, it would be MAD for one side to risk starting a new conflict if, in so doing, it invited its own destruction. As the Chernobyl incident of 1986 was to indicate, it wouldn't need much of a disaster to launch a nuclear winter that would see the elimination of the planet's atmosphere. And so, despite repeated superpower jostling for position in the decades following the Second World War, there was a fundamental recognition that, even if one side should 'win' a nuclear conflict, it could at best achieve a Pyrrhic victory because the other side was bound to have inflicted massive devastation in the process of 'losing'. Such a conflict was unlikely to be contained and so, through a process of escalation, a genuine Domesday scenario loomed large. As a consequence, international diplomacy appeared to be developing by the 1950s into a great game of bluff, counter-bluff and double bluff all set against a climate of terror. Because both sides had to project the impression that they were in fact serious and that this was *not* a game of bluff, an atmosphere was created in which propaganda could only flourish.

This was an expensive and highly risky competition. The high costs of maintaining a nuclear arsenal and of developing missile delivery systems to carry them across continents (with the race extending into Outer Space in the 1960s), meant there was a need to justify year after year such consistently high peacetime military expenditure to domestic audiences in both the USSR and the USA. The Atlantic community under the umbrella of NATO (formed 1949) existed on the rationale that disarmament after the First World War was a major cause for the Second World War; we had trusted our enemies last time by disarming whereas they had betrayed that trust and had attacked Poland and Pearl Harbour so that we must now be constantly on our guard and ready. (Eventually, admittedly, Russia had also been attacked – but that was only after collusion of the 1939-41 Nazi-Soviet Pact.) For western taxpaying voters, a genuine 'enemy' was required and, as Soviet actions in the suppression of Eastern Europe seemed to indicate – Hungary 1956, Czechoslovakia 1968, Poland 1981 – one had clearly been found. The Great Russian Bear was thus transformed into the Red Bolshevik Menace.

From 1946 onwards, and for a period lasting four decades, the rhetoric of the free world and the slave once again came to dominate public discourse about international conflict. The Truman Doctrine of 1948 served to narrow this down to a black and white confrontation between two seemingly incompatible ways of life:

> One way of life is based upon the will of the majority, and is distinguished by free institutions, representative government, free elections, guarantees of personal liberty, freedom of speech and religion and freedom from political repression. The second way of life is based upon the will of a minority imposed upon the majority. It relies upon terror and repression, a controlled press and radio, fixed elections, and the suppression of personal freedoms.

Yet on both sides, sustained military preparation was justified in accordance with the maxim that 'he who desires peace must prepare for war'. Those words had been written by the Roman writer Vegetius in the fourth century and they now assumed even greater significance as nations which purported to cherish peace and disarmament found themselves having to accept reluctantly continued military preparation to safeguard their way of life. This combination of theoretical and historical justification for maintaining a nuclear balance was a significant area in the propaganda battle for the hearts and minds of war-fearing citizens.

At the root of this battle was, indeed, fear. The problem was that fear of 'The Bomb' and possible global thermo-nuclear annihilation undoubtedly helped to fuel a pacifist mentality which belied the advice of Vegetius. Especially in war-ravaged Europe, caught between the two extra-European superpowers, peace movements such as the Campaign for Nuclear Disarmament began to emerge as a direct response to the mounting superpower nuclear tension of the 1950s and early 1960s. Official propaganda therefore had to ensure that fear of the enemy was sustained at a higher level than fear of the bomb. Both in Russia and America, as well as in their alliance blocs of NATO and the Warsaw Pact, it was imperative to convince people that fear of the enemy was genuine, legitimate and justified. This in turn would legitimate and justify the need to sustain a nuclear arsenal that would have to be at least the equal of the other side, in which case there might never be a use for it. And so the nuclear arms race continued through its inescapably logical course.

This climate of fear – or balance of terror – was played out in the media. So long as 'The Enemy' had 'The Bomb', he would always be feared by decent, peace-loving citizens, whether they be Soviet or American. Propaganda exploited these fears with such themes as 'nuclear weapons cannot be disinvented' (technological determinism), 'because they are pointing weapons at us we must point the same weapons at them' (deterrence), 'if they attack us first, we have effectively lost' (first strike capability) and so on. The other side had always to be portrayed as aggressive, militaristic and repressive – as a genuine threat to peace and freedom however such concepts were defined by either side.

On this aspect, it might be thought that the Soviet Union, with its state-controlled media and thus its greater capacity to shape the information and opinions of its citizens concerning the intentions of the outside world, enjoyed a considerable advantage over its democratic rivals. This was certainly so on the domestic front within the borders of the Soviet Union and in its Moscow-imposed allies. It held this advantage until the 1980s when new communications technologies were finally able to penetrate the Iron Curtain and provide alternative images of what 'The Enemy' was really like which ran counter to the 'accepted view' decreed by the Communist Party of the Soviet Union (CPSU). Until then, however, it was possible for the CPSU to maintain an information environment that was just about hermetically sealed, an environment in which the official Soviet world-view could prevail, while it simultaneously exploited the very freedoms cherished by the West.

Paradoxically, that same sealed environment provided the United States with advantages of its own in its propaganda when it came to painting a particular image of 'the enemy'. It meant that the 'freedom-loving' public could only perceive the Soviets as being afraid to permit alternative ways of seeing and believing, and thus by way of contrast reinforce their views about the undesirability of

communist totalitarianism. Because the Soviet authorities refused
to permit a free press, because they restricted travel beyond their
own borders – and even within them – and because they had a secret
police to enforce these repressive laws, they were indeed behaving
like the enemy of democratic principles. And because the view *from*
Moscow was clearly orchestrated by the CPSU authorities and not
by the Russian 'people', this in turn made it difficult for 'we, the
people' to accept a view *of* Moscow that was different from that
presented by *Washington*. So when President Nixon said that 'it
may be melodramatic to say that the United States and Russia
represent Good and Evil, but if we think of it that way, it helps to
clarify our perspective on the world struggle' or when President
Reagan spoke of the Soviet Union as an 'Evil Empire', it was tricky
for Moscow to provide an alternative or acceptable point of view.

They did try, with a concerted propaganda campaign which insisted that they were nowhere near as dangerous as the Americans
made them out to be. Indeed, in Cold War battlegrounds beyond
Europe and North America, they were not without success.
Regardless of their own difficulties with Peking following the
communist take-over of China, the Soviets were able to exploit the
vulnerability of newly independent countries emerging from
centuries of colonial rule in the 'Third World' during the 1950s
and 1960s. Although the United States had always professed itself
to be anti-imperialist – citing its own revolutionary history of
independence from British rule – its commitment to capitalism
enabled the Soviets to portray a Marxist-Leninist view of a free-
market enterprise system as a form of imperialism under an
economic disguise. Former colonies in Africa and Asia therefore
had a choice – which was something they had not enjoyed before.
They could not survive in an increasingly interdependent world
economy defined by the Bretton Woods system unless they became
part of that system which, the Soviets argued, would merely perpetuate their *dependence* upon the western capitalist powers rather
than encourage their *independence* from them. But there was now
at least an alternative. Moscow would help – with economic
subsidies, with advisers and arms supplies to aid their struggle and
with guidance on how to provide political and social stability in
the transformation from colonial dependency to a Marxist-Leninist
version of independence that would dismantle the differences
between the fortunate rich and the less fortunate, exploited poor. If

the British were also trying to achieve their own version of the future in the transformation from Empire to Commonwealth, the Soviets argued that former colonies needed to look no further than the uprisings in Kenya or Malaysia to see the disastrous consequences of that particular route. Contrasting the 1951 Festival of Britain with the Great Exhibition of a century earlier, it was easy to argue that Britain was a country with a great future behind it. Equally, the French were waging colonial wars in Algeria and South Vietnam and their defeat merely reflected their degeneracy. Nor was the United States, despite all its protestations, above all this with interference in Iran, the Philippines, Guatemala, Nicaragua, El Salvador, Chile and elsewhere. Moscow therefore offered a new way forward, a way that could once and for all provide an alternative to the exploitation of oppressed peoples, a socialist paradise in which everyone would benefit equally.

To reinforce these messages, the Soviet Union launched a propagandist onslaught, orchestrated by Agitprop (the Administration of Agitation and Propaganda of the Communist Party Central Committee) and Cominform (established in 1947 to replace the now defunct Comintern). Every available media were utilized, as appropriate to local conditions, from books and pamphlets to press, radio and film. No matter how sophisticated the methods and media used, however, it is important to remember that the Soviets always regarded language as a fundamental aspect of policy to secure Marxist-Leninist 'historical imperatives'. Words as weapons in this ideological struggle thus assumed an active and highly potent role in defining such concepts as 'peace', 'disarmament', 'independence' and 'liberation' in an attempt to seize the initiative from, and set the perceptual framework about, 'the West'. The world was conceived in terms of a struggle between communism and anti-communism. Hence the Cold War started when 'American imperialism sought to nullify the victory of the forces of progress in the Second World War and to impose its diktat on mankind'. The objective was quite simply to control the terms of the debate on international affairs and to set the agenda of international discourse. A major strategy in this once again was to play on fear, both within the West and, within the Third World, fear of the West. For this, 'Front' organizations were required so as to disguise the fact that Moscow was conducting the orchestra: far better to have foreigners playing the tune in their own countries than musicians with a Russian accent. Fear of nuclear war was exploited by such various front organizations as the World Peace Council, founded in 1949, which supported the North Korean invasion of South Korea in June 1950 and was also responsible for disseminating fabricated charges of US germ warfare in that conflict. Other 'agents of influence' such as sympathetic journalists, academics and even intelligence officers operating in the West were cultivated by Moscow while massive disinformation campaigns were also launched by the KGB to disguise the real strength of the Soviet armed forces while exaggerating the threat posed by the West. It was a 'divide and rule' approach designed to divert attention from Soviet intentions. According to some estimates, by 1960 the Soviets were spending the equivalent of $2 billion dollars on communist propaganda world-wide.

To counter this onslaught, the Americans responded vigorously on two fronts that were closely connected: the domestic and the international. In 1948, the Smith-Mundt Act revitalized the American post-war information services 'to promote a better understanding of the United States in other countries, and to increase mutual understanding between the people of the United States and the people of other countries'. This statement in fact resonates of 'cultural propaganda' – or 'cultural diplomacy' as the British and French prefer to call it; the Americans prefer 'public diplomacy'. Usually, such activity involves the dissemination of literature and other cultural products such as visiting speakers, films, travelling theatre groups and orchestras, the promotion of language teaching and other 'educational' activities such as student exchange schemes. All are designed to create over time 'goodwill' towards the country subsidizing the activity. The Europeans had already been engaged in this type of 'national self-advertisement' for some 50 years, with the British entering the field relatively late in the day with the formation of the British Council in 1934. The Americans, however, tended to leave this type of activity to private 'philanthropic' or commercial concerns, and when one bears in mind the universal attractiveness of such American products as Coca-Cola, Levi jeans or McDonalds, or Hollywood films and American music, it is an approach which commanded its supporters. As Walter Wanger pointed out in 1950, Hollywood represented a 'Marshall Plan of Ideas' in 115 countries around the world where 72 per cent of the films being shown were of American origin. Hence, in the context of the Cold War, such cultural activity was assuming an increasingly political significance. Wanger put it bluntly: 'Donald Duck as World Diplomat!'. Propagandist, more like. Marxist scholars argued that media products like films and later television programmes carry ideologically coded messages that attack indigenous cultures and create aspirations to emulate the culture which produced them. This, claimed the critics unable to counter effectively with attractive products of their own, was 'Coca-Colonialism' – a 'cultural imperialism' designed to homogenize the world into a global village where American values and perspectives prevailed.

Regardless of the validity of whether this activity was a conspiracy by an American military-industrial complex, or merely the coincidental consequence of American economic power and prowess in popular culture products, successive political administrations in Washington were concerned to promote directly American beliefs and outlooks abroad. This had first become apparent in 1950 when President Truman launched his 'Campaign for Truth' against communism following the outbreak of the Korean War, with $121 million appropriated by Congress. Such increased expenditure on propaganda was to be merely the psychological component of a massive rearmament programme that was all based on an infamous 1950 policy document known as NSC 68, in which Soviet intentions were identified quite simply as world domination:

> The Kremlin is inescapably militant. It is inescapably militant because it possesses and is possessed by a world-wide revolutionary movement, because it is the inheritor of Russian imperialism, and because it is a totalitarian dictatorship ... It is quite clear from Soviet theory and practice that the Kremlin seeks to bring the free world under its domination by the methods of the Cold War.

The document went on to state that the Soviets were to be countered by the rapid build-up of political, economic and military strength in order to create 'confidence in the free world'. While the military prepared for a surprise Soviet atomic strike, the American propaganda machine was cranked up to justify the consequences to tax-payers and to reassure NATO and other alliance partners that they would not be overrun, that communism would be, and could be, 'contained' if not 'rolled back'. To this end, West Germany was admitted into the NATO fold, while the US State Department did all it could to help Hollywood's overseas markets in the recognition that films served as 'ideas ambassadors'. The difficult problem of movies which depicted the darker side of the American way of life – crime and gangster movies and the like – was overcome since the Soviet Union and its allies banned even those.

Cultural activity, however, was a long-term process. What was also urgently required was a short-term strategy based upon news and information to counter rapidly any Soviet-inspired misinformation about US intentions. To this end, several decisions were taken. In 1950, the Voice of America (VOA – the USA's official external broadcasting service) was transmitting 30 programme hours daily in 23 different languages around the world. By 1955, VOA was broadcasting about 850 hours per week as part of an all-embracing international propaganda campaign conducted by the United States Information Services (USIS). One of its officials subsequently admitted that 'we frequently fell to the temptation of broadcasting bitterly sarcastic, almost vitriolic, anti-Stalinist attacks'. Yet this did not prevent Senator Joseph McCarthy from bringing the VOA under his anti-communist scrutiny and the mud thrown in this period probably contributed to the VOA cut-backs of the late 1950s.

In 1951, the President had also created a Psychological Strategy Board to advise the National Security Council and in 1953 a personal adviser on psychological warfare was working at the White House for President Eisenhower, Truman's successor. Government-sponsored research into psychological warfare was also stepped up and even civil defence programmes at home which played on fears of the bomb came within its remit. In 1953, American information activities were separated from the State Department and the USIA (US Information Agency) was formed. The VOA, as the radio arm of USIA, was given a clear objective, namely 'to multiply and intensify psychological deterrents to communist aggression'. Indeed, the degree to which propaganda and psychological warfare were now operating hand in hand with American policy at the highest levels was reflected by Eisenhower's belief that:

> We are now conducting a cold war. That cold war must have some objective, otherwise it would be senseless. It is conducted in the belief that if there is no war, if two systems of government are allowed to live side by side, that ours, because of its greater appeal to men everywhere, to mankind, in the long run will win out. That it will defeat all forms of

dictatorial government because of its greater appeal to the human soul, the human heart, the human mind.

How such statements were received in Moscow remains unknown. But in the West, Moscow was now being viewed through American filters and such filters were incapable of permitting an alternative perception of Soviet intentions. So when Soviet leaders insisted that they were not threatening anybody, nor had they ever done – that they were only interested in defending their homeland against invasion and chaos, in Finland 1940, in Hungary 1956, even in Afghanistan much later – all the West could hear were Khrushchev's famous words: 'we will bury you'. In the manufacture of consent during the Cold War, it might appear that each side was shouting blindly at the other, yet the reality was an alarming and highly dangerous failure to communicate effectively beyond the propaganda barrage.

Part of this can be explained in terms of a mirror image. When the Soviets and Americans viewed one another, they tended to see the dark side of their own characteristics which they reflected back at their view of the other. This isn't a recipe for genuine mutual understanding, but it is conducive to an effective domestic propaganda campaign feeding off paranoia. In the United States, the start of the Cold War was accompanied by a hate-inspired anti-Soviet propaganda campaign that permeated all aspects of American life, especially between 1947 and 1958. This was orchestrated by the Senate's Internal Security Committee and the House of Representative's Un-American Activities Committee (HUAC), founded in 1938 to weed out Nazi agents. Culminating in the sordid McCarthyite 'witch-hunts' of the early 1950s, this campaign created a climate of fear in which sympathy for the 'Enemy' was equated with sympathy for the Devil. The conversion of a former wartime ally into a peacetime enemy was fuelled by media representation of post-war events in a specifically hostile light. The 'Red Menace' was not just a threat to Europe and Asia: it threatened the very existence of the 'American way of life' itself. Books, magazines, films and even the new medium of television were scrutinized by self-appointed watchdog groups of red-hunters, often sponsored by the Federal Bureau of Investigation, to create an atmosphere in which no view of the Russians other than as demons could be tolerated. It was a campaign which, by comparison, made the Second World War search for Nazi 'Fifth Columnists' pale into insignificance.

The new 'Enemy Within' now became all members of American society who had ever shown any sympathy with communist, socialist, or even liberal causes – regardless of the wartime alliance. More ominously, anyone who protested against government measures came to be labelled 'a subversive'. As one cinema newsreel stated in its coverage of public protests in New York in 1949: 'Union Square in New York was the backdrop for these scenes of Red violence. From their ranks will come the saboteurs, spies and subversives should a Third World War be forced upon America'. The growing number of television viewers from 1948 onwards could witness the menace for themselves as people previously unconcerned with political affairs were sucked into the climate of fear from the (dis)comfort of their own living rooms. They were told that the media were full of Soviet spies and communist lackeys, which merely brought the media into line. Hollywood suddenly became keen to demonstrate what we would now call political correctness by making a succession of anti-communist movies, such as *The Woman on Pier 13* (1949, originally entitled *I Married a Communist*) and *I Was a Communist for the FBI* (1951). Films can also serve as mirrors of their times and it is possible to identify Cold War concerns that would have resonated with contemporary audiences in many popular movies of this period, from *High Noon* (1952) to *On the Waterfront* (1954).

Science fiction films are an especially rich genre for analysing such themes as 'the enemy' or 'the invader' as metaphors for reflecting contemporary fears of hostile aggression and invasion. Alien invaders needn't automatically look like bug-eyed monsters; their appearance could be deceptive. In *The Invasion of the Body Snatchers* (1953) the aliens take control of the body and minds of citizens from small town America who thereafter start behaving mechanically and collectively in what is a suspiciously American perception of what a communist society would look like. Compare this version with the remake in 1978 – the period of detente – in which the invaders are more clearly extra-terrestrial than Russian. In the science fiction film *Them!* (1954) about giant flying *red* ants taking over the sewers of Los Angeles, the invaders have been created by mutation following nuclear test explosions. The 'fear of the bomb' genre of films and the 'fear of invasion' genre came together perfectly in *The Day the Earth Stood Still* (1951) in which an ostensibly benign alien humanoid (played by Michael Rennie) brings with him a robot ('Gort') with destructive powers to enforce his message that mankind must abandon its course towards self-annihilation through the development of nuclear weapons. The message of disarmament in this film was tempered by the fact that the Rennie character was prepared to use force if reason did not prevail. Nuclear themes were tackled directly in other films such as *On the Beach* (1959) or in Stanley Kubrick's satirical masterpiece, *Dr Strangelove, or How I Learned to Stop Worrying and Love the Bomb* (1964).

Spies were also everywhere in the movies: how else could the technologically inferior Russians have secured the A-bomb unless traitors had supplied them with the secret? Many lives were ruined in this media-fest. In 1953 Julius and Ethel Rosenberg paid the ultimate price in the electric chair at the height of this epidemic hysteria. The spy movie genre survived throughout the Cold War, most notably in the 'James Bond' and 'Harry Palmer' films and those based upon novels by writers such as Graham Greene and John Le Carré. But the anti-communist menace was most pronounced in the early 1950s. Of this unfortunate period in American history, cultural historian Fred Inglis has written: 'The combination of popular passion, rigging of the legislature, and the hysterical complicity of the press turned the state into the liberal-capitalist version of totalitarianism'.

Nor was the battle confined to American soil. Cold Warriors were keen to take the campaign into the Soviet Union and Eastern Europe. On one programme from the early 1950s, 'The Longines Chronoscope: a television journal of the important issues of the hour', Congressman Emanuel Celler (with a significant slip of the tongue) stated:

> There is no doubt that Russia is winning the propaganda battle. If I may say it, I'd like to use a 'T Bomb', a bomb of truth, and explode it all over Europe particularly where the communists are in control ... I'm in favour of economy, but when it comes to waging war, er, waging rather peace, we cannot spend enough.

'The Crusade for Freedom' was launched, ostensibly to promote the ability of freedom-loving peoples in Eastern Europe to shake off the Soviet militaristic yoke by providing them with 'objective' news and information through the newly-created Radio Free Europe. Radio Liberation (later Liberty) was set up to cater purely for Russian audiences. As the popular singer, Bing Crosby, said on one fund-raising film shown in America's cinemas:

> I want to tell you something I found out over in Europe. We've got plenty of good friends behind the Iron Curtain – probably 50 or 60 million of them. Naturally, they're not Russians, they're not communists. They're freedom-loving peoples in the captive countries who refuse to believe the big red lies the commies tell them. And do you know why they don't believe those lies? It's because we, you and I and millions of other private US citizens have found a way to pierce the Iron Curtain with the truth. And that way is Radio Free Europe, the most powerful weapon in the Crusade for Freedom. You know we're actually helping to prevent World War Three. But that way takes dollars. Truth dollars. All we can spare.

In fact, public subscription alone proved insufficient to subsidize this campaign, and so the CIA decided to back it secretly. Ronald Reagan, then best known as a Hollywood 'B' movie actor who had done his bit to weed out communists from Hollywood, added his support: 'The Campaign for Freedom is your chance and mine to fight communism. Join now by sending your contributions ... or join in your local communities'. It emerged much later that, together, Radio Liberty, the VOA, the BBC World Service and German service Deutsche Welle were collectively nicknamed 'The Voices' by the KGB.

With the death of Stalin in 1953, the Soviet Union also experienced a significant domestic propaganda campaign in the form of Khrushchev's 'de-Stalinization' programme and his denunciation of the former leader's 'cult of personality'. This chiefly took the form of expanding the system of political education from around 4 million pupils in 1953 to just under 40 million at the time of Khrushchev's dismissal in 1964 to create the 'New Soviet Man'. Sporting prowess assumed a new significance in international competitions such as the Olympic Games and even chess tournaments. This remained a considerable factor in demonstrating national prestige, with the Soviets even recruiting athlete-soldiers to test the limits of human endurance not just on earth but, later, in space. In 1967, they launched the Cosmonauts Number Zero project to participate in medical experiments. Likewise, Soviet prowess in medical achievements was a key element in demonstrating the all-round superiority of the Soviet superman.

At the 20th Congress of the CPSU in February 1956, Khrushchev confirmed the acceptance of 'varying roads to socialism', namely a loosening of Moscow's previous iron grip on its Eastern European satellites. Although the discrediting of Stalin of which this was a part was originally supposed to be a secret policy, news of it quickly spread and created repercussions in Hungary where many saw an opportunity of creating socialism 'with a human face'. When Russian military force suppressed the 1956 uprising, it was a chink in the armour of the Soviet-inspired view of the Eastern bloc as a happy band of willing fellow travellers. Western propaganda exploited it as such, stepping up its broadcasts beyond the Iron Curtain. Khrushchev responded in spectacular style by appearing on CBS television in 1957, telling American viewers of his intentions to engage in what he called 'peaceful competition'. Television was heralding in a new age of international diplomacy, allowing politicians to address the public of other countries directly. But until television achieved majority penetration in advanced societies after the 1960s, international radio remained the most significant medium in the international battle which, in the context of the Cold War, was a far cry from the notion encapsulated by the BBC motto that 'Nation Shall Speak Peace Unto Nation'. Hence the continuing Soviet need for the jamming of western broadcasts that became a characteristic of the ebbs and flows of Cold War tension. By transmitting a continuous 'buzz-saw' noise on the same frequency as the offending broadcasts, the Soviets hoped to seal their citizens off from the alternative interpretations offered by the opposition and thus sustain their own view of international events. The competition must not be too equal and peace must be on the terms of the new Soviet men. The western powers did not engage in jamming Russian broadcasts, although considerable resources were poured into to monitoring them constantly.

As for television broadcasting, which began in Russia in 1949, it was not until the 1970s that it became a truly mass medium covering most of the Soviet Union. Between 1960 and 1981, the number of domestic TV sets rose from just under 5 million to around 75 million (a rise from 5 per cent to 90 per cent of the population) and it was only really then that it superseded the press and radio as the principal sources of news and information. Like those media, however, television broadcasting was rigorously controlled by the State, from the granting of licenses and finance to the selection of media personnel, from providing access to news gatherers to the supervision of journalistic training. If all that failed to produce the desired result at the pre- or self-censorship stages, there was also the recourse to straight and direct control by the Politburo of the Central Committee, the ruling body of the State, and its censorship agency, GLAVIT. The Politburo also appointed the head of the State-owned news agency, TASS, and its radio network, GOSTELRADIO, as well as the editors of the leading newspapers such as *Pravda* and *Izvestia*. In 1978, the editor-in-chief of *Pravda* stated bluntly: 'Our aim is propaganda, the propaganda of the party and the state. We do not hide this'. The first Molniya television communications satellite, launched in 1965, threatened to extend the international propaganda war into new types of media as well as into Outer Space.

Such a battle would at first be confined to industrialized countries. As decolonization proceeded apace in the 1950s and 1960s, the newly independent countries in Africa, Asia and Latin America invariably had higher priorities – such as health, food, political stability – than acquiring advanced media systems such as television services. Interestingly, many domestic radio and television services around the Third World evolved out of a local demand created following the spillage of signals from armed forces networks established to entertain and inform foreign military personnel from advanced countries stationed in those nations. There was, however, a growing feeling that such services could serve a greater function than mere entertainment; that they could invariably help economic development. The problem was that the world was divided into rich and poor, developed and underdeveloped, media 'haves' and media 'have-nots'. Moreover, many newly independent countries possessed illiterate or poorly educated populations, and radio especially offered a comparatively inexpensive route to informing and educating their peoples. But a further problem was that once a domestic radio infrastructure was established, it became a target for external broadcasting and thus became prone to involvement in the ideological struggle of the Cold War. Indeed the very debate about international communications became entangled in the divide, with the Americans arguing for a free flow of information while the Soviets felt this would jeopardize their position in the competition. Moscow backed Third World calls through UNESCO for a New World Information Order to redress the balance of western (especially American) media domination.

Washington, seeing this a tool for preserving authoritarian regimes afraid to admit western media products and values, eventually withdrew from UNESCO in 1985, to be followed by the UK.

If by 1962 anyone was still in doubt, the Americans and Russians demonstrated just how far they remained prepared to go to the brink of nuclear confrontation over Cuba. Washington, invigorated by the new administration of John Fitzgerald Kennedy, was keen to show that it still regarded Central and South America as their backyard where no communist should tread, even though the worst excesses of the McCarthy period were past. But, by going so close to the brink, the Cuban missile crisis served as a severe shock, a classic example of the dangers of a failure to communicate effectively instead of through the fog of mutually antagonistic propaganda. Significantly, in the aftermath of the crisis, Washington and Moscow agreed to establish a direct 'hot-line' so that their leaders could communicate directly with one another to avoid any future misunderstandings in crises that were now characteristically propaganda-driven.

This is not to suggest that the public confrontation diminished. One USIA official warned in the early 1960s that 'unless there is a suicidal nuclear war, the balance of power between ourselves and the communists will be largely determined by public opinion'. Many officials were now arguing that propaganda was becoming as important to diplomacy as gunpowder had been to the conduct of war. The problem was that it was becoming increasingly difficult to ascertain precisely where the word-weapons were coming from thanks to increased covert involvement by the secret intelligence services. To undermine Fidel Castro's regime, for example, the Americans launched covert 'black propaganda' transmissions to Cuba from the CIA's Radio Swan (although in 1985 this became a 'white' service in the form of Radio Marti transmitted from Florida. TV Marti began in 1990). The Russians also retained their faith in black propaganda, which they termed 'active measures', and in front organizations, disseminating forged documents in the aftermath of the downing of the U-2 American spy plane over Soviet air space in 1960. Covert activity was felt to be 'more forceful than diplomacy but less hideous than war'. The advantage of black activity was that it was, by definition, supposed to be emanating from sources other than the covert but true one. It therefore enjoyed considerably more latitude with such concepts as 'the truth' than its white counterpart, which was ostensibly subject to greater international agreements concerning the fostering of internal unrest in other countries. By 1962, Soviet radio was broadcasting 1200 hours a week to foreign countries, of which only 250 were directed at Western Europe. Moscow Radio now had a rival in Peking Radio but, to the Americans, Sino-Soviet antagonism was secondary to the massive increase in communist international propaganda that began increasingly to exploit the growing western youth movements of the 1960s. Accordingly, by 1965, the USIA's budget was increased to $100.3 million.

The VOA did have an ally in the BBC World Service, which was generally regarded as a more reliable source of 'objective information', but Anglo-American relations had also come under much strain during the Suez crisis of 1956. There was also a recognition that the shadowy world of intelligence activities was somewhere that the white services, such as the VOA and BBC, dared not tread if they were to preserve their credibility. The Americans accordingly renamed psychological warfare into psychological operations while Soviet 'active measures' continued to spread *dezinformatsia*. This became a great game between the CIA and KGB to discredit the other side – by spreading rumours that one side was involved in this or that dirty deed (such as biological and chemical experiments, assassinations, fomenting uprisings and so on) which was to last well into the 1980s. The story, for example, that AIDS was an offshoot of American biological warfare experiments – which was picked up by newspapers all around the world – was a KGB plant. So was another 1980s story that wealthy Americans were plundering children in Third World countries for 'spare-part surgery' back home. We know about such things now thanks to Soviet defectors and the end of the Cold War, although what the CIA was doing in this field still remains obscure. One example did come to light in 1985 when a CIA propaganda officer (John Stockwell) admitted fabricating a widely-reported story that Cuban soldiers who had raped some girls in Angola had subsequently been caught, tried and executed by firing squad. Even the photograph of the 'firing squad' was a fake. In early 1995, *The Times* reported that American academic research centres in Moscow were front organizations for the CIA. Future historians will need to be wary when scouring the international media of this period as primary sources for their research since such stories abounded, making it difficult if not impossible for contemporaneous readers to identify which story was real and which was a propaganda plant.

Psychological operations were, then, no longer being confined to the traditional battlefield, for the battlefield had become the global information environment. They were still used in low intensity conflicts – in the colonial and guerilla wars, for example – which required high-intensity propaganda, and they were to be tried in the escalating conflict in Vietnam. The time-honoured techniques of leaflet dropping and clandestine radio broadcasting were now accompanied by more sophisticated experiments such as the placing of messages in bars of soap and on ping-pong balls dropped over enemy lines. Blocks of ice containing animal blood were even dropped by parachute over the Vietnamese jungle, where they would melt leaving all the indications that a pilot was injured but missing somewhere – a ploy designed to divert North Vietnamese forces on a wild goose chase. In the Vietnam war, however, the major propaganda battle was to be fought not in theatre itself but on the domestic front.

President Kennedy had proved himself a master of the new medium of television. Indeed, such was his skill as a media politician – the most effective since Roosevelt – that many myths about his administration still belie the actual historical record (resurfacing in Oliver Stone's 1989 film *J.F.K.*). Kennedy's youthful and dynamic image, combined with his ability to find the appropriate snappy phrase before the cameras (which we now call 'sound-bites') made for an attractive leader of the western world as it attempted to stem the advance of communism. He was quick to see that the space race would be perceived world-wide more in terms of prestige through technological achievement, and he launched an American space programme designed to steal the thunder of the Soviets following their successful launch of the first extra-terrestrial vehicle, Sputnik I, in 1957. He was not to see that race won with the American moon landing in 1969. Nor, following his assassination in Dallas in 1963, was he to see the disastrous outcome of the war he had done so much to escalate in South-East Asia. Even in death, Kennedy's love affair with the camera was captured on film, the famous Zapruder footage. Little could he have known that the war he helped to escalate when it was captured on television was, for many people, to lie at the root of what would be America's first significant military defeat.

Shortly after Kennedy's death, the World Rule of Law Centre commissioned a study in 1964 by John Whitton and Arthur Larson who stated unequivocally that 'propaganda helps to cause war'. They continued: 'that propaganda in itself increases the danger of war is no mere theory or rhetorical flourish. There is convincing historical evidence of the actual hastening of war by deliberate propaganda techniques'. They then went on to cite numerous examples of where this had occurred in an attempt to advocate 'disarmament in the war of words'. As we have seen, the escalation of propaganda since 1945 undoubtedly contributed to significant international friction. But, in a sense, Whitton and Larson missed the point. Wars are not caused solely, or even mainly, by propaganda. They are caused by people in power who have to balance possible risks against potential gains in order to achieve their aims by means other than peaceful ones. Once they have balanced the risks, then the propaganda comes into play. Propaganda can escalate a conflict but it usually comes after the policy has been decided. The Cold War, once it was under way, demanded that policy and propaganda be conducted hand-in-hand. Many propagandists working in various western information agencies argued that the Soviets always held the initiative because their propaganda was so interwoven with their policy. The western democracies had to learn that, in order to survive an ideological confrontation, they would need to fight fire with fire.

Moreover, the increasing intrusiveness of the mass media into political life required greater attention to presentational skills on the domestic front, giving rise to the recent age of media politics. Propaganda could no longer operate in a vacuum divorced from social or political realities. But if the policy arrived at was one of peace, the propaganda which would follow from it had the potential to reinforce it. It was Clausewitz who argued that war was the continuation of politics by other means but, in the Cold War, propaganda became the continuation of politics by other means. In terms of a possible nuclear confrontation, propaganda became the essential means by which the superpowers could fight each other verbally rather than physically. But in a confrontation between a nuclear and a non-nuclear power, as in Vietnam, the former dared not use the bomb for fear of being branded an irresponsible nuclear thug and the enemy of civilization whereas the latter had to use every weapon that it could muster. With the arrival of television, a significant new weapon had been found.

The Vietnam conflict crept on to American television screens rather like it has done in this chapter, that is gradually, almost serendipitously, reflecting the extent of the US military build-up there. In 1963, there were 16,000 American troops and about 20 American foreign correspondents in Vietnam. By 1968, these figures had risen to half a million men and 637 journalists. It was the first war fought out before a mass television audience, and its impact upon American (and world) public opinion is often said to have been decisive. Images of burning monks, napalmed children, executed Vietcong and deadly helicopter gunships appeared nightly in the living rooms of civilian homes far removed from the fighting and made Vietnam the most visible war yet seen in history. The relationship between television and war has been greatly debated ever since. Would the First World War have lasted as long as it did if television cameras had been present in the trenches? Yet Vietnam lasted much longer than that earlier conflict, despite the presence of television. Even so, ever since, there has been a widely-held belief that television helped America to lose the war in Vietnam. So precisely what role did television play?

From a propaganda point of view, the conflict can be broken down into three main stages. The first, from 1941-63, in which the Americans played only a minor role to the French through a small number of military 'advisers', received scant media attention in America. The second, from 1963-8, saw a massive escalation of American military involvement by the Kennedy and Johnson administrations and a corresponding increase in media coverage. It was during this period that the Joint United States Public Affairs Office (JUSPAO) was established to meet the needs of newsmen who, for the most part, supported the war. Hordes of inexperienced journalists attempting to make a reputation for themselves proved to be easily 'managed' by JUSPAO, which exploited their dependence on news from the fighting fronts in the north. Military censorship was not much in evidence in what has since been termed by Daniel Hallin as 'the Uncensored War'. Certainly, this was the least censored major war of the twentieth century, the exception to the rules on war reporting which had been the norm since the Crimean conflict. One significant consequence of this abnormality was the gradual opening up of a credibility gap as a few journalists started to check the 'facts' issued by official American sources in Saigon. They found an increasingly wide discrepancy between

JUSPAO's official battle accounts and casualty figures and their own observations in the field. The official early evening briefings – timed to facilitate reporting by domestic TV news bulletins – earned the nickname 'Five O'Clock Follies' as the credibility gap widened from around 1965. This in turn was exploited by Hanoi, where journalists were permitted to see only what the authorities wanted them to see. The North Vietnamese began to realize that, despite inferior military equipment and technology, the propaganda tradition of communist warfare could exploit democracy's cherished freedoms and its new love affair with television. If Hanoi could win over the journalists and other high-profile visitors, or at least make them sceptical about America's ability to win, then the war could be won in New York, Chicago, Los Angeles, San Francisco and, above all, Washington.

The third phase of the war was 1968-75. The 1968 Tet Offensive is frequently said to have been a significant turning point. The media coverage during and after that offensive supposedly reflected the mounting hostility of American newsmen towards United States involvement. General Westmorland, the American commander, was to state in 1979:

> The American media had misled the American people about the Tet offensive and when they realised that they had misjudged the situation – that in fact it was an American victory – they didn't have the courage or integrity to admit it.

Television pictures of the time of Tet certainly did portray a view different from that being conveyed by the political and military authorities in Washington and Saigon. Walter Cronkite, the distinguished and respected anchorman of CBS News, watched with disbelief as the Vietcong stormed the American embassy in Saigon, exclaiming: 'What the hell is going on? I thought we were winning the war'. The credibility gap had now reached America itself. President Johnson felt that, with the loss of faith by people of Cronkite's standing and influence, he should not stand for the 1968 presidential election. True, polls indicated that he was losing more and more of middle America's support, while young America took to the streets in protest. Anti-war propaganda by a growing vocal minority – fuelled, of course, by Moscow – now jostled with the patriotism of the majority, while the media attempted to steer a middle course in the tradition of objective reporting. None the less, as Professor Hallin has pointed out:

> Before Tet, editorial comments by television journalists ran nearly four
> to one in favour of administration policy; after Tet, two to one against.
> Before Tet, of the battles journalists ventured to describe as victories or
> defeats, 62% were described as victories for the United States, 28% as
> defeats, 2% as inconclusive or as stalemates. After Tet, the figures were
> 44% victories, 32% defeats, and 24% inconclusive.

So a change had taken place but it is a change that has been
exaggerated. The American media did not necessarily become anti-
war after 1968; they merely became less willing to accept
uncritically the official version. The official propaganda line, in
other words, had lost its credibility – while the media have since
shouldered a large proportion of the blame for in fact doing their
job more efficiently than they had before 1968.

President Nixon, who was elected in 1968 on the ticket of
ending the war, was soon to reveal what he meant by this by
extending it into Laos and Cambodia and by extensive bombing of
the north. The number of American forces was reduced gradually
as a concession to public opinion while bombing offered the hope –
as it had done in 1940 and 1943 – of victory through air power. Yet
as the Second World War had shown, bombing even on the scale
the Americans were prepared to adopt in 1969-73, does not destroy
the morale of the enemy; quite the reverse in fact. It was an attempt
to demonstrate to domestic opinion that the military was capable
of hitting the enemy – a propaganda of the deed – at a time when it
was losing the propaganda battle and the conventional military
struggle. The continuing return home of dead young American
conscripts in body-bags belied the official pronouncements that
the war against a fanatical, but inferior, enemy was being won.
Repeated media coverage of such homecomings sapped the domestic
will to continue the fight while alienating public confidence in
central government's ability to tell the truth – a process which
received further confirmation during the Watergate scandal. As for
Vietnam, the hearts of the American people were no longer in the
war either, and Nixon bowed to the inevitable in 1973 when the
last US troops were pulled out of Vietnam. Nixon resigned to avoid
impeachment over Watergate shortly thereafter, while Saigon fell
to the communists in 1975.

The United States took a long time to come to terms with its defeat in Vietnam. During the war itself, only one feature film dealing directly with the war was made by a Hollywood studio: *The Green Berets* (1968), produced by and starring the patriotic movie star, John Wayne. Overtly propagandistic in its support for American involvement, the film was boycotted by anti-war groups. Despite this, it proved a box-office success – which does raise some doubts as to the validity of the thesis that the Vietnam war was lost on the domestic front by a hostile media. On this, William Small, Director of CBS News in Washington, felt that

> When television covered its 'first war' in Vietnam, it showed a terrible truth of war in a manner new to a mass audience. A case can be made, and certainly should be examined, that this was cardinal to the disillusionment of Americans with this war, the cynicism of many young people towards America, and the destruction of Lyndon Johnson's tenure of office.

On the last point, there can be little doubt. The 1960s saw democratically elected politicians becoming increasingly sensitive to what they saw as the power of television to sway public opinion. Whether television in fact possesses such power has preoccupied academic researchers ever since. But the point is that many politicians *believe* that it is invested with such qualities and, although that belief may say more about them than it does about television's actual impact upon society, it does mean that politicians rather than the media have largely shaped the agenda for debating the subject. And so, a real war, uncensored, enacted every day for ten years in full colour on 100 million TV sets throughout America, might indeed appear to be a recipe for disaster in terms of domestic public opinion. Before 1968, surveys reveal that a majority of those viewers were encouraged to support the efforts of their boys 'over there' by the coverage. Thereafter, however, following prolonged exposure to the horrors, and supposed media hostility, did such coverage undermine popular support? Some research indicates that prolonged media exposure to media violence leads to the inoculation of people's sensitivities, turning off their minds rather than the TV sets. The pictures may be horrific, but were they having an impact? The students may have chanted 'the whole world is watching' in their anti-war demonstrations, but was television capable of converting the desensitized, the indifferent or the patriotic into like-minded souls? It has to be remembered that the war went on for five more years after Tet – as long a period as it had been going on before the offensive. What impact did television therefore really have between 1968-73? Those who argue that its impact was significant need to remember that this was a period which saw Nixon elected and re-elected. Yet although the academic jury may still be out on this issue, many politicians and military personnel were none the less convinced that it *had* had an impact, that television had stabbed America in the back, and this belief has had significant consequences for the way in which later wars were reported.

Vietnam certainly reveals some of the dangers of war in the television age. Reporters and cameramen were in fact unable to present a 'true' image of the war by virtue of the circumstances in which they operated. The 'limitless medium' does in fact suffer from several significant limitations. Whisked in and out of combat zones by any helicopter on which they could hitch a ride, reporters in Vietnam were looking for the kind of exciting footage demanded by their editors without searching for a context in which the action needed to be seen. Visual excitement on the small screen does not automatically make for adequate or contextualized reporting, especially with television companies back home competing for ratings in short, sharp newscasts. Bias, naturally enough, affects the entire reporting process – from what the camera was pointed at in the first instance to how the film was subsequently edited and packaged and even to how the images and messages were received by individual members of the public. Although there were comparatively few censorship restrictions on what newsmen could cover in Vietnam, they often acted as their own censors by not including material that might offend the senses of taste and decency amongst their audiences. If the horrific images emanating from Vietnam had any impact at all, it was likely that it was their *cumulative* impact which served to shape popular perceptions about the war over a period of time rather than in any specific military 'turning point' coverage. None the less, scenes of a little naked girl screaming in pain from napalm burns or the execution of a Vietcong suspect by Saigon Police Chief Loan are the very stuff of which atrocity propaganda is made. The problem in Vietnam was that such atrocities were being committed by 'our side' rather than by the enemy. The My Lai massacre may not have been filmed, but the very fact that it happened reinforced the overwhelming visual 'evidence' that the war was about something more than the authorities pretended. The comparative shortage of equivalent material from the enemy side – the difference between rigid media control and unfettered media access – meant that Americans began to fight amongst themselves about the respective merits of the war, and many could only draw one conclusion. In short, television helped to simplify a complicated war. By its very nature, it relies upon sensational coverage, generalization and selection. It killed off the old myth that 'the camera never lies'.

In 1970, in a famous article, the distinguished British broadcaster Robin Day wondered about the new age of televised warfare. He wrote:

> Television has a built-in bias towards depicting any conflict in terms of the visible brutality. You can say, of course, that that is what war is – brutality, conflict, starvation and combat. All I am saying is that there are other issues which cause these things to come about, and television does not always deal with them adequately ... One wonders if in future a democracy which has uninhibited television coverage in every home will ever be able to fight a war, however just.

It might equally be said that the conduct of diplomacy is incompatible with the needs of television, as the Cold War 'era of negotiations' between 1969 and 1975 revealed. Television cameras can film leaders or decision-makers rolling up to a meeting in limousines, it can film them getting out of their cars and going into their meetings and, if the diplomats are media-sensitive (still a rare breed), it can capture appropriate 'sound-bytes' encapsulating intentions. But the round-table negotiations which follow are rarely conducive to entertaining television. As the non-televisual period of detente between the superpowers unfolded in the 1960s and 1970s, television news instead settled into a pattern of picture-led reporting of disasters, earthquakes, coups and terrorist activities – confirming the medium as best suited to event-based reporting and entertainment rather than as an issue-based mechanism capable of providing detailed, contextualized analysis. This would not matter so much but for the fact that most people were now gaining most of their information about what was happening in the world from television rather than from the older media of press and radio. By its inherent predisposition to simplify, television thus became an ideal medium for propaganda, as terrorist groups around the world recognized.

Vietnam had demonstrated that wars are precisely the kind of events that are good for television. But whether television was good for war was an altogether different matter, discussed at length by an American military now busy looking for explanations for military defeat against an inferior opponent. During the war in Vietnam 350,000 Americans had been killed or wounded, and there was no homecoming parade for the survivors. A deep sense of national mourning set in and the administrations of Presidents Ford and Carter reflected this loss of national confidence in a period which saw the Soviets actually threaten to overtake the Americans in the arms race. As America looked in on itself in the second half of the 1970s, this in turn gave them a lead in international propaganda, as strategic arms limitations talks crept on to the agenda in which the Soviets appeared to be the victim, not the aggressor. Their most spectacular propaganda coup of this period was the highly effective international campaign it orchestrated against the American deployment of the neutron bomb that would have shifted the balance back in America's favour. The neutron bomb was depicted as an inhumane, but typically capitalist, weapon capable of destroying people but which left everything else – the economic as well as the military infrastructure – intact for subsequent exploitation. Precisely how much other popular agitation against the US during the late 1970s was inspired by Soviet agents of influence working in western and Third World media or with terrorist groups will remain unknown until the KGB archives are opened fully. On the other side, despite the Freedom of Information Act, much CIA activity from this period also remains shrouded in mystery. But Soviet leader Leonid Brezhnev is on record as saying in the 1970s that 'the ideological struggle is becoming ever more acute, and imperialist propaganda ever more subtle'.

The Soviet invasion of Afghanistan in 1979 was a stark reminder to the western world that a militaristic enemy was still very much in existence. A new injection of western confidence was needed and the decade's close found it in the forms of two determined leaders: Margaret Thatcher and Ronald Reagan.

As the Soviets became embroiled in their own Vietnam, the Americans continued to examine the reasons for their defeat. In popular culture, movies began the reassessment, tentatively at first with films like *Coming Home* (1978), *The Deer Hunter* (1978) and *Apocalypse Now!* (1979) but, reflecting the new confidence of the

1980s, these gradually became more gung-ho, culminating in the 'Rambo' series of films in which the hero asks: 'do we get to win this time?' Ironically it was a question not far removed from one being asked by the US military: '*how* do we get to win next time?' Despite all the research that was appearing pointing to confusion about US war aims and high casualties being significant factors influencing public opinion – not the media coverage – the myth of media responsibility took root. Next time would indeed be different.

In 1982, the British showed how. The conflict that erupted in the South Atlantic following the Argentinian invasion of the Falklands Islands was to provide a model for any democratic government wishing to conduct a propaganda war in the television age. As British diplomats in Washington and New York worked hard to secure the safe passage of Resolution 502 through the United Nations (calling for the withdrawal of Argentinian troops prior to any further negotiations over the issue of sovereignty), a Royal Navy Task Force was quickly mobilized and despatched south. It was important for the British to have the United Nations, as a forum for world opinion and the 'international community', sanction the British action if the Thatcher government was to portray the idea of a 'just war'. The Argentinians were presented as invaders who had violated international law and abandoned the negotiating process. There could be no appeasing of dictators – and stories of missing Argentinian dissidents were issued to confirm that the regime of General Galtieri was the nasty dictatorship the British claimed it to be. The Argentinians had no historical claims to South Georgia, but this had not deterred them from invading that island and was thus 'proof' of the aggressive actions of a right-wing totalitarian regime that violated human rights. Ever since President Carter's renewed emphasis on human rights in the late 1970s, this issue had provided a significant plank for international propaganda: a yardstick by which 'good' and 'bad' regimes could be judged. And ever since the Iranian seizure of American hostages in Tehran in 1979, American politicians had been wary of regimes which resorted to this particular form of terrorism. Were not the Argentinians now holding 1800 Falkland Islanders against their will? The Americans were thus left in no doubt that their sympathies should now lie with their NATO partner – a democratic regime fighting the excesses of dictatorship and with whom they had enjoyed a special historical relationship over such issues. For the

British, American co-operation was vital, particularly in the sphere of intelligence, even at the risk of President Reagan abandoning his anti-communist crusade in Latin America that was to have been spearheaded by Argentina. Getting the Americans to side with the British was thus no straightforward matter. The British campaign in the USA in April 1982 proved every bit as important as that conducted between 1914-17 or 1939-41.

With Resolution 502 safely through the United Nations with American support, the Thatcher government had to confront the question of domestic morale in a real war fought 8000 miles from home in the television age. Equipped with some degree of experience of media management derived from the 'Troubles' in Northern Ireland, and with the 'Vietnam effect' very much in mind, there would be no uncensored war in the South Atlantic. Only 29 journalists and crew were permitted to accompany the Task Force – all British; the foreign media were to be served by the Reuters representative. Even that small number was only agreed to reluctantly by a Royal Navy holding on to its reputation as the 'silent service'. The compensation was that the journalists would all be totally dependent upon the navy in two vital aspects: travel to and from the war zone, and communicating their copy from the Task Force back to London. The opportunity for near complete military censorship was achieved. Reports could only be compiled on the basis of what military personnel on the spot were prepared to say or show, and could only be sent home via military channels. At each stage, the blue pencil censors were at work. After stories reached London – and one was delayed longer than Russell's despatches took to reach London from the Crimea in the 1850s – they were subjected to another censorship stage (or 'security review') prior to release. A third phenomenon was also closely observed, that of 'bonding' between reporters and soldiers. Journalists dependent upon the military for their safety, let alone their copy, soon came to identify closely with the troops who shared their confined sea-borne quarters and their anxieties. Ironically, therefore, when the BBC back home tried to treat the enemy's case objectively, it was criticized by the government for being 'unacceptably even-handed'. Mrs Thatcher informed Parliament:

> I know how strongly many people feel that the case for our boys is not being put with sufficient vigour on certain – I do not say all – BBC programmes. The Chairman of the BBC has assured us, and has said in

> vigorous terms, that the BBC is not neutral on this point, and I hope that
> his words will be heeded by the many who responsibilities for standing up
> for our task force, our boys, our people and the cause of democracy.

Churchill would have been proud of her. The government was at least happier with the attitude of the domestic tabloid press, which threw itself wholeheartedly behind the war effort, although its excesses (such as *The Sun*'s headline of 'GOTCHA!' greeting the sinking of the Argentinian battleship *Belgrano*) were perhaps more appropriate to eighteenth-century scandal-sheets rather than a modern British journalistic tradition. The alarmed could take some comfort in the wartime decline of *The Sun*'s circulation.

The fact that the war was short, lasting barely two months, helped to sustain the patriotic mood that swept the country. After the war, the House of Commons Defence Committee which investigated the media coverage conceded that there had been more to censorship than mere 'operational security', namely the 'furtherance of the war effort through public relations'. During the war itself the philosophy underlining this appeared to take the form that late news is no news for the media, which in turn is good news for the military. With some film reports taking three weeks to reach London, the BBC was forced to use pictures from other sources. When Argentinian footage was used to fill the vacuum created by British censorship, the BBC was accused of disseminating enemy propaganda. When footage from British journalists did finally arrive, it had been sanitized by the censors. Phrases such as 'horribly burned' were cut out, news of setbacks such as the loss of *HMS Sheffield* were delayed, even the substitution of the word 'cleared' for 'censored' were all part of an attempt to present a particularly one-sided view of a war with little bloodshed. As one public relations officer told an ITN correspondent with the Task Force: 'You must have been told you couldn't report bad news before you left. You knew when you came you were expected to do a 1940 propaganda job'.

This type of comment revealed the eternal tension between the military and the media in wartime: secrecy versus publicity. The Ministry of Defence's spokesman, Ian McDonald (whose slow, deliberate, and expressionless nightly appearances on television made him a national figure and earned him the tag of the 'speak-your-weight machine') epitomized the traditional military preference for secrecy. His policy was never to lie deliberately but never to endanger the safety of the troops. He also knew that, thanks to the increasing internationalization of the media, the Argentinians would be watching. If a denial served to deceive the enemy, then well and good. But tension with the media increased when the military deliberately used them as instruments for deception. On this issue, the Chief of the Defence Staff, Sir Terence Lewin, stated:

> I do not see it as deceiving the press or the public; I see it as deceiving the enemy. What I am trying to do is to win. Anything I can do to help me win is fair as far as I'm concerned, and I would have thought that that was what the Government and the public and the media would want, too, provided the outcome was the one we were all after.

The press may have disagreed, but whether the public would have done so is another matter, especially as polls revealed a considerable majority of public support for the war. The cheerful mood of despatches from the fleet, combined with the jingoism of the tabloids ('UP YOURS, GALTIERI!' and 'ARGIE-BARGY' ran other *Sun* headlines) and high domestic morale, seemed only to justify the military's restrictions on the media. The overall result was that the British public received comparatively little information – and some disinformation – about what was happening when it was happening. Despite several graphic voice reports of the action, there were remarkably few television pictures of the war until it was all over and the islands had been re-taken. But the notion that the British military had enjoyed a good media war with a supportive and compliant public needed to be tempered by one event afterwards. When a Ministry of Defence official, Clive Ponting, released documents showing that the British government had indeed lied over the direction in which the *Belgrano* had been sailing when it was attacked by a British submarine, he was arrested and tried under the 1911 Official Secrets Act. The jury refused to convict him.

It appeared, then, that an answer had been found not only to Robin Day's question about democratic war and its relationship to television but also that the British had stumbled upon an antidote to the 'Vietnam effect'. As former US Secretary of State, Henry Kissinger, commented: 'If we could have got the support for our Vietnam policy that the prime minister has for her Falklands policy, I would have been the happiest man in the world'. But, to Mrs Thatcher, nothing short of total, uncritical support had been acceptable. While she became determined to tackle the BBC, she had in fact made the same mistake as her political hero, Winston Churchill, in not being able to trust the democratic media in wartime. Patriotic journalists, especially those working alongside fighting soldiers from their own country, do not want to reveal information that might be of value to the enemy because of an identification of shared risks and shared interests. But within a democratic frame-work, they demand the right to retain their critical judgement. They know that their reports have an important bearing on civilian morale, yet they reserve the right to criticize. Governments that attempt to censor views, as distinct from news, are their natural enemies. In the Falklands conflict, there remains the suspicion that the Thatcher government confused *national* interests with *political* interests, equating them as one and the same, when healthy democracy demands that they be kept separate. It is easier, and perhaps more acceptable, to do this in wartime, when the media serve as a fourth arm of national defence. But the dangers of restricting the normal flow of opinion – critical or otherwise – in times of peace is a challenge to democracy that must be resisted.

The problem since the 1980s is that the accepted definitions of conflict are changing. One such change is the 'low intensity conflict' which the Americans found themselves in shortly after the Falklands war. The US invasion of the small Caribbean island of Grenada in October 1983, ostensibly to 'rescue' American students from Cuban-backed communists on the island (fear of hostage-taking again), saw the next significant development in the post-Vietnam, post-Falklands military-media dynamic. Operation Urgent Fury was to be undertaken with the media excluded altogether. It was too dangerous, said the Reagan administration, dodging the issue of whether it was more dangerous a precedent for an open democratic society not to allow the media to report freely on events of national concern. But Grenada was not 8000 miles away. Several journalists responded to the official media black-out by hiring fishing boats to sail to the island, only to be intercepted by US naval ships and planes. Seven who did make it ashore quickly found themselves under house arrest and were unable to file any copy, a frustrating experience at the best of times but even more so as they observed events in a very different light from the versions being disseminated by VOA and other official sources (such as US psy-ops). One later wrote that 'Reality was the first casualty of the Grenada "war" and there was something strangely Orwellian about the whole affair – as if "1984" had arrived early'. Although after massive media protests, the Pentagon later relented and organized journalists into pools, by then the invasion was all over, or rather the 'rescue operation' successfully completed (with returning students filmed kissing the tarmac as they arrived home on American soil) and the popularity of President Reagan enhanced sufficiently to see him re-elected the following year.

Reagan's first administration had been particularly hawkish towards the Soviet Union and its communist allies. Many feel that 'the Great Communicator', as he was known, enjoyed his greatest propaganda success with the announcement of the Strategic Defence Initiative (SDI or 'Star Wars') designed to protect the United States from a nuclear attack. Whether or not SDI was realizable – and there was a good deal of domestic and overseas propaganda surrounding it implying that it was more real than imagined – it scared the Russians who knew that they could not compete with the Americans financially or technologically. Following the death of Brezhnev in 1982, the Soviet leadership underwent a crisis as former KGB chief Andropov followed him to the grave only to be replaced by the weak Chernenko who was unable to extricate the Soviet Union from the quagmire of Afghanistan. With both Thatcher and Reagan reinstated in further terms of office, there then arrived on the Soviet scene a leader in the form of Mikhail Gorbachev. He was, as Thatcher informed Reagan, a Russian with whom the West could finally do business. Together, they ended the Cold War.

The West did not really 'win' the Cold War. If anything, the Soviet Union lost it by default. After almost 70 years of communist rule, the Soviet economy had singularly failed to deliver its promises. The arms race, for all its expense, had contributed to the end of this war rather than its outbreak. By 1985, Gorbachev recognized that wide-sweeping economic reconstruction was necessary – *perestroika* – but in order to promote debate about how this should be done, he also introduced the concept of *glasnost*, or openness. This was a radical departure for a regime which had depended for its preservation on leading public opinion rather than following it. We can now see that it opened the floodgates to greater freedom of opinion within the Soviet Union which led five years later to the triumph of democracy and the collapse of the CPSU. That had never been Gorbachev's intention, despite the 'Gorbymania' of the West at the time seeing it that way. Yet if *glasnost* is now seen as ringing the death-knell of Soviet authoritarianism – with its increased news coverage of mistakes and problems, the reporting of bad news, even the 'space bridge' chat shows between ordinary American and Russian TV audiences – Gorbachev was bowing to the inevitable march of communications technology. The 1980s saw a massive expansion in international satellite television broadcasting and the arrival of such global news services such as Cable News Network (CNN). Direct Broadcasting by Satellite (DBS) provided alternative ways of seeing and perceiving what was happening in the outside world, which was made further possible by the secret and easy importation of foreign radio and television programmes on small audio and video-cassette formats. Fax machines were to provide another route. Many Soviet officials seemed more afraid of DBS and CNN than they were of SDI. In a sense they were right, since CNN and DBS were among the new technological realities of the 1980s. News of the 1986 Chernobyl disaster, for example, reached Soviet audiences from foreign sources and prompted Moscow to re-think completely its domestic propaganda policy. With hopeful signs that the West was now proving more co-operative than confrontational (such as in arms reductions talks), the jamming of the BBC World Service, VOA and even RFE and RFL was halted in 1987 and 1988. A long-standing ban on the unofficial use of photocopiers was lifted while the state control over the mass media was eased to permit greater internal communication and discourse. Former dissidents were permitted to return while others were released from the Gulags. At last, the old Cold War enemy was extending to its citizens the type of freedoms which the West had insisted were fundamental human rights. Few noted the irony that this was taking place at a time when the US was searching for ways of restricting its media from covering conflicts such the American invasion of Panama in 1989. In that same year, the Soviets withdrew from Afghanistan. The Bear may still have had its claws but it had lost its teeth. The ultimate twist came during the attempted coup of 1991 when Gorbachev, under house arrest in the Crimea, was able to listen to what was happening in Moscow via the very same BBC World Service which he had stopped jamming a few years earlier. Meanwhile, the rest of the world was watching his eventual successor, Boris Yeltsin, climb aboard a tank to lead the forces of resistance in support of Gorbachev – live on CNN.

Part Six

The New World Information Disorder

Chapter 25

The Gulf War of 1991

With the Cold War effectively pronounced over by 1990, there was much talk of an 'end of history' prompted by the writings of Francis Fukuyama. But history does not end; one historical period merely gives way to another in which the past continues to loom large. The continued survival of communist regimes in places like Cuba and North Korea and, in a slightly different way, the increasingly consumerist People's Republic of China – especially after the suppression of the Tiananmen Square uprising in 1989 – served as a salutary reminder that the old world had not yet completely capitulated to the new. Nonetheless, the historic events of the late 1980s and early 1990s – the fall of the Berlin Wall, the advent of democracy in Poland, Romania, Bulgaria, Hungary, the Czech and Slovak Republics, combined with the Soviet decision to withdraw their troops occupying those countries – did seem to herald the conclusion of what had appeared to be the unfinished business of the twentieth century. Moreover, all this monumental change was televised in full view of a global audience, giving rise to speculation that the televising of events in one uprising encouraged the process of change and reform elsewhere in Eastern Europe. If this was true – and the leaders of Polish Solidarity amongst others are on record as saying it was a major factor – then it may be said that television was to the end of the Cold War what radio had been to its beginning and, indeed, to its perpetuation.

The most significant of all these events was, of course, the disintegration of the old Soviet Empire by 1991. At last it seemed to have gone the same way as its older European equivalents, to be replaced by the Commonwealth of Independent States (CIS). For regions like Ukraine, this was the long awaited opportunity to sever its ties with Russia; the CIS was arguably even looser as an association of nation-states than the British Commonwealth of Nations. For invaded nations like Afghanistan, Soviet troop withdrawal created a power vacuum that was to be filled by the Taliban who were to later haunt the United States. So talk of the 'triumph' of the West in the Cold War was soon tempered with anxiety about what would happen next to a world which had experienced – even, by comparison, 'enjoyed' – the certainties of a bi-polar order in which enemies and friends could be clearly identified.

Change bred all sorts of new doubts and anxieties. For example, would the forces of nationalism resurface or would they crumble under the pressure of internationalism, especially now that 'globalization' had become a new buzz-word linking the concerns of all nations to describe such universal concerns as environmental issues, global warming, pollution, the spread of AIDS and drugs, and nuclear proliferation? Or would the Islamic crescent now replace the hammer and sickle as the West's bogeyman? Samuel Huntington wrote of a possible 'clash of civilisations' while other scholars, who had failed to anticipate the end of the Cold War, groped around to explain the new international circumstances. 'Islamic Fundamentalism' was a phenomenon that had been appearing more and more in the western media throughout the 1980s and it was usually connected, in an almost Pavlovian reaction, with international terrorism. However, in the two decades prior to the September 11th, 2001 terrorist attacks on New York and Washington, this appeared to be only an episodic or random problem. It had framed the western media coverage of the 1979 Iranian revolution, the American bombing of Libya in 1986, Lebanon throughout the 1980s, and the downing of Pan Am 107 over Lockerbie in 1988. These parameters had made the 'accidental' shooting down of an Iranian passenger plane by the *USS Vincennes* less of an atrocity than the 'deliberate' Soviet interception of Korean Air Lines flight 007. So when President Bush Snr talked about a 'New World Order' at the start of the 1990s, no one was quite sure what it meant but it did at least appear to signify a point of departure from the East–West tensions and nuclear confrontation of the recent past. Something different was certainly happening, as developments in South Africa and, later, Northern Ireland seemed to reveal. But whether it consisted of Order or Chaos remained to be seen.

Hopes that order would prevail were raised in the aftermath of Iraq's invasion of Kuwait in August 1990. In the six months that followed, the Bush administration was able to forge a coalition of almost thirty nations from both the developed and developing world operating ostensibly in the name of UN resolutions designed to withstand inter-state aggression. This remarkable diplomatic achievement was to be followed by a remarkable military operation when, following Iraq's refusal to withdraw from the oil rich country it now claimed as its nineteenth province, coalition forces under American command launched Operation Desert Storm in January 1991. The war 'to liberate Kuwait', which lasted barely six weeks, proved to be a decisive military victory without the triumph of seeing Saddam Hussein removed from power. Although this had never been one of the stated aims of the coalition at the time, it was to preoccupy successive administrations in Washington for more than a decade, until President Bush's son was elected president in 2000. Then, following the 9/11 attacks, an 'axis of evil' was identified that included Iraq (as well as Syria and North Korea) and US foreign policy was adjusted to implement what was openly described as 'regime change'.

In the meantime, the Gulf War of 1991 provided a classic example of how to project a desired view of conflict in the new international informational environment that had emerged during the 1980s, coupled with the lessons learned from Vietnam, the Falklands, Grenada and Panama. Vietnam, in particular, featured prominently in the Gulf War. It was mentioned by Reagan's successor and former vice president George Bush in his opening and closing statements about the war. Most of the senior American commanders, including General Schwarzkopf, were Vietnam veterans who were determined that the same mistakes would not be repeated again. This required clear and realizable military objectives, minimal political interference from Washington, a short war with low coalition casualty figures – and tight controls on the media coverage. The latter would not be easy. More than 1,500 journalists from around the world flocked to the region equipped with the latest technologies, including transportable satellite dishes, portable telephones (that were then still the size of a house brick) and laptop computers that were potentially capable of circumventing the official channels of communication through which journalists were supposed to transmit their copy back to their home editorial bases.

Given that the mass media were to be the principal conduit through which the propaganda war was to be fought, the capability of journalists to circumvent the military version of events was, at least in theory, significant.

Nowhere was this better illustrated than in Baghdad. Saddam Hussein, who also believed in the Vietnam Syndrome, decided to allow journalists from coalition countries to remain behind once the bombing started so that they could report from the Iraqi capital under fire in the hope that anticipated stomach-churning television footage of civilian casualties would repel western audiences to the point of protesting that the war should stop. Just like the North Vietnamese, the Iraqis hoped to win the war on the domestic fronts of their enemies, and they even tried Vietnam-style propaganda ploys such as the parading of captured coalition airmen on Iraqi television. Allowing western journalists to stay behind in an enemy capital under fire seemed, as David Frost pointed out in disgust, the equivalent of Dr Goebbels permitting British and American journalists to remain in Dresden while allied bombers torched the city. It was certainly a recognition of how the media were no longer regarded as simple observers of conflict but as actual participants on a new front: media warfare.

But Saddam miscalculated. He underestimated the resolve of western public opinion to support the war, with polls in Britain and America – the two leading military contributors – holding steady at between 70-80% approval ratings. He also perhaps overrated the power of television to alter that support, not least because the coalition, in launching the largest air strike since the Second World War, chose not to bomb the Iraqi capital indiscriminately. This, the coalition insisted, was not a war against the Iraqi people, but a war against the regime of Saddam Hussein that had ordered an invasion of Kuwait. Instead, only 'smart' weapons such as cruise missiles and laser-guided bombs dropped from Stealth fighter-bombers were used against military and other specific targets in Baghdad. And these invariably hit their targets with accuracy unprecedented in the history of aerial bombing. On the opening night of the war, broadcast live by CNN reporters from the Al-Rashid hotel, viewers were able to hear (if not yet see) how such precision bombing took out the Iraqi Defence Ministry building, the telecommunications tower, the power stations and so on. Back in the USA, it was early evening prime time and what one CNN journalist described as like watching a 4th July fireworks display attracted the largest television audience in broadcasting history to date. Then, within a matter of days, the coalition military machine began releasing spectacular video footage taken by cameras located on the noses of 'smart' weaponry as they glided with uncanny accuracy through the doors, windows and ventilation shafts of their intended targets before the screen went blank. Within ten days, CNN and other international news organizations were able to transmit live pictures of cruise missiles flying along the streets of Baghdad as though they were following an A-Z grid map of the city to hit their strategic – not civilian – targets.

It was all sensational footage, but it was also highly misleading. The overall impression was that the coalition possessed the capability of winning the war in a clinical, almost bloodless, air campaign with minimum casualties to both sides, especially where civilians – 'innocent women and children' – were concerned. Many critics argued that this wasn't a real war at all, but rather a 'video game war' staged for the entertainment of a global TV audience which had been primed by months of justificatory propaganda about Saddam Hussein being a 'new Hitler' who needed to be taught a lesson by freedom- and peace-loving nations. But, as we should by now appreciate, appearances can be deceptive. It turned out subsequently that, in fact, only about 8% of the weapons used against Iraq were 'smart'. The vast majority of bombs used were of the old-fashioned 'dumb' variety, dropped by B-52 bombers from the Vietnam era from heights of around 30,000 feet on the Iraqi troops occupying Kuwait or on those standing in reserve in Southern Iraq. These killing fields, where the war was effectively fought and won, were well away from the TV cameras. The real war, as distinct from the media war, in which between forty to eighty thousand Iraqis died, was not captured on film or videotape. Like the new generation of 'Star Wars' weaponry being deployed, such as cruise missiles or the F-117A bombers that were invisible to radar, this was Stealth TV.

Despite the Baghdad loophole, then, the coalition was able to create a media management system that was highly conducive to the effective deployment of its official propaganda lines. Rooted in a misperception of the past, it was to provide a template for the future. The deeply-felt myth that America had lost the Vietnam War because of a hostile and uncensored media resurfaced during the Gulf War through the creation of a 'media management' system. This system was based upon some dubious assumptions other than the Vietnam Syndrome. One was a belief in the power of television to alter public opinion, that its role was more than a simple observer of events but was rather a catalyst capable of altering the course of those events. During the build-up to war known as Operation Desert Shield, this received some credibility through the 'loudspeaker diplomacy' conducted by Presidents Bush and Saddam Hussein via CNN. It was also to receive further reinforcement by events at the end of the war when shocking images of the coalition's destructive power on the Iraqi army were a factor in ending the war when it did. Because Saddam continued to be a thorn in the side of the West, many people in the years that followed queried why the coalition failed to 'finish him off' when they had a chance to do so in 1991. 'Regime change' was not, however, on the official agenda at that time. But avoiding further casualties certainly was. It may just be, therefore, that more often than not democratic politicians are influenced more by a *fear* of television to influence public opinion – the so-called 'CNN Effect' – than the actual ability of the medium to wield this influence. They share this assumption with dictators who fear the power of television so much that they try to rigorously control it. In the climate of 1989-91, this was perhaps understandable.

These assumptions nonetheless prompted the creation of a media management system which saw a minority of journalists allocated to media 'pools' attached to military units in the field while the rest – the vast majority – were holed up in hotel rooms in Riyadh and Dharhan. These 'hotel warriors' could attend daily briefings by the leading military participants where they received the official line from the American, British, French, Saudi and Kuwaiti spokesmen. The Joint Information Bureau (JIB) was created to cater for their journalistic needs, and they could also use material from the pool despatches coming back from the front – once, that is, it had been subjected to 'security review'. Because the first month of the war consisted mainly of air strikes, the pool reports mainly consisted of stories about life amongst the troops on the ground waiting for combat – pretty unexciting stuff from a media point of view. Some journalists – dubbed the 'unilaterals' – decided to break free from their official minders and tried to find out if anything else other than the official version was actually happening, but most reporters were deterred from emulating this by the knowledge that a CBS crew had gone missing at the start of the war near the Kuwaiti border and were probably being held in Iraqi captivity. The Iraqis had a track record of executing foreign journalists as spies. Most journalists therefore accepted the official line, and even those with the troops in the field conformed to the guidelines issued to them for fear of giving away their positions to the enemy. The American-led coalition was therefore able to ensure that the outside world received the predominantly official version of what was happening, that the coalition was winning with minimum 'collateral damage' and with little loss of life.

A clue that not all was as it appeared emerged at the end of January when Iraqi forces crossed the Kuwaiti border and occupied the Saudi coastal town of Ras Al-Khafji for several days. If the Iraqis were being bombed into submission by superior air power, how was it that they were able to launch a ground attack against coalition-held territory? There is even the possibility that the Iraqis only attacked this strategically insignificant town because they had seen pictures of it unoccupied on global television news services! Moreover, the coalition's tight media arrangements seemed to have broken down as American spokesmen in Riyadh claimed that Saudi forces were re-taking the town when the pictures taken by some unilateral crews depicted mainly US marines in combat. Although Khafji was re-taken, the Iraqis had scored a minor propaganda victory by proving that they were capable of more than merely 'taking it'. In addition, they could hit back with Scud missiles, not just against coalition forces in Saudi Arabia but also against targets in Israel. While the use of these indiscriminate terror weapons against America's 'Zionist lackey' in the region were designed to provoke an Israeli retaliation in order to fragment the coalition and unite the Arab world behind Iraq, strenuous efforts were made by the allies to dissuade Israel from such a course. Great play was made of the new high-tech American Patriot missiles and their ability to intercept the Scuds as they were deployed to Israel, whereas after the war it became known that they were nowhere near as effective as the coalition had made them out to be at the time. Admittedly BDA – bomb damage assessment – is not an instant science, although the media want quick results. For this reason, the military acronym should really mean Broadcasting Damage Assessment.

The wartime duel between the Scuds and the Patriots encapsulated many of the propaganda themes deployed during the war. The Scuds were old-fashioned legacies from the Cold War era, inaccurate and therefore indiscriminate, reflecting the brutal, callous and desperate nature of the despotic regime deploying them. The Patriots, on the other hand, were from a new era, designed by a technologically advanced military power that placed great emphasis on clinical accuracy as a means of avoiding the unnecessary loss of life. Moreover, for journalists becoming increasingly frustrated at their inability to report on the war for themselves because they were so heavily dependent upon images of the air war supplied by the coalition military, the Scuds provided a new lease of life. At last reporters were able to film for themselves the Scud–Patriot duels over Saudi and Israeli cities, and there followed the somewhat ludicrous sight of western reporters commentating live from rooftops as their newsrooms back home pleaded with them to go below to the safety of the air raid shelters. The 'reporter-as-star' had arrived, with one even earning the nickname the 'Scud Stud' and the 'Satellite Dish'. In Jerusalem, certain news organizations initially claimed live on air that the incoming Scuds were carrying chemical weapons as watching audiences saw heroic reporters staying at their posts donning gas masks. Jerusalem, a holy city for the Arabs as well as Jews, was at no point targeted during the Gulf War.

Such spectacles may have made for exciting live television, but militarily they were something of a sideshow. The Scuds were a nuisance, but they deflected public (and, admittedly, some military) attention away from the real conflict – which was precisely why the coalition failed to stop the media 'Scudfest'. But even that story lost its novelty value after a week or so. The media, which had been mesmerised by the coalition's high-tech weaponry to the point of becoming its cheerleaders, were beginning to show signs of impatience as the war 'dragged on'. This 24-hour television war demanded more than just the same old footage and the time had to be filled with something. That something turned out to be endless 'talking heads' of retired military officers speculating on what or would not happen next to serve the needs of this 'infotainment'. After three weeks, such speculation was substituting for hard news as the media anticipated the ground war that would hopefully supply more exciting material.

It was during this period that some of the better informed media pundits guessed that when the allied attack came it would take the form of a rapid knock-out push to the west of Kuwait which would then swing eastwards in an attempt (in the words of one commander) to 'cut off and kill' the occupying enemy forces from their Iraqi homeland. This was what actually did happen but, until it did, there was so much media speculation that, if Iraqi intelligence was looking to the media for clues, it must have been hopelessly confused. Although coalition military spokesmen despaired of such speculation, professing to prefer hard facts (if not all the facts), they did in reality use the media as part of the deception plan about the coalition's real intentions. This plan was to give the Iraqis the impression that the land war would take place following a seaborne invasion of Kuwait by the US marines in the hope that it would deflect Iraqi forces away from the real onslaught. Nobody said this explicitly to journalists; more subtle hints were provided. For example, in the build up to the land war, reporters were provided with improved access to the marines and to the ships in the Persian Gulf, with a corresponding increase in the amount of media coverage given to those areas. Attention was diverted away from the Saudi desert. Stories concentrating on Saddam's 'eco-terrorism' – the release of oil into the waters of the Persian Gulf and its effect on the local wildlife – were prominent. At the same time, there was a stepping up of atrocity stories about the Iraqi occupiers of Kuwait, such as the execution of brave Kuwaiti resistance fighters, rapes and pillage. It subsequently came to light that a prominent atrocity story about Iraqi troops snatching Kuwaiti babies from hospital incubators and throwing them callously onto the floor to die was in fact perpetuated by the American public relations firm, Hill and Knowlton, which was in the employ of the Kuwaiti government-in-exile. During Desert Shield, they had also primed a young Kuwaiti woman to testify before a televised United Nations hearing on the brutality of the Iraqi occupation. She turned out to be the daughter of the Kuwaiti ambassador to the United States.

The coalition, as it entered the final stages of the air war, was worried that it too might be charged with committing atrocities. As air strikes against Iraq's military-industrial infrastructure continued, the risk of causing civilian casualties was high. Some early speculation that the coalition was missing some of its intended targets was fuelled by CNN reporters in Iraq who reported that they had seen the country's only 'baby milk plant' destroyed following a coalition air strike. The coalition claimed that it was a chemical weapons facility. How could journalists unversed in the minutiae of such technology distinguish between what they thought they had seen and what military intelligence knew it to be? The Iraqis, came the reply, did not normally escort reporters to bombed military installations, so why change that policy now? 'Propaganda' shouted the military; western journalists were spreading Iraqi propaganda. Saddam had used chemical weapons in 1988 against his own people (in fact the Kurds) and during the Iran–Iraq war, and he was now developing nuclear weapons. (Although this was a prominent propaganda theme during the Gulf War, post-war investigations were to in fact confirm its validity.) Yet because coalition leaders, and especially President Bush, had made much of the fact that the war was not being fought against the Iraqi people but against the Ba'athist regime of Saddam Hussein, it had laid itself open to charges of brutality should mistakes occur.

On 13 February 1991, any remaining illusions about a blood-less, clinical war were shattered when two laser-guided bombs smashed through the roof of the Al-Firdos installation in the Amiriya suburb of Baghdad. Around 400 civilians – mainly women, children and old men – were killed in the attack. The Iraqis, who maintained that this kind of barbarism had been going on since the start of the war but had notably failed previously to escort western journalists to such sites, realized that they had a potential propaganda bombshell on their hands. As first light approached, the journalists were woken from their beds in the Al-Rashid hotel and escorted to the scene of the devastation. They saw firefighters struggling with the smoking building as rescue workers brought out the dead. The bodies had been so badly burned that they were barely recognizable as human beings. The reporters were then taken to the local hospital where the charred remains were paraded for the cameras. All prior Iraqi censorship restrictions were lifted that day; the Iraqi minders told the reporters that they could film and say anything they liked.

The graphic images that were filmed, however, were not broad-cast by most western media organisations. They were deemed likely to offend the 'taste and decency' of western audiences, and the most shocking images were edited out (or 'self-censored') by the broad-casters themselves, even though the coalition's media management system had been bypassed. Even so, the message carried even by the sanitized pictures that were transmitted was at such variance from the coalition's previous pronouncements about minimal 'collateral damage' that it prompted many to attack the messenger. *The Daily Mail*, for example, dubbed the BBC as the 'Baghdad Broadcasting Corporation' while CNN reporters were accused of treachery. While coalition spokesmen insisted that they had hit what they were aiming at, that it was a command and control bunker rather than a civilian shelter, the images depicted many dead civilians and their anguished mourning relatives. The more hysterical newspapers explained that Saddam must have deliberately placed innocent people in the bunker as a callous sacrifice on the propaganda battlefront. The pictures did alter slightly the coalition's targeting schedule for Baghdad, but public support for the war held firm in the West. Saddam's ploy had therefore failed, and the so-called Vietnam Syndrome about television's capacity to alter public support by showing the true horrors of war had been exposed.

Nonetheless, fear of what further horrors television might show in the coming land war remained. When coalition forces actually began their push into Iraq and Kuwait on 24 February, a news black-out was imposed. But coalition forces advanced so rapidly as Iraqi forces crumbled before them that the embargo was soon lifted – in other words because the news was better than expected. The deception plan had worked; Iraqi guns were pointed out to sea. Due to the rapid advance, journalists in the pools accompanying the troops experienced extreme difficulties in getting their reports back to Riyadh with the result that there were few pictures of the ground war until it was virtually all over after 100 hours. Some reporters broke away from the battlefield and raced into Kuwait City to set up their portable satellite systems and film the liberation in scenes reminiscent of Paris in 1944, although this time they were reported live. But by that stage, the real war was being fought elsewhere as the Iraqis had already decided to 'withdraw' from the Kuwaiti capital. The coalition insisted that they were in 'retreat', not just with their military equipment but also with the loot they had plundered. They were therefore still legitimate military targets. Allied warplanes attacked the two main Iraqi convoys racing north out of Kuwait City, and one – the road to the Mutlah Gap – became known as the 'Highway of Death' when journalists came across it after the bombardment. The other convoy on the coastal road to Basra, equally devastated, was not filmed.

There have been some suggestions that President Bush, himself a World War Two veteran aviator, decided to halt the convoy bombings when he did because he was worried that the eventual television coverage of the 'Highway of Death' might shock western public opinion too much. The pictures that did emerge – on 1 March – were certainly appalling, suggesting a one-sided massacre from the air. But President Bush had announced the 'cessation of hostilities' two days earlier, on 27 February, the day after Kuwait City's evacuation and liberation and about the same time, therefore, that the convoys were being attacked. It is thus possible that the coalition military at the scene warned Washington in advance that devastating pictures were about to emerge. If so, it is a striking testimony to the pervasiveness of the Vietnam Syndrome about the role of television in wartime upon democratic politicians. But it also enabled the much vaunted Republican Guard to escape and, more significantly, for Saddam Hussein to survive in power.

One of the striking aspects about the footage taken of the 'Highway of Death' was the absence of corpses. Now it may well be that, once again, television companies self-censored the pictures, or that coalition censors ordered the exclusion of the gruesome shots. This didn't stop *The Observer* from publishing Kenneth Jarecke's now famous still photograph of a charred Iraqi soldier sitting upright in his burned out vehicle – on 10 March, long after the battle. (No American news organization would publish that photograph until years later.) But even print journalists noted the shortage of bodies on the scene as compared to the large number of burned out vehicles. It may well be, therefore, that many Iraqis had fled the convoys as they were being attacked, and simply evaporated away into the desert in their attempts to get home.

If so, this was due in no small measure to the coalition's combat theatre propaganda directed at the Iraqi troops. The use of psychological operations (PSYOPS) by the Americans was extensive. Having gone into decline after Vietnam, in the 1980s the American PSYOPS capability had been revived by President Reagan. In the Gulf War, some 29 million leaflets were dropped over Iraqi lines, which meant fifty–sixty for every Iraqi soldier believed to be in the area. In addition, PSYOPS loudspeaker teams accompanied front line forces shouting out instructions on how to surrender safely.

Radio transmissions from land-based and airborne transmitters aboard a converted EC 130 (the 'Volant Solo') broadcast under the name 'The Voice of the Gulf'. These broadcasts warned that the 'Mother of All Battles' would turn out to be the 'Mother of All Defeats' in their efforts to encourage desertion, defection or surrender. Although the precise figure is unknown, around 70,000 Iraqi soldiers surrendered because of the coalition's success in getting this message across by various means. This made the coalition, and especially the Americans who dominated the PSYOPS campaign, feel that they had demonstrated a desire to save lives – even enemy lives – rather than conduct a brutal campaign, not least because – although again estimates vary – more Iraqi soldiers may have been saved than slaughtered. PSYOPS thus entered the new decade with a renewed reputation for altering the face of battle without the need for mass slaughter. Despite popular suspicion – and indeed some political nervousness and even some surviving military qualms about its use – PSYOPS had become a 'combat force multiplier' capable of saving lives on both sides at cheaper costs than modern high-tech weapons and with an additional moral premium that persuading people to stop fighting and surrender was more acceptable than sending them home in body bags.

One question mark about this was caused by the uneasy relationship between military PSYOPS in its white form and CIA-backed PSYOPS in its covert form. The latter consisted of black radio transmitters posing as Iraqi stations manned by internal enemies of Saddam Hussein. Because no one could supposedly detect the genuine source of messages broadcast by these stations, they were able to deviate from the official coalition line that Desert Storm was about the liberation of Kuwait and not about the overthrow of Saddam Hussein, which was never a declared war aim in 1991. Black radio stations therefore carried messages encouraging an internal revolt inside Iraq, but when signs of success in doing this appeared towards the end of the war in the form of the Kurdish and Shia uprisings, no actual military support was forthcoming from the West. This was another classic example of the dangers of policy and propaganda getting out of step. The very covert nature of black propaganda, the fact that it is unattributable and even unaccountable, does make it a dangerous survivor from the era of Total War and Cold War. Whether it was an appropriate weapon for democracies in the years that followed remained to be seen.

Chapter 26

Information-Age Conflict in the Post-Cold War Era

The Gulf War was hailed as the 'first information war' partly because of the effective use of new technologies, especially satellites, computers and communications, in support of the war effort. The ability of the coalition to take successful 'command and control' of the battlefield, to achieve information and communications dominance while at the same time depriving the enemy of his eyes and ears, prompted claims that a Revolution in Military Affairs (RMA) was underway. Although the Gulf War was one of the most one-sided conflicts in military history because of this, we should of course always be cautious about labelling anything a 'first'. It would, however, be fair to say that the Gulf War was the first real-time or live television war, propelling the twenty-four-hour rolling news service CNN into prominence. The media were such a prominent feature of the propaganda effort on all sides that the illusion was given of an information overload in terms of the war coverage.

But the term 'information war' was assuming a new meaning. Information had always been a crucial ingredient of military tactics and strategy, whether relating to weather or terrain or intelligence about enemy troop sizes, movement and morale. The high-tech side of the coalition's war effort may have been decisive against Iraq, but tanks and troops and planes were still required to expel physically the enemy's forces from Kuwait. In the years that followed, however, it became clearer that the very nature of international crises was changing, and that new military doctrines for dealing with them would be required. Instead of *inter*-state conflicts like the Gulf War, a series of *intra*-state conflicts broke out around the world which attracted high-profile media attention not least because, since they were effectively civil wars, they produced dramatic images of human suffering that played to the heart and evoked cries for the international community to 'do something' to stop the terrible tragedies being played out before a global television audience. This in turn prompted a new debate about the ability of television footage to drive foreign policy decisions, now labelled the 'CNN Effect', although this term also encapsulated other 24/7 news services like BBC World, Sky News and Fox News.

While many people at the time argued that dramatic television news coverage was a major factor in prompting international responses to the crises in Northern Iraq after the Gulf War (Operation Provide Comfort) or in Somalia in 1992 (Operation Restore Hope), subsequent research has tempered this argument. After all, despite months of shocking pictures from Rwanda beginning in April and May 1994, including scores of bodies floating down rivers and the hacking to death of a woman, for twelve weeks 'of terrifying tribal genocide the Clinton administration and other western governments ... actively resisted the flow of horrific pictures that documented the mass slaughter'. A twenty-year-long civil war in Sudan likewise was left largely to pursue its own course: 'Somalia without CNN', in the words of one official.

To summarize briefly the research into the so-called 'CNN Effect', the findings are as follows. When leading politicians have a firm foreign policy, they can and do resist the images if non-intervention is the policy. This was the case with the Clinton administration and Bosnia until 1995, and with Rwanda. In fact, despite claims that 'television got us in, and got us out too', it was also the case with Somalia since the horrific images of death and starvation mainly post-dated the decision to become involved with a humanitarian mission and pre-dated the appalling imagery of a dead US Ranger being dragged through the streets of Mogadishu. Television news usually follows the decisions of policy makers, not the other way around. This partly helps to explain why there were so many camera crews on the Mogadishu beachhead when the US marines stormed ashore; they had been told the Americans were coming because that policy-decision to intervene had already been made. But if there is no policy, or if the policy is weak or still forming, that is when dramatic images can have an impact. This would appear to have been the case in 1995 when the Americans launched air strikes against the Serbs, and again in 1999 over Kosovo.

Summarizing the emerging thinking about information warfare

is more difficult. At first it was preoccupied with communications systems – the largely computer-based command and control capabilities that enabled the coalition to win the war against Iraq so completely. Alvin Toffler argued that the way societies waged war reflected the way they made peace. He suggested three 'waves' of societal development. The first wave was agricultural, the second industrial and the third was informational. So, whereas agricultural societies in the ancient world waged seasonal warfare to enable the farmer-soldiers to return to their land in time for the harvest, second wave industrial societies waged industrial war with the primary targets of mass production being the object of mass bombing and mechanized killing. Hence the First and Second World Wars were second wave warfare. With the triumph of free market liberal capitalist democracy at the end of the Cold War, the information age had arrived fully, encapsulated by the arrival of the internet. Third wave societies thus began to think about warfare in ways similar to the way they made profits in normal times of peace. If computers were the essential tool of this new world information and economic order, especially following the invention of the World Wide Web in 1992, then the way to harm adversaries was to attack their information systems. So, whereas factories and shipyards had been the targets of World War Two 'strategic' bombing, power stations, radio towers and television stations had become the primary targets of third wave information warfare. A completely new terminology emerged to describe the new thinking: 'cyberwar', 'computer network attack and defence', 'electronic warfare', 'info-bombs' and 'info-warriors'.

At first this all seemed to belong more in the realm of science fiction than military doctrine. After all, the ongoing Balkan wars of the 1990s revealed that the old-fashioned war propagandists were still very much in business. It is comparatively easy for an outsider to identify such a strong propaganda climate within another society. However, if one is actually living through it, such dispassionate analysis becomes virtually impossible. It is like breathing oxygen; one knows it is there, but it is difficult to see it for what it is. The sharper manifestations of its existence – print, television and radio products, posters, music – are like condensation. For the previous forty years, the Yugoslavian political climate had been shaped by a Soviet-style communist propaganda regime that attempted to forge a national identity upon an ethnically heterogeneous population.

With the death of Tito and, moreover, the collapse of the Soviet Empire between 1989-91, both the internal and external cement of this sense of national and international identity crumbled. Into the vacuum flooded a heady mix of a modern political power struggle, ethnic polarization and historical revisionism. This was rationalized by the Serbs as an assault (chiefly by the Muslims) on their 'rightful' position from both within Yugoslavia and from without (epitomized by the German recognition of Croatia). The internal–external threat nexus was reinforced by the role of Turkey, the only Muslim member of NATO. Hence it became a 'war for survival' on the part a Serb nation which was fighting not just against the 'forces of evil' but also on behalf of the 'Christian (orthodox) civilized' world. It was more unfinished business.

The creation of Yugoslavia in 1919 out of the remnants of the Austro-Hungarian Empire was always along dubious ethnographic lines. An artificial patchwork of regions in which Serbs were sometimes in the majority but – outside of Serbia itself – usually in the minority, meant that once the country began to disintegrate, ethnic identity became a rallying cry for the Serbian 'Democratic' Party. It was in this regard that historical legitimacy for the creation of a unified Serb state, dating back 600 years, began to be frequently evoked. And so, an ethnic-nation-under-siege mentality took root in which Serbs were defending themselves against Croatian and Muslim extremists, who were aided by outside foreign forces, in a war of ethnic survival. This became the framework through which events were generally perceived, and from which no dissent was permitted.

Within this climate, especially as the state degenerated into civil war, many of the propaganda themes were entirely in accord with classic propaganda 'wars' of the past. These can be summarized as follows: pride in the Serbian army, admiration for its professionalism, soliloquies for its fallen 'heroes', non-discussion or dismissal of claims about breaches in the rules of war and law, praise for its commanders, and continuing public support for its efforts. Then there was the demonization of Croatian and Muslim 'extremists', complete with atrocity stories about their barbarous behaviour (including rape, and the murder of 'innocent women, children and old people'). Such barbarous behaviour was said to have been motivated by fanatical forces, including criminal mercenaries and the mujahidin. There were also evocations of historical, cultural and religious slogans to demonstrate that this latest conflict was merely part of a longer struggle of ethnic survival against internal and external threats, especially Muslim 'terrorists' who were inspired by jihad (i.e. connecting the enemy within to an enemy without). Other external 'inspirations' for the aggression against the Serbs related to the Hapsburg and Nazi periods, including the Vatican, Turks, and Islam generally. German recognition of Croatia was cited as further evidence of the European Union's adherence to this 'conspiracy'. In short, an Islamic–Catholic axis had 'conspired' to drive the Orthodox Serbs to extinction.

To the outside world, however, it was not the Serbs who were seen as the victims. Indeed, they were regarded as the aggressors. It has to be said that the complexity of the conflict exposed the inability of television news in particular to provide a clear picture of events as they unfolded. Instead, the conflict was reported in somewhat simplistic terms of 'bad guys' (the Serbs) versus 'good guys' (the Bosnians) when in fact all sides (including the under-reported Croatians) were capable of atrocious behaviour. When claims of atrocities did occur, one would have thought that, in the new global information environment, it would have been much easier than before to verify or discredit such claims. However, when international journalists wanted to check for themselves one alleged atrocity about necklaces being made from the fingers of Serbian babies, they were quite simply refused access to the scene of the 'crime'. The famous ITN footage of emaciated Muslim prisoners of war, which caused an international outrage in 1992, was banned on Serbian TV. The difficulties of accurate or clear reporting in such a climate were further illustrated in 1994 when a market place in Sarajevo was mortar bombed, causing numerous Bosnian casualties and horrific (if, again, self-censored) television coverage. The Serbs claimed that Muslim forces had done this themselves to evoke international sympathy, a claim that subsequently proved to be not wholly without foundation.

After nearly five years of a war the like of which Europe thought it had relegated to the past, the final straw came in the summer of 1995. This was when the 'safe havens' created by the UN in its token peacekeeping intervention (SFOR) up to that point fell to the Serb forces. All sides were keen to steer the media coverage in their favour, not just within areas under their control but on the international arena as well. The Bosnian Muslims now had an ideal opportunity and they provided increased foreign journalistic access to their civilians on the march from the fallen 'safe havens' of Srebrenica and Jeppa to demonstrate once and for all that it was they, indeed, who were the victims in this conflict. Serb protests that they were merely retaliating for Bosnian army attacks (off-camera) were drowned beneath the sea of devastating footage of Bosnian civilian suffering. Washington could resist no more – an example of where the 'CNN Effect' did occur – and, following a series of air strikes on Serb army positions, the Americans bombed President Milosevic to the negotiating table and at last brokered a peace agreement known as the Dayton Peace Accords.

An interesting twist to this entire story emerged when veteran BBC reporter Martin Bell argued in his memoirs that the reporting of the Balkans conflict had been too detached and that it had accordingly failed to prompt serious international intervention to stop the slaughter. That a supposed objective reporter working for a public service broadcaster should call for a 'journalism of attachment' in order to make the media an actor or participant in, as distinct from mere observer of, international crises is indicative of the widespread belief in the CNN Effect amongst journalists, let alone officials. They believed that television could make a difference. From our perspective, it also served to illustrate that, despite all protestations about being above propaganda, the media were in fact much more a part of the problem than the solution. Bell was motivated by a desire to reverse this situation but, in doing so, he was effectively arguing for the media actively to serve a propagandist role: propaganda for peace.

To a large extent thereafter, the Balkans fell off the media map until 1999. But that did not mean the propaganda in the region stopped. In military circles, the conviction was emerging that 'victory is no longer determined on the ground, but in media reporting'. As one observer pointed out, 'this is even more true in peace support operations where the goal is not to conquer territory or defeat an enemy but to persuade parties in conflict (as well as local populations) into a favored course of action'. This was the real significance of Operations Joint Endeavour and Joint Guard, the NATO-led multinational force designed to implement the Dayton agreements. The experience of SFOR and IFOR in Bosnia between 1995 and 1999 in terms of 'shaping the information space' in support of the mission was to have considerable impact on the development of the 'information warfare' (IW) concepts emerging out of the Gulf

War experience and the doctrine of 'information operations' (IO) that was to supersede it in the second half of the 1990s.

This is not to suggest that NATO was yet capable of conducting an integrated information operations campaign in the Balkans during this period. Far from it. But the three strands of NATO's Balkans information activities – Public Information (or, as the Americans called it, Public Affairs), Psychological Operations (PSYOPS) and Civil–Military Co-operation (CIMIC) – were to subsequently become essential ingredients of information operations thinking. That they were able to do this by the turn of the millennium is due to the success of these three informational 'tools' as they were deployed in Bosnia after 1995. It was not all smooth sailing, but the restoration and maintenance of peace after four years of bitter fighting in the former Yugoslavia, combined with the slow and painful rebuilding of civil society in the region, owed a great deal to NATO's recognition of communications and information, both within the country and beyond, as central to the success of the peacekeeping mission.

Many critics called this 'nation building'. This was an important and controversial development, and a far cry from the old assumption that states should not intervene in the internal affairs of other nation-states. Indigenous media reform was certainly a major strand of the process of attempting to create a climate of peace and reconciliation in Bosnia, although this was very much felt to be the responsibility of non-military and non-governmental organizations. But, so long as there was a NATO presence, there remained a need for SFOR to communicate not only with local media, however hostile they remained but also, because of this, directly with the local populations, as well as with the international media presence in the region. Centred on Sarajevo, the Coalition Information and Press Centre operated along by now well-established NATO Public Information principles, namely a proactive campaign designed to tell reporters as much of the truth as could be told (within constraints of operational security and force protection), as accurately and as timely as possible. Daily press conferences, regular press releases and the arrangement of interviews with commanders became its routine work while the overriding message in the early days was that SFOR was not an invading force, that it was well led, well equipped and ready to respond through the use of force if necessary.

To this end, a weekly newspaper was printed, *The Herald of*

Peace, which became *The Herald of Progress* under SFOR with a circulation of around 100,000 by 1997. The German component of the Psychological Operations Task Force contributed a monthly magazine with a similar circulation, *Mirko*, targeted at younger audiences. Following IFOR's use of five radio stations, SFOR continued with three, particularly Radio Mir, broadcasting news, information, music and entertainment for eighteen hours a day. Spot bulletins were also produced for television while millions of posters and handbills were peppered throughout the region. As in the aftermath of any modern civil war, unexploded landmines remained a constant menace and so a major campaign of mine awareness was launched to inform the local populace, especially the children, of the dangers of wandering into minefields or how to identify different types of mines. Join-the-dot colouring books depicting these were issued to schools, and DC Comics was commissioned to produce a special issue of the Superman comic warning of the perils of playing near minefields. A classic example of how such well-intentioned propaganda can backfire, this comic had to be withdrawn when it was discovered that some young children were deliberately walking into minefields in the hope that Superman would come and save them.

Nonetheless, Bosnia revealed the possibilities of what could be done with information as a 'tool' in the same way that Desert Storm had revealed the significance of information as a 'weapon'. But in the new international environment, the major obstacle to realizing this were old and increasingly inappropriate Cold War structures and ways of thinking about what the role of the military should be when war fighting was now to be but one of its functions. Intra-state conflicts may be battlefields for the indigenous warring parties but, when international forces are deployed to do something to stop the fighting, they become 'operational spaces' in which communications skills become key. Prior to an intervention, it is essential to explain in advance why external forces are coming to counter any indigenous propaganda that they are in fact invading. This was a major challenge in Somalia in 1992. Once troops were on the ground, communicating with locals in a country where local media were either hostile or absent was conducted mainly by PSYOPS personnel. In Somalia, Radio Rajo ('Hope') was established to do this, to explain when and where humanitarian convoys were distributing food relief or to give even more basic messages such as requests to stay off the roads at certain time so that the convoys could get through. During Operation Restore Democracy, the operation to restore democratically elected President Aristide to power in Haiti during 1994, the upgraded Volant (now Commando) Solo airborne broadcasting platform transmitted messages onto local television and radio frequencies under the umbrella of 'Radio Democracy'. Although an actual military invasion was pre-empted on that occasion, it remained essential to communicate with a largely illiterate population about how to behave once the troops arrived. PSYOPS teams then produced leaflets, posters, news sheets, radio and television programmes to explain US intentions to local audiences in an attempt to lubricate military operations taking place in the midst of civilians.

What used to be called peacekeeping missions were now being described as 'operations other than war'. The extent to which many western armed forces have professionalized their approach towards these new kinds of operations meant that PSYOPS had to adapt the traditional 'Surrender or Die' messages disseminated to enemy soldiers or the 'Resistance is Futile' messages targeted at enemy civilians. Essentially, there were two reasons for this. The first is that international interventions, as they succeeded the peace-keeping operations of the Cold War, no longer involved merely keeping opposing warring factions apart. Soldiers were tradition-ally trained to fight soldiers. Now they had increasingly to interact with civilians. The second factor is that the traditional battlefields of the past, where soldiers knew the Rules of Engagement and the limits of their ability to behave in certain ways, have transformed into a new kind of environment where new skills other than war fighting are necessary if the objectives of the intervention are to be achieved. In other words, in operations like the 'humanitarian intervention' in Kosovo in 1999, or Bosnia before it, the real work begins after the battle in order to pre-empt the need for further military action.

Since the armed intervention by NATO air power to expel the Serb armed forces from Kosovo from March to June 1999 and the establishment since then of KFOR, the region tends only to make the headlines when things go wrong. Without getting distracted into debates about whether 'bad news' defines the media's agenda, NATO attempted to avoid such headlines by an ambitious inform-ation campaign designed to stabilize the region's ethnic hatreds and assist in the restoration of Kosovo's civic society. This continues to involve three strands. The first is designed to 'retrain' the soldiers to operate within a difficult psychological climate in which civilian hatred runs deep and wide. The second is directed at the 'hearts and minds' of those very civilians divided by centuries of ethnic hatred and indoctrination. The third strand has an even more ambitious aim, namely the rebuilding not just of Kosovo's infrastructure but also of its psychology. It is nation building on a par with the political re-education of Germany and Japan after 1945, although it is rarely admitted as such.

During the actual war-fighting phase of Operation Allied Force, the conduct of PSYOPS assumed similar characteristics to Desert Storm. More than 100 million leaflets were dropped against various targets. In Kosovo itself, VJ (Yugoslavian Army) forces received warnings that they were about to be attacked unless they left the area. This technique was copied from Kuwait when leaflets warning of impending attacks by Daisy Cutter bombs and B52s were successful in clearing the battlefield of enemy forces. In Kosovo, however, the Yugoslav army was a very different proposition to that of Iraq's largely conscripted forces. The Yugoslav army did not flee. Highly skilled in deception and camouflage techniques, it moved around with considerable skill to avoid the destructive power of the NATO air campaign. Anyone who can recall the defiance of Serb forces as they were televised leaving Kosovo at the end of the campaign will appreciate that this PSYOP campaign had little or no impact.

A second target audience was the Serb population. The PSYOP campaign here also had little or no impact. Leaflets were dropped over cities like Belgrade and Novi Sad suggesting that NATO was not fighting the civilian population but rather the Milosovic regime. This personalization of the campaign, if anything, prompted an outburst of patriotic support for Milosovic from people who had just months earlier been demonstrating their opposition to his regime. 'We are all targets' became a rallying cry that saw defiant civilians rally to bridges to test NATO's claim that they were targeting only military and political installations. A skilful domestic propaganda campaign which emphasized that the Kosovo Albanians were fleeing the country due to the NATO bombing rather than the alleged Serb 'genocide' in Kosovo eventually saw Serb State television attacked, but even here RTS was off the air for barely four hours. Regular street concerts by traditional music and rock bands maintained the atmosphere of defiance against NATO=Nazis.

Kosovo can also be justifiably described as the first internet war. In Serbia, it was estimated that a maximum of 50,000 of its ten million population had access to the internet, with less than 1,000 in Kosovo itself. It was not therefore a decisive factor in the conflict, but it was a new one. The internet was to Kosovo what television had been to the Korean war. However, it is axiomatic of both the internet and of emerging information warfare thinking that with comparatively limited resources a widespread global impact is possible. The Kosovo Liberation Army certainly recognized this by their establishment of a website long before the conflict with NATO began. The self-proclaimed Kosovo government in exile ran its own site from Geneva. When the Serbs closed down the independent radio station B92, it merely moved to a different location in cyberspace, based in Holland, and continued its protests. With only the thinnest legal backing, and arguably an actual violation of both the UN's and NATO's charters, NATO governments justified the campaign largely in moral terms, as a humanitarian mission to rescue the Kosovans from genocide. With Britain at the forefront of the information campaign, the war was framed in terms of the Labour government's so-called 'ethical foreign policy'. Whereas the majority of people within NATO (with the notable exception of Greece) backed their government's war effort and accepted it as a 'just war', and had the television images of fleeing refugees to reinforce their support for it, the kind of people who used the internet for accessing information behind the journalistic gatekeeping of new stories may not have been quite so sure. It was these very voices of dissent, that were absent from the traditional media coverage of the war, who seized upon the internet as a medium of transmitting their reservations around the world.

The Serbs certainly demonstrated an understanding of all this by devoting considerable resources towards internet communications during the Kosovo conflict. They saw the World Wide Web as a unique instrument for waging their own information war against NATO and for getting their message across to a global public, while refuting or challenging the arguments of their adversaries. Indeed, from the moment the NATO bombing commenced on 24 March 1999, and as it extended into targeting Serbia's military–civil infrastructure, including Serbian television and radio transmitters and stations, it was perhaps their only weapon of retaliation. Serb attacks took place on NATO's own home page and anti-NATO hackers disrupted the website of the White House. One individual in Belgrade was able to cause considerable damage by e-mailing 2000 messages a day, some containing the Melissa and more pernicious Papa macro viruses, to NATO's website using 'ping' bombardment strategy to cause line saturation.

What was now being labelled asymmetric warfare had arrived. This phrase essentially means that militarily strong nations like the United States, which can unleash overwhelming firepower, are nonetheless vulnerable in certain areas that weaker opponents can exploit. Information in the global media 'space' is one such area unless the voice of the enemy can be silenced. Attacking Iraqi or Serb radio towers may have been controversial, but this was all part of this thinking. However, when western news organizations send journalists into countries under fire, they provide an opportunity for those countries to publicize their point of view in the very countries attacking them. Moreover, the internationalization of the telephone system means that individuals can either phone family and friends around the world and, if computers attached to modems are available, all sorts of words and images can follow. Battle spaces had thus become extremely porous places in which it is almost impossible to prevent or censor the flow of information out of the actual combat zone, especially now that battlefields had now become operational spaces, whereas in the past the military had been able to control the flow of news and information from the area of fighting.

Given the importance of credibility in the successful conduct of PSYOPS, NATO's deployment in Kosovo of one leaflet in particular is worthy of mention. This was a leaflet depicting the Apache attack helicopter with the phrase 'Don't wait for me'. Given that the Apache was never deployed during the air campaign because of orders to fight the war from above 15,000 feet, the failure to deliver what was promised in the messages was symptomatic of a defective PSYOP campaign that failed to break either Serb military or civilian morale. After the Gulf War the Kurds and Shias had risen up against Saddam Hussein, only to be crushed by Iraqi armed forces. No such counterpart took place in Serbia, although of course within a year Milosovic had been removed by a 'velvet revolution' in Belgrade. Meanwhile, NATO had expanded its Balkan commitments through its occupation of Kosovo where the real challenge for the information campaign was all too apparent once the fighting stopped.

The most important element in such a nation-building exercise is time. The allied campaign to 're-educate' Germany and Japan out of their militaristic tendencies after the Second World War arguably took a generation, plus the rewriting of constitutions, school text books and press laws, to infuse a democratic way of thinking. One of the key debates of the Cold War surrounded the rights and wrongs of interfering in the internal affairs of other countries. With Kosovo branded a 'humanitarian intervention', such debates have resurfaced, especially with subsequent international interventions in East Timor, Macedonia, Sierra Leone and Afghanistan. But it is possible to see military forces in places like Kosovo as an occupying force, with the attempts to rebuild civic society in these countries as being tantamount to a 're-educational' campaign. Whether they succeed in reconciling centuries of hatred, for example between Kosovar and Serb, really does depend upon how much time the information campaign is given to achieve its objectives.

That, of course, is a political decision and is very much dependent upon the longevity and attitudes of the new governments that have displaced the ones causing the trouble in the first place. In the meantime, NATO and other authorities on the ground continue their efforts to restore peace and reconciliation. The warm glow surrounding the conduct of PSYOPS since the Gulf War has chilled in the light of the Kosovo experience but it still continues to enjoy an increasingly central position as emerging Information Operations doctrine unfolds. At the time of writing, the working definition of Information Operations remains: 'actions taken to affect adversary information and information systems while defending one's own information and information systems'. This is very much a conflict variant of command and control warfare. Despite the initial preoccupation with systems and machines, people are what matter because if wars begin in the human mind, that is where the determination to end them takes place. And so, central to the thinking is the importance of 'influence operations' or what is becoming known as 'perception management': the new euphemism for propaganda. It is within this spectrum that PSYOPS is being placed – dangerously in my view – alongside deception activities. Deception is as old as the Trojan Horse, an accepted part of war fighting. But it is also a form of psychological operations. The danger lies in the fact that the broadening nature of PSYOPS in the previous decade has meant an increasing interface with media operations. It is essential for PSYOPS and media operations to be kept separate, albeit co-ordinated; a press conference is not, and never should be, a psychological operation in the strictest sense. Critical to the success of PSYOPS is credibility, and if PSYOPS are lumped in with deception operations, that credibility is bound to be undermined.

Part of the difficulty in new thinking about the Revolution in Military Affairs is the need to win within a global information environment. Operational security has become increasingly difficult, as the range of information disseminators from a conflict area has broadened out from the media to the general public. New communications technologies such as mobile phones and laptop computers are affordable and accessible to ordinary people and so it is not just the unpredictable media that needs to concern the information operators. Battlefields have become conflict spaces in which assistance to civilians is frequently the reason for military intervention. It is in these spaces that the military now have to *compete* with their information; they are no longer able to monopolize or confine the information flows. As such, tactical information – such as that contained in PSYOPS products – has a strategic significance, which merely makes the issue of credibility even more important. It is not just that citizens in Belgrade could pick up a leaflet dropped minutes earlier and turn to display it to a CNN camera crew. They can now take it home, scan it into their computer and send it as an email attachment to anyone on the internet. Hence just as power supplies, television stations and radio transmitters have become the primary targets of information-age warfare, perception is a vitally important and worldwide conflict space.

If modern, liberal, free-market capitalist democracies decide for whatever reason to deploy their armed forces, they cannot do so behind closed doors. Correspondingly, their behaviour has to reflect not just the political imperatives but also the very ideology for which they are risking their lives. Under such scrutiny, casualties – on both sides – need to be kept to a minimum, mistakes need to admitted quickly, and credible and accurate information needs to be released as soon as operational security allows. Quite simply the world has changed and the military are still a little old-fashioned in their thinking about what their role now is. Effectively, they have become heavily armed social workers and, although they may not like this new function, they need the new skills required to operate in humanitarian and other interventions. The new skills are not just required during the military phase of any such operation; they have already demonstrated that they are pretty effective at this anyway. But before the battle, considerable planning to prepare the way is required and when the information processors are brought into the planning loop – as in the Gulf – then information dominance can ease the path to victory. What is now required is an equally sustained effort once the fighting has stopped. Rehabilitation takes time and effort.

PSYOPS is an essential part of this effort, together with other forms of 'perception management' that constitute the spectrum of persuasion which modern armed forces must undertake in support of both traditional and emerging missions. But because of the information explosion, adversary reliance on information technology also requires a need to target such communications and information systems. Conversely, one's own information systems need to be protected from attack. The post-Cold War shift of American military information systems into the civilian domain have thus created new vulnerabilities, encapsulated by the fear of what has been called 'an electronic Pearl Harbour'. By extension, the need is now to think of rebuilding former adversaries in terms of an electronic Marshall Plan.

It should come as no surprise to find the instruments of 'soft' power assuming an increasingly central role in pre- and post-conflict scenarios. The reorganization of the United States Information Agency in 1999, which saw USIA and Voice of America fully reintegrated into the US State Department, is recognition of the latter. The hidden assumptions behind this, however, relate to wider political and (usually) unspoken imperatives about the need to promote democracy, in all its forms, worldwide. Many senior political figures in the western world are very much taken by the assertion that democracies do not fight other democracies. If the enemies of democracy are therefore non-democracies, then it follows that every effort should be made to reduce the number of potential enemies, or what are sometimes called 'rogue states'. Hence the psychological warfare stations targeting specific 'enemies', such as Radio and TV Marti directed at Cuba, or Radio Free Asia directed at North Korea and China, continue their work under the umbrella of 'soft' power information campaigns. Radio Free Europe continues as well in an effort to consolidate democratic ways of thinking in the former communist countries of Eastern Europe. In what has now been labelled 'international information', the victors of the Cold War see a newly invigorated and potentially decisive instrument for consolidating a New World Information Order.

In the new terrain that has been identified for war-fighting and democracy building alike, the concept of Information Operations that is emerging assumes strategic dimensions across the full spectrum of conflict (the RMA) and diplomacy alike (prompting what might be called a Revolution in Diplomatic Affairs). Old forms of thinking still prevail as this terrain continues to be mapped out. The paradigm shift for the new world is simply too great a leap in faith to make fully as yet. However, the acquisition, transmission, storage and transformation of information makes IO a target, a weapon, a vulnerability and an integrated strategy all at the same time. This strategy will continue to require the capacity for greater physical destruction than an adversary, both in traditional terms and in new ways that utilize the digital revolution to its full advantage, whether it be in ways of protecting information systems from virus attack or the insertion of logic bombs into adversary systems. And because of the increasing inter-relationship between civilian and military information infrastructures, homeland defence becomes a pre-requisite in light of vulnerabilities to hacker attacks from adversaries that are increasingly difficult to identify in a world which may be witnessing the triumph of democratic systems but which is also seeing new and often individualistic adversaries rather than state actors.

Within this thinking, 'influence operations' to either pre-empt future adversaries, to defeat them in the case of conflict, and to consolidate triumphal value systems once victory is achieved, assumes a central role. The objectives are to support foreign policy, deter aggression and support democratic reform. What raises some doubt from the sceptics who liken this thinking to Orwellian 'mind control' is indeed an old philosophical conundrum faced by PSYOPS practitioners since the First World War. To put it simply, is it better to persuade an adversary to lay down his weapon and to desert, defect or surrender than it is to blow his head off? A hundred years ago, before the advent of mass slaughter that characterizes industrialized warfare, there were many who would have said 'no' to this question. Lord Pononby's belief that 'the defilement of the human soul is worse than the destruction of the human body' needs to be re-written to ask whether the injection of democratic values into people's minds is a better guarantee of protecting human rights, respecting minorities and other peoples' differences than bombing them into thinking like 'us'. This suggests that a simple choice has to be made. That choice is whether to conduct 'perception management' operations in support of one set of values at the expense of another.

This is not an easy choice to make. It is vulnerable to accusations of 'cultural imperialism' or 'coca-colonialism', especially if the choice is being made in Washington as the self-proclaimed capital of the democratic world. Non-democracies will accuse the USA of arrogance in assuming that its political system and values are superior to those of others who choose not to adopt the same system and values. No doubt the retort would be: 'whose choice?' – government or people? If non-democratic governments are not prepared to test their moral position by letting the people decide in free and fair elections, then they merely confirm their position as 'rogue' or authoritarian regimes that constitute the 'natural' enemies of democracies. The retort would be a fair one if not for Florida during the 2000 presidential election.

However, regardless of whether the George W. Bush Jr. administration reverses these trends, the international information effort now being conducted by the US is founded on the premise that the US should and can make a difference in world affairs. In attempting to shape the international environment to best serve US interests, the programme is predicated on the assumption that democratization will continue to thrive on a worldwide basis. The campaign in Kosovo was but one small piece of this jigsaw. The bigger picture is to deter conflict whenever possible (including by high profile visible threats of use of force but preferably by avoiding the actual deployment of force). In order to achieve this, greater use of 'soft' power will be required at the cultural, political and economic levels of inter-state relations on a local, regional and global basis. But the choice has indeed been made. Only time will tell if the belief that democracies really do prefer trade to war is a valid universal assumption or whether it is in fact an assumption that says more about the American value system than the realities of international affairs or of human nature.

Chapter 27

The World after 11 September 2001

The terrorist attacks on New York and Washington on '9/11' prompted a major debate in the United States about 'why they hate us so much'. Clearly American assertions about being a 'force for good in the world' had failed to convince the terrorist network behind the attacks identified as al-Qaeda ('the base') led by Osama bin Laden, a Saudi businessman who had been simmering with anti-American resentment since the Gulf War and the arrival of American troops into the Holy Land of Mecca. The World Trade Centre had been attacked before, in 1993, although subsequent American targets had been outside the USA – on the American embassies in Nairobi, Kenya and Dar es Salam in 1998, and on the *USS Cole* in the Yemeni port of Aden in 2000. But the hijack of four domestic commercial passenger jets, full of aviation fuel, and the successful strikes on the twin towers of New York and on the Pentagon – that symbol of American military might as the world's sole superpower in its very own capital city – was of a much different order, with the deaths of innocent civilians on a much greater scale.

It was a classic asymmetric attack. Moreover, in the 16 minutes between the strikes on the first and second towers, New York's newsrooms had scrambled their helicopters and were able to capture the second plane hitting its target live to a global audience. It was therefore also a spectacular example of the 'propaganda of the deed'. The initial American reaction was to hunt down the perpetrators, and the 'war' on international terrorism was declared, although wars are usually defined in international law as being between two or more nation states. Within a month, on 7 October, American planes began bombing al-Qaeda strongholds in Afghanistan where their Taliban sponsors had also been identified as a

target for 'regime change'. American and British special forces were
inserted on the ground to conduct a manhunt for al-Qaeda and
Taliban fighters, working alongside local forces in the Northern
Alliance. A $25 million reward was offered for the capture of bin
Laden and the Taliban leader, Mullah Omar. The operation, initially
dubbed a 'crusade' under the label of 'Infinite Justice' – both spectacular propaganda own-goals – was quickly re-labelled 'Enduring
Freedom'. By December, the Taliban had fled the Afghan capital,
Kabul, and dispersed in the mountains. Captured prisoners were
taken to the American military base at Guantanamo Bay, Cuba,
and the slow process of rebuilding Afghan civil society began.

The conflict in Afghanistan was but a small part of the 'war'
against terrorism. Other fighting 'fronts' were in the realms of
intelligence, law enforcement, finance, homeland defence, diplomacy – and propaganda. In Afghanistan itself, PSYOPS teams
dropped more than 80 million leaflets declaring that 'The Partnership of Nations is Here to Help'. Commando Solo was deployed to
broadcast radio messages into the region, especially after Taliban
radio was bombed and taken off the air. The Taliban had banned
television, which meant that most people in Afghanistan had never
seen the images of the twin towers collapsing. It was therefore
imperative that the Americans explained why they were in the
country, not as an invading force like the Russians before them (or
even the British before that) but to seek justice for the crimes committed against them. Rather, they suggested, it was the Arab al-
Qaeda fighters who were the foreign invaders holding the country
to ransom by payrolling the Taliban. An important ingredient of
this campaign was the humanitarian aid dropped by the ton in
yellow packets. The Taliban countered by warning that the food
was either poisoned or that the packets were really cluster bombs
(which were also yellow). The colour was changed to blue. The
coalition was clearly attempting to divide Afghan civilians from
the Taliban leadership with messages such as: 'Do you enjoy being
ruled by the Taliban? Are you proud to live a life of fear? Are you
happy to see the place your family has owned for generations
become a terrorist training site?' Leaflets were dropped over towns
depicting a Taliban whipping a woman dressed in a burkha and
bearing the words: 'Is this the future you want for your women and
children?' Other messages tried to convey a sense of solidarity
between the ordinary people of the USA and of Afghanistan. As

one leaflet declared: 'No one should tell you how to live. The Partnership of Nations will help rescue the Afghan people from the Taliban criminals and foreign terrorists.'

The Taliban understood the 24/7 global news cycle and they also realized the importance of a new media player, namely Al Jazeera, the Qatar based television station founded in 1995 and dubbed the 'Arab CNN'. Five hours ahead of London and 10 ahead of Washington, Taliban spokesmen were able to set the daily news agenda with stories about 'collateral damage' or how they had shot down American helicopters. Al Jazeera was given exclusive rights to bin Laden videotaped interviews which were then relayed by other stations to western audiences. The time difference meant that London and Washington were on the defensive responding to such claims. It was not until the creation of Coalition Information Centres in London, Washington and – most crucially – in Islamabad that this situation was reversed. But, by then, a lot of damage had been done to the coalition's cause. Serious doubts had been cast on the veracity of American claims about al-Qaeda's responsibility for the 9/11 attacks, on the identity of the hijackers, even the so called 'evidence' from the crash sites. Rumours were rife that 4,000 Jews failed to turn up for work on the day of the strikes, that footage of celebrating Palestinians aired on CNN had in fact been taken during the Gulf War, and that the strikes were really a CIA–Mossad conspiracy to provide a pretext for war in Afghanistan motivated by the Bush family's oil interests. This mixture of rumour, gossip and misinformation from Palestine to Pakistan was picked up in the western media and, where it wasn't, on the internet. The global information environment had become so porous and so fast that the waging of any strategic information campaign could no longer merely be confined to the traditional mass media front. This did not prevent the White House from trying to deny the American people access to the 'enemy' point of view, but when commercial television stations were asked not to run the bin Laden tapes, for fear that they might contain coded messages to terrorist 'sleepers', this merely provided their opponents with further 'evidence' of western hypocrisy about purporting to promote democratic values, such as freedom of speech.

The early rounds of the propaganda war had clearly gone to the terrorists. In the Islamic world, in particular, simmering anti-American resentment resurfaced focusing especially upon American

support for Israel. The downgrading of US public diplomacy since
the Reagan Administration had meant that explanations of US
foreign policy issues were being dominated by its opponents. In
Pakistan, extremists took to the streets parading a poster which
superimposed bin Laden's face over a photograph of the twin
towers being hit, suggesting that in those circles there was no
doubt about who had been responsible for the strikes. While denying that this was a 'clash of civilizations', western propagandists
had clearly missed a trick by failing to focus on previous US
support for Muslim communities in Kuwait, Bosnia, Kosovo and
East Timor. US foreign policy was, instead, accused of being selective, pro-Israeli and therefore anti-Palestinian, self-interested,
driven by Texan oil barons and anti-Islamic – indeed anything but
a force for good in the world. This shocked many Americans,
especially footage of some Palestinians actually celebrating as they
watched the twin towers footage. 'It was taken during the Gulf
War!' came the retort, which was not true but widely believed as
the misinformation spread throughout the internet.

The World Trade Centre was the most symbolic of targets. People
from scores of nationalities were among the 3,000 dead, including
almost 100 Muslims. But the building not only symbolized the
triumph of free market liberal capitalism, it also represented
modernity itself. In this respect it was an attack on the modern
world and everything it represented by a group of fanatics who
were deeply concerned at the erosion of tradition in their own
societies. Fifteen of the nineteen dead hijackers were Saudi citizens,
men who were deeply resentful of the presence of American military
bases in their Holy Land since the Gulf War. In this respect, the
'war' against international terrorism is a clash of ideas in much the
same way as the Cold War was a battle of ideologies. As such, it
would require a more coherent propaganda – or perception management – machinery than the one which had failed the Americans so
badly in the 1990s. In 2002, an Office of Global Communications
was established within the White House to co-ordinate this campaign, Voice of America broadcasts in foreign languages including
Arabic were increased, and greater funding was provided to cultural
exchange programmes with citizens of Islamic countries. In the
Pentagon, it was announced that an Office of Strategic Influence
had been created shortly after 9/11 but when, six months later, it
was revealed that among its functions would be military deception

through the media, there was an outcry amongst the press and it had to be closed down.

In this new battle for hearts and minds, propaganda – however it is termed – will play a central role, especially if the 'war' against international terrorism lasts for a long time. Many people ask whether the world has changed since 11 September, but certainly many aspects of American foreign policy have changed. The identification of an 'axis of evil', the openly declared desire to foster 'regime change' in places like Iraq, the determination to 'hunt down' terrorists and their supporters, and the renewed emphasis on preventing 'weapons of mass destruction' from reaching undesirable hands may well be understandable reactions to 9/11 but they do create enormous challenges from a democratic propaganda point of view. Image and reality must go hand-in-hand if a nation's actions are to be perceived in a desired way. Otherwise, the world's sole surviving superpower will merely be seen to be wielding what has become another dirty 'p' word, namely power.

In December 2002, American PSYOPS teams began dropping leaflets on Iraq warning its soldiers not to fire on coalition aircraft. Commando Solo broadcasts encouraged Iraqi soldiers to desert the regime of Saddam Hussein. American resolve to destroy the first target of the 'axis of evil' prompted many to question the link between Iraq and the events of 11 September but the debate over weapons of mass destruction, and whether Iraq might one day supply them to al-Qaeda, placed the realm of foreign policy into the 'what if?' category rather than its more traditional pragmatism for dealing with what had already happened. This makes it even harder for the propagandists because they are forced to deal with a world as it might be rather than with constructing justifications for actions that have already taken place. In such a world, image may have nothing to do with reality. And in a world where image is everything, reality has nothing to do with 'facts' or 'the truth'. The only truth is power.

Chapter 28

Epilogue

In the previous edition of this book, published in 1995, the epilogue began with the stark assertion that we are in an age of propaganda. This is even more appropriate to the twenty-first century than to all the other centuries before it, as outlined in this book. But the somewhat optimistic tone in that earlier edition now has to be tempered in light of the experience of the so-called 'war' against terrorism. Then, the epilogue suggested that there was nothing for democracies to fear about either the prominence of propaganda or the necessity of conducting it on behalf of democratic values. The picture is now a little more mixed. I would still maintain that we need more propaganda, not less. We need more attempts to influence our opinions and to arouse our participation in the democratic process, which depends for its survival upon public opinion. This is even more the case in light of declining electoral turnouts and the debacle of the 2000 presidential election in the United States. We need more propaganda about issues of universal concern to all human beings, regardless of race, creed, colour or nationality. We need more propaganda to counter the hate-inspired propaganda of certain factions attempting to undermine peaceful co-existence between peoples. That this was not done effectively in certain parts of the world after the end of the Cold War may indeed have been one of the root causes of the 11 September attacks.

Eighty years earlier, Walter Lippmann had written:

> Within the life of a generation now in control of affairs, persuasion has become a self-conscious art and a regular organ of popular government ... It is no longer possible ... to believe in the original dogma of democracy; that the knowledge needed for the management of human affairs comes up spontaneously from the human heart. Where we act

on that theory, we expose ourselves to self-deception, and to forms of persuasion that we cannot verify.

So, in an age of propaganda, the only course of action open to us is to learn to identify it for what it is – merely a process of persuasion that forms a part of everyday life. It can be used for good or ill, just like any other form of communication, but its very pervasiveness in contemporary society is a reflection not just of the multiplicity of media but also of the plurality of mediators who exist for getting us to think – and do – something which serves their vested interests.

Those interests may, or may not, coincide with our own. If they do, we tend not to label it as propaganda. They become our shared value system, our common set of 'truths'. It is only when we meet someone from outside this system, whose views of the world are quite different from our own, that we can begin to appreciate that there may be another way of looking at things. We can accept or reject that different way, but we ignore it at our peril. In a globalized, communications-rich environment it is unlikely that it can be ignored anyway. There are those who equate globalization with Americanization, and they don't like it. The attempt in the United States after 9/11 to understand 'why they hate us so much' at times failed to give due emphasis to the enormous amount of support Washington has from around the world in the fight against international terrorism. But the agonizing also reflected a failure of American propaganda to project itself as a benign 'force for good in the world'. The Romans hadn't really worried too much about this aspect of their power in the ancient world and nor had the European empires of more recent times. But the communications revolution had changed the environment in which power now had to operate. In its democratic manifestation, it now needed to be explained. It could no longer be left to speak for itself.

When, for example, nothing was done about Radio Mille Collines in Rwanda which called for the massacre of Tutsis, the dangers of leaving the information environment to those who would abuse it was plain for all to see. However, despite sympathetic western media coverage for the plight of the Chechens in the winter of 1994-5, western governments were slow to put pressure on Moscow to stop the 'slaughter'. The Russians tried to exclude the international media altogether from the second Chechen war. They argued that the Chechens were not freedom fighters but terrorists, and the seizing of an opera house full of citizens in the late summer of 2002 seemed to confirm the view of the Moscow government as being right all along. But in propaganda battles, it is not so much a struggle for being right but for being credible. They are battles between competing truths. Nowhere is this more evident than in the Middle East where Israel struggles to portray itself as the only democracy in the region to evoke the sympathy of like-minded governments and where the Palestinians talk of 'justice' from the Zionist 'invaders'.

Ultimately, therefore, propaganda is about sides. Whether or not something is branded as 'propaganda' depends upon which side you are on. The democratic tradition has evolved through a 'strategy of truth' although that does not mean the whole truth can be, or is, told. This is particularly the case in wartime, where information that could assist an enemy is held back or suppressed on grounds of 'operational security'. But it would indeed be delusional to assume that morale is not a factor. And it is the same for peacetime as it is for wartime. The prominence of 'spin doctors' in modern politics is the latest example of Lippmann's analysis, which brings us back to the role of the media and whether they are part of the state propaganda machine. In authoritarian states this is certainly the case, but what about democracies where the media are free to say whatever they like, within legal constraints relating to libel or national security? This brings us to what Noam Chomsky and Edward Herman have called the 'manufacture of consent'. These leftish scholars have provided a 'propaganda model' to analyse the systemic bias of the American media, identifying five factors which determine what kind of news is published or broadcast thanks to a sort of American media–government complex. The factors are: (1) the increased concentration of ownership of the mass media by an ever smaller number of corporations whose motive is profit rather than any sense of duty to inform the public; (2) increasing media dependence on advertising revenue; (3) media dependence on government sources or huge corporate or elite expert sources for their information; (4) a media preoccupation with responding to negative events; and (5) anti-communism. These factors, they argued, serve to marginalize dissenting or alternative voices and to allow dominant public and private interests undue access to the mass media.

Whatever the validity of this model – and it does tend to see the world as a sort of top-down conspiracy at the expense of journalistic practices as they operate on the ground – it does serve to remind us that dominant ideologies and corporate interests which benefit from those ideologies are always happy to use propaganda via whatever media are available. The same is beginning to happen to the internet. Time Warner buys CNN and AOL, America's biggest internet service provider. The Chinese government continues to find ways of building a great firewall to 'protect' its citizens from the free flow of global information, and disinformation, available on the World Wide Web. The increased use of media advisers by democratic governments, such as the hiring of the Renton public relations group for the war against terrorism while the US government built its official propaganda machine, is a recognition that even democratic politics is now as much about presentation as it is policy. This may be lamentable, but it is a reflection of the need to do something proactive, to 'package' politics almost as a marketing exercise.

In the war against terrorism, there is a need for western liberal democracies to package their very value systems. The 9/11 attacks signalled a twin strike against the United States as the world's surviving superpower, and modernity as achieved in developed capitalist nations when the bi-polar world collapsed. But although 9/11 increased a general sense of vulnerability against weaker opponents who were prepared to commit suicide to achieve their goals (whatever they might be) it really revealed the vulnerability of democracy itself as a way of life and as a way of doing politics. And if democracies are to engage in propaganda – or whatever they prefer to call it – either at home or abroad, that propaganda must be based upon democratic principles. These include persuasion rather than coercion, telling as much of the truth as can be told without jeopardizing lives, respect for individual rights and freedoms for all peoples, tolerance of minorities and so on. In the United States, it may have once been the case that these 'truths' were held to be self-evident, but they are not in many other parts of the world. The export of democratic values – to Bosnia, Kosovo, Afghanistan or anywhere else where nation building takes place after an enforced regime change – may well be seen as another form of cultural imperialism. They will be resisted by people who only see modern democratic political systems as selective in their so-called humanitarian interventions, self-serving in their foreign policies and morally corrupt at home.

This book began with the suggestion that it is the intention behind propaganda that needs scrutiny, not just the propaganda itself. It is intention that has caused and prolonged wars. It is intention which can prevent them. Increased use of persuasive techniques intended to benefit humanity as a whole requires some fundamental rethinking about how we popularly regard propaganda. Differences of opinion between people and nations are inevitable, but they can only remain a healthy aspect of civilized society if violence, war and terrorism are avoided. Since 9/11, we need peace propagandists, not war propagandists – people whose job it is to increase communication, understanding and dialogue between different peoples with different perspectives. A gradual process of explanation can only generate greater trust, and therefore a greater willingness to understand our perspective. And if this dialogue is mutual, greater empathy and consensus will emerge. We might not always like what we see about others but we need to recognize that fear, hypocrisy and ignorance are the enemies of peace and peaceful co-existence. The historical function of propaganda has been to fuel that fear, hypocrisy and ignorance, and it has earned itself a bad reputation for so doing. But propaganda has the potential to serve a constructive, civilized and peaceful purpose – if that is the intention behind conducting it. We must all become propagandists on behalf of those very characteristics that genetically and anthropologically link all people to the human species. Only then might we really begin to see an end to history. It may, however, be a long time coming.

Bibliographical Essay

The study of propaganda requires a multidisciplinary approach, but as the emphasis of this book is historical I have relied on a wide variety of works too numerous to mention here. Wherever possible, I have used primary source materials (in translation when available), such as Roman inscriptions and the works of classical historians, medieval songs and chronicles, modern printed propaganda, film and documentary evidence, and television.

Certain general works are useful starting points, such as Oliver Thomson's illustrated *Mass Persuasion in History* (1977) and Anthony Rhodes's *Propaganda* (1976). A seminal work by a sociologist is Jacques Ellul, *Propaganda: The Formation of Men's Attitudes* (1957), but the same author's *The Technological Society* (1964) is an invaluable compendium. More recently, two psychologists have tackled the subject from a contemporary point of view in Anthony Pratkanis and Elliot Aronson, *Age of Propaganda: The Everyday Use and Abuse of Persuasion* (1991). Another psychological perspective is offered by G.H. Jamieson, *Communication and Persuasion* (1985). Guy Arnold's *Brainwash: The Cover-up Society* (1992) is better than its title. The best single-volume introduction is edited by 'old masters' Harold Lasswell, Daniel Lerner and Hans Speier, *Propaganda and Communication in World History* (1979). Other invaluable works include T.H. Qualter's *Propaganda and Psychological Warfare* (1962) and his *Opinion Control in the Democracies* (1985), Elias Canetti's *Crowds and Power* (1963), Sam Keen's *Face of the Enemy* (1986), F.H. Hartmann's *The Conservation of Enemies* (1982), Garth Jowett and Victoria O'Donnell's *Propaganda and Persuasion* (1986) and Charles Roetter's *Psychological Warfare* (1974). I, personally, dislike Laurence Rees's *Selling Politics* (1992); the BBC TV programmes it was written to accompany ('We Have Ways of Making You Think') were better. No examination of this topic can avoid Walter Lippmann's seminal *Public Opinion* (1922). Useful approaches to related persuasive techniques such as advertising include: A. & J. Trout, *Positioning: The Battle For Your Mind* (1987), S. Fox, *The Mirror Makers* (1984) and W. Schramm (ed.), *The Science of Human Communication* (1963). Vance Packard's *The Hidden Persuaders* (1957) was the classic of its time about advertising, as was J.A.C. Brown's *Techniques of Persuasion* (1963).

General histories of warfare rarely give much attention to propaganda, but certain key works provide invaluable insights for the student of propaganda and morale. These are H.W. Koch's illustrated *History of Warfare* (1987), Sir Michael Howard's *War in European History* (1973), Michael Waltzer's *Just and Unjust Wars* (1977), Geoffrey Best's *Humanity in Warfare* (1980) and John Keegan's *History of Warfare* (1993). The latter is a useful corrective to studies of war dominated by Clausewitzian theories.

For the ancient period Arthur Ferrill's *The Origins of War* (1985), W.K. Pritchett's *The Greek State at War* (2 vols, 1971, 1974), W.W. Tarn's *Alexander the Great* (1948), Sir Ronald Syme's *The Roman Revolution* (1939) and J.F. Gardner's *Leadership and the Cult of Personality* (1974). Essential studies of ancient uses of persuasion are: M. Billig, *Arguing and Thinking* (1987), G.A. Kennedy, *The Art of Persuasion in Greece* (1972) and his more recent *Classical Rhetoric* (1980). An important new contribution is Anton Powell, *Roman Poetry and Propaganda in the Age of Augustus* (1992).

Michael McCormick's *Eternal Victory: Triumphal Rulership in Late Antiquity, Byzantium and the Early Medieval West* (1986), though highly specialized, is an important contribution to our knowledge of ceremony and ritual in the Dark Ages.

For the medieval period, J.F. Verbruggen's *The Art of Warfare in Western Europe during the Middle Ages* (1977) is invaluable as it attempts to examine the psychological aspects of warfare, particularly for the later Middle Ages. Phillipe Contamine's *War in the Middle Ages*, first published in France in 1980, provides an even more general view. John Beele's *Warfare in Feudal Europe, 730-1200* (1971) is a good introductory work. For the Norman Conquest, R. Allen Brown's edition of documents, *The Norman Conquest* (1984) is essential. For the Crusades, T.P. Murphey's edition of papers, *The Holy War* (1976) is also valuable. For the fifteenth century, see Malcolm Vale's *War and Chivalry* (1981). Two documentary compilations provide insights into contemporary views: Louise and Jonathan Riley-Smith's *The Crusades: Idea and Reality 1095-1274* (1981) and the older *The Crusades: A Documentary Survey*, edited by James A.

Brundage (1962).

For the early modern period, J.R. Hale's *War and Society in Renaissance Europe* (1985) is an excellent introduction. By far the most useful work on printing is Elizabeth Eisenstein's two-volume masterpiece, *The Printing Press as an Agent of Change* (1979). On early Tudor propaganda, Sydney Angelo's *Spectacle, Pageantry and Early Tudor Policy* (1969) remains invaluable, as does C.E. Challis's *The Tudor Coinage* (1978). Sir Geoffrey Elton's *Policy and Police* (1972) contains a chapter on Thomas Cromwell's propaganda activities. Roy Strong has provided the most useful examination of Elizabethan propaganda in his *The Cult of Elizabeth* (1977), which should be read in conjunction with his earlier works, *Portraits of Queen Elizabeth I* (1963), *The English Icon: Elizabethan and Jacobean Portraiture* (1969) and *Tudor and Jacobean Portraits* (1969). See also P. Erlanger's *The Age of Courts and Kings* (1967). On Elizabeth's military affairs, see C.G. Cruikshank, *Elizabeth's Army* (1946). The Thirty Years War is best dealt with by two works, Herbert Langer's 1978 book of that title and the older book by E.A. Beller, *Propaganda in Germany during the Thirty Years War* (1940). Henry Kamen's *European Society, 1500-1700* (1984) provides useful background and insights into the period as a whole. The best work on France in this period is Joseph Klaits, *Printed Propaganda under Louis XIV* (1976). G. Boyce, J. Curran and P. Wingate have edited a useful collection on the origins and development of the press, *Newspaper History from the 17th Century to the Present Day* (1978), which also contains a valuable bibliography. Tim Harris's *London Crowds in the Reign of Charles II* (1987) is a model for microcosmic studies in the early modern period; George Rudé's, *The Crowd in History* (1964) remains a classic.

On the American Revolution see Carl Berger, *Broadsides and Bayonets: The Propaganda War of the American Revolution* (1961), Solomon Lutnicj, *The American Revolution and the British Press, 1775-83* (1967), Kenneth Silverman, *A Cultural History of the American Revolution* (1976), and D.M. Clark, *British Opinion and the American Revolution* (1930). Still useful are Philip Davidson, *Propaganda and the American Revolution* (1941) and Arthur Schlesinger, *Prelude to Independence: the Newspaper War in Britain* (1958). On the French revolutionary period, attention is still drawn to Robert Holtman's *Napoleonic Propaganda* (1950), M. Agulhon's *Marianne into Battle* (1981) and Clive Emsley's *British Society and the French Wars* (1979).

For the nineteenth century, Philip Knightley's *The First Casualty: The War Correspondent as Hero, Myth-maker and Propagandist* (1975) remains as good a starting point as any, especially on war correspondents and censorship, and John Mackenzie's *Propaganda and Empire, 1880-1960* (1984) throws much new light on the British scene. On censorship, see R.J. Goldstein, *Political Censorhip of the Arts and the Press in 19th Century Europe* (1989).

For the twentieth century, there is a veritable wealth of published works far too numerous to mention here. Much has been pioneered in the works of Nicholas Pronay. The shortest available introduction is Ken Ward's *Mass Communications and the Modern World* (1989). However, certain important works cannot be overlooked, most notably Michael Balfour, *Propaganda in War 1939-45* (1978), Nicholas Reeves, *Official British Film Propaganda in the First World War* (1986), N. Pronay and D.W. Springs (eds), *Propaganda, Politics and Film, 1918-45* (1982), K.R.M. Short, *Film and Radio Propaganda in the Second World War* (1983), Richard Taylor, *Film Propaganda* (1979), Robert E. Herzstein, *The War that Hitler Won* (1979), C.R. Koppes and G.D. Black, *Hollywood Goes to War* (1987), J. Leyda, *Kino* (1960), P. Kenez, *The Birth of the Propaganda State* (1985), Anthony Aldgate and Jeffrey Richards, *Britain Can Take It* (1986), David Welch, *The Third Reich: Politics and Propaganda* (1993) and Clive Coultass, *Images for Battle* (1989).

Since this book first appeared in 1990, several major new contributions have appeared. Philip Bell made an important contribution to our knowledge of the Second World War propaganda with *John Bull and the Bear: British Public Opinion, Foreign Policy and the Soviet Union, 1941-45* (1990) and an important American work is by H. Winkler, *The Censored War: American Visual Experience in World War Two* (1992). The First World War has received new contributions in the form of P. Buitenhuis, *The Great War of Words: Literature as Propaganda, 1914-18 and After* (1989) and Gary Messinger, *British Propaganda and the State in the First World War* (1992). Both acknowledge, as all works dealing with the First World War must do, the earlier work of Harold Lasswell, *Propaganda Technique in the World War* (1927). Lord Ponsonby's best-selling *Falsehood in Wartime* (1927) provides an indication of popular misconception of the real nature of propaganda.

The Cold War has received recent attention in Fred Inglis, *The Cruel Peace: Living through the Cold War* (1991) and Robert B. Bathurst, *Intelligence and the Mirror: On Creating an Enemy* (1993). Black radio propaganda's origins are discussed by L.C. Soley in *Radio Warfare: OSS and CIA Subversive Propaganda* (1989). Older works include James Aronsen, *The Press and the Cold War* (1970) and J.C. Clews, *Communist*

Propaganda Techniques (1964) and Richard H. Scultz and Roy Godson, *Dezinformatsia: Active Measures in Soviet Strategy* (1984). See also P. Biskind, *Seeing is Believing: How Hollywood Taught Us to Stop Worrying and Love the Fifties* (1983). Science fiction films from the period are reasonably well served in John Brosnan's *The Primal Screen* (1991), a largely personal labour of love, as is Stephen E. Pease, *Psywar: Psychological Warfare in Korea, 1950-53* (1992). V. Kortunov, *The Battle of Ideas in the Modern World* (Moscow, 1979) and Georgi Arbatov, *The War of Ideas in Contemporary International Relations* (Moscow, 1973) reveal how the Soviets viewed the ideological struggle in the Cold War. A more dispassionate analysis is to be found in Marian Leighton, *Soviet Propaganda as a Foreign Tool* (1991). The Gorbachev era is covered by L. Bittman, *The New Image Makers: Soviet Propaganda and Disinformation Today* (1988). The reference in the text to the early 1960s work of Whitton and Larson is *Propaganda: Towards Disarmament in the War of Words* (1964). A new study of international radio is P.C. Wasburn, *Broadcasting Propaganda: International Radio Broadcasting and the Construction of Political Reality* (1992) which complements K.R.M. Short (ed.), *Broadcasting over the Iron Curtain* (1986) and Laurien Alexandre, *The Voice of America: From Detente to the Reagan Doctrine* (1988).

Vietnam has been best served by Daniel Hallin, *The Uncensored War: The Media and Vietnam* (1986), Peter Braestrup, *Big Story: How the American Press and Television Reported and Interpreted the Crisis of Tet 1968 in Vietnam and Washington* (1977), Michael Arlen, *Living Room War* (1982) and C.R. Wyatt, *Paper Soldiers* (1993). The subsequent film treatment of the war has been covered by Gilbert Adair, *Hollywood's Vietnam* (1987). Bruce Cumings' *War and Television* (1992) should have been called 'War on television' as he rails against the medium.

The Gulf War has produced a plethora of works of mixed quality, but attention is drawn to David E. Morrison, *Television and the Gulf War* (1992), Douglas Kellner, *The Persian Gulf TV War* (1993), Bradley S. Greenberg and Walter Gantz (eds), *Desert Storm and the Mass Media* (1993), John R. MacArthur, *Censorship and Propaganda in the Gulf War* (1992) and Hedrick Smith, *The Media and the Gulf War: The Press and Democracy in Wartime* (1992) as correctives to my own work (listed below). The best insight so far into what was really happening in the Gulf War, as distinct from the media images, is Rick Atkinson's *Crusade* (1994).

On modern military-media relations, A. Hooper's *The Military and the Media* (1982) has now received an invaluable supplement in the form of Jacqueline Sharkey, *Under Fire: U.S. Military Restrictions on the Media* *from* Grenada to the Persian Gulf *and a short pamphlet by Steven Badsey, *Modern Military Operations and the Media* (1994). Sharkey's well-researched 1993 book in fact also contains chapters going back to Vietnam and the Falklands. But David E. Morrison and Howard Tumber's *Journalists at War: The Dynamics of News Reporting in the Falklands War* (1988) contains the best insight into the experience of the reporters with the Task Force in the South Atlantic – sociology in the service of future historians. A general view of that conflict is Valerie Adams, *The Media and the Falklands Campaign* (1986) and a good read is to be found in Robert Harris, *Gotcha! The Media, the Government and the Falklands Crisis* (1983), although the House of Commons Defence Committee's first report on *The Handling of Press and Public Information during the Falklands Conflict* (2 vols, 1982) is perhaps the best starting point. Derrik Mercer, Geoff Mungham and Kevin Williams, *The Fog of War: The Media on the Battlefield* (1987) is not only vital for the Falklands but also for case studies elsewhere.

Equally variable in quality are works by media studies scholars who have yet to embrace the notion of propaganda as a central concern. Most who have tend to rely on the works of Noam Chomsky but such works as *Manufacturing Consent: The Political Economy of the Mass Media* (1988, with Edward Herman), *Beyond Hypocrisy: Decoding the News in an Age of Propaganda* (1992, also with Herman), *Deterring Democracy* (1991) and *Necessary Illusions: Thought Control in Democratic Societies* (1989) need to be read with caution. A short lesson on cock-ups in history rather than conspiracies needs to be issued with these as a health warning to students, especially those who believed that Oliver Stone's film *J.F.K.* was historically accurate. That said, they do stimulate the forewarned and they do provide compelling evidence of the mainstream American media's inability to accommodate opposing or dissenting viewpoints. Inside explanations of how the media actually work tend to come from practitioners from within the system, especially Mort Rosenblum's *Who Stole the News? Why We Can't Keep Up With What Happens in the World* (1993), Peter Arnett's *Live from the Battlefield* (1994), and Robert Weiner, *Live from Baghdad: Gathering News at Ground Zero* (1992). For a British perspective on reporting in the Gulf War, see John Simpson, *From the House of War* (1991), Patrick Bishop, *Famous Victory* (1992), Ben Brown and David Shukman, *All Necessary Means* (1991) and Alex Thomson, *Smokescreen: The Media, The Censors, The Gulf* (1992).

On combat morale, readers should consult John Keegan's *The Face of Battle* (1976), F.M. Richardson's *Fighting Spirit* (1978) and Richard

Holmes' *Firing Line* (1985). And on possible futures, see Alvin and Heidi Toffler, *War and Anti-War: Survival at the Dawn of the 21st Century* (1994). As that book borrowed from the first edition of this one, I am happy to reciprocate.

My own contributions to this subject are principally *The Projection of Britain: British Overseas Publicity and Propaganda, 1919-39* (1981), *British Propaganda during the First World War* (1982, with Mike Sanders), *A Call to Arms: Propaganda and Rearmament in the 1930s* (1984, pamphlet and film produced by the InterUniversity History Film Consortium), *Britain and the Cinema and the Second World War* (1988, as editor) and *War and the Media: Propaganda and Persuasion in the Gulf War* (1992).

Invaluable journals are *The Historical Journal of Film, Radio and Television, Public Opinion Quarterly* and *Media Studies Journal*.

Since the last edition of this book, several important works have appeared. These include Susan Carruthers' *The Media at War* (2000), Nancy Snow's *Propaganda Inc: Selling America's Culture to the World* (2nd edition, 2002), Alvin Snyder's *Warriors of Disinformation: American Propaganda, Soviet Lies and the Winning of the Cold War* (1997) and Walter Hixson's *Parting the Curtain: Propaganda, Culture and the Cold War* (1997). Historians continue to produce excellent works, such as Nicholas Reeves' *The Power of Film Propaganda: Myth or Reality* (2000) and James Chapman's *The British at War, Cinema, State and Propaganda 1939-45* (2000). But now that the internet is more widely available, bibliographical searches have become simple. There are also numerous websites that are becoming valuable resources, many of which can be accessed via my own at www.leeds.ac.uk/ics/phillink.htm.

These are but a fraction of the works I have consulted over the years, not to mention the huge amount of documentary material, published and unpublished, in a whole host of places. But special mention must be made of the debt all propaganda historians owe to David Culbert, the series editor of the monumental collection of documents, *Film and Propaganda in America* (5 vols, 1990-3). But to all authors who have dedicated their time, energy and attention to this area, living and deceased, my thanks.

Index